Kashrut and Jewish Food Ethics

Jewish Thought, Jewish History: New Studies

Series Editor
GREGG STERN

ACADEMIC
STUDIES
PRESS

Kashrut and Jewish Food Ethics

Edited by
SHMULY YANKLOWITZ

Boston
2019

This book was created in partnership with the rabbinic members of Torat Chayim.

Library of Congress Cataloging-in-Publication Data

Names: Yanklowitz, Shmuly, 1981- editor.

Title: Kashrut and Jewish food ethics / edited by Shmuly Yanklowitz.

Description: Boston : Academic Studies Press, 2019. | Series: Jewish thought, Jewish history: new studies | Includes bibliographical references and index.

Identifiers: LCCN 2018036413 (print) | LCCN 2018038201 (ebook) | ISBN 9781618119056 (ebook) | ISBN 9781618119032 (hardcover : alk. paper) | ISBN 9781618119049 (pbk. : alk. paper)

Subjects: LCSH: Jews—Dietary laws. | Kosher food industry. | Jewish ethics.

Classification: LCC BM710 (ebook) | LCC BM710 .K2646 2019 (print) | DDC 296.7/3—dc23

LC record available at https://lccn.loc.gov/2018036413

Book design by Kryon Publishing Services (P) Ltd.
www.kryonpublishing.com
Cover design by Ivan Grave.
On the cover: *Cows in a Pasture*, Marie Diéterle Van Marcke de Lummen. Museum of Fine Arts, Boston, reproduced by permission.
Photograph © 2019 Museum of Fine Arts, Boston

Published by Academic Studies Press
28 Montfern Avenue
Brighton, MA 02135, USA
press@academicstudiespress.com
www.academicstudiespress.com

This book is dedicated to the humble, tired, invisible food worker. These are the men and women who labor in the fields, who toil in the kitchens, and who spend their days working in backrooms sight unseen. They provide us with sustenance, yet we rarely see them. We rarely give our thanks. Too often they are left out of the narrative of *kashrut* and out of the consciousness of the kosher consumer. May we rectify this oversight together.

ABOUT TORAT CHAYIM:

Torat Chayim is a rabbinical association of Orthodox rabbis committed to fostering a more pluralistic and progressive future. Its rabbinic members—men & women—work together to foster Torah-rooted progress in the Jewish community and in society at large.

The name Torat Chayim was chosen because Torah is about rootedness and Chayim is about dynamism. We want a Torah that is strongly rooted in tradition and that is also responsive to—and pushing us forward in—our time. Further, Torah is about life. It is about ethics, human dignity, and the perpetuation—and sanctification—of life. We embrace a life-affirming, dignity-affirming Torah, and work to ensure that Torah only adds to—and never detracts from—human dignity and the sanctity of life.

Thank you so much for everything!
Wishing you all the best,

Table of Contents

Introduction
Rabbi Dr. Shmuly Yanklowitz   ix

SECTION 1

Kashrut Dynamics

1. On the Ethics and Politics of Kosher Food Supervision   1
   Rabbi Aaron Leibowitz
2. Are You Really Eating Kosher? On Camouflage, Hypocrisy,
   and Hiding Behind the Kashrut Laws   10
   Rabbi Dr. Nathan Lopes Cardozo
3. Milk and Meat: The Dangerous Mixture   14
   Rabbi Dr. Nathan Lopes Cardozo

SECTION 2

Bridging Kashrut with Ethical & Spiritual Concerns

1. The Moral Underpinnings of Kashrut   18
   Rabbi Dr. Shmuly Yanklowitz
2. Eating Our Way from Holiness to Justice: Kashrut as a Bridge
   Between Competing Value Systems   27
   Rabbi Dr. David Kasher
3. Increasing Holiness in Life: Towards an Expanded Kashrut   33
   Rabbi Dr. Irving (Yitz) Greenberg

SECTION 3

Spirituality of Eating

1. Eating as a Sacrament: The Eating Table and the Coffin   43
   Rabbi Dr. Daniel Sperber
2. Food for Thought: Hasidic Wisdom on Spiritual Eating   49
   Rabbi Dr. Ariel Evan Mayse
3. Holy Eating in Jewish Thought and Practice   66
   Rabbi Hyim Shafner
4. Too Much of Everything is Just Enough: Eating as a
   Spiritual Practice in a Culture of Abundance   78
   Rabbi David Jaffe

SECTION 4
Health & Consumption

1. Towards a Jewish Nutrition Ethic: The Theology, Law, and
   Ethics of Healthy Eating   87
   Rabbi Daniel R. Goodman
2. Why Are We So Hungry? Our Betrayal of Eating, Being Satisfied
   and Blessing and The Way Back!   119
   Rabbi Daniel Landes
3. Your Grains, Your Grape Juice, and Your Oil: Coming to
   Terms with Unhealthy Foods Venerated by Jewish Tradition   126
   Rabbi Asher Lopatin

SECTION 5
Worker Rights, Equality, & Hunger

1. The Divine Image: Theological Reflections on Jewish Labor Law   134
   Rabbi Dr. Ariel Evan Mayse
2. Judaism and The Crisis of the Rural Village in the Global South   154
   Rabbi Micha Odenheimer
3. Let Them Have a Little Bread   167
   Rabbi Marc Gitler

SECTION 6
Animal Welfare

1. תשובה בעניני צער בעלי חיים   171
   Rabbi David Bigman
2. Animal Suffering and the Rhetoric of Values and *Halakhah*   182
   Rabbi Dov Linzer
3. The Commandments Were Only Given for the Purpose
   of Refining People   209
   Rabbi Dr. David Rosen
4. The Case for Limiting Meat Consumption to Shabbat,
   Holidays, and Celebrations   218
   Rabbi Aaron Potek

SECTION 7
Environmentalism, Conservation, and GMOs

1. Ethical Eating and the Impact on our Environment   235
   Rabbi Dr. Mel Gottlieb
2. Humanity and the Tree of the Field: Conservation as a Commandment 244
   Rosh Kehillah Dina Najman
3. Divine Wisdom or Altering Creation? A Torah Perspective on GMOs   252
   Rabbi Gabe Greenberg

Conclusion
Rabbi Dr. Shmuly Yanklowitz   266

Index   270

Introduction

The volume of essays you hold in your hands is a dynamic survey of the inter-section between Judaism's concern with ethics, empathy, and the environment. Contained in these pages are rabbinic reflections on the nature of Judaism's timeless concern with upholding the integrity of *kashrut* in all its dimensions. As we all know, *kashrut*—as an organized ontological system—is focused on the Jewish laws of food consumption. The vaunted "Thou shalt not consume" and so forth. But even more so than a rigid classification of allowances and pro-hibitions, the notions of *kashrut* reflect the extent to which Judaism views itself as an integral component of society and faith.

Historically, the essential application of the boundaries of *kashrut* were limited given the inadequate freedom of the Jewish community in the Diaspora. Pre-modern sensitivities to the feelings of the environment, or animal con-sciousness, were never fully considered in the ways they are today. Such feel-ings are understandable considering the significant external pressure on Jewish communities throughout the world struggling to survive in environments hostile to their existence. It has only been in the postmodern era, and especially in the early years of the twenty-first century, where the proliferation of interest in food ethics, animal welfare, and the questions of whether there truly is an ethical ecology of Jewish food ways materialized. Given the increasing power, privilege, knowledge, and modern sensitivities of Jews in modern society com-bined with the least restrictive flow of information in human history, the need for contemporary inquiry regarding the application of *kashrut* is fundamental to Judaism's continued role as a force for progress.

Put simply, for Jews today, the most vigorous place to create intellectual synergies regarding the traditional observance and current societal moral dynamics has been the laws of *kashrut* and the Jewish values protecting the earth and the dignity for all creatures.

But what does this mean in practice? Since the turn of the millennia and the rapid advances in technology, globalized markets, and atomized politics, pressing issues have emerged in the American and Israeli Jewish communities around ethical issues related to food consumption. All of these contemporary issues, including worker rights, animal welfare, environmental protection, among others, intersect with basic Jewish food ethics. As a people who respects the ancient laws, but also look forward to a more repaired world, our ability to heal a fractured world hinges on the vitality of applying the latent ethical proscription as described by our wisest sages. On a more personal level, since the beginning of my rabbinical career, and even during my studies, I've been fascinated by the interrelation of *kashrut* to topics that seem to go outside the direct scope of the laws. Usually, when one imagines the extent of a kosher law, one looks to a symbol on a food package: Is this permissible or is it not; this is the normative dialectic. But as I devoted more time in studying the minutia of *kashrut*, the way it balances and counterbalances base desires with refinement, satiation with respect for the worker, and freedom from overconsumption of any litany of products, the more I came to realize that this broad topic—actually, a conglomeration and amalgamation of hundreds of smaller topics brought together through a singular ethical framework—is indispensable for the development of the mind and the soul.

Furthermore, I wanted to learn more about the elasticity of *kashrut*. I wanted to look beyond symbols, procedures, and didacticism and explore the major world problems that *kashrut* can solve. Fortunately, throughout my career, I have been privileged to come into contact with thinkers more thoughtful and knowledgeable in the subject than myself. These thinkers, all of them so humble and powerful in their intellect, guided me in my journey. Yet, I knew that there was more to add to the literature of this topic. Indeed, to further the intellectual potential of this line of inquiry, I decided the time was right to call on some of the brightest Jewish minds—my colleagues—to lend their thoughts on this significant pedagogical exploration. It was these essays—from a range of academics and professionals in the field alike—which led to the creation of this book. I realized that I was not alone and that others were grappling to combine their Jewish values with their ethical food sensitivities.

Who is this book for? As one should be able to discern from the contents within, this volume is not an academic book in the strictest sense. More often than not, the need for an accessible work from scholars in the field superseded the impulse to make this a purely academic book. While there are elements of classic academia within the pages, the chance to let loose these novel ideas took precedence. Thus, rather than spend time examining the minutia of *kashrut* in contemporary practice, the editorial decision was made to use this book as a springboard for an ethics-based theological treatise that should leave readers with more questions than answers. Utilizing such an approach is manifest within this book's purpose, which is to poke, prod, and explore the manifold dimensions of *kashrut* while appraising it's traditional, moral role in Jewish philosophy. The intellectual style is to embrace academic thought but present the material in an accessible and more popular style.

The path of this book is non-linear, by which I mean that we don't begin with the Torah proscriptions for *kashrut* and move on through history. Rather, this book is grouped thematically by topic that begins with exploring the dynamism of *kashrut* and ending with essays pondering the status of genetically modified organisms, conservation, and the environment. In this manner, we go from the particular to the general, first by exploring the theory behind the topic at hand, before moving to the role of the self, and finally charting the role that *kashrut* plays in the world beyond Judaism. In between are sections dedicated to animal welfare, hunger, and spirituality. A more thorough breakdown follows:

In the first section of this book, titled *"Kashrut* Dynamics" features essays that consider the political tribulations (Rabbi Aaron Leibowitz) and social potential (Rabbi Dr. Nathan Lopes Cardozo) of kosher supervision and practices. Leibowitz, currently a member of the Jerusalem City Council, and a *mashgiah* by trade, cared so deeply for reform in the *kashrut* industry that he created his own supervision agency, Hashgaha Pratit. Dedicating years of his life to the project, his approach to this topic is deeply personal, and it shows. Rabbi Dr. Cardozo's two contributions here, though each brief, are dense nuggets of wisdom that allow readers to break down preconceived norms while reorienting them for deeper assessment of the epistemological function of certain normative traits of *kashrut*. Why should one separate the eating of milk and meat together, besides the obvious reason we are told to? Even more so, does the label on a package of kosher food truly mean it's kosher?

The second section, titled "Bridging Kashrut with Ethical & Spiritual Concerns," directly follows the lines of thinking introduced in the first section while expanding the definitions of what ethics and justice mean in a modern context. My lone contribution to this edition is included in the section and, indeed, it provides the spark that I hope readers will pick up throughout the course of the book: What really is the moral underpinning of *kashrut*? But even more so, how we do learn these values and incorporate them into daily life? The other essays in this section both explore the values of holiness and the expansion of *kashrut*'s ethical principles in all we do (Rabbi Dr. Yitz Greenberg) and how these ancient ethics influence applications of justice in the modern world (Rabbi Dr. David Kasher).

The locus of the third section of the book spirituality, particularly the spirituality of eating (this thought lends the section its title). Eating, to the mundane mind, seems banal and base: We have to eat to live, so what does this have to do with spirituality? As it turns out, the vein of thought that explores interconnectedness between eating and Jewish spirituality runs deep throughout the tradition, especially Hasidic hermeneutics of blessings and ritual. And to be sure, to explore the intrinsic holiness of something as ordinary as a table (as Rabbi Dr. Daniel Sperber does) allows readers to begin imagining that there are more avenues to spirituality than through rote expression of following the laws of *kashrut*. Elsewhere, this section focuses on the damages of overconsumption (Rabbi Dr. Ariel Evan Mayse and Rabbi David Jaffe) as well as the religio-historical intent of eating with the spiritual self in mind (Rabbi Hyim Shafner).

Moving on, the fourth section examines the health aspects of *kashrut*, while dispelling the inexplicable notion that a kosher diet is somehow healthier than other diets. Opening the section is a powerful call of an ethic guided by Jewish theology and law (Rabbi Daniel Goodman), followed by a more personal essay into the challenges of staying healthy while adhering to *kashrut*. Furthermore, the assumption that restrictions of a kosher diet may have health benefits is challenged; at the least, it is certainly inconclusive that a kosher diet is inherently healthier than any other diet. And as Rabbi Lopatin points out in his contribution, a normative *kashrut*-observant diet is saddled with ritual foods high in carbohydrates, fats, and sugar. Related to the issue of nutrition is the tragic dyad of hunger and obesity. In a fascinating juxtaposition, readers are presented with a stark analysis moral conflict of societies that fetishize food and overeat while millions of people suffer from food deprivation (Rabbi Daniel Landes).

The fifth and sixth sections of the book conjoin topics that concern the hidden dimensions of *kashrut*: labor law (Mayse) and how it affects small farmers in poor, rural villages in the Global South (Rabbi Micha Odenheimer), the welfare of animals raised for slaughter (Rabbi David Bigman, Rabbi Dov Linzer, and Rabbi Dr. David Rosen), limiting consumption of meat (Potek), and the emotional response of hunger and how to remedy it worldwide (Rabbi Marc Gitler).

The final section looks at *kashrut* through the tripartite lens of the environment (Gottlieb), nature conservation in Jewish thought (Rosh Kehillah Dina Najman), and the permissibility of genetically modified crops (Rabbi Gabriel Greenberg).

Make no mistake, the essays contained in this volume are rich in detail and offer new paradigms for issues of *kashrut* that have swirled in the ether for generations. In the following pages, readers will have the unique opportunity to delve into the minds of some of the brightest Modern Orthodox thinkers of this generation. Almost all contributors to this book are rabbinic members of Torat Chayim, the Progressive Orthodox rabbinical association. I'm grateful to the group and to each member for their inspiration and support. Each contribution in this volume is a unique addition to Orthodox discourse and to the broader discourse of Jewish food ethics. The mix of tones and voices present here, from extended academic discourses, short, sermonic pieces, Hebrew responsa, and forward-thinking explications of *halakhah* coalesce into a singularly pluralistic and diverse tome. I'm humbled and excited to see such an extraordinary caliber of thinkers and leaders contribute to a work which will be a valuable resource for decades to come.

Indeed, I believe this volume will serve as an invaluable guide for those committed to *kashrut*, for those committed to Jewish food ethics, and for those thinking about the intersection between tradition and progress, law and values, and ritual and ethics. It's a first, and necessary, leap.

Shmuly Yanklowitz
Scottsdale, Arizona
April 2018

Section 1   Kashrut Dynamics

CHAPTER 1

On the Ethics and Politics of Kosher Food Supervision

Rabbi Aaron Leibowitz

Hours before candle lighting, our *mashgiah* (kosher supervisor) gets a phone call from one of our locations. The hummus joint near the Shuk in Jerusalem has a problem. They just realized that they can't soak the chickpeas, the main ingredient in hummus, properly before a holiday immediately followed by Shabbat. (For reference, soaking chickpeas is fine for twenty-four hours, but forty-eight hours will ruin the beans.) How will they have beans for cooking hummus right after Shabbat for their Saturday night business? Thank God we managed to find a solution, but the remarkable thing was that they called at all, knowing full well we would have no way of catching them coming in on a holiday to put up the beans. To us, this was a success story. The gratification we feel when our strict supervision catches a possible breach in our standards is great, but the knowledge that we have nurtured a commitment to high standards on the part of the client is true vindication.

In 2013, I set out to create the most ethical and professional kosher supervision agency in Israel. It has been a fascinating journey, revealing multiple layers of politics, social dynamics, and ethical issues. In this chapter, I uncover some of these dynamics while also exploring their complexities.

We will see that Jewish law regarding trust, *ne'emanut*, is an intricate system that sets out to define objective categories regarding people's character. When they are applied in a modern and diverse Jewish society they can seem out of place and challenge solidarity and unity. Politics complicate things even further, in the diaspora on a communal level, but especially in Israel where the law of the land comes into play.

Trust: It's Complicated.

When a customer asks if a restaurant is kosher, there are many interests at play. On the simplest of levels, we can assume two primary motives: The business owner wants to make a sale, and the customer wants a reliable answer. The kosher-supervision industry ostensibly comes to serve as an objective third party in order to address the gap between these interests.

But what is the interest of the supervisory agency itself? Clearly any time they remove their supervision from a client they lose business. On the other hand, their product has value to the extent that it can deliver reliable standards to the end user, the kosher consumer. Clearly these conflicting interests should require an honest agency to closely manage its own ethical standards. Let us also look at the consumer's motives. Is it possible that the public may not want reliable supervision as much as they want many kosher places to eat? To what extent is consumer behavior generally considered and careful in the face of the complexities of commercial *kashrut*? Studies show that when the public is faced with complex decisions herd mentality tends to take over. Might that not be the case in regard to *hashgaha* (kosher supervision)?

When we understand that there are not singular motivating factors we must ask; how does one assess ethical character and trustworthiness in the face of personal and perhaps conflicting interests?

Halakhah Trustworthiness

The *halakhah* sources make clear that there is a judgement call involved in assessing one's trustworthiness. Note that Maimonides posits that our assumptions in regard to someone's reliability change in regard to time and place:

> At the time when *Eretz Yisrael* was entirely Jewish, one could buy wine from every person and have no suspicion, whereas outside of Israel one could only buy from someone held to be Kosher. But in our day, no matter where one is, one may only buy wine from a person held to be kosher.[1]

The *Shulhan Arukh*, from the Sephardic tradition, and the Rema's notations, from the Ashkenazic tradition, discuss what is required for reliability and

---

1 Maimonides, *Mishneh Torah, Hilchot Ma'achalot Asurot,* 11:25.

how our assumptions may shift when we are discussing a private person versus a merchant:

> When one is suspect in eating [a certain] forbidden food, whether forbidden by Torah or rabbinic law, they may not be relied on regarding [the *kashrut* of] that same food.[2]
>
> And some say that even from a person who is not suspect but is not held to be kosher either it is forbidden to buy wine or the other things that are liable of prohibition. But if one is a guest by such a person, one may eat by him.[3]

The *halakhah* recognizes that a reputation of honesty has value for a merchant, and this consideration can enhance our willingness to rely on a merchant's word under certain circumstances:

> One may buy pomegranate wine which is sold for medicinal purposes from the merchant, even if it is not from the barrel, even though it is more valuable than wine, because [people] are strict about it [for its medicinal properties], [the merchant] will not damage his own reputation. (And so with anything one buys from a professional, he will not damage his reputation).[4]

We should note that this *halakhah* is only applied when the fraud can be discovered, like in the case of grape wine being passed as pomegranate wine. This becomes a primary source for kosher supervision based periodic inspection. The fact that the business values its reputation, coupled with the fact that cheaters may be caught, can generate a reasonable assumption of trust. The ability to make a dynamic assessment of trustworthiness finds a radical application in a unique responsa of Rabbi Moshe Feinstein of blessed memory. He was asked about elderly parents who were living with their non-observant children in the former Soviet Union. The question was whether the elderly and infirm eat their grown children's food if their son or daughter tells them it has been properly prepared to be kosher. He commented:

> I proposed that there is room to be lenient for many people. If the father knows and trusts his daughter or his daughter-in-law, and believes that she

---

2 Rabbi Yosef Karo, *Shulhan Arukh, Yorah De'ah* 119:1.
3 Rema, ibid.
4 Rabbi Yosef Karo, *Shulhan Arukh, Yoreh De'ah* 114:5.

will not try to mislead him and give him something forbidden, because he knows her nature with total clarity and she has proved herself many times that she does not try to mislead him, for she does want to cause him grief or because she is by nature honest, then he can rely on her and eat anything she cooks for him that she says is kosher meat, cooked in the pots and dishes that she uses only for him.[5]

So the *halakhah* recognizes that an assessment of context and circumstance is appropriate when coming to determine trustworthiness. Rabbi Feinstein, for instance, issues his ruling specifically for the infirm behind the iron curtain, and instructs that it is specifically for those difficult circumstances. At the same time, he is willing to issue this ruling within the *halakhah* discourse, indicating that in his view there is a dynamic standard.

Kashrut and Modern Jewish Diversity

As we saw in the last source, the social dynamics around trust in *kashrut* are especially sensitive because they live in the space between different sectors of the Jewish People, those who keep kosher and those who do not. Taken at face value we could assume that the primary goal of kosher supervision is to address this gap. The simplest case of this would be a non-Orthodox business catering to the Orthodox consumer. The *halakhah*, as presented above, clearly states that one may not trust someone who does not keep kosher regarding *kashrut*. At the same time, this seems to set us up for a disturbing equation.

Can we honestly conduct ourselves as if one who is observant is more honest than one who is not? It goes without saying that this is not the reality and yet that is how this standard could appear. Is this rule ethically sound? Should we be concerned with the problematic message it may send?

We have also seen that business interests effect one's status regarding trustworthiness. A store owner is more suspect than a private home, and a pharmacist is more trusted due to the professional stake in their reputation. What happens when kosher supervision itself becomes a business? Is the fact that the agency represents *halakhah* and *kashrut* enough to guarantee that it employs and is run by people of character? The early *halakhah* sources were concerned with honesty in the face of financial interest despite the fact that they addressing a wholly observant community well before the enlightenment and secular Judaism.

---

5 Rabbi Moshe Feinstein, *Igrot Moshe, Yoreh De'ah 1, Siman 54.*

Despite the fact that an agency may represent the religious morality surrounding *kashrut*, can we be sure there is a moral commitment to honesty and truth to mitigate any personal or organizational interest? When money is involved may we not require some form of supervision over the supervisors?

Political Interests

Here we must also consider the political dynamics present in modern *kashrut*. In many communities, there is a *kashrut* committee which brings together local rabbis to oversee the local *kashrut* standards. This committee can quickly come to hold a monopoly on the local supervision industry. There are different ethical opinions regarding monopolies, both in *halakhah* and in general ethics. At the same time, monopolies often breed corrupt practices at the expense of the public. A local *Vaad* (rabbinic committee) may block competition in order to maintain community standards. At the same time, this move is also in their financial interest. Conflict of interest is a basic consideration in the determination of *ne'emanut* (trustworthiness) and may be a consideration in regard to the *Vaad* itself. Competition between reliable agencies would likely incentivize local *hashgaha* providers to be more transparent, fairly priced, service oriented, and even reliable.

In Israel, these dynamics are even more problematic as there is a single national monopoly. The "Law to Prevent Fraud in Kashrut" passed in 1983 prohibits any business from using the word "kosher" without governmental certification. The Chief Rabbinate of Israel and its local councils are the only authorized agency permitted to provide supervision and certification in Israel. Those private agencies that do exist are only permitted to provide additional supervision to more severe standards for the ultra-Orthodox community, and only to businesses that have the *Rabbanut* certification as well. The monopoly of the Chief Rabbinate has bred severe corruption, due to lack of oversight, transparency, and competition. A recent report by the state comptroller found the *Rabbanut* guilty of false reporting, cronyism, weak standards, and other questionable practices.[6]

This law is also part of a larger controversy regarding the monopoly that the Chief Rabbinate has on all religious services including marriage and divorce. As I write these words, battles rage in the Knesset over a law that would give them a monopoly on conversion as well, placing even alternative orthodox

---

6 Justice Joseph Shapira, Israel State Comptroller report, 67b 2017.

conversions outside the law. I believe that the political and capital gains of the ultra-Orthodox-controlled Chief Rabbinate themselves create a conflict of interest, allowing them to maintain a substandard level of supervision in the name of what they see as a greater good. In order to suggest practical methods for maintaining higher ethical standards we need to go back and consider the underlying issues involving *hashgaha*.

Core Concerns Regarding the Reliability in *Kashrut*

The core concerns present in supervision seem to come down to three primary issues:

1. Is there the requisite knowledge for maintaining *kashrut*? We have all heard statements to the tune of: It's only cut up vegetables and a dressing, what could *not* be kosher? Or, of course it is obvious to anyone who maintains strict standards that the salad may not be kosher, due to tithes, infestation, wine vinegar, and a number of additional issues. Modern industrial *kashrut*, with its myriad compounds and ingredients, makes this even more sensitive.

2. Does the person I seek to trust care about *kashrut* as much as I do? We all know that a waiter would never lie about a peanut to someone with an allergy, because they themselves know it to be true and deadly. Might not one who does not believe in *kashrut* fudge the truth, in the case of a mistake in the kitchen for instance? If one does not believe it to be important perhaps they will think 'what they don't know won't kill them?'

3. The business interest is of significant concern to the *halakhah*, as we have explained. This extends to other foreign interests as well. Is there a way for us to address all the concerns that lie behind the *halakhah*, within the framework of *halakhah*, while creating a more socially-positive dynamic?

From Fraud Busting to Trust Building

Behind the complicated concerns we have brought to fore there is one simple question of profound social import: Can I trust you? From an idealistic perspective, if we seek to move towards a more utopian society, we would hope to be increasing the instances where we may answer yes. An expert in *kashrut* supervision once characterized to me his core responsibility as catching their clients when they lie. It is hard to argue with this logical conclusion. Yet, I would ask if we may recast the ultimate goal of *kashrut* supervision as one of building trust through inspection, transparency, and constructive communication? While the inspection is *halakhically* required, and provides the bedrock of reliable supervision, how might we recruit the partnership of the business in maintaining strict standards?

Bestowing trust need not imply that I trust you with my life, we need not all be lifeguards or surgeons. Trust can be broad or narrow, and employing mechanisms that build and maintain trust is not the same as no trust. The awareness that no party is perfectly trustworthy shifts our attention to systems that are designed to enable trust, indeed, to build trust.

By enhancing and reinforcing trust we create a stronger civil society. Ethics and trust have a reciprocal relationship, to the extent that I perceive that there are people of character before me, committed to the highest ethical standards, to that extent I am willing to trust. This also works in the other direction, by building an effective framework that maintains transparency, and healthy communication, we reinforce the ethical commitments to truth. It is important to see that the core value at stake is that of truth. Once we see this we can begin to appreciate that there is a shared value being protected here, a value that is important to those who do not keep kosher as well. This insight allows us all to get on the same side.

Building the concept of kosher supervision around trust building and social solidarity can also create a profound shift in the attitude of the business owner. The *kashrut* agency becomes an ally in building social capitol, something considered a valuable asset in modern business.

Power Dynamics vs. Professionalism and Communication

Kashrut supervision must aspire to the highest levels of professionalism and professional communication. The agency must view itself as a resource for the business and the consumer. The agency brings the requisite knowledge, the *halakhah* care, and the professional know-how in creating full transparency. Removal of certification due to non-compliance is not a threat, rather it is in service of truth, in service of the social capitol which the agency serves. Here *kashrut* is not only protecting the *halakhah* standard and the consumer, it is serving the interests of all the businesses being supervised. This orientation can change the entire tenor of the relationship, recruiting the good will of the business who views the agency as an important ally.

In Israel, the legal monopoly and its enforcement paradigm have cast *hashgaha* as a power dynamic. Training courses for supervisors teach that it is important to create a crisis early in the relationship, bringing a business to a halt, and showing them who is boss. The lack of uniform standards, and the lack of professional practices and standards breed resentment and suspicion. Quickly, the client learns that his role in the relationship is to not get caught. The quality of the trust that the business has in the *kashrut* agency is damaged, and the relationship is no longer about truth, it is adversarial, not reciprocal. The poor reputation of the Chief Rabbinate in Israel does not help.

Communication skills for staff become a crucial component in this work, especially due to the intense sort of interactions that can occur. Whenever a critical conversation around a breach of standards occurs there is a tremendous amount of fear present. The business owner is concerned for his business and livelihood and is often personally invested and protective of his realm, and the *mashgiah* (kosher supervisor) is carrying the significant responsibility towards the community, the agency, and of course towards heaven. This often deteriorates into a power dynamic, full of threats and anger, undermining whatever trust has been built. Clear ethical boundaries, with synchronized expectations, and professional communication become a major skill set. Being able to use nonviolent language, maintain uncompromised red lines and standards, and communicate clearly the needs of the agency, are of utmost importance.

Even more so, *kashrut* agencies must aspire to the highest ethical practices and standards. Supervisors must not be permitted to receive gifts of food from clients. Businesses should be handled by multiple supervisors. All prices and standards should be advertised and transparent. All fiscal transactions should be conducted by the agency, not the supervisors, indeed it should be prohibited for the supervisor to collect funds. Regular and formal feedback should be solicited from all clients regarding the *mashgihim*, and any complaints should be addressed seriously and objectively. All agencies should subject themselves to external reviews. *Mashgihim* must be trained in communication skills and this should be a significant metric in measuring their success.

In addition, competition should be encouraged. This will place higher demand on the public as the need to educate themselves regarding which agencies are reliable become ever more vital to daily living. Encouraging informed consumerism is something that strengthens civil society and will also improve the quality of *kashrut*. When private agencies compete for public trust, but also on pricing and service, it may be harder for an agency, but everybody else wins. Including Torah.

When we seek to use *halakhah* to wield power we damage the public image of Torah. Allowing Torah, which is supposed to represent truth, become associated with arm twisting and corruption is a travesty. When the rabbinic community becomes obsessed with power and control it reflects fear and weakness. Rabbi Jonathan Sacks said that "Religion doesn't need and should never seek power."[7] Indeed by insisting on a monopoly as the only authority we undermine truth and even God. There is a heresy present when we do not trust that things can work well without us needing to be in control.

---

7   Rabbi Lord Jonathan Sacks, BBC Radio Thought for the Day, 22nd September 2010.

Are You Really Eating Kosher? On Camouflage, Hypocrisy, and Hiding Behind the Kashrut Laws

Rabbi Dr. Nathan Lopes Cardozo

"With devotion's visage
And pious action
We do sugar o'er
The devil himself"[1]

Kosher animals, as is well known, can be identified by two *simanim* (physical signs). They must chew their cud, and their hooves must be wholly cloven.[2] In order to be kosher, the animal must possess both *simanim*. The Torah goes out of its way to emphasize the fact that an animal in which only *one* sign is present cannot be considered kosher in any way. Consider the verse:

> The camel, because it chews the cud but does not part the hoof, it is unclean to you. And the rock-badger, because it chews the cud but does not part the hoof, it is unclean to you. And the hare, because it chews the cud but does not part the hoof, it is unclean to you. And the swine, because it parts the hoof and is cloven-footed, but does not chew the cud, it is unclean to you.[3]

Carefully reading this text makes us wonder. Why did the Torah need to state that these non-kosher animals either chew their cud or have cloven hooves? After all, *that's* not what makes them spiritually "unclean." On the contrary, having one positive sign seems to suggest that perhaps they could

---

1 *Hamlet*, Act III, Scene I.
2 Deuteronomy 11:2–3; 14:6–8.
3 Leviticus 11:4–7.

be kosher. If the Torah would have only mentioned the negative indicators in these animals that clearly identify them as non-kosher, we would have known enough: Not kosher.

Moreover, why are the kosher signs mentioned *before* the non-kosher signs? Wouldn't the reverse order be more accurate? Surely their non-kosher signs bear more relevance in a discussion of why these animals are not kosher! In what way, then, do the kosher *simanim* make the animal *more* non-kosher than the non-kosher signs themselves?

Rabbi Ephraim Shlomo ben Chaim of Luntshitz, the *Kli Yakar* (1550–1619), gives us a most illuminating explanation for why the Torah specifically chose this wording. In his opinion, we might have thought that, indeed, the non-kosher aspects of these animals make them impure, but the kosher signs somehow moderate that impurity. Instead, the Torah comes to tell us that the kosher signs of non-kosher animals make them *all the more* unclean.

Why? Because animals with only one kosher sign represent negative character traits—namely, hypocrisy. The camel, the rock-badger, the harem, and the swine all give the *appearance* of being kosher. The first three can demonstrate their "*kashrut*" by emphasizing that they do, after all, chew their cud. The swine, too, can show its cloven hooves in order to "prove" its virtue. They all, therefore, have the ability to hide their true natures behind a façade of purity. Only on close inspection do we realize that these animals are unclean.

These animals wave a kosher flag but hide unclean cargo. This is much worse than possessing both non-kosher *simanim*. Animals with both non-kosher *simanim* don't try to "deceive" us about their impurity, but rather openly and honestly declare where they stand. With them, there is no hypocrisy and there are no misleading impressions. For this reason, the Torah first mentions the kosher signs of these animals, because it is these deceptive signs that make them even more unclean.[4]

When reading the story about the multicolored garment, Jacob gift to Joseph, the Torah states, "and his [Joseph's] brothers saw that their father [Jacob] loved him more than all his brothers, so they hated him and could not speak with him peacefully."[5] Rashi comments on this verse: "From their faults we learn their virtues, for they did not speak one way with their mouths and think differently in their hearts." Even as they erred, we see their honesty.

---

4 See *Leviticus Rabbah* 13:3.
5 Genesis 37:4.

To be sure, the issue of hypocrisy and religious integrity presents a most severe problem: For what is ghastly about evil is not so much its apparent power but its uncanny ability to camouflage. In our days, when every human deed and thought is the object of suspicion, man begins to wonder whether it is at all possible to live a life of integrity. Is piety ever detached from expediency? Is there not a vicious motive behind every action? Are we not smooth-tongued and deceitful even when we appear to be honest?

This is also true on a practical level. One of the functions of *kashrut* is to protect the animal from pain even during the slaughtering.[6] This is accomplished by the many strict laws of *shehitah* in accordance with *halakhah*. Attacks on this method, by several European countries or political parties, are nothing but expressions of anti-Semitism camouflaged by so-called animal rights arguments.[7] In fact, we see constant and severe violations of these rights in their own abattoirs, where animals are horribly mistreated and sometimes mercilessly killed.[8]

Yet, in all honesty, however, how many of our "glatt kosher" kitchens, including my own, are still truthfully kosher? A haunting question, from which we cannot hide. We cannot deny that even in Jewish slaughterhouses, where proper *shehitah* is done, there have been serious violations of another law: *tza'ar ba'alei hayyim* (the Torah's prohibition against inflicting unnecessary pain on animals). How are these animals handled just before the *shehitah* takes place? Are they treated with mercy when they are put on their backs so as to make the *shehitah* easier? (This can easily be accomplished with the known Weinberg Pen, or by other methods.) What if chickens or other fowl are kept under the most unacceptable conditions, such as in overcrowded containers? Are these animals and chickens still kosher, even if the *shehitah* was one hundred percent accurate? Since when is the actual *shehitah* more important than the laws of *tza'ar ba'alei hayyim*? It seems self-righteous and duplicitous on the part of

---

6 See Maurice D. Harris, *Leviticus: You Have No Idea* (Eugene, OR: Cascade Books, 2013), 38; Jordan Curnutt, *Animals and the Law: A Sourcebook* (Santa Barbara: ABC-CLIO, 2001), 177.

7 See Cnaan Liphshiz "Why Kosher Butchers in Western Europe Are Preparing to Close Shop." Jewish Telegraphic Agency. November 28, 2017. Accessed March 28, 2018. https://www.jta.org/2017/11/27/news-opinion/world/why-kosher-butchers-in-western-europe-are-preparing-to-close-shop.

8 See Dale-Harris, Luke. "Revealed: Exported EU Animals Subject to Abuse and Illegal Conditions." *The Guardian*. March 01, 2017. Accessed March 28, 2018. https://www.theguardian.com/world/2017/mar/01/revealed-exported-eu-animals-subject-to-abuse-illegal-conditions.

ultra-religious Jews to insist on glatt kosher *shehitah*, with all its stringencies, when the animals are badly treated prior to *shehitah*, in defiance of *halakhah's* requirements? Are they not as *treif* (non-kosher) as any other animal that is not slaughtered according to *halakhah*? Can we hide behind the laws of *shehitah* and then look the other way when the laws of *tza'ar ba'alei hayyim* are violated? Is that any less hypocritical?[9]

The laws of *shehitah* and *tza'ar ba'alei hayyim* were meant for Jewish communities who would eat meat occasionally, not for the huge industry we have today where these laws can no longer be properly applied. That being the case, wouldn't it be appropriate and advisable for religious Jews to become vegetarians? Since the massive growth of the meat industry, in which thousands and thousands of animals are slaughtered daily, it has become more and more difficult, if not impossible, to treat animals humanely, as Jewish law requires.

Judaism fully recognizes this problem of hypocrisy. It is difficult, if not impossible, to know whether one acts out of self-interest, or out of absolute integrity. But as long as the question hounds us, and we admit to possibly being the victim of our own camouflage, and we try to extricate ourselves from this malaise, we have done what is humanly possible. Our greatest problem is when we are no longer disturbed by our ability to hide from our own camouflage. Once hypocrisy begins to be a state of mind, it becomes real evil. "The true hypocrite is the one who ceases to perceive his deception, the one who lies with sincerity."[10]

---

9 The realities of modern factory farming make the issue of treifot extremely complex. See Michoel Zylberman, "The *Kashrut* of Commercially Sold Milk," *Journal of Halacha and Contemporary Society* 54 (2007): 93–113. http://aleph.nli.org.il:80/F/?func=direct&doc_number=000460694&local_base=RMB01, fn. 18.

10 André Gide, *The Counterfeiters*, tr. from French by Dorothy Bussy (New York: Vintage Books Edition, 1973), 427.

CHAPTER 3

Milk and Meat

The Dangerous Mixture

Rabbi Dr. Nathan Cardozo

There is one law in the Jewish tradition that no doubt has puzzled scholars and laypeople alike: that which prohibits the mixing of milk and meat. Its source is found in the Torah,[1] but no clue is provided as to its meaning. Strangely enough, it is this mysterious law that has had the greatest influence on the daily life of Jews for thousands of years, right up to the present day. It divides the Jewish kitchen into two sections—meat and milk—and has far-reaching implications: two sets of pots, pans and cutlery, which are kept separate in every way. This law encompasses much of Jewish life and has turned Judaism into something distinct.

What could be the reason behind this prohibition? While one might argue that many other Jewish dietary laws try to infuse people with sensitivity, this can hardly be said about the law of milk and meat. We might, for example, contend that the animals and fowls that we are forbidden to eat are those that are aggressive and carnivorous, and the Torah wishes us to distance ourselves from such traits. But the mixture of milk and meat doesn't seem to highlight any particular unwanted characteristic.

There is another strange dimension to this law. It is not only forbidden to consume a mixture of milk and meat, but the blending of these food categories, in the form of cooking, baking, and other such processes, is also forbidden, even if they will not be consumed.[2] One is obliged to destroy this mixture. This is reminiscent of the law on Pesach that forbids not only the consumption of *hametz* (leavened bread) but even having it in one's possession.[3] While one may still sell the leavened bread to ensure against benefitting from the

---

1 Exodus 23:19, 34:26; Deuteronomy 14:21.
2 BT *Chulin* 115b; *Shulhan Arukh, Yoreh De'ah* 87:1; *Pitchei Teshuva* 2.
3 Exodus 12:19, 13:7; BT *Pesahim* 29a.

prohibited substance, this is not permitted in the case of a milk and meat mixture. The obligation to destroy this combination of milk and meat seems, therefore, to indicate an acute matter that doesn't allow for any compromise. Why should this be?

Kabbalah

According to Jewish tradition, God created the world with the specific purpose of having human beings sanctify it. We are asked to infuse the world with the divine spark that is found within ourselves, since we were created in the image of God.[4]

To enable the creation of the universe, God had to withdraw the *Ein Sof* (infinite spiritual light). Only in this void, or darkness, would physical existence become possible. In kabbalistic tradition this principle is called *tzimtzum* (self-withdrawal or self-constriction) and is one of the most difficult concepts to understand in kabbalistic philosophy.

Once human beings were created, God informed them of their task to ensure that this withdrawn light would (at least partially) return. This would be possible by means of sanctification. By connecting all physical elements with the *Ein Sof*, this withdrawn light would return, and the universe would be lifted from its purely physical dimensions. This was to be accomplished through the fulfillment of good deeds, the commandments, and the study of Torah. Ultimately, everything would return to God, the Infinite Source.[5]

One way to grasp this concept is to imagine a circle that is open on top. The initial point of creation is to the right where the circle starts, and the motion of time begins. The circle itself symbolizes the path on which the world must journey until it will, on completing the circle, re-enter the initial open space on top—the moment when the purpose of all existence has been fulfilled and time comes to an end.

---

4 Genesis 1:27.
5 One may wonder why God wished to create a physical world if, after all, it was intended to revert back to spirituality. The kabbalists respond by saying that the division between the spiritual and the physical, originating with the act of creation, allowed for the capacity of longing, the urge and drive to bring unity to that which has been divided. This, they believe, is the greatest good that God wanted to bestow. Love, the quality that provides people with the highest form of joy, is, after all, the result of two components longing to become one. See Friedrich Weinreb, *De Bijbel als Schepping* (Wassenaar, Holland: Servire, 1963).

The circle has, however, another important feature. It symbolizes the confines within which the world must travel to return to its original Source (symbolized by the open space on top of the circle). As long as the world moves *along* and *within* the line of the circle, it will finally be connected with the original Source. But if it will break through and run wild, it will no longer be able to bring itself back into the confines of the circle, never to return to the Original Source and consequently failing to fulfill its purpose. This means devastation and chaos.

The line of the circle itself must also be seen as symbolizing the dividing line between that which is permitted and that which is forbidden. Everything *inside* the circle is assured of the possibility to return to its Source and is therefore permissible. There is still a connection with the Original Source (symbolized by the open space on top), regardless of how far removed from it something may be. Consequently, the dividing line is the border between that which is permitted (inside) and that which is forbidden (outside).

There is another kabbalistic idea, which teaches that what is more material, and therefore "independent," lies closer to the outside (borderline) of the circle. All that is less material and more dependent on God is nearer to the center of the circle and therefore closer to its original Source. "God is a circle whose center is everywhere and circumference nowhere." When looking in the Creation chapter, we find that a certain evolving process took place, which led to the appearance of the animal world at the end of the six days of Creation, just before the arrival of Adam and Eve[6]. This evolving process reveals a constant increase in "independence"—greater mobility and physicality. While the plants are still completely dependent on the Divine Source, having no say of their own, the small insects and creatures are more autonomous. This independence increases drastically with the creation of the larger animals on the Sixth Day.[7]

The Animal World

The superior animal must be seen as the most autonomous creature within the corporeal world. Unlike a human, the animal is not blessed with a divine soul and has no part in a spiritual, moral existence. While it is highly autonomous, it is nevertheless completely bound by the physical world in that it cannot

---

6 Genesis 1:25–27.
7 Much of the original sources mentioned by the Kabbalists were never cited, and thus, we do not know exactly from where they receive them originally.

rise above the laws of nature. In this sense, it is the most developed physical creature in the world. Consequently, it is the animal that walks on the borderline of our circle.

This has far-reaching consequences. Since the animal has developed to the outermost line of the circle, it treads a dangerous path: one more step and it will find itself outside the line. It will then run wild and lose its connection with the Source on top of the circle. This must be prevented at all costs, since it would lead to chaos. In other words, this animal is never to become a "super-animal," through over development. It must not become more physical than it already is. To emphasize the point: animal flesh is not to become "super-flesh," developing beyond the limits of the circle border.

Milk

You may now begin to understand the danger of mixing milk with meat. The animal is the most advanced of all physical creatures. It finds itself on the border of the circle. Any addition to its physicality will force it out of the circle. It will sever its connection with the Source and become overdeveloped, creating "super-flesh."

But what is milk? Milk is no doubt the most important nutrient for human and animal body development. It is nourishment par excellence. It contains all the ingredients that enable proper physical development.

Since milk is the substance that promotes body development, it would be a fatal mistake to add this nutrient to fully developed meat. The milk would continue to advance the meat's expansion beyond its proper borders. This would suggest a wish to overdevelop the already optimally developed flesh of the animal. It would be as if one wanted to make the animal world break out of the circle and sever its connection with its Source, which would indicate denial of the very purpose of this world. This may also explain the ruling that one is not only forbidden to consume a mixture of milk and meat but is also obligated to destroy this mixture even if there is no intention to consume it. Its existence is a denial of the foundation of God's plan for His creation and is therefore forbidden.

Section 2 **Bridging Kashrut with Ethical & Spiritual Concerns**

CHAPTER 1

The Moral Underpinnings of Kashrut Rabbi

Rabbi Dr. Shmuly Yanklowitz

As a child, I didn't think much about what I ate. I wasn't concerned with the cost, or nutritional value. I certainly never thought about the quality of the *kashrut* or about the ethical dimensions that were involved in bringing the food to my table. It wasn't that I disregarded those concerns per se, I was just oblivious. When I began adhering to the laws of *kashrut* on a strict basis, I experienced an awakening. Never before in my life had I applied so much self-restraint. When I was younger, I never paused to consider what I was eating; now I think about each bite as an opportunity to fulfill a moral imperative.

Yet, the contemporary reality of *kashrut* poses pronounced difficulty for me. As my personal evolution continued, I felt the need to keep kosher based on my commitment to the Torah. I view the commitment to the timeless ritual of holy kosher laws as central to Jewish survival and continuity. Yet my kosher diet did not reflect any particular ethical pursuit per se, and was merely connected to my being only by necessity of the tautology of keeping kosher because the Torah says that is the ethical purist of the laws. My deeper awakening of kosher consciousness only emerged after I realized that the mechanisms of *kashrut* were touchstones for a much deeper value system. Indeed, I began to realize that the opportunities for food consciousness were vast. I began to appreciate the deeper temporal dimensions of *kashrut* (as a vision): its overall effects on human health, worker treatment, animal welfare, care for the environment, and the scourge of poverty. Corresponding to the ethical call of kosher law, a personal spirituality of consumption began to stir within my soul. Consequently, I wondered why this spiritual element seemed absent from the broader Judaic consciousness. For instance, why, as demand for kosher meat grew, did kosher slaughter follow the trend of the non-kosher meat industry towards mass industrial production methods, with animals often penned in for extended periods of time in the harshest conditions? How could a community as demanding and painstakingly particular about the laws of *kashrut* allow for such treatment of animals, deemed so inhumane in secular culture?

Something deeply troubling, spiritually unsettling took hold in the Orthodox Jewish community. Could a different voice—steeped in the love of Torah and *mitzvot*, reverent toward the sages and sensitive to the pace of change—call for a kosher consciousness to emerge? Or better yet, to revive?

Animal Welfare and *Kashrut*

To those who know my work as an advocate for animal welfare, it may come as a surprise to learn that my grandfather was a butcher. Though he has long since passed, I clearly remember his passion for service and his love of animals, even though he thought that his obligation to the world was to use their flesh as food. The juxtaposition of a benign, kindly gentleman flaying the flesh of an animal into the stuff of deli meats and finger foods for family gatherings has not been lost on me. That is why, today more than ever, I believe that advocating for animal welfare is a significant part of the contemporary Jewish enterprise. In truth, I think of my grandfather often when engaging in my work as a rabbi and activist.

A brief snapshot of what is happening today: What was once the purview of family or small farm-owned operations has grown into a sinister Goliath of bureaucracy and mechanized slaughter. Yet, the ethical reality of *kashrut* can't be upheld under strict scrutiny. Over and over again, we find corruption among *kashrut* agencies and kosher companies, we find neglect for animal suffering in kosher slaughterhouses, we find the abuse of workers in kosher establishments. How could this be so pervasive if Torah commentators throughout the ages had described *kashrut* as a vehicle toward attaining higher holiness? The first command of the Torah—in the Garden of Eden, no less—was about the ethics of food consumption. Indeed, the emergence of moral consciousness—eating from the Tree of Knowledge of Good and Evil—was born in this first act of food consumption. Today, therefore, each ethical food choice we make has the potential to be a *tikkun* (a holy repair) on that first historical mistake in the Garden of Eden.

In the depths of Jewish tradition and law, there is one refrain that echoes through each and every story, each and every law: to do what is *yashar v'tov*, what is right and good; to uphold the banner of justice and treat all our fellow human beings with dignity and respect. For millennia, the purpose of living a Jewish life has been to uplift the soul to perform its heavenly duties here on earth and bring about positive change to a world occupied with conflict, exploitation, and woe. This need to exercise the everyday potential of the soul expands to all facets of life, yet nowhere is this more immediate than in the food industry. In the Torah, there is a serious emphasis on what products are consumable and which are forbidden.

Nachmanides (Ramban) wrote that a person can be *naval birshut ha-Torah* (a disgusting person with the permission of the Torah). It is not enough, he argued, to follow the letter of the law. If we wish to be moral and holy, we must go further. His specific example, in fact, is one who keeps kosher but is morally oblivious and gluttonous with kosher meat.[1] *Kashrut* is indeed about far more than some technical ritual preparation laws. Rav Joseph B. Soloveitchik has been credited with the expounding on the thought that *halakhah* is a "floor not a ceiling."[2] We fulfill the basic ritual requirements but that is only the beginning of considering the moral and spiritual dimensions involved with each religious act.

Still, sadly—and too frequently— the businesses and certifying agencies the Orthodox Jewish community relies on to uphold the high standards of *kashrut* have failed. Whether it be through the exploitation of undocumented workers and minors or unethical business practices, these organizations repeatedly let down the Jewish community and denigrate the sacred practice of *kashrut*. This leaves the Jewish community in a terrible bind. We require both ritual and moral excellence from businesses who provide us with food. Yet, the kosher certification agencies we rely on for guidance and spiritual security are unwilling to take even the most basic step of ensuring the most basic moral responsibilities of our food providers. Their moral standards are, sadly, now equivalent to the secular corporate standards of factory farming in twenty-first-century America.

In that vein, I'm reminded of a story about Rabbi Israel Salanter, the nineteenth-century founder of the *mussar* movement, who was asked to certify a *matzah* factory. As *matzah* is the primary food symbol of Passover, its production is strictly regulated. Companies that make *matzah*, prepare for months before sending their product out; with much money at stake.

---

1 Commentary on Leviticus 19:2.
2 Quoted in *Covenantal Imperatives: Essays by Walter Wurzburger on Jewish Law, Thought and Community*, 17.

So, as one can imagine, having a properly certified operation for *matzah* is vital for business. Yet, after inspecting this particular factory at great length, Rabbi Salanter declined the certification. Everyone was shocked. Surely, all the ingredients were correct and in proper order? The process to make the *matzah* was performed to the letter of the law. How could the *matzah* be denied? For Rav Salanter, the certification was denied due to how the factory treated its workers. They were overworked, made to work in brutal conditions without a though to their care. This ethical reason was reason enough for Rabbi Salanter to deny a much-desired (and undeniably lucrative) kosher certification.[3]

Such a commitment to ethical concerns, while technically separate from the kosher laws themselves, shows that additional—but dynamic—moral mandates are always interwoven with ritual law. Admittedly, when we don't remember that we are here to respect and cherish the works of the Divine, we concede our moral primacy as human beings. But we cannot merely point fingers at the producers. Jewish consumers motivated by *halakhah* understand that the consumer is the ultimate enabler of the producer's abuse.

Indeed, if we are serious about the underlying ethical dimensions of *kashrut*, then we must demand change. The progress that's already been made is only a small step toward ensuring that the kosher industry returns to its position as a moral enterprise. For too long, ethics and business practices in the kosher food industry have been treated as separate spheres. This approach needs to end and with haste. Making forthright and righteous choices at the grocery store is our most powerful asset. By taking positive steps towards reducing the harm in our consumer choice, we are saying, in essence that transparency and kindness to workers is essential, that not giving in to corporate bullying is crucial, and that we are empowered to be the positive change in the world. At the heart of the matter is the notion that the institutions that control kosher certification exist to serve *our* communal needs, not their bottom line. It is entirely within our power to demand more from them.

Though it may sound counter-intuitive to some, *kashrut* should be viewed as a vehicle for social progress. Once we pause and examine the holiness of our food, we see layers of moral truth hidden within each bite. It is a holy enterprise to be concerned with the *kashrut* standards, the worker treatment, animal welfare, the environmental process, whether something is certified fair trade, or

---

3 See Howard N. Lupovitch, *Jews and Judaism in World History* (New York: Routledge, 2010), 175; Irving M. Bunim, *Ethics from Sinai: A Wide-Ranging Commentary on Pirkei Avos*, vol. 1 (Jerusalem: Feldheim, 2002), 219.

has the proper nutrition or is sustainably produced. Each pursuit brings us one step closer to fully walking in the path of God. When we arrive at the insight that the world was not created for us alone and that we are not entitled to consume whatever we wish, we reach a powerful Torah ideal, one that may be the most spiritual ideal of all. We share this beautiful world with a remarkable diversity of life. We are only one aspect of this biosphere. And when we respect it for what it is, we venerate that which brought it forth from the far reaches of time and space.

Hearing the Cries of Workers

Our concern goes beyond the Jewish community. Indeed, we need societal change. We must be sure that the workers who are cooking, cleaning, and serving food in our country are being paid properly. Firstly, they should be paid what they are owed. Secondly, the legal standards for pay must be adjusted. Raising the minimum wage to a living wage helps poor families move out of poverty, spurs job creation, and stimulates economic growth and thus it is our Jewish obligation to lead this fight for justice. Rema—Rabbi Moses Isserles— taught that when one is involved in a communal issue of public monies one must engage (act and vote) l'shem shamayim (for the sake of heaven; i.e., for the right reasons not based on self-interest).[4] It is crucial that Jews fall out on the right side of this national debate as advocates for systemic change for the poor.

Consider this: Raising the minimum wage is actually a *mitzvah*. Rambam articulated that ensuring others have work that can sustain them is the highest rung of the hierarchy on how to give *tzedakah*.[5] In Jewish thought, *tzedakah* does not mean charity but justice. We rectify social wrongs and fulfill our obligations through the giving of *tzedakah*. By raising the minimum wage, we are enabling others who work to move out of deeper poverty. The Rambam is dealing here with private voluntary giving; this value is all the truer when being applied to a system of legislation, as the mission of the Jewish people is to perpetuate our most precious values of the good and the just into broader society. Our messianic dream is the creation of a society where Torah values are actualized in the world to create a more just and holy civilization.

The rabbis already limited the wealth of owners selling essential food to help the poor through the laws of *onaah*. The owner could not keep more

---

4 *Choshen Mishpat* 163:1.
5 *Mattanot Aniyim* 10:7.

than one-sixth profit in order that others could be sustained as well.[6] For the Talmudic rabbis, the value of maintaining an orderly just society where the needs of all can be met outweighs the full autonomy of owners to maximize their profits to no end.

The primary wage responsibilities fall upon employers. Rabbeinu Yonah, the thirteenth-century Spanish rabbi, taught:

> Be careful not to afflict a living creature, whether animal or fowl, and even more so not to afflict a human being, who is created in God's image. If you want to hire workers and you find that they are poor, they should become like poor members of your household. You should not disgrace them, for you shall command them respectfully, and should pay their salaries.[7]

What Rabbeinu Yonah taught through this piece was that when we hire a worker and find that they are still poor after we pay them, then we must treat them as "members of our households" (*b'nei beitekha*). If we choose to become an employer, then we must take responsibility to ensure our workers do not live in poverty.

Yet, when we look at the minimum wage in its current state, its existence is a collective violation of the Biblical prohibition of *oshek* (worker oppression): workers remain poor while they work to their full capacity.[8] The previous verse tells us that we must not be enablers of social wrongs (*lifnei iver*) linking the two responsibilities of fair wages and Jewish activism. Now is the time for a collective Jewish intervention to ensure that those who work can live comfortably.

Imagine, if you will for a moment, the plight of an unwed mother living in the Southeast side of Washington, DC. Abandoned by an abusive boyfriend, shunned from family and left to fend for herself and her child, Mother struggles to pay the bills. Her hourly income to support herself and her child should be around $30 to meet their most basic needs. Though she has a job to provide for her family, she is only paid the minimum wage in Washington (which, due to ballot initiatives, is slowly rising to $15 per hour).[9] That gap of nearly $15

6 BT *Bava Batra* 90a; *Choshen Mishpat* 231:20.
7 *Sefer HaYirah.*
8 Leviticus 19:13; see also Deuteronomy 24:14–15.
9 Jackson Brainerd, "State Minimum Wages: 2018 Minimum Wage by State," accessed March 27, 2018, http://www.ncsl.org/research/labor-and-employment/state-minimum-wage-chart.aspx.

means that despite all the hard work Mother puts in to care for her child, life is economically unsustainable.

But even beyond the big urban areas, income inequality is stark and unrelenting as the cost of living is enormously high. Indeed, reducing the gap between what one earns and one needs to live is one of the most crucial moral issues that needs to be addressed in contemporary society. Many of the problems that face sustainable growth has to do with the issue of fair wages and a reasonable income. The mechanism by which we improve our communities depends on how willing we are to fight for a more equitable compensation structure that allows all those who work to lead decent and productive lives.

Adapting to New Environmental Realities

Behavioral change is difficult, particularly around food consumption. Further, it can be frightening to reimagine our lifestyles. Leadership theorists speculate that we should not operate from fear and past models when attempting to "weather the storm." For instance, during the early months of the Great Recession (circa 2007–2012), there was a systemic breakdown in institutional leadership and the role of dynamic thinking. A commentary in the *Harvard Business Review* summed up the difficulties succinctly:

> The danger in the current economic situation is that people in positions of authority will hunker down. They will try to solve the problem with short-term fixes: tightened controls, across-the-board cuts, restructuring plans. They'll default to what they know how to do in order to reduce frustration and quell their own and other's fears. Their primary mode will be drawing on familiar expertise to help their organization weather the storm.[10]

History is filled with stories of leaders who adapted to change and those who refused and were engulfed by history. Joseph interpreted Pharaoh's dreams to mean that seven years of abundance would be followed by seven years of famine, and so the grain surplus was stored during the years of abundance and helped save Egypt during the succeeding famine.[11] Joseph could have become

---

10 Ronald Heifetz, Alexander Grashow, Marty Linsky, "Leadership in a (Permanent) Crisis," *Harvard Business Review,* https://hbr.org/2009/07/leadership-in-a-permanent-crisis.

11 Genesis 41:25–30.

acquiescent, as Egyptians were used to regular flooding from the Nile that annually replenished the soil, seemingly guaranteeing a perpetual plentiful food supply. He understood, however, that eventually there would come a time of scarcity, and acted accordingly. On the other hand, the last king of Babylon, Belshazzar, ignored the literal "writing on the wall"[12] at his peril and decided to celebrate what he thought would be a long, secure reign. In reality, a large force of Persians and Medes were about to overthrow him and bring about the downfall of Babylon.

Today, there are signs of great change on the horizon, and we look to our leaders to have the vision of Noah. For many years, scientists have warned of the consequences of climate change and the impact of humanity on that change. Unfortunately, at Kyoto (1997) and Copenhagen (2009), world leaders largely failed to address this looming crisis in a meaningful way. In 2013, scientists made another effort, with a stark prediction. In late September of that year, the world's leading climate scientists (through the Intergovernmental Panel on Climate Change, a United Nations-sponsored group) issued a dire warning: there is a limit to the carbon emissions issued by humans that, if exceeded, will irrevocably put the world on a course toward cataclysmic climate change. Unfortunately, this level may be reached within a few decades unless there is a radical reduction of greenhouse gas emissions. Thomas F. Stocker, co-chair of the Group, noted that "Climate change is the greatest challenge of our time. In short, it threatens our planet, our only home." Sadly, many climatologists have concluded that the UN group was optimistic in its calculations.

Former President Barack Obama endorsed the conclusions reached by this and other UN panels, but his efforts to achieve the reduction requiring the development of technology that would trap carbon dioxide emissions underground has met with strong political opposition. Indeed, in 2017 President Donald Trump allowed the United States to back away unilaterally from the non-binding Paris Agreement meant to stave off more environmental damage by developed nations.[13] For Trump, the Agreement harmed American business at the expense of protecting the environment. And although the criticism from the international community was high, the United States' departure has begun. Only time will tell of the consequences. But as we view these startling

---

12 Daniel 5:25–28.

13 Michael D. Shear, "Trump Will Withdraw U.S. From Paris Climate Agreement," *New York Times*, June 1, 2017, accessed March 27, 2018, https://www.nytimes.com/2017/06/01/climate/trump-paris-climate-agreement.html.

events, we also have the ability to ponder the question of whether our leaders, in facing dramatic change, shall be like Joseph or Belshazzar.

It is our obligation to not retreat in fear of challenges. Rather, we must prepare for them and adapt to new realities. Sometimes we must look outside of our own "arks" to properly—emotionally and practically—prepare for the new world we are embracing.

CHAPTER 2

Eating Our Way from Holiness to Justice

Kashrut as a Bridge Between Competing Value Systems

Rabbi Dr. David Kasher

By the middle of the book of Exodus, the reader of the Torah might reasonably presume that the central value in this religion is to be: justice. In the great revelation of the Ten Commandments, the Israelites are immediately given some of the basic moral rules of the social order: "Do not kill"; "Do not steal." Just one chapter later, in the Covenant Code of *Parshat Mishpatim*, the concern with social justice has already taken on a level of great specificity. There are laws governing the fair treatment of slaves,[1] assigning liability for damages to persons or property,[2] and ensuring the equal treatment of rich and poor in the legal system,[3] among many others. The project of constructing a society organized around principles of justice is well underway. By the time we arrive into the book of Leviticus, it is clear that there is another value competing for dominance in the religion of the Israelites: holiness, or *kedusha* (קדושה).

Now, we have certainly seen holiness before in the Torah. In the first usage of the term in the book of Genesis, it has the connotation of 'distinct,' or 'separate,' when it is applied to the Shabbat as follows:

> God blessed the seventh day and sanctified it (*vaykadesh oto*), because on
> it God ceased from all the work of Creation that God had done.[4]

---

1 Exodus 21:2.
2 Ibid., vv. 12–36.
3 Ibid., 23:2–3.
4 Genesis 2:3. See, for example, the interpretation of Rabbi David Kimhi (the "RaDaK," 1160-1235, Provence), who also authored *Sefer Ha-Shorashim*, a dictionary of Hebrew roots, in his

וַיְבָרֶךְ אֱלֹקִים אֶת-יוֹם הַשְּׁבִיעִי, וַיְקַדֵּשׁ אֹתוֹ: כִּי בוֹ שָׁבַת מִכָּל-מְלַאכְתּוֹ, אֲשֶׁר-בָּרָא אֱלֹקִים
לַעֲשׂוֹת.

Holiness also appears to have something do with closeness to God, who is the source of the sacred. This is the impression we get from the first appearance of the word in the book of Exodus. In Moses' encounter with the Burning Bush, God tells him:

> Do not come any closer. Remove your sandals from your feet, for the place on which you stand is holy ground (*admat kodesh*).[5]
> וַיֹּאמֶר, אַל-תִּקְרַב הֲלֹם; שַׁל-נְעָלֶיךָ, מֵעַל רַגְלֶיךָ--כִּי הַמָּקוֹם אֲשֶׁר אַתָּה עוֹמֵד עָלָיו,
> אַדְמַת-קֹדֶשׁ הוּא.

We continue to see references to holiness, here and there, throughout the book of Exodus, and it is clear that this is a value to be pursued. So we are told that the Israelites are to be "holy people" to God,[6] and even that they will be known as a "holy nation."[7]

It is not until the construction of the Tabernacle and the appointment of the priesthood that holiness truly comes into center stage in the Biblical text. The Tabernacle, meant to serve as a dwelling place for God on earth, is called a *mikdash* (מקדש), or "sanctuary"—literally a "holy thing."[8] And the High Priest, who oversees the sacrifices offered there, is to wear a golden headband, on which will be engraved: *Kodesh l'Hashem* (קדש להי)—*Holy to the Lord*.[9] By the time we are several chapters into Leviticus, which first presents itself as a book devoted to detailing the work of the priests and the rituals of the Tabernacle, we have fully entered into a religion of holiness. The sacrifices themselves are described, again and again, as "holy"; the inner chamber of the Tabernacle is "The Holy of Holies"; and the priests themselves, dressed in their "holy garments" are the official representatives of this holiness. The most explicit description of their role is given in Leviticus 10:

---

interpretation of this verse: ויקדש אתו, שיהא קדוש ומובדל משאר הימים (*vayekadesh oto*—that it be *kadosh*, and separated from the rest of the days). See also the word's listing in the Brown-Driver-Briggs Hebrew and English Lexicon: 1. *set apart as sacred, consecrate, dedicate* . . . .**d.** 7th day (by God) Genesis 2:3 (2nd ed.), 451.

5 Exodus 3:5.
6 Ibid., 22:30.
7 Ibid., 19:6.
8 Ibid., 25:8.
9 Ibid., 28:36.

To distinguish between the sacred (*hakodesh*) and the profane, and between the impure and the pure. And to teach the Children of Israel all the laws that the Lord spoke to Moses.[10]

וּלְהַבְדִּיל, בֵּין הַקֹּדֶשׁ וּבֵין הַחֹל, וּבֵין הַטָּמֵא, וּבֵין הַטָּהוֹר. וּלְהוֹרֹת, אֶת-בְּנֵי יִשְׂרָאֵל, אֶת-כָּל-הַחֻקִּים, אֲשֶׁר דִּבֶּר ה אֲלֵיהֶם, בְּיַד-מֹשֶׁה.

It is clear by now that holiness is to be an essential feature of this new religious community. And it is equally clear that the priests will be the mediators of this holiness, sanctifying themselves in order to enter into the holy place and carry out the holy rites on behalf of the people. What remains unclear is what exactly this holiness is, and whether or not the people themselves will have any access to it. So far, holiness seems entirely outside of them. God is holy; the Tabernacle and its offerings are holy; perhaps the priests themselves are holy men—but all of these things stand at a distinct remove from the average Israelite. So how are they to fulfill the charge to become "holy people"? Is such a thing even possible?

* * *

The first indication that the Children of Israel are able to move holiness from the priesthood into their own lives comes in Leviticus chapter eleven with the listing of kosher and non-kosher animals. This is the first set of laws we have in Leviticus that are not directly connected to the sacrificial rites. Instead, we get the categories of mammals, fish, birds, insects, and reptiles that may or may not be eaten. The passages are rather technical and detail-heavy, until we come to the end, when we get this sweeping statement of the purpose of these dietary restrictions:

> For I the Lord am your God: you shall sanctify yourselves and be holy, for I am holy. You shall not make yourselves unclean through any swarming thing that moves upon the earth. For I the Lord am the One who brought you up from the land of Egypt to be your God: you shall be holy, for I am holy.[11]
>
> כִּי אֲנִי ה, אֱלֹקֵיכֶם, וְהִתְקַדִּשְׁתֶּם וִהְיִיתֶם קְדֹשִׁים, כִּי קָדוֹשׁ אָנִי; וְלֹא תְטַמְּאוּ אֶת-נַפְשֹׁתֵיכֶם, בְּכָל הַשֶּׁרֶץ הָרֹמֵשׂ עַל-הָאָרֶץ. כִּי אֲנִי ה, הַמַּעֲלֶה אֶתְכֶם מֵאֶרֶץ מִצְרַיִם, לִהְיֹת לָכֶם, לֵאלֹקִים; וִהְיִיתֶם קְדֹשִׁים, כִּי קָדוֹשׁ אָנִי.

These verses make it quite clear that the practice of keeping kosher is meant to sanctify the practitioner. Just as the priests will have to monitor what animals

---

10 Leviticus 10:10–11.
11 Ibid., 11:44–45.

are offered in the temple and how they are prepared carefully, so the whole Children of Israel will monitor what animals come in their bodies. Remember, just a chapter earlier, we read that the priests were supposed to teach the people how to distinguish between the pure and the impure, the sacred and the profane. Why was that necessary if the sacrifices were to be handled exclusively by those same priests? Now, it becomes clear that the people will use what they have learned from the priests in order to make such distinctions in their own food preparation. One gets the sense that the body has become the new sanctuary, with every person treating their own mouth and stomach as a kind of mini-altar, on which only holy things can be placed.

Holiness, then, already made a remarkable transition from the official realm of the Tabernacle into the personal sphere of eating. Through our food choices, we purify and sanctify ourselves. Here is the first hands-on method that we, the common people, have for becoming holy.

* * *

Yet, these decrees are only a first step for we have still not answered the question of what holiness is, and why we ought to seek it. Is sanctity really just about maintaining bodily purity? Eating is undoubtedly one of the basic human activities, but it seems unlikely that our entire quest for personal holiness would begin and end with food. The careful reader of the lines above, however, will see that they are pointing us toward a much broader destination. For while the words, *"You shall be holy, for I am holy,"* are first stated here, they are most famously repeated further on, as the opening to Chapter Nineteen of Leviticus:

> Speak to the whole Israelite community and say to them: You shall be holy, for I, the, Lord your God am holy.[12]
>
> דַּבֵּר אֶל-כָּל-עֲדַת בְּנֵי-יִשְׂרָאֵל, וְאָמַרְתָּ אֲלֵהֶם-קְדֹשִׁים תִּהְיוּ: כִּי קָדוֹשׁ, אֲנִי ה' אֱלֹקֵיכֶם.

The language is almost the same. This time, however, the injunction to be holy like God comes as the introduction to an entire corpus of laws, one of the longest in the Torah, often referred to as—what else?—"The Holiness Code."

The character of these laws, however, are surprising here in the middle of Leviticus. For they, for the most part, do not focus on the sacrifices or purities and impurities. Instead the Holiness Code contains commandments like the following:

---

12 Ibid., v. 2.

You shall revere your mother and father ... I am the Lord your God.[13]

אִישׁ אִמּוֹ וְאָבִיו תִּירָאוּ, וְאֶת-שַׁבְּתֹתַי תִּשְׁמֹרוּ: אֲנִי,ה׳ אֱלֹקֵיכֶם.

You shall leave the [the corner of your field, and the fallen fruit of your vineyard] for the poor and the stranger. I am the Lord your God.[14]

לֶעָנִי וְלַגֵּר תַּעֲזֹב אֹתָם, אֲנִי ה׳ אֱלֹקֵיכֶם.

You shall not steal. You shall not deal deceitfully or falsely with one another ... I am the Lord.[15]

לֹא, תִּגְנֹבוּ; וְלֹא-תְכַחֲשׁוּ וְלֹא-תְשַׁקְּרוּ, אִישׁ בַּעֲמִיתוֹ ... אֲנִי ה׳.

You shall not insult the deaf, or place a stumbling block before the blind ... I am the Lord.[16]

לֹא-תְקַלֵּל חֵרֵשׁ-וְלִפְנֵי עִוֵּר, לֹא תִתֵּן מִכְשֹׁל; וְיָרֵאתָ מֵּאֱלֹהֶיךָ, אֲנִי ה׳.

You shall not render an unfair judgment: do not favor the poor, nor show deference to the rich, with justice shall you judge your kinsman ... I am the Lord.[17]

לֹא-תַעֲשׂוּ עָוֶל, בַּמִּשְׁפָּט-לֹא-תִשָּׂא פְנֵי-דָל, וְלֹא תֶהְדַּר פְּנֵי גָדוֹל: בְּצֶדֶק, תִּשְׁפֹּט עֲמִיתֶךָ.
אֲנִי, ה׳.

Respect; charity; honesty; compassion; justice—these values are all through the Holiness Code. Lofty principles, to be sure, but what do they have to do with holiness itself? This body of rules seems more reminiscent of the laws we received just after the revelation at Sinai, before we started dealing with the Tabernacle, than anything we have seen so far in Leviticus; that seems to be precisely the point. This pivot is a return to a religion centered around justice, the one we thought we were getting before we took a turn into the arcane realm of Holiness. For the priests have been, ever since the glory days of Mount Sinai and the subsequent downfall of our worshipping the Golden Calf, redirecting us away from the ethical message of the Covenant to a new, singular focus on Sanctity and the purity required to maintain it.

And it is *kashrut*, the kosher laws of Chapter Ten, that serves as the bridge between these two paradigms by shifting the priestly responsibility for maintaining holiness over to us through personal dietary laws. Our bodies act as the medium by which the transcendent and external realm of holiness is—quite literally—internalized. Once that transference has been achieved, Leviticus moves on to redefine the holiness we seek: the construction of a just society.

---

13 Ibid., v. 3.
14 Ibid., v. 10.
15 Ibid., vv. 11–12.
16 Ibid., v. 14.
17 Ibid., vv. 15–16.

However—and this is key—Leviticus never leaves holiness behind. The message is not: forget the sacred and focus on the ethical. Rather, the message is: true holiness *is* manifested through justice. We find the sacred and the pure not only in the Tabernacle, and not only in our bodies, but out in the real world, in living human society. We encounter holiness in the respect with which we treat one another, in the way we care for the most vulnerable among us, and even in the gritty work of resolving conflicts with fair laws. Holiness is not so mysterious, after all. For it is bound up in the pursuit of all the just principles that make for a well-functioning and compassionate society.

What about God? Does this vision of holiness not reduce the sacred to mere ethical humanism? Don't we lose, in the midst of such pragmatic calculations, the transcendent encounter with Divinity that the priests had been so carefully cultivating? No, not if the wording of Leviticus itself is to be taken seriously. For note that all the laws we listed end with the phrase, *"I am the Lord your God."* Just so, the kosher laws were meant to keep us holy, *"for I am holy."* And this is also the language of the Holiness Code: *"be holy, for I, the Lord your God, am holy."* These practices are not merely good in themselves, but also because they serve as acts of imitating God. *"Just as God is merciful and compassionate,"* goes a Talmudic saying, *"so you should be merciful and compassionate."*[18]

This merging of justice and holiness is a radical move, but also a brilliant one for two reasons. First, it resolves a problem we started with. That is, we knew that God was supposed to be holy, and that we were charged with becoming holy like God—but how? What was this mysterious force called "holiness?" Now we have an answer. For if God's holiness is intertwined with God's justice, then we have a principle we can actually understand and attempt to emulate. We can actively seek holiness, even without intermediaries, because it consists of practices that makes sense to human beings and directly apply to human life. And it was sanctifying our eating, that most human of all activities, which first made that direct contact with holiness seem possible.

But the other great advantage that this synthesis provides is that it addresses a classic tension in religious life. For there have always been some voices that preach service towards mankind as the primary goal of religion, and other voices that describe the ideal religious life as one of pure devotion to the sacred. What then, the religious seeker is left to wonder, is the true spiritual path? Is it to go out and attempt to repair a broken world? Or to stay intensely focused on clinging to God? Are we to live our lives in pursuit of justice, or of holiness? The great breakthrough of Judaism was to figure out a way to answer: both. Both at once.

---

18   BT *Shabbat* 133b.

CHAPTER 3

Increasing Holiness in Life

Towards an Expanded *Kashrut*

Rabbi Dr. Irving (Yitz) Greenberg

The Torah is a covenant (*brit*) of redemption. Its central purpose is the repair and perfection of the world through a process called *tikkun olam*. In his master work, *Halakhah Man*, Rabbi Joseph B. Soloveitchik writes that the Torah opens with a Chapter on Creation *not* to teach humanity about cosmology or metaphysics. Instead, the purpose of the Creation narrative is to teach that repair of the flaws of creation is the ultimate hope/yearning of a *halakhah* person. In this way, we understand that God recruited the human being to repair the unfinished, imperfect aspects of Creation.[1] And, even further, we see that *Torat Moshe* is the founding document of that divine-human partnership to perfect the world.

Indeed, the central concept of the Torah is that as a collective, the Jews will create a just society through "justice and law"[2] within which human life will be treated with all the dignity and fairness that it deserves. All of humanity is tasked with this responsibility for the globe, starting with the covenant of Noah.[3] According to the prophets, the goal for the eventual coming of the Messiah is to overcome poverty, hunger, oppression, war, sickness, and all the enemies of life.[4] The "eventual outcome will be they will do no evil or destructive acts in my whole Holy Mountain (i.e., planet Earth)"[5] When that state is achieved, then God's presence will be manifest to all (" … the earth will be full of knowledge of God.")[6] The Jews will serve as a "covenant nation,"

---

1   Joseph B. Soloveitchik, *Halakhah Man* (Philadelphia, Jewish Publication Society, 1984) 99–110, especially 99–101.

2   Genesis 18:18.

3   Genesis 8–9.

4   See Isaiah 66:12 (poverty); Isaiah 49:8–10 (hunger); Isaiah 11:4; Ezekiel 37: 24–27 (oppression); Isaiah 2:3–4 (war); Isaiah 35:5–6 (sickness).

5   Isaiah 11:9.

6   Ibid.

a pacesetter, and guide to "light (the path forward) for the nations."[7] Therefore, all the actions, legislation, and policies of the Jewish nation should be guided by covenantal standards and directed toward the realization of the ultimate goals which are to maximize life and uphold its dignity.

For the same purpose, the actions of every individual are to be reshaped into covenantal actions to advance the goal of maximizing life; in every moment of life, there is a need to act. In every situation, however, there is a choice to act on the side of life (improving quality of life) or on the side of death (degrading the quality of life). The Torah, I contend, prescribes covenantal actions to steer us toward life (or quality of life) to the maximum point of realization possible given the realities of current societal standards and entrenched interests. In this theological approach, the *halakhah* is the code of covenantal actions which move us toward life. That the *halakhah* regulated more and more aspects of life, implies a deep theology. No acts of living are intrinsically morally neutral or without consequences for the overall equilibrium of life in the society or in the individual's life. If done one way, an act of life like eating (say: eating healthy food) strengthens life. If done another way, eating (say: consuming only processed foods, or with too much salt and sugar added, or excessive fat and calories) harms life. Eating overfished species tilts the tide of environment toward death for that species. *Every act in life* is potentially re-shapeable to maximize life and quality of life. This philosophy applies to ritual actions as well, in that every ritual action should nurture life and every encounter with God should strengthen reverence for life. A classic expression of this approach is found in the act of eating and the laws of *kashrut*.[8]

Eating and Holiness

Eating is a central human activity. One cannot live without eating or without an adequate diet; hunger and malnutrition are the enemies of life. Much of

---

7 Genesis 11–12; Isaiah 42:6–7.
8 The argument for these claims about the centrality of world repair (*tikkun olam*), the full-ness of human dignity and the supremacy of life in the Torah are fleshed out at length in my forthcoming book, *The Triumph of Life*, especially chapters 1–3. The covenantal approach to upholding life and to world repair is articulated in depth in chapters 6–8. In this volume, I also argue that the next step in maximizing life is to give upholding quality of life the weight we know give to upholding the quantity of life (*pikuach nefesh*—saving life—overrides all but three of the commandments). Giving greater weight to upholding the quality of life is also a *tikkun* for the degradation of quality of life widely inflicted in the *Shoah*. See also ibid., chapter 11.

the quality of life is shaped by the practices and social interactions of eating. Therefore, the Torah sought to place eating within the zone of holiness, that is where there is the presence of God. The sanctification was primarily expressed by ensuring that the process of eating was suffused with reverence for life.

The initial vision was that humans and higher forms of life, ideally, should not live by killing other higher forms of life. In the Garden of Eden—in the portrait of the ideal world—humans and all higher organisms are instructed: "I have given you every herb bearing seed ... and every tree, on which is fruit yielding seed; to you it shall be for food."[9] According to Isaiah, this ideal reverence for life will be restored in messianic times. In the era of world perfection, according to the prophet, animals as well as humans will live at this ideal level.[10]

Yet, the covenant of redemption operates in the real world, the flawed, imperfect reality that humanity inhabits. The covenantal method starts with what is and seeks to move it, step-by-step, toward the final perfection. In the process, the Torah often compromises with the entrenched evils of reality in order to enable people to move from where they are towards the goal. In the real world, meat eating is ubiquitous. Whether out of acknowledging the entrenched nature of the eating, or recognizing the hunting, carnivorous nature of humans and predatory animals, the Torah compromises and permits the consumption of animal flesh. To uphold the ultimate vision, however, meat eating was surrounded with restrictions. This is to say that in the eating of meat, there is an incremental step (or acknowledgment) of the goal of not eating higher organisms.

Strikingly, the covenantal compromise with meat eating is the Torah's choice to illustrate God's decision to enter into a covenantal relationship with humanity. Initially, the Lord insisted that humans must live up to the ideal standard. When "... the Lord saw that the wickedness of man was great in the earth," a Great Flood was inflicted to wipe out the evildoers and, as it were, start over again. At this point, the Lord turns decisively from the way of perfection (or else!) and to the covenantal way toward perfection. First, the Divine pledges that all natural laws will be fixed and upheld. Never again will natural laws be overridden to punish humanity for doing the wrong action (for this is coercive).[11] Instead, God works in partnership with humanity, accepting humans with their flaws and limits, instructing and inspiring instead of forcing people to

---

9   Genesis 1:29–30.
10 Isaiah 11:6–7.
11 Compare Genesis 6:5–7 with Genesis 8:21–24.

do good.[12] Covenantal behaviors begin with the actual standard operating procedures of the society but move the behaviors towards the ideal (to the extent possible). Thus, covenantal behaviors are often *not* the ideal, but the best possible under the circumstances. What saves this compromise from being a sellout of the ideal is the Divine knowledge that in future generations—starting from a different level or in a culture with higher standards—covenantal behaviors will be redirected to a higher level, and a level much closer to the ultimate ideal.

* * *

Kashrut

What we have come to call *kashrut* is the codification, over the centuries, of actions intended to turn eating into a covenantal act. I contend that the laws regulating what species/food types can be eaten are primary expressions of the concept of regulating eating to advance us toward the covenantal goal of increasing life in the world. By this measure, *kashrut* is the first example of prescribed covenantal behaviors in the Torah. These laws are incorporated into the covenant with Noah, which is the covenant with all of humanity. The Torah feels keenly that permitting the killing of animals for food weakens reverence for life. In fact, the text couples permission to eat animals with a warning against killing humans (which becomes easier to do when the taboo against killing all higher life is weakened).[13] Therefore, the first kosher laws apply to all of humanity. All human beings were instructed not to eat blood for "the life force is in the blood."[14] This prohibition is an acknowledgment that life is sacred and its dignity is rooted in God, independent of human standards or needs. Humans, in principle, should not squander (nor have a right to dispose of) other animals' lives. Similarly, all humans (and not only Jews) are prohibited from eating flesh of *living animals*. Such actions are cruel and lack respect for the animal's life.[15]

The Israelites—as the vanguard for humanity on the Messianic journey—were held to a higher standard of reverence in the Mosaic/Sinaitic covenant.

---

12 Genesis 9:1–17.

13 Genesis 9:5–6.

14 Leviticus 17:11–12. The Israelites poured the blood of the sacrifices onto the altar as a ritual of atonement for the "sin" of eating meat.

15 This is one of the seven commandments given to the sons of Noah, that is all humanity. See BT *Sanhedrin* 59a.

If an animal was to be killed, the act of killing had to be done swiftly, painlessly[16], and individually (rather than industrially), as a sign of reverence in the act of taking a life.[17] The number of species permitted to be eaten was sharply reduced for Jews. All permitted species were non-predators. Animals who live by killing would be distanced from the holy people who seek in all actions to express reverence for life.

In the Temple, a holy place where God was more intensely present, the number of species permitted to be sacrificed was reduced even further. The message is that the closer to God one was (psychically speaking) the less exceptions permitting killing were allowed. Finally, the Torah alludes at the clash of eating meat with the commitment to uphold life by stating "do not boil a kid in its mother's milk."[18] The Oral Law fleshes out this awareness by comprehensively restricting any combination of meat (food generated by the death of an animal) and milk (food that is a key source of life, commonly and especially in the form of mother's milk.) It is prohibited to cook them together, eat them together, or to derive any benefit at all from any combination of meat and milk.[19] Later communities and traditions built on these notions to emphasize the contradiction of sacredness of life and the lower standard of eating meat to spell out extreme avoidance of using the same dishes or pots or kitchen sinks to prepare these foods.[20]

* * *

Increasing Holiness Areas in Life

The expansion of *kashrut* from an initial blood prohibition for humanity to an elaborate set of restrictions as to species permitted to eat is paralleled in the broader *halakhah*, the code of covenantal behaviors. The laws governing the

---

16 In *shehitah*, the death stroke cuts the jugular vein first. This cuts off the blood supply to the brain, bringing loss of consciousness and an end to pain. In pre-modern times, the other forms of killing, the animal died more slowly and suffered more. The modern development of stunning an animal before killing challenges the supremacy of *shehitah* as a method of reducing pain. However, this issue is too complicated to deal with in this essay.

17 Deuteronomy 12:21, as interpreted in BT *Hullin*, chapter 1 et seq.

18 Exodus 23:19, 34:26; Deuteronomy 14:21.

19 BT *Hullin* 115b.

20 Of course there are other possible interpretations of these laws, but I am focusing on the sense of "contradiction" between milk (life) and meat (death) which was turned into minutiae of avoiding any contact between the two in preparing or serving food. See *Shulhan Arukh*, *Yoreh De'ah* 87–97, the chapters on meat in milk. For a comprehensive statement of the biblical/rabbinic dietary system as a statement of reverence for life, see Jacob Milgrom, *Leviticus 1–16: A New Translation with Introduction and Commentary* (New York: Doubleday, 1991), 735.

treatment of women were revised by the sages to elaborate their rights as free women,[21] to protect their rights over property which they brought into the marriage and in the *ketubah* which guaranteed a financial settlement protecting them against poverty in the event that they were divorced. While the Rabbis did not challenge the patriarchal system in which women were both secondary and protected, they ameliorated women's dignities beyond the dominant social priorities in the Biblical period. We see this again with how the treatment of Hebrew slaves was improved, in the Biblical and Talmudic eras, in all areas: type of work, hours of labor, conditions of support, and so on.[22]

Elsewhere, I argue that these expansions reflect the role of the Oral Law to recalibrate covenantal actions in later generations in order to bring them closer to the ultimate ideal, the messianic standard. To this I add that there was a theological factor in this expansion. The rabbis concluded that God had self-limited again to shift the divine and human roles in the covenant. By self-"reduction," God became hidden, less visible, and less controlling in life and history in order to call humans to a higher level of responsibility in the covenant. There would be no more heavenly revelation or prophetic messages straight from God. Instead human minds (i.e., the rabbis) studied past revelation texts and analyzed historical events to tell the people what God wants of them now.

God had become less "visible" and domineering in order to come closer to people. Thus holiness—which in biblical times was visible but "concentrated" in such places as the Holy Temple—was now present in many areas of life but had to be uncovered. Holiness—God's presence as *Shekhinah*—could now be discovered in the home, in the kitchen, in the bedroom, in deeds of loving-kindness, in learning Torah, and in prayer congregations all around the world.[23]

It is my contention that we are living in another such age of Divine *tzimtzum*—becoming more hidden in the world. In this era, God self-reduces and is totally hidden in order to summon humans to take on full responsibility of the covenant of redemption. Projecting the rabbis' insight: God, totally hidden, is present everywhere, but the Presence must be uncovered by human insight and actions. Humans are called to find God in secular areas everywhere in the world. Simultaneously, we encounter holiness in these areas if we uncover the presence of God by bringing out the depth dimension of life in these secular areas. The time has come to uncover the presence of God in all areas of food

---

21 Exodus 21:10; BT *Ketubot* 47b and 48a–b.
22 Leviticus 25:39 and *Mekhilta*; ibid., *Kiddushin seriatim*.
23 This is discussed at length in Chapter 8 of *The Triumph of Life* (forthcoming).

and food preparation by expanding the laws of *kashrut* to deepen the dimension of life in all these areas.[24]

Expanding *Kashrut*

Recently, out of search for the intensification of life experiences, food and food preparation have become a high visibility, trendy, and mass market phenomenon. There is great interest in enriching activity, in deepening the flavor and character of food as well as discovering healthier eating patterns. Much of these interests are perceived as secular activity. Nevertheless, acting on the covenantal principle of finding the holy in the secular, we need to expand the *halakhot* of *kashrut* to intensify respect for life among those who keep traditional kosher—and those who do not.

The ever-increasing provision of meat as living standards rise is stressing the environment and threatening the quality of life on earth. The growth of industrial farming and animal husbandry has broadened availability of reasonably-priced food. On the other hand, large-scale farming has led to excessive use of fertilizer which pollutes water sources and farming techniques which exhaust or erode soil. Industrial animal husbandry has led to crowding, cruelty, and reduced the quality of life for the animals raised only to die. The related environmental degradation has become a threat to all life. For Jews, as people who believe that eating should be a covenantal behavior supporting life, neutralizing or reversing these trends is our first priority. Given the broad rise in standards of food adequacy and the fact that in many developed countries there is a large variety of vegetarian foods available, we might reassert the classic push toward systemic vegetarianism. Prohibiting meat eating and ending the endless slaughter of countless animals, could be a major contribution to rebalancing the Earth toward life.

In the past, failure in the preparation process (bad slaughter or using sick animals, let's say) made a kosher animal unfit for consumption. Extending this model, current practices such as making veal more tender by starting calves to make them anemic or preparing pâté de foie gras by aggressively force-feeding geese should be prohibited as an assault of the dignity of life. Overfishing and/or eating endangered species should be similarly prohibited, for this pushes the planet toward death instead of life. Raising chickens in crowded conditions, they cannot move or they bite off parts of the neighbors is a violation

---

24 Ibid., chapter 13 (forthcoming).

of the prohibition of causing pain to animals. We can uphold life by designating such foods (or eggs which are the product of such crowding) to be unfit for human consumption. God, whose "compassion is all God's creatures,"[25] is driven out by such cruelty. On the other hand, practical steps to improve conditions—organic farming, expanded use of plant derivatives and equivalents, individualized slaughter, and humane husbandry—bring us closer to God and, consequently, God closer to us.

We also must look to the image of God of those who prepare the food. Were the conditions of the work degrading? Were the conditions unjustifiably stressful? Dangerous to preparers' health? What about exposure to pesticides and weed killers endangering the health of workers in food packing plants and crop agriculture? When we respect life more intensely, then such violations disqualify food from eating. There is a story of Rabbi Israel Salanter, who said: anti-Semites spread vicious reports that Jews bake blood of children into their *matzahs*. This is false. Alas, our true sin is in spilling the blood of *overworked or underpaid workers* in the process of preparing food.[26]

Reverence for life should extend to the eaters as well. Choosing healthy food is a rigorous requirement of holy eating. Being aware of harmful ingredients, avoiding sugar, excessive fat, and salt, adding elements like iodine or folic acid to prevent illnesses or birth defects, directly fulfill the command to "choose life." These considerations expand the covenantal parameters of those who observed the laws of *kashrut*. In accordance with the universal focus of this new stage, however, these applications are for all people as well as to all foods that are eaten.

From another perspective, we can apply the *halakhah* of increasing quality of life to the act of preparing food. A master chef brings out deeper flavors and food by cutting or preparing it in a certain way. Others develop a richer taste by juxtaposing to foods of varying ingredients, textures, and aromas. Even reshaping the aesthetic experience by positioning food on a plate or varying portion sizes brings out wonders of the food. This is an intensification of life; a dimension of holiness. This constitutes uncovering the delights which the Creator has built into the edible vegetation of the world. This process brings us closer to the One who generated wondrous food in the first place. As long as these

---

25 Psalms 135:9.

26 See Bonnie Margulis, "Worker Justice and Ethical Kashrut." *Interfaith Coalition for Worker Justice of South Central Wisconsin.* April 7, 2014. Accessed October 9, 2017. http://worker-justice.org/2014/passover-reflection-2014/.

pleasures are not enhanced at the expense of another's life or pain, say, boiling a lobster or eating a snake alive in order to freshen the taste, then these activities bring us closer to the Divine infrastructure of existence. Quite possibly these enhancements help us meet the Talmudic test that a person will be held accountable in the afterlife for every permitted pleasure that he/she passed on in this world.[27] In short, increasing the embrace of life through joy should be a hallmark of holy secularity in this new age.

Lastly, there is the social dimension of eating. Eating together, conversation and fellowship while dining, lead to knowing the image of God of the other. Preparing food for another—as an active service, commitment to love—and all such actions are elements of savoring life, deepening relationships and growing in depth of living. All such actions are holy for they deepen the quality of life and uncover the presence of the hidden Divine. Special meals on national celebrations—such as Israel Independence Day grills, Fourth of July barbecues, or even a charity of community dinner—also add a connection to a higher cause. They are reminders that we have a commitment to move the planet towards freedom and perfection. Thus, the secular realm of living is suffused with sacred values and its quality of life is deepened. In that depth dimension of life, we meet the image of God, of the other, and we connect to the hidden Divine ground of our existence.[28]

Through this proposed expansion of *kashrut*, we can reassert the proper understanding of what it means to be an observant Jew. A *halakhah* Jew (religious Jew) is not one who keeps the whole inherited tradition unchanged (this is the *haredi* definition) nor is it that we observe parts of the tradition which others are dropping because of modern influences (this is the Orthodox denominational definition).

There are two defining characteristics of a holistic, religious Jew. Firstly, religious Jews bring the whole tradition with us and learn from it even as we find new applications or make changes in order to live lives of holiness in new circumstances. Secondly, religious Jews hold themselves to the highest standards possible that exist right now. Despite the reverence for life in *kashrut*— those who keep kosher, as a group, are not holding themselves to the highest standards of respect for animals and for the environment as are being upheld by proponents of eco-kosher, organic farming, and other food ethicists.

---

27 JT *Kiddushin* 48B, h. 1.
28 *The Triumph of Life* (forthcoming), chap. 13.

The definition of *kiddush ha-Shem* is that those who are close to God set higher standards of behavior which impress and inspire others. They make God beloved because people admire the higher standard behaviors and credit God for inspiring people to act that way. An expanded *kashrut* offers a way for *kashrut* observant Jews and all people who seek to eat in holiness (more ethically and more respectfully of life) to do so.

The Spirituality of Eating

CHAPTER 1

Eating as a Sacrament–
The Eating Table and the Coffin

Rabbi Dr. Daniel Sperber

Eating in traditional Jewish thought is a sacrament: a strict and pious endeavor. There are a variety of benedictions made before and after eating and drinking different kinds of food and drink, which reflect the understanding that God's sovereignty over all that is in this world; we acknowledge his beneficence for granting us of the fruits of his creation. With this in mind, we may better understand a variety of rules and customs connected with eating, some of which we will touch on here. But, for the purposes of this chapter, let us look at a seemingly banal aspect of eating: the table.

Where can one find holiness in this seemingly mundane inanimate object? The table at which a holy Sage studies constitutes a fine advocate for him after his death, as it were, because of the holiness that was absorbed from the sacred books he studied over a lifetime. This is somewhat similar—in thought if not in *halakhah* practice—to the fact that the table—*bima*—on which a Torah scroll is placed to be read in the synagogue has a degree of holiness that falls into the category called *tashmishei kedushah* (implements of sacrality).[1] However, we might question why the table at which he *ate* should serve in a similar such capacity. And in order to answer this question, we need briefly to examine the status of the table used for eating, and the sacramental nature of eating.

A key to understanding this thought is found in the Talmud: "The altar of wood was three cubit high, and the length thereof two cubit . . ." (Ezekiel 41:22).

---

1 See *Shulhan Arukh, Orah Hayyim* 154:3; *Mishnah Berurah* ad loc. note 10.

And the verse continues, "This is the table that is before the Lord."—The verse opens by referring to the altar and ends by calling it a table! R. Yohanan and R. Eleazar both stated: "As long as the Temple existed, the people of Israel atoned for their sins through the altar. But now [that there is no Temple] a person's table atones for him."[2]

And similarly, in the *Zohar*: "A person's table supports and purifies him from all his sins … "[3] In other words, our table has taken the place of the altar, and instead of offering sin-offerings on the altar, through behavior at the table and suitable thoughts, and an attempt to act with holiness and in purity, we can expiate our sins, and remedy our failures.

In this vein, we read in the *Magen Avraham*[4] following that which is written in *Sefer Hasidim*:

> One must not kill lice on the table at which one eats, and one who does so, it is as though he had killed on the altar, *for the table is an altar.*[5]

Within this symbolic context, we may well understand rabbinic admonitions against standing or sitting *on* a table, and not to put children on them, because "the table is like unto an altar," and the verse in Psalms 23:5 says, "Thou preparest a table before Me … "[6] This probably goes back to *Sefer Hasidim*, which relates as follows:

> A certain child stood jumping over the table upon which his father would keep his books. And the table was not merely for his books, but also when he wished to eat bread, he would remove the books until he finished eating. And the boy stood on the table and climbed down and cut the sole of his foot on a knife. And the father said, "It was my sin that caused [his wound], for I let my son climb on the table which had on it books."[7]

---

2   BT *Berakhot* 55a. Also: BT *Hagigah* 27a; BT *Menahot* 97a.

3   Exodus, *Terumah* 154a.

4   Rabbi Abraham Gombiner, to *Shulhan Arukh, Orah Hayyim* 167, subsect. 6.

5   See sect.107, ed. Margaliot, 136. Note, not "like an altar" but "is an altar" (though in R. Yona's Sefer ha-Yirah, ed. Zilber, 62, the formulation is: "like an altar").

6   See Yishai Mazlumian, *Sefer Segulot Raboteinu* (Holon, 2013), 387 (citing *Shulhan ha-Tohar* by R. Aaron Roth, Satmar 1933, chapter 2; and R. Yehoshua Friedman, *Rivevot Efraim*, vol. 6, sect. 95).

7   No. 920, ed. Margaliot, 501.

See also *Yosif Ometz* by Yosef Yuspa Neurlingen, where he adds that:

> One may not seat or stand a child on the *shtender* upon which one places
> *mahzorim* and prayer books, for they are dedicated to holiness (*meyuhad*
> *li-kedushah*).[8]

Neurlingen goes even further to state, in the name of Rabbi Eliezer of
Metz, that those benches on which one seats youths in the synagogue, their
owners may not bring them back home in order to use them for sitting, even if
they were to substitute them with better benches, for one may not reduce their
holiness, and he who is careful (i.e., stringent) in this respect may he be blessed.
This notion, of course, leads us into a whole additional *halakhah* area of *maalin
ba-kodesh ve-ein moridin*, one ascends in holiness, that is increases holiness, but
does not descend—that is decrease the status of an object's holiness.[9]

Following this same line of thought we find in *Kitzur ha-Shelah*:

> Just as at the altar one gave a portion [of the sacrifice] to God, so too [at the
> table] one must give a portion [of one's food] to the poor. And if there are
> no poor people at hand, since one fully intends to give to the poor person
> should he appear, it is as though one had entertained a poor man at his table.[10]

Similarly, in Responsa *Hitorerut ha-Teshuvah* by Rabbi Shimon Sofer,[11] we
read that the practice of his father, the Ktav Sofer (Rabbi Shmuel Benyamin
Sofer) was to throw pieces of bread to those who participated in his meal,
explaining that such was the practice at the altar, namely, throwing the blood of
portions of sacrifices offered on the altar. And this he did despite what is stated
expressly in the *Shulhan Arukh*[12] that one may not throw about pieces of bread,
for this constitutes contempt of food (*bizion okhlin*). Presumably he thought
that reenacting part of the Temple practice could not be considered an act of
contempt.

Against this background in mind, we may well understand the passage in
Mishnah Avot 3:3, in the name of Rabbi Shimon:

---

8   Second ed. Jerusalem 1965, 16, sect. 64, who refers us to *Sefer Hasidim*.
9   See, for example, *Shulhan Arukh, Orah Hayyim* 154; BT *Berakhot* 28a; BT *Megillah* 9b; BT
    Yoma 12b; BT *Horayot* 12b.
10 Yehiel Michel Epstein, Jerusalem ed. 54–55.
11 Budapest 1923, sect. 171.
12 *Orah Hayyim* 171:1.

If three have eaten at one table and have not spoken over it words of the Law, it is as though they had eaten of the sacrifices of the dead (cf. Psalms 106:28), *for it is written, "For all tables are full of vomit and filthiness without God"* (Isaiah 28:2). But if three have eaten at one table and have spoken over it words of the Law, it is as if they had eaten from the table of God, for it is written, "and he said unto me: This is the table that is before the Lord" (Ezekiel ibid.).

Indeed, the Shelah—Rabbi Isaiah Horowitz—insisted that there be Torah discussions at the table "with either a *halakhah* ruling or a new explanation of a verse or an *aggadah*"[13] explaining that this was like that which the *Maamad* priests did alongside the sacrificing priests, when they read the story of Creation.[14] This also explains the customs to recite a Psalm before the grace after meals (Psalms 137 on weekdays; 126 on the Sabbath, etc.) as in so doing we recall the Psalms that the Levites would sing in the Temple.

We understand the passage in *Midrash Lekah Tov* (to Exodus 40:30): "And he set the laver between the tent of the congregation and the altar and put water there to wash withal." From here they learned that immediately after one washes one's hands [for the meal] one must make the benediction. The author of the *Lekah Tov* was referring to the sections in the Talmud where we learn of the necessity closely to conjoin the handwashing with its benediction.[15] For the laver was close to the altar, and he who delays making the benediction of washing his hands over and above the time it's taken to walk twenty-two cubits—the distance from the Nikanor Gate to the area of sacrifice and back; this is considered an "interruption" (*hefsek*), meaning he must repeat the process.[16] Indeed, the obligation to wash one's hands before eating bread (and other foods) was derived from the verse in Exodus 30:18–19:

Thou shalt make a laver of brass … , and thou shalt put water therein. For Aaron and his sons shall wash their hands and feet thereat.

So, we learn from *Eliyahu Rabbah*:

We have learned [the rule of] washing hands from the Torah from Moses and Aaron, as it is said, "And thou shalt make a laver … For …

---

13 *Shaar ha-Otiyyot*, 86b.
14 *M. Taanit* 4:3.
15 *BT Berakhot* 42a; *YT Berakhot* 1.1.
16 See Rema to *Orah Hayyim* 166:71, and Derishah, ibid.

[they] shall wash their hands ... thereat." From here Rabban Gamliel [derived that he should] eat [even] non-consecrated food *(hullin)* in a state of purity.[17]

Likewise, the Rema writes that:

It is a *mitzvah* to bring to the table salt before one cuts the bread, for the table is like unto an altar, and the eating like a sacrifice, and it is said, "[And every oblation of thy meat offering shalt thou suffer the salt of the covenant of thy God to be lacking from my meat offering:] with all thine offerings thou shalt offer salt" (Leviticus 2:13).[18]

And, finally, we may point to the practice of covering, or even removing, knives from the table when making the grace after meals. This we find in *Sefer ha-Rokeah:*

One covers the knife at the time of the Grace after Meals, recalling the verse (in *Deut.* 27:5), "[And there shalt thou build an altar unto the Lord thy God, an altar of stone:] thou shalt not lift up any iron tool upon them." And in the *Mekhilta* (*Yitro*, ed. Horovitz-Rabin, 244): From here R. Shimon ben Eleazar would say: The altar was created to lengthen a person's years, and iron [tools] were created to shorten a person's years. It is not suitable that the shortener should be wielded over the lengthener. And the table is like an altar ... [19]

And in this context, we may further note that the *Mekhilta*,[20] interprets the verse, "And thou shalt sacrifice upon it" [i.e., the altar] as meaning "next to it" or "at its side," but not on it.[21] This custom is brought in the *Shulhan Arukh:*

It is the custom to cover the knife during the Grace after Meals, and it is the practice not to cover it on Shabbat and festivals.[22]

---

17 Ed. Ish-Shalom, 72; On Rabban Gamliel's ruling, see Gedalyahu Alon's classic study in his *Mehkarim be-Toldot Yisrael.* vol. 1, Israel 1957, 158–69.
18 *Orah Hayyim* 167:5
19 Sect. 332, ed. Shneurson, 230.
20 Exodus 20:21, ed. Horowitz-Rabin (Jerusalem, 1960), 242.
21 See B. ha-Levi Epstein, *Torah Temimah* ad loc., 219–20 note 118. So the slaughtering knife was also not on, or over, the altar, but beside it.
22 *Orah Hayyim* 180:5.

The *Magen Avraham* ad loc. explained why not to cover it on Shabbat and festivals: "We do not build altars on Shabbat." He also adds that the knife to be covered must be of metal, referring to Rabbeinu Bahya's *Shulhan she Arba* also noting that the *Levush*, of Rabbi Mordechai Yaffe made no distinction between the Sabbath and weekdays. The *Shulhan Arukh ha-Rav*, brings a different reason for the distinction between Sabbaths and weekdays, explaining that the knife represents "the powers of Esav, and on Sabbaths and festivals the Satan has no strength to attack us."[23] The *Nefesh Hayyah* questions the Magen Avraham's reason,[24] arguing that since one does not build an altar during the night,[25] one should not need to cover the knife at night, something that finds no mention in our sources. Rabbi Shalom Spalter, in an article in *Or Yisrael*,[26] suggests that this is why the *Shulhan Arukh ha-Rav* gave an alternative reason for this practice.[27]

In sum, in the eyes of the Rabbis of old, eating was not merely a mechanism to feed the body and sate one's hunger, but was seen as a sacramental act symbolizing expiation of sin and a reenactment of the Temple's sacrificial ritual and therefore required suitable behavior, pure thoughts and both God's permission to partake of his creation, and thanks to Him for giving us the means to preserve our life in order to serve Him in faith and rectitude. Hence, that the sages, who, indeed, ate in piety and in strict accordance with the relevant laws—the table at which they sat and held their meals could serve, as it were, as a suitable witness as to his place of worthiness in the World to Come.[28]

---

23 *Baal ha-Tanya*, 180:6.
24 Rabbi Reuven Margaliot (Tel Aviv, 1954) to the *Shulhan Arukh* ad loc.
25 BT *Shavuot* 15a.
26 19/2 (68), Nissan 5774, 2013, 332–3.
27 See the continuation of his discussion.
28 See further for additional material on the sanctity of the table *Be-Noheg she-ba-Olam*, Jerusalem (n.s. no author, but probably R. Mosheh Rachelsohn), 110–17.

CHAPTER 2

Food for Thought

Hasidic Wisdom on Spiritual Eating

Rabbi Dr. Ariel Evan Mayse

Legend recalls a time that Rabbi Israel of Kozhenits, a Hasidic master renowned for his wisdom and spiritual talents, was visited by a wealthy but miserly individual. The skinflint asked only to be served bread, water, and salt in the Rebbe's home. The Kozhenitser Maggid demanded that he accept nothing less than the richest meal befitting someone of his stature. Rabbi Israel's disciples later asked their teacher, known for his Spartan ways, why he had insisted on giving his stingy guest such royal fare. "Because," said Rabbi Israel, "if he had contented himself with bread and water, he would have thought that the poor may suffice with rocks. But now that he has tasted of this sumptuous food, he will remember that others must be sustained at a higher level as well."[1]

This Hasidic tale reminds us that eating should be an experience of empathy and compassion, a chance to remember those who are less fortunate. Sitting down to table certainly involves *mitzvot bein adam la-makom* (ritual commandments between people and God), but it also includes *mitzvot bein adam le-havero* (ethical commandments between people and people)—eating includes concomitant obligations toward both God and humanity, blending the religious and ethical dimensions of our lives. Gluttony and over-consumption are acts of arrogance and immodesty and such behavior is unbecoming of a religious person. But this Hasidic story is repercussive precisely because it also includes a warning against misguided asceticism. Such pious denial, though perhaps well-intentioned, may cause an individual to close his heart to the suffering and need of others; strict piety may become yet another form of callous

---

1 See Martin Buber, *Tales of the Hasidim*, trans. Olga Marx (New York: Schocken Books, 1975), 292.

self-obsession. This balanced appreciation is rather characteristic of the Hasidic approach to the life of the spirit. As the late Elie Wiesel poignantly summarized, Hasidism teaches that: "The way to heaven … the way to God leads through your fellow man."[2] One who seeks only to fill his own stomach will surely forget the needs of others, but a similar pitfall awaits the pinched ascetic whose ears and heart are closed to the suffering of those around him.

This chapter explores key teachings from the Hasidic masters on eating as a spiritual practice, highlighting their relevance for our contemporary devotional lives. As is clear from the other contributions to this volume, Hasidic thinking on this subject emerges from a line of Jewish tradition stretching deep into antiquity. The book of Leviticus in particular, the heart of the Torah, frames all eating—and consumption of meat in particular—in terms of sacrificial offerings that were eaten within certain sacred boundaries both temporal and physical. This thrust continues in rabbinic law and theology, for the intricate laws of the blessings recited over food found in chapter six of the tractate *Berakhot* reveal the extent of rabbinic investment in eating as a spiritual act.[3] The Talmud suggests that the one's conduct at the table atones for our sins after the destruction of the Temple.[4] We find references to sages who continued to eat their food in a state of ritual purity even after the destruction of the Temple rendered many such laws obsolete.[5] The Talmud recounts a story about pietists who, in their mourning, refused to eat anything that had once been offered in the Temple.[6] This practice is ultimately rejected as untenable, but a brooding voice of discontent remains to declare that all of our eating contains within it a broken-hearted acknowledgment of the imperfection of this world. The Tosefta teaches that we should always leave out one dish from a meal in order to remind ourselves of this fact.[7] When one sits down to a fully-laden table it is easy to forget that ours is a world of fracture, imperfection and want. But denying any and all pleasure from eating is equally unjustified. Indeed, say the

---

2 Elie Wiesel, *Somewhere a Master: Further Portraits and Legends* (New York: Simon & Schuster, 1984), 151.

3 On this subject, see David Kraemer, *Jewish Eating and Identity Through the Ages* (New York: Routledge, 2007).

4 BT *Hagigah* 27a: "This is the table that stands before the LORD" (Ezekiel 41:22). The verse begins with the altar and ends with the table. R. Yohanan and Reish Lakish both taught that when the Temple stood, the altar atoned for one's sins. Now one's table atones for his sins.

5 BT *Hagigah* 19b.

6 BT *Bava Batra* 60b.

7 JT *Bava Batra* 2:17.

sages, one who fasts unduly—like the Nazir who abstains from wine and fruit of the grape—sins by not partaking in the beauty of God's creation.[8] The rabbinic answer to this tension is to embrace eating, but to do so within sacral boundaries.

Medieval Kabbalists developed new food rituals and reinterpreted traditional practices in their quest to frame eating as an act with the power to transform the human being and even to impact the flow of blessing through the Godhead by uniting the *sefirot*.[9] This reached its peak in Safed Kabbalah, where elaborate *yihudim* (unifications) were developed to accompany eating, especially that of the Sabbath and holiday. On the whole Jewish mysticism developed a rather robust relationship with eating as an act of spirit and cosmic significance, although Kabbalistic literature reveals some draw toward fasting, a characteristic held in common with medieval Christian and Sufi pietism.

Rabbi Israel Baal Shem Tov (d. 1760), the charismatic religious leader from whose teachings the Hasidic movement emerged, totally rejected those earlier forms of Jewish pietism that recommended strict asceticism. The Baal Shem Tov outlined a religious path founded in open-heartedness and joy rather than moribund guilt and fasting, explicitly critiquing one of his early disciples who insisted on starving himself.[10] Eating, explained the Baal Shem, was another type of opportunity to serve God, because food and drink contain within them sparks of holiness waiting to be redeemed. This devotional idea undergirds the sacral quality of communal meals in Hasidism.[11] The fellowship of seekers assembles around the Sabbath table—a gathering that is serious, but not solemn—in order to listen to the *rebbe* speak words of Torah, to eat together, and to sing with a single heart. Such meals are among the height of one's communal religious life.

---

8   BT *Taanit* 11a.
9   See Rabbi Joel Hecker, including his *Mystical Bodies, Mystical Meals: Eating and Embodiment in Medieval Kabbalah* (Detroit: Wayne State University Press, 2005).
10 Moshe Rosman, *Founder of Hasidism: A Quest for the Historical Ba'al Shem Tov*, second revised edition with a new introduction (Oxford; Portland, OR: The Littman Library of Jewish Civilization, 2013), 114–15; and see also Immanuel Etkes, *The Besht: Magician, Mystic, and Leader* (Saadya Sternberg. trans) (Waltham, MA: Brandeis University Press, 2005), 139–41.
11 Allan Nadler, "Holy Kugel: The Sanctification of Ashkenazic Ethnic Foods in Hasidism," in *Food and Judaism*, eds. Leonard J. Greenspoon, Ronald A. Simkins and Gerald Shapiro (Omaha, NE: Creighton University Press, 2005), 193–211.

Raising the Inner Spark

The robust approach to religious service offered by Hasidism is rooted in an expansive vision of the cosmos as filled with God's vitality. This theology of divine unity, a kind of mystical monism or "panentheism," is a cornerstone of Hasidic spirituality. "There is no place devoid of the One," quoted the Baal Shem Tov from the *Tikkunei Zohar*, teaching also that we must be ever-mindful of the prophet's words: "The whole world is full of His glory" (Isaiah 6:3). God's sacred vitality inheres within *all* aspects of the cosmos, animating and sustaining the physical realm as an ever-flowing river of divine energy. Therefore, said the Baal Shem Tov, each individual is called to seek God's presence everywhere and in all moments. Such service includes even seemingly mundane deeds, from ordinary conversations to this-worldly activities like eating and drinking.[12] These pursuits are transformed into acts of divine worship when approached with the right kind of contemplative awareness, thus linking all moments of one's life—like the notes of a *niggun*—into a single mellifluous chain of service before the One.

Rabbi Menachem Nahum of Chernobyl (c. 1730–1797) was among those Hasidic thinkers who adhered most closely to the Baal Shem Tov's spiritual path.[13] His homilies reveal a mystical thinker firmly committed to seeking God's presence in every deed. The following teaching, reflective of his religious ethos, depicts eating as a central practice for unlocking and uplifting the divine illumination hidden within the cosmos:

> The world and everything within it, both great and small, was created by the word of God. "By the word of God were the heavens made, and all their hosts by the breath of His mouth" (Psalms 33:6). That word also sustains them and gives them life. "You enliven them all" (Nehemiah 9:6). Were it not for the life force within each thing, it would vanish from existence.

---

12 Louis Jacobs, "The Uplifting of Sparks in Later Jewish Mysticism," in *Jewish Spirituality: From the Sixteenth-Century Revival to the Present*, ed. Arthur Green (New York: Continuum, 1987), 99–126; Moshe Idel, "The *Tsadik* and His Soul's Sparks: From Kabbalah to Hasidism," *The Jewish Quarterly Review* 103 (2013): 196–240; Seth Brody, "'Open to Me the Gates of Righteousness': The Pursuit of Holiness and Non-Duality in Early Hasidic Teaching," *The Jewish Quarterly Review* 89 (1998): 3–44; and Tsippi Kauffman, *In all Your Ways Know Him: The Concept of God and* Avodah be-Gashmiyut *in the Early Stages of Hasidism* (Ramat-Gan: Bar-Ilan University Press, 2009) [Hebrew].

13 Arthur Green is currently in the final stages of a full translation of Rabbi Menahem Nahum's major work, *Me'or Eynayim*, to be published in the Yale Judaica Series. See also his forthcoming *Da'at: Spiritual Awareness in a Hasidic Classic*.

But [we see things that are] in a broken state in this lowly world, having come about through the sin of Adam and the generations that followed. Sparks of fallen souls became encased in things of this world, including food and drink. There is nothing in this world that does not have a holy spark within it, proceeding from the word of the blessed Holy One, making it alive.

That divine spark is the taste within the thing, that which makes it sweet to the palate. "Taste and see that Y-H-V-H is good" (Psalms 34:9). This means that when you taste or see something good, it is Y-H-V-H, the holy spark garbed within that thing, appearing before the eye ... Therefore, when you eat something, the spark within it is joined to your own life-energy, and you become nourished by it.

When you have complete faith that this spiritual sustenance is indeed God's presence hidden within that thing, you will turn your mind and heart entirely inward. Linking both those aspects of yourself to the sustenance coming from that spark, you will join them all to the Root of all, that One from whom all life flows. Then you bring that broken, exiled spark before God, causing great delight. The whole purpose of our religious life is to bring those holy sparks out from under the "shells," those broken places, into the realm of the holy. Thus is holiness raised from its broken state.[14]

The rabbinic dictum of God forming the world through ten "utterances" is often interpreted in the Hasidic tradition to mean that the letters of this divine speech remain within the physical world as an enlivening force. This vitality is God's continuous presence in the physical world, the pulsing sacred core that animates all corporeal things, including inanimate food, by granting them continued life and existence. Over the generations, this inner divine vitality has become increasingly obscured through humanity's misdeeds. We redeem and heal this fractured world through acts of devotion like prayer and study. But when approached with the correct level of contemplative attention, ordinary deeds like eating and drinking expand the boundaries of holiness to encompass

---

14 *Me'or Eynayim*, translated in Arthur Green, *Speaking Torah: Spiritual Teachings from Around the Maggid's Table*, with Ebn Leader, Ariel Evan Mayse, and Or N. Rose (Woodstock, VT: Jewish Lights, 2013), vol. 2, 70–71.

every moment of our lives. Each gesture of spiritual service has the power to raise up a unique spark, illuminating with an extra measure of divine light world one step at a time.

Regarding eating as a sacred practice allows us to draw energy from the reservoir of divine vitality within the food. In this homily Rabbi Menachem Nahum described this vitality as the food's taste (ta'am), an ethereal quality within that is at once indescribable and decidedly real to the experience of the palate. Like the meaning included within a word (also ta'am), an item's taste is infinitely greater than the sum of its ingredients, thus representing the boundless vitality of the Divine.

Tasteful appreciation of this inner nature cannot take place if one simply consumes food with a purely utilitarian sense of purpose, treating food as a commodity to be ingested and then ignored. It certainly does not happen if one bolts down one's food with a sense of piggishness and greed. To uplift the spark, to raise up the sacred vitality within the food, we must approach it—and ourselves—with respect and attention. We must appreciate its specific flavors and its unique composition, seeing the food on our plate as specific expression of God's infinite Being.

I doubt that such a contemplative process is possible when we consume highly-processed comestibles. Such one-dimensional food grants little in the way of nutritional value—spiritual or physical—and it damages our bodies while robbing us of sustenance. The kind of thoughtfulness and attention explored by Rabbi Menachem Nahum requires food that nourishes on multiple levels. It need not be rare or expensive, of course, but it cannot be an aggregate of processed chemicals with little or no connection to the fertility of the earth.

The Hasidic masters speak often of hibbat ha-kodesh, an attitude of tender belovedness toward all things sacred.[15] For this reason they stress the importance of doing things related to the mitzvot by hand (and not by proxy), since this personal involvement deepens one's religious experience and heightens the spiritual resonance of the deed. Translating such Hasidic wisdom on the practice of eating into our contemporary world means expanding such attention to all elements of food production and consumption.

---

15 See also Rabbi Moses Isserles's gloss to Shulhan Arukh, Orah Hayyim 242:1.

Presence in the Act of Eating

Actualizing Rabbi Menachem Nahum's advice about raising up the divine spark and the inner vitality expressed in the food's taste requires further consideration. Just how are we meant to go about doing this? The key, say the Hasidic masters, is focused presence and concentration throughout the process of eating. This is a cardinal element of Hasidic spirituality, for the Baal Shem Tov laid forth a religious path that demands contemplative attention in each and every one of our actions. Hasidic devotion pivots on the notion of *kavvanah*, of heartfelt intention, in religious service and ordinary deeds alike.

The Baal Shem Tov illustrated this point by means of a striking reinterpretation the verse: "Whatever comes to your hand to do, do it with your strength" (Ecclesiastes 9:10), which appears in a book that seems to condone this-worldly pleasures in the face of life's absurdity.[16] From this verse he gleaned the following spiritual message: whatever you are doing—be it prayer, Torah study, or the simple act of eating a piece of fruit—perform the action with the fullness of your being and infuse it with the totality of your reflective, contemplative power. Binding inner realms of the heart and mind together with action has the power to transform an ordinary deed into a direct experience of the Divine glory. Like the fabled character Enoch, described in the Midrash as a cobbler who stitched together heaven and earth, the deeds of the contemporary seeker bind spirit to body and transform the ordinary into the sublime. Eating, thus construed, is a quiet but awe-inspiring revelation of God's splendid majesty.

Distraction is among the greatest enemies of the spirit in the modern era. Quickly consuming fast food, or gulping down a repast while watching a movie, checking email and scanning the news is anathema to the project of sacred eating. Eating correctly requires complete focus, inwardness and attention. In a homily from the school of the Maggid of Mezritch, we read: "On the table place the showbread, before Me always" (Exodus 25:30). Scripture also says: "You shall eat, eat and be sated, and praise the name of Y-H-V-H, who has acted wondrously with you" (Joel 2:26) ...

We know that God created the world through Torah, and through Torah all the worlds continue to exist. The life-energy within each thing consists of the letters of Torah; within them is the inward light of Endlessness (*Ein Sof*), hidden within the letters that sustain all ... This is the meaning of "You shall eat, eat"—eat of the life force of Torah, the sustenance within the food, "and be

---

16 See *Keter Shem Tov ha-Shalem* (Brooklyn: Kehot Publication Society, 2004), no. 91, 52–53.

sated." Once you are sated by words of Torah, becoming a full vessel, then you will absorb the life-energy within the food ...

If you attain that energy within the food, your soul will be sustained by its spirit, while your body is nourished by the physical foodstuff itself. Thus, are soul and body joined together. Then "you shall praise the name of Y-H-V-H, who has acted wondrously with you," since this union of spirit and flesh is truly a wonder, sustained by this food.

Our sages taught that as long as the Temple stood, the altar was there to atone for us. Now it is a person's table [and the way we eat at it] that atones (BT *Hagigah* 27a). Surely, they were referring to those who eat in this way, seeking out the life-energy and the holy sparks within the food [joining them] to their souls, allowing them to serve the Creator ...

Thus "On the table place the showbread" (*lehem ha-panim*). This means "the bread of inwardness" (*lehem ha-penimi*), the life-energy within the food. Place this upon your table; then it will be "before Me always," called "This is the table that is before Y-H-V-H" (Ezekiel 41:22).[17]

The complexity of life, the fusion of physical matter and spiritual energy that is expressed in food, is a remarkable wonder worthy of our amazement. As we come to appreciate this gift, we open our eyes to the possibility of eating in the presence of God. Like a sacrifice on the altar, our consumption of food is a sacral moment. We integrate its vitality into our souls, allowing the spark to become a part of us. This energy, these sparks of holiness from amid the shattered world, infuse us with flow of vitality on which we draw in our quest for inspiration and meaning.

This Hasidic source suggests that a life of practicing Torah should necessarily lead one to a respectful appreciation of food's great power. The author reminds us that God created the world by means of the Torah, echoing a classical midrash often quoted in medieval Kabbalah, and therefore the imprint of God's sacred Word endures within all aspects of the cosmos. We are attuned to find the traces of Torah through constant study, which imbues our every action with deeper significance. This posture finds expression in the structures and rhythms of *halakhah* that guide our lives. Hasidism continued many older kabbalistic food rituals and created some new ones as well, but much of the spiritual project of Hasidism may be described as an attempt to renew Jewish life by granting traditional structures with new religious meaning. *Halakhah* is

---

17 *Orah le-Hayyim,* as translated in Green et al., *Speaking Torah,* vol. 1 (219), no. 91 (2004): 52–20.

a quest or "journey" (*halikhah*) toward *devekut*, communion with the One, a goal that should be reflected in all aspects of Jewish law.

Interpreted with this spiritual paradigm, the many and varied *halakhot* around eating take on new resonance. Many of these laws aim to draw our attention to the sacred task at hand. Blessings are, of course, key to cultivating this consciousness. The Talmud suggests that food is like Temple property (*hekdesh*) until it has been redeemed through a blessing.[18] One must come to know exactly *what* lies before him, becoming aware of the origins, ingredients and the cooking process, in order to be able to offer the correct blessings before and after eating. This attentiveness requires focus and concentration. When eating bread, the staff of the traditional meal, we enter into a greater state of ritual purity in order to be able to better sanctify our meal. Finally, the rabbis declared that one should not eat many important foods while standing up, nor should one eat while walking along the road. Food is to be the center of one's attention, physical and contemplative.

The Dangers of Lustful Over-Consumption

Philosophers, scientists, and religious thinkers have long explored the pleasure-seeking dimension of human existence. Different people find their delight in various forms, but many of us are drawn to the pleasures of the table. There is, of course, nothing wrong with enjoying one's meal—indeed, the pleasure taken in eating can be a reflection of one's deep, thoughtful engagement with the inner vitality within the food. But we know all too well that we may be easily lulled into deceiving ourselves that we are eating spiritually, when we're really just gorging on sumptuous delicacies. Such critique is found among the writings of the early *mitnaggedim*, the opponents of Hasidism, who felt that the Hasidic masters were serving their own cravings rather than worshiping God. Yet thinkers from within the Hasidic camp also issued warnings about the dangers and difficulties of serving God through the physical realm:

> Y-H-V-H said to Moses: Behold I will rain down upon you bread from heaven. The people may go forth to gather it, each day's portion on that day, so that I may test them to see whether they will follow My teaching or not. On the sixth day they shall prepare what they have gathered, collecting double what they did each day ... " (Exodus 16:4-5).

---

18   B. *Berakhot* 35a, and the MaHaRSHA ad loc.

To understand how these holy verses apply to every person and at all times, we must recall the two ways of serving God.

There are some people who have no heart for either knowing or serving the Creator except when they study Torah, pray, or engage in some commandment. But as soon as they go to fulfill their own bodily needs, like eating, drinking, and all the rest, they turn into fools, completely unaware of how to link their thoughts to divinity. [We need rather] to take unto ourselves hints of wisdom, so that we never be separate from our Creator, even in physical matters. We must be aware that there is nothing in the world that does not contain sublime lights, letters of Torah. Scripture points to this in saying: "Go eat of My bread" (Proverbs 9:5). This tells the enlightened how indeed to serve God, to raise up letters of Torah even from the physical act of eating bread.

I have explained this also on the verse "At the time of eating, come nigh (Ruth 2:14). "Nigh" refers to *malkhut* [the kingdom of God on earth] (BT *Zevahim* 102a). Even when eating bread and the rest of what is on our table, we should "come nigh" to these limbs of *shekhinah*, dwelling in those lower realms. This is "*My* bread," letters of Torah-bread garbed in the physical bread that we eat … . One who serves the blessed Holy One in this way, uplifting letters of Torah from the earthly world, is called one who eats "bread from the earth" (Psalms 104:14) …. The other, who awakens the heart to God's service through Torah and prayer, engages in "bread from heaven."[19]

Rabbi Zeev Wolf of Zhitomir, the author of this homily, explains that some seekers may attain divine rapture while studying Torah and praying, but they lose that expansive consciousness the moment they approach the table. The mundane act of physical consumption drags them away from sacred service, and they see the two realms as totally separate. Attachment to pleasure prevents one from discovering the spiritual amid the physical, and individuals who cannot find such divine meaning in the corporeal must indeed devote themselves to worship and prayer.

Hasidic thinkers understood that there is indeed great danger in becoming too attached to the this-worldly pursuits. The great Maggid of Mezritch (d. 1772) warned his disciples that any residual desire or lust for food will derail

---

19 *Or ha-Me'ir*, translated in Green et al., *Speaking Torah*, vol. 1, 192–93.

the project of sacred eating.[20] The more one allows oneself to yearn for the food and the pleasure it will bring, the more such consumption is for oneself rather than spiritual eating in the service of the Divine. Food, recommends the Maggid, should be approached with a kind of indifference or equanimity, breaking down any lust or attachment for the food and seeing it only as a kind of vessel for holiness.

But the sermon quoted above presents another, more expansive modality of service. This understanding transforms ordinary eating into a holy act. By adopting this approach, one comes to serve God always, lifting up the divine vitality of the world and bringing it toward the innermost regions of the soul. Such service diminishes the exile of the *shekhinah* (divine presence) and heals some measure of the fractured world by summoning forth God's sublime light hidden within the cosmos.

Hasidism thus calls for restraint on one hand, admitting that, for some individuals, sitting down to table is a distraction from one's higher purpose. But Hasidism also calls us to embrace eating as an act of sacred service. How do we, as modern readers, juggle these values? So many of us exist within a society of comfort and consumption that would have been totally unimaginable to the Hasidic masters of Eastern Europe. So many of us live immersed in a kind of gross materialism and over-consumption that nears mockery of the notion of serving God amid the physical. But perhaps the Hasidic masters would ask us to see the that key to healing is not found in the immoderate rejecting of food, but in reorienting our attitude toward eating and food production toward an approach that is more holistic, thoughtful and compassionate. This means toward our own individual lives, but also into the broader context of the world.

Expanding the Sacred Community

Hasidic teachers used food and the occasion of eating as opportunities for transformative education. Hasidic masters generally imparted Torah to their disciples in the context of a communal meal on the Sabbath. This setting was no mere coincidence, of course, for the shared act of eating, an intimate form of public social engagement, brings people together into a sacred community and cultivates a powerful spiritual *communitas*. In a sermon from Rabbi Elimelekh of Lizhensk (1717–1786/87), a Hasidic thinker much concerned with questions of education, we read:

---

20 *Mevasser Tsedek,* translated in Green et al., *Speaking Torah,* vol. 2, 89–90.

"I will bring you bread, to strengthen your hearts; then you will go on ... " (Genesis 18:5). A *tzaddik* who wants to benefit the world must do so through relationships with other *tzaddikim*. By feeding them in holiness the *tsaddik* draws down a great flow of benefit. That is the meaning of "I will bring you bread, to strengthen your hearts"—by this eating you will fortify your hearts with holiness. The heart is the place where holiness resides as it says—"that we may obtain a heart of wisdom" (Psalms 90:12). When you do this, you will impact yet others, as the verse continues—"Then you will go on"—you [the receivers] will pass on this benefit to others as well. Think about this.[21]

Food, says Rabbi Elimelekh, is an important vessel for spiritual instruction. Feeding one's disciples gives them a type of sustenance that is literally incorporated into the fiber of their being. The intimacy fostered in this moment opens the heart of student and teacher alike, clearing a channel through which blessing and instruction may be communicated. But each act of eating—and the decisions surrounding it—places us within a community or network far beyond than our immediate circumstances. Rabbi Yosef Hayyim of Baghdad (1834–1909), known as the *Ben Ish Hai* after one of his major works, offers the following reflection on the blessing recited after a meal that did not include bread, one of the five grains, wine, or certain choice fruits:

The blessing after foods is ["Blessed are You, Y-H-V-H, our God, Ruler of the cosmos,] Creator of many souls [and their needs, all the things You have created, animating them with the soul of all life. Blessed is the Life of all the worlds."] It alludes to repairing souls (*tikkun nefashot*) that were reborn in plants, living creatures or some other species. They were reborn there because of their sin and are repaired and ascend from there by means of this blessing.

This is its explanation [of the blessing]: "Blessed are You, Y-H-V-H, our God, Ruler of the cosmos, Creator of many souls"—[referring to] His many creations—"and their needs, all the things You have created"— that is, because of their need they must be reborn in one these species, each person according to the transgression. Therefore, we, through the power of this blessing, must "animate them with the soul of all life," wherever it [i.e., the soul in need] has been reborn. Thus [the we conclude]:

---

21 *No'am Elimelekh*, Green et al., *Speaking Torah*, vol. 1, 105.

"Blessed is the Life of all the worlds"—it is wondrous that something so great is performed through us.[22]

The chapter from which this excerpt is taken emphasizes the capacity of human speech, and blessings in particular, to impact the cosmos and the Divine. When uttered in a state of joy and contemplative focus, words repair the rift between the different aspects of the Godhead by uniting the *sefirot*, infusing the divine superstructure with effluence and vitality. Our words have this power because God created the world through language, and human speech mirrors— or better, embodies—this same quality of sacred speech.

Reading this text in a contemporary register, it suggests that our connection to the broader worlds via food is not only a matter of metaphysical importance. It has profound moral implications as well, for the way we choose to eat has a tremendous impact on the world around us. All of life is bound up in a single web of soulful energy and vitality. Each decision around food either contributes to healing and rebirth, or it adds to the entropy of the cosmos. The choice is ours, and it includes everything from the formal blessings to the sorts of food we buy and their global impact.

Many centuries earlier, Maimonides reminded his readers of a related ethical point in a well-known passage in his laws of Yom Tov. Rambam emphasizes that one should make room for those less fortunate as part of any fitting holiday repast:

> And while one eats and drinks himself, it is his duty to feed the stranger, the orphan, the widow, and other poor and unfortunate people, for he who locks the doors to his courtyard and eats and drinks with his wife and family, without giving anything to eat and drink to the poor and the bitter of soul—his meal is not a rejoicing in a divine commandment, but a rejoicing in his own stomach. It is of such persons that Scripture says, "Their sacrifices shall be to them as the bread of mourners, all that eat thereof shall be polluted; for their bread is for their own appetite" (Hosea 9:4).[23]

---

22 *Ben Ish Hai* (Jerusalem: 1985), *Helek ha-Halakhot, Shanah Rishonah, Mattot,* no. 16, 311. I wish to thank my colleague and friend Rabbi Ebn Leader for drawing this source to my attention.

23 *Mishneh Torah, Hilkhot Shevitat Yom Tov* 6:18, translated in Isadore Twersky, *A Maimonides Reader* (New York: Behrman House, 1982), 108–9. See also *Mishneh Torah, Hilkhot Megillah ve-Hannukah* 2:17, translated in Twersky, *Maimonides Reader,* 118: "It is preferable to spend

If one does not care for the others of the community, inviting them to share in our repast, then cooking pleasant food is nothing more than crass and self-absorbed gastronomic delight. We begin the Passover Seder with the recitation of *kol dikhfin yeytey ve-yekhol*—"let all who are hungry come and eat." But how many of us recite these words more than once a year? In thinking about the boundaries of our sacred community, we must remember those who have less to eat, who are in need of sustenance.

Sustainable Practices and Ethical Consumption

I take it for granted that spiritual eating cannot emerge from food produced by corrosive or damaging industries. Our quest to lift up the sparks through tasting food and engaging with it deeply should lead us to ask the following ethical questions: How did it come into being? Where did it come from, and what was involved in its production? How did it get there? Who helped bring this into being? How much effort was invested, how many tears and sweat went into the production of this bread? Were any people harmed in allowing me to eat? And finally, what are the environmental footprint and social impact of this food? Spiritual eating must involve a holistic approach to food production.

Rabbinic sources are aware that food production, like all industries, exerts a toll on the environment and the surrounding areas, including the residents. This price is to be limited and controlled, and the damage must never be allowed to run unchecked. The second chapter of tractate *Bava Batra* describes how various industries may damage property (both public and private) and explore the circumstances under which one may prevent another from damaging his livelihood. The contemporary reality begs us to find a corollary between the endless plastic bags that destroy life, both human and animal, and the wheat chaff that sweeps across another's field and thereby ruins it. Toxic pesticides could easily be understood as what the Talmud describes as "arrows" launched from one property to another, either intentionally or even unwillingly, which then cause damage to property and to life. And the labor laws in the sixth and seventh chapters of *Bava Metzia* clearly demand far better treatment for our agricultural workers, including undocumented immigrants.

---

more on gifts to the poor than on the Purim meal or on presents to friends. For no joy is greater or more glorious than the joy of gladdening the hearts of the poor, the orphans, the widows, and the strangers. Indeed, he who causes the hearts of these unfortunates to rejoice, emulates the Divine Presence, of whom Scripture says, 'to revive the spirit of the humble, and to revive the heart of the contrite ones' (Isiah 57:15)."

Rather than artisans or even day-laborers, we conveniently treat these individuals as if they were foreign slaves rather than dignified guest workers created in the image of God.

We must also unshackle ourselves from an industrial meat industry that is terribly damaging to the environment as well as cruel toward the animals that are grist for the mill. *Halakhah* forbids causing undue suffering to animals under any circumstances, including raising and slaughtering them for food. I say "undue" because Jewish law has often defined this prohibited suffering as anything not *le-tzorekh ha-adam*—for a human need. Perhaps this caveat must be revisited in the contemporary world, as it is often invoked to justify enormous cruelty to animals. This includes ordinary dairy cows and egg chickens in addition to foodstock, not to mention animals raised for purposes such as *foie gras*. Rav Moshe Feinstein's courageous *teshuvah* regarding veal was a step in this direction,[24] as was Rabbi Moshe Shmuel Glasner's (1856–1924) thoughtful and provocative acceptance that we must prohibit something permitted by Jewish law if contemporary society has deemed it unbecoming or immoral.[25]

In this quest to prevent cruelty to animals we are guided by something more than the limited definitions of Jewish law, Rav Asher Weiss, addressing the Talmudic question as to whether *tza'ar ba'alei hayyim* is *de-orayta* or *de-rabbanan*,[26] writes as follows:

> The fundament of this matter seems simple to me ... one is obligated to fulfill God's will even in such matters that are not counted among the 613 commandments, because they were not stated explicitly as injunctions in the Torah. Nevertheless, we are enjoined to do them, since they represent the will of the Torah ... [The sages] claim in *Bava Metzia* that not causing pain to animals is a biblical commandment, but do so without bringing any source from this prohibition! In the words of our teachers, the medieval and later authorities, we find eleven different ways of explaining the [biblical] origin of the prohibition ... This proves that certain commandments, which are not formulated as either a negative or positive injunction, may be a biblical commandment because they are the very will of the Torah.[27]

---

24 See *Iggerot Moshe, Even ha-'Ezer*, vol. 4, no. 92; and *Noda be-Yehudah, Yoreh De'ah*, no. 10.

25 See the introduction to his *Dor Revi'i*, and Yaakov Elman, "Rabbi Moses Samuel Glasner: The Oral Torah," *Tradition* 25.3 (1991): 63–69.

26 See BT *Bava Metzia* 32a-33a; BT *Shabbat* 128b.

27 *Minhat Asher: Bereshit* (Jerusalem: 2004), *Ca-Yera*, no. 21, 130–1.

This point is more radical than it may seem at first blush. Rabbi Asher Weiss has made the claim that there is a deeper ethos that undergirds the project of Torah, driving forward the jurisprudence of *halakhah* but not restricted to its internal or definitions. This higher law, as it were, is what we aim to express through our formulation and application of rabbinic law, but it is not defined nor necessarily coterminous with their details. God desires us to show compassion to animals, to express kindness and prevent suffering. This ethical posture is so fundamental to the project of Judaism that we have no need to settle on a specific scriptural proof text in order to prove that it is of central, even biblical importance. God cannot accept the suffering of animals. Those who choose to eat meat must do so with this in mind.

Finally, eating with a sense of spirit, integrity and responsibility also means adopting an expansive vision of *Bal Tashhit*, the interdiction against wanton destruction that should inform our contemporary agricultural systems. The medieval *Sefer ha-Hinukh* gives the following explanation of the roots of this commandment and its relevance to one's private life and public deeds:

> The commandment not to destroy fruit-bearing trees during a siege includes all forms of destruction ...
>
> The root of this commandment is well-known. It is to teach our souls to love that which is good and worthwhile, cleaving to this [path]. Thus the good shall cleave to us [in return], and we will distance ourselves from all wicked and wasteful matters. This is the path of the pious and people of the spirit, who love peace and rejoice in that which is good for created beings, bringing them close to the Torah—they do not destroy even a single mustard seed, and are pained by all loss and destruction that they see. If they can prevent any kind of destruction, they do so with all of their might. Such is not true of the wicked, brethren of the damaging demons, who rejoice in destruction and themselves seek to destroy.
>
> The way (*be-middah*) a person comports himself (*moded*) is returned (*modedin*) unto him—it cleaves to him forever, as it says, "[One who mocks the poor blasphemes his Maker; and] one that rejoices in calamity shall not be unpunished" (Proverbs 17:5). One who longs for good, taking joy in it, shall be connected to goodness forevermore. This is indeed well-known.[28]

---

28 *Sefer ha-Hinukh*, no. 529.

Preserving and safeguarding this *mitzvah* cultivates a vision of kindness, love, and respect for the world around us. Rather than feeling indifference to waste or apathy toward loss and privileging immediate pleasure and expendability, this medieval Jewish legal source calls us to remember that all waste and destruction is antithetical to God's vision. Food production—and distribution—need not be scaled in such a way that they lead to environmental degradation and massive waste. On the contrary, our choices about eating and our attitude toward the food-producing systems may be a source of blessing and an opportunity to develop a path of goodness and compassion. Such is the beckoning call extended by the Torah.

Tzeidah le-Derekh

The slow food movement has gradually gained momentum over the past five decades. Seeking to reverse our industrialized society's staggering alienation from the food that it consumes, advocates of slow food emphasize the significance of community, sustainability, cultural preservation, and attentiveness to environmental protection. My goal in this brief paper has been to provide some food for thought regarding Hasidic wisdom and the contemporary "spiritual food" movement. These mystical sources give us a spiritual language grounded in the values of devotion, compassion, attentiveness, presence, sustainability, and community. Hasidism reflects on eating as an opportunity for spiritual service, a moment in which we serve God and unlock the finest elements of the human soul. Aspects of this process are internal, taking place within the mind and heart of the seeker, but the notion of eating as a sacred act entails a greater commitment to fostering connections between people and cultivating openhearted compassion toward all others. Such positive engagement with food and its healing qualities comes neither from gluttony nor denial, but through a balanced approach in which eating is embraced as an act of sacred devotion.

CHAPTER 3

Holy Eating in Jewish Thought and Practice

Rabbi Hyim Shafner

Rabbi Johanan and Resh Lakish both said: At the time when the Temple stood, the altar used to make atonement for a person; now their table makes atonement for them.[1]

Eating is the first act we engage in after birth and it follows us constantly throughout our lives. It is often a magnet for our emotions and a screen for the projection of our inner conflicts. The Torah opens with a commandment and its trespass (in the Garden of Eden), with the most basic of human conflicts, that of desire and control, obedience, and rebellion. It is eating that serves as the stage for this drama. Sigmund Freud famously identified the mouth, it's sucking and eating, as the very first cathectic location, the first erogenous zone. Though it is not genital, and therefore not generally viewed as sexual, Freud understood that eating involves desire and relationship, and from it blooms a person's first feelings of pleasure and satiation, anger, and frustration. (Indeed, some Hasidic sources see eating as even more primordial, more powerful, and more self-defining than that mother of all yearning, sexuality, and perhaps even, ultimately, as its source.[2])

The Torah realizes that eating is a powerful act, potentially both productive and destructive, and offers instruction for harnessing this act. In Deuteronomy, eating gives way to a practical *mitzvah*, the only blessing that is commanded in the Torah, *birkat hamazon*, the grace after meals: "And you shall eat and be satisfied and bless the Lord your God on the good land which God has given you … guard yourself lest you eat and are satisfied … and forget the Lord your God who took you out of the land of Egypt."[3]

---

1 BT *Hagigah* 27a.
2 See Rav Tzadok Ha-Kohen Mi'-Lublin, "*Ayt ha-Okhel*," supplement to *Pre Tzadik* (Jerusalem, 2005).
3 Deuteronomy 8:10–14, author translation.

While blessings after food (and per the rabbis, before eating as well) serve as tools in our quest to harness eating, more may be required to truly utilize consumption as an instrument for the spirit. The border between eating and indulgence is subtle: If eating is permitted, is indulgence then permitted? What about gluttony? From the Torah's point of view is all that is not forbidden, permitted? If food is kosher, may one eat wantonly? Though it has become a modern Jewish theological platitude, isn't it true that we Jews are anti-ascetic or, at least, non-ascetic?

A closer look at the Talmud reveals that this is not necessarily the case. Some have argued that indeed the Rabbis of the Talmud were champions of religious asceticism.[4] What theology fueled rabbinic asceticism is unclear. Some hold that the rabbis' acetic views were less a religious path in and of itself and more an instrument toward a passionate religious life, a life so dedicated to study that everything else, especially the physical, was beside the point.[5] Given the Talmud's varied approaches to asceticism we must assume that the places in which the Talmud does promote an acetic life are not celebrations of asceticism as a value in and of itself but asceticism as a tool for deepening one's religious commitments and narrowing one's vision to hone in on the spirit.

Another approach to the Talmud's contradictory presentation on asceticism is the thesis that when the Talmud wants to address complex theological questions it offers statements which reflect varied positions on a spectrum, describing opposite attitudes. For instance, with regard to asceticism the Talmud, BT *Taanit* 11a, states:

> Shmuel said: Whoever sits in observance of a fast is called a sinner, as it is inappropriate to take unnecessary suffering upon oneself. The Gemara comments: Shmuel holds in accordance with the opinion of the following tanna, as it is taught in a *baraita*: Rabbi Elazar HaKappar the Great says: What is the meaning when the verse states, with regard to a Nazirite: "And he will atone for him for that he sinned by the soul [nefesh]" (Numbers 6:11). But with what soul did this Nazirite sin? Rather, the Nazirite sinned by the distress he caused himself when he abstained from wine, in accordance with the terms of his vow. And are these matters not inferred a fortiori? And if this Nazirite, who distressed

---

4 See Eliezer Diamond, *Holy Men and Hunger Artists: Fasting and Asceticism in Rabbinic Culture* (Oxford, UK: Oxford University Press, 2004).

5 Ibid., 12.

himself by abstaining only from wine, is nevertheless called a sinner and requires atonement, then with regard to one who distresses himself by abstaining from each and every matter of food and drink when he fasts, all the more so should he be considered a sinner.

Conversely, Rabbi Elazar says: One who accepts a fast upon himself is called sacred, as it is stated with regard to the Nazirite: "He shall be sacred, he shall let the locks of the hair of his head grow long" (Numbers 6:5). Here too, one can apply an a fortiori inference: And if this Nazirite, who distressed himself by abstaining from only one matter, wine, is nevertheless called sacred, then with regard to one who distresses himself by abstaining from every matter, all the more so should he be considered sacred.

On the question of eating specifically, the Talmud takes a similar approach but here it presents contradictory approaches practiced by the same Rabbi. The Talmud relates that the table of Rebbe was replete with delicacies, equal to that of the Roman emperor Antoninus:

Rabbi Yehudah said in the name of Rav, this (aforementioned Biblical verse) refers to Antoninus and Rebbe, for there was never missing from their tables, not even radishes, lettuce, or cucumbers, not in the summer and not in the winter.[6]

Yet another Talmudic passage relates:

When Rebbe was on his deathbed he raised his ten fingers toward heaven and said, 'Master of the Universe, You know that I engaged with all my ten fingers in Torah and did not take pleasure (from the world) with even my pinky.'[7]

It seems on one hand, Rebbe had a table of great indulgence, yet on the other he resisted indulgence entirely. Various latter commentaries have attempted to resolve this contradiction between indulgence and asceticism in Jewish thought. Some approach this dichotomy by siding with one narrative or the other, others instruct that one's ascetic sensibility must limit and guide the

---

6 BT *Berakhot* 57b, author translation.
7 BT *Ketubot* 104a, author translation.

desire for indulgence, while still others, especially the Hasidic mystics, take the view that there is a synergy to be had between these dialectical poles.

Maimonides—Healthful Intent

Maimonides, in keeping with his life philosophy around the perfection of human character through the golden mean, strikes a balance. He writes that a person should engage in worldly pursuits but must direct their heart and all they do solely to know God. Eating and drinking, labor, and sexual intercourse, all of these should not be practiced only for one's pleasure or gain alone, but as a means to develop a healthy body and obtain support in order to have the ability to know God and raise children who will be, "Wise among our people." Even at the time that one sleeps, says Maimonides, if one sleeps in order to have the energy and health to serve God, even one's sleep is a service to God.[8]

In keeping with this spiritual orientation, Maimonides instructs: "When one eats and drinks … one should not intend only to have pleasure, and thus eat only what is sweet … but one should eat only for bodily health. Therefore, one should not only eat and drink what their palate desires like a dog or a donkey, but should eat foods which heal one's body, whether sweet or bitter … "[9] For Maimonides, one may engage in the pleasures of this world but only with a higher motive.[10] If the intent is to use the health, energy, and monetary gain from engaging in the pursuits of the physical world to know and serve God, then all of these things are, by extension, acts of Divine service.

Jewish mystics and hasidic thinkers take a different path than Maimonides. Generally, they develop ways to engage in eating and other physical pursuits of pleasure in which the act itself becomes a kind of Divine service, not only by association, as Maimonides sees them, but intrinsically so. There are many views within this school of thought and we will examine several of them. Additionally, practical methodologies and instruction for achieving this state of sanctity are outlined.

---

8 Moses Maimonides, "Hilchot De'ot" in *Mishneh Torah*, chapter 3, author translation.

9 Ibid.

10 In truth, Maimonides' phrasing is equivocal. He writes: "A person must direct his heart and all he does solely to know God … when one works one should not have in mind *only* to accumulate money … (italics and translation mine). One answer might be that Maimonides would hold as long as one primarily has the intent to come to know God through physical matters, one would also be permitted to do these acts for the pleasure they engender.

Rabbi Menachem Nachum—Holy Taste

In contrast to Maimonides, Rabbi Menachem Nachum of Chernobyl (1735–1798) approaches the dialectic between indulgence and asceticism through sanctifying the act of eating via the pleasure of a sweet taste:[11]

> Everything was created by God through speech, as the verse states, "By the word of God were the heavens created (Nehemiah 9:6) ... " If not for the (Divine) life force within the speech (that is imparted in the physical) nothing would exist.[12] This Divine life force within our food is the taste that is sweet to the palate ... When a person eats or drinks, the spark (Divine life force which is the taste in the food) becomes part of that person's life power (חיותו של האדם) and gives them energy. If we believe with complete belief that this (taste which enters us) is spiritual sustenance and is God's Divinity, may He be blessed, which is clothed in (the food) and if we are mindful of this ... then we also lift this spark of Divinity which was in exile (in the physical) up to God ... For this is the main aspect of our service to God (author translation).[13]

Rabbi Menachem Nachum continues to state that this idea is also true of all other physical elements, namely the pleasure we get from the Divine spark that resides within them. He adds that each person has a different mission in the world which only they can accomplish; sparks of the Divine that only that person can raise up from the spark's "exile" in the realm of the physical. Thus, each person desires different tastes according to their particular unique potential for service to God that only they can do. For example, one desires a particular food and taste because the sparks in those foods resonate with the root of their individual soul. Therefore, this individual alone has the ability to raise up those particular sparks in that food, physical endeavor, or indulgence.[14]

On this thought, Rabbi Menachem Nachum continues:

---

11 Rabbi Menahem Nahum Twersky, *Me'or Eynayim*, beginning of *Parshat Mattot*.

12 See also the first chapter of *Sha'ar ha-Yihud V'ha-emunah* by Rabbi Shneur Zalman of Lyadi.

13 In addition, he also includes the idea of using the energy for good and of making blessings as tools for elevating the sparks within the food.

14 Though Rabbi Menachem Nachum does not mention it here, many places in *Hasidut* are explicit about the notion that only when eaten in a permissible way or when an act is done in a permissible way, is one able to unlock the sparks and elevate them. See *Likutey Amarim*, chapter 8.

One who acts with asceticism and refuses to take pleasure from the world is called a sinner, as one opinion in the Talmud states, in tractate [BT] *Taanit* 11a, for, this (taking pleasure from the physical world) is also a service of God, just as is studying Torah, or praying or donning *tefillin*, or any other mitzvah, because God created the world through the Torah.[15] Through the Torah the world functions, and in everything (physical) there is Torah, as we know. All believers must believe that there is nothing outside of God's service, save that it must be done according to the Torah, eating that which has been permitted. It must be done for the sake of accomplishing and not for one's own pleasure, in the way that we have described ... And even if one's intent is not perfect, nevertheless one accomplishes something spiritual thereby.

Here, Rabbi Menachem Nachum develops a profound notion. He not only sanctifies the pleasure of eating itself, but the "sweet taste" is now seen not as a stumbling block—as it is for Maimonides—but as *the* Divine aspect of the food. He frames eating in personal terms, as an individual's unique holy capacity to elevate a food through its enjoyment. Pleasure is no longer the enemy of the soul nor is a stumbling block (as conceived by Maimonides) but, surprisingly, it is the *source* of the holy.

Rabbi Israel Baal Shem Tov—Like Draws Out Like

The German philosopher Martin Heidegger (1889–1976) said that the most essential question in philosophy is: Why isn't there nothing?[16] This realization, that the simplest state of things is not existence but non-existence, is important for understanding the kabbalistic notion of Creation. Rabbi Israel Baal Shem Tov, the famous founder of *Hasidut*, paints a slightly different picture of the elevation of Divine sparks in food. Instead of eating for the sole purpose to garner energy to serve God or focusing on taste as a Divine manifestation, the Baal Shem Tov utilizes the blessing—the uttering of God's name itself—in order to sanctify the food directly. Our access to God's name enables us to draw God out.

The Baal Shem Tov, quoting Rabbi Isaac Luria, writes that God's creation of the world by speaking was not a cause of the creation, but is existence

---

15 See Zohar 1:5.
16 Martin Heidegger, *An Introduction to Metaphysics* (New Haven, CT: Yale University Press, 1959), 7–8.

itself. Existence itself, he writes, is a kind of soul, a Divine life force (manifest through God's word), without which things would not exist. The Baal Shem Tov continues:

> When a person makes a blessing on a food with intent and uses God's name, the person stirs up and draws out the Divine life force in the food which created it. Since he uses God's name, the Godliness in the fruit, its Divine force, is drawn to the Godliness the person invokes by blessing in God's name, for, like is drawn to like. This Godly life force then gives spiritual sustenance to the person's soul. … Through this process we raise up the sparks of holiness.[17]

The Baal Shem Tov's method of sanctifying our eating is one that is accessible, both through the recitation of a blessing, and also through the linkage to the highest of realms which draw the Divine close. In contrast to Rabbi Menachem Nachum, the Baal Shem Tov provides us with a specific spiritual tool: the blessing. No longer is the blessing only a way of asking permission for the food, but the blessing links the physical and the spiritual, our personal, very human, act of eating, with the Divine that can pervade even the physical universe.

Rabbi Tzadok Ha-Kohen of Lublin—Practical Methodologies

Rabbi Tzadok Ha-Kohen (Poland), a Hasidic rebbe who passed away in 1900, places eating in the center of the spiritual life. In his philosophy, Rav Tzadok suggests several practical approaches to eating in holiness. The first is not to take direct benefit from what one eats, but a different kind of pleasure, one that is centered cognitively around kindness and giving. Further, he writes that: "The beginning and foundation of *Hasidut* is in sanctifying what one eats. If one does not eat in holiness and becomes full thereby, this leads to sin. Through eating in holiness, one merits the light of God's face."[18]

Rav Tzadok states that such holiness can be accomplished by seeing physical pleasure as Hillel saw it in this midrash:[19]

---

17 Rabbi Israel ben Eliezer, *Keter Shem Tov* (Zalkevo, 1794), *Parshat Ekev*, 2, author translation.
18 Rabbi Tzadok Ha-Kohen Rabinowitz of Lublin, *Divrey Halomot* (Jerusalem: 2000), 5.
19 Rabbi Tzadok, *Pre Tzadik* (Jerusalem, 2005), *Parshat Va-Yeshev*.

This (aforementioned verse) applies to Hillel the Elder who once, when he concluded his studies with his disciples, walked along with them. His disciples asked him: "Master, whither are you bound?" "He answered them: To perform a religious duty." "What," they asked, "is this religious duty?" He said to them: "To wash in the bath-house." Said they: "Is this a religious duty?" "Yes," he replied; "if the statues of kings, which are erected in theatres and circuses, are scoured and washed by the man who is appointed to look after them, and who thereby obtains his maintenance through them—nay more, he is exalted in the company of the great of the kingdom—how much more I, who have been created in the Image and Likeness; as it is written, For in the image of God made He man" (Genesis 9:6)? Another exposition: "The merciful man doeth good to his own soul" applies to Hillel the Elder. Once when he had concluded his studies with his disciples he walked along with them. His disciples said to him: "Master, whither are you bound?" He replied: "To bestow kindness upon a guest in the house." They asked: "Have you a guest every day?" He replied: "Is not the poor soul a guest in the body? Today it is here and tomorrow it is here no longer."[20]

According to Rav Tzadok, one minimizes physical pleasure and sanctifies it, not through avoiding tasting the food,[21] or feeling pleasure from eating, but by cultivating Hillel's perspective as presented in the above midrash. Rav Tzadok assumes the same to be true of Rebbe, whose table was full but who said about himself that he did not take pleasure from this world. He concludes with the midrash that Hillel only felt physical pleasure as one who bestows kindness on a guest in his home.

The soul in this framework is the guest. Instead of feeding oneself, that is one's body, one feeds their guest: the soul. Just like feeding a guest does not bestow taste pleasure on the host, so too here the taste pleasure goes to another. But another kind of more spiritual, more giving, pleasure is left for the host, the body. Feeding the self is not a *mitzvah* but feeding the other always is. Here, selfishness transforms into selflessness. It is a subtle perspective change, but a profound one. By cognitively moving the self out of the center, we achieve a move toward the other.

---

20 See *Leviticus Rabbah* 34:3 in *Soncino Midrash Rabbah* (trans. H. Freedman & Maurice Simon) (New York: Judaica Press, 1983).

21 Rabbi Nachman of Breslov did this as a young boy by eating with only his two front teeth, see *Sichos ha-Ran*, no. 246.

"I am going to do kindness with the guest in my house," says Hillel. The students' question is instructive, "Do you have a guest every day (as you leave the study house to eat or tend to your needs every day)?" Hillel's answer affirms that the soul is indeed a guest, it is here and then will not be. He seems to want to move them to this place with the strange leading questions. Not just that he is not selfish but he sees the self and soul as temporary guests, bringing into focus the existential reality of our temporality, our transient nature. I indulge when I see myself as real, as the center of things. I desire, therefore I am. But if the I is only a guest, then I am also a host, and I am not really myself, at least not entirely so. I am here and then gone. There are two aspects to Hillel's cognitive gesture. I am temporary and what I see as I, is not really I. It is other.[22]

A second method of sanctifying eating that Rav Tzadok employs is based on the verse: "And you shall be sanctified and be holy ... "[23] The Talmud expounds on this verse: "and you shall be sanctified," this refers to washing our hands before we eat, "And be holy," this refers to washing after we eat."[24]

Rav Tzadok interprets the waters of washing in this piece of Talmud not only as a ritual law but also metaphorically to mean that if we wash our hands by engaging in Torah study and the performance of commandments, and eat in a holy way, then God will then be forced to sanctify us after our meal. Through this lens, we see that Rav Tzadok views the process of eating in holiness not only as a way of avoiding sin that might be produced by our meal and its subsequent satisfaction, but as a process that actively sanctifies humanity. A complete turnaround in the conception of eating and physical indulgence. The indulgence itself, if done in the correct manner, infused with Torah, produces a higher level of spirit.[25]

Further, Rav Tzadok offers a third practical tool for the sanctification of one's eating. He sees the desires and indulgences of this world as taking up the same space in the heart as Torah. There is no room for both, says Rav Tzadok. If the heart is filled with Torah there will not be "space" for the desires of this world to enter, but if the heart is filled with the crass pleasures of the physical the obverse is true, there will be no room for Torah. [26]

---

22 See also *Mishnah Avot* 1:14: "It is Hillel who says: 'If I am not for myself who will be for me and if I am for myself what am I ...'"
23 Leviticus 11:44.
24 BT *Berakhot* 53b.
25 Rav Tzadok, "Ayt ha-Okhel," supplement to *Pre Tzadik* on Genesis, section 1.
26 Ibid., 4.

The fourth practical tool that Rav Tzadok offers is slowing down and eating with attention and mindfulness. Rushing is bound up with physical desire because: "The essence of the seizing power of desire is fervid rushing, for a person wishes to consume quickly and fill themselves up ... the Torah's language for eating is, "to enter," as in "entering to eat,"[27] with intent and preparation ... not like a glutton who grabs and eats."[28]

Rav Tzadok's fifth piece of advice for holy eating is to realize how miraculous eating is. God created the food and its taste. Taste is subtle; a powerful sense yet hard to quantify. That we have a desire to eat, to consume, to put things in our bodies is amazing, without which we could not survive. This pleasurable act gives us the energy we need to live. When we recognize that all of this is from God, that our most physical desire comes from God, then we see that this desire itself is something very lofty, like a divine sacrifice, and the food we eat is sanctified.

When we eat in this way, according to Rav Tzadok, it is like bringing a sacrifice to God. But when we eat thinking only of our own desires, we are then only bringing the sacrifice to our physical bodies, which are temporal. Thus, *Pirkei Avot* refers to such eating as *zivchey matim,* sacrifices brought to the dead. When engaged in a physical act like eating, to focus on one's physical self and forget the Godly self is tantamount to idolatry, to sacrifices to the dead, and the physical body destined for death. [29]

Rav Tzadok Ha-Kohen—On Eating Meat

Additionally, Rav Tzadok distinguishes between our ability to raise up the Divine light in vegan foods and, conversely, in animal products. Drawing on the Talmud's statement that only a Torah scholar may meat,[30] he explains that plant-based food can be raised up spiritually just by eating it with the faith that it was created by God as expressed in the blessing before consuming it.[31] Meat, on the other hand, was brought on an altar in the temple as a sacrifice to God. The act of eating meat therefore requires some sort of altar. Rav Tzadok suggests that only the table of a Torah scholar can replace the altar, since in a post exilic world God dwells in the *beit midrash,* the house of study.

---

27 See *Mishnah Berakhot* 1:1.
28 Ibid., 5.
29 Ibid., section 6.
30 BT *Pesahim* 49b.
31 Ibid., section 8.

Today, holiness is encountered through study, not the action of sacrifices. The Torah indeed is compared to fire, and this mirrors the sacrificial fire of the temple altar, now transformed into the home table on which the fire of Torah is brought, along with the meat to be eaten. The scholar now stands in the place of the high priest and raises up the animal to God through their eating.

Eating meat, explains Rav Tzadok, is an animalistic act: It involves the tearing of flesh, but precisely by utilizing our animalistic nature and eating meat in holiness we raise up the lower parts of our soul, the animalistic, physical life sustaining soul, to a higher place. This serves a much higher purpose in kabbalah than the raising up of something that is already holy. The further from holiness something is the more kinetic spiritual potential it has.[32] Thus eating meat properly may be a more difficult and dangerous spiritual act, reserved for a Torah scholar, but it also offers greater potential for spirituality.

Practical Advice

It is important that we draw on these thinkers not only to understand Judaism's approach to spiritual eating on a theoretical level but on a practical one also. We can bring these ideas into our own meals in simple ways. The following is an example, but certainly there are many more approaches to be explored in our personal practice of eating.

It is important, firstly, to bear in mind Rav Tzadok's fundamental idea, mentioned above, that eating is not just to sustain ourselves but is itself one of the highest forms of serving God, a path to the spiritual, "light of God's face." When shopping and making choices regarding which foods to buy, choose a healthy option over a less healthy one (Maimonides). When cooking or preparing the food, articulate your intent to relate to the food as more than a way to fill your hunger. If the food is for the Sabbath, say to yourself, "this food is for the honor of the holy Shabbat," if for weekday consumption say to yourself that the food is for the honor of supporting other family members who will consume it and use the energy for good acts, or if for yourself articulate how the food will be for energy to serve God and do positive deeds in the world (Maimonides).

Before taking your first bite, approach the food, look at your plate of food and take a breadth (Rav Tzadok Ha-Kohen). To take a moment before eating to look at our plate of food and think about the act as a Godly one, through

---

32 Ibid., section 9.

which one can access the Divine, can be a key to unlocking a vast storehouse of spirituality. Reflect on how strange and miraculous the food is, that some things we can eat and others we cannot, that food tastes good, is nutritious, gives us energy, and that it grows on trees and has the potential within it to reproduce itself though seeds.

Make a blessing, and when you do realize that it comes from God and is sustained in existence by God's word and God's energy. Using God's name in the blessing imagine drawing out the Divine energy in the food (Baal Shem Tov).

Taste the food. It is your unique taste of the food, perhaps different than everyone else's. Reflect on how the holy work that you can do, since each soul has unique resonances, and your taste buds have unique taste, is not the work that can be accomplished by another (Rabbi Menachem Nachum). And as you continue to eat and feel the pleasure of the food, think about how you are actually providing to another, providing life to our soul, a Godly part of ourselves that is visiting from above (Rav Tzadok Ha-Kohen).

Now take a break in your eating and speak some words of Torah, transforming the table into an altar through the holy words. Finish with a blessing afterward, expressing thanks to God for the food, the land, and all the goodness.

Conclusion

Too often, we eat mindlessly. We eat without thought, attention, or regard for how miraculous the food in front of is and how miraculous our lives are. Eating, the Hasidic Rabbis have taught us, is a door to the spirit. Do not become discouraged after a meal eaten without higher attention. It just takes a moment of focus, just a bit of tuning into some or several of the above insights, to render our meal one that is tied to higher purpose. May we merit to truly fulfill the words of the Torah: "Eat, be satisfied and bless the Lord your God ... "[33]

---

33 Deuteronomy 8:10.

CHAPTER 4

Too Much of Everything is Just Enough

Eating as a Spiritual Practice in a Culture of Abundance

Rabbi David Jaffe

The Baal Shem Tov—the founder of the modern Hasidic movement—and his followers made *Avodah B'Gashmius*, serving God through the physical world, a central part of their spiritual program. Prayer, Torah learning, and *mitzvot* are pathways for spiritual practice, but so is the way a tailor sews a button on a shirt, or how one dresses, dances, or eats. The way we relate to food—how we produce it, acquire it, store it and consume it, has long been a focus of Divine service. Food is a metaphor in the Torah for all economic activity, consumption and, indeed, desire itself, as seen in test of the Tree of Knowledge of Good and Evil (Genesis 3:1–15). Food, in the form of *manna*, is later used by God to test the Israelite's faith after leaving Egyptian bondage.

Why food? Perhaps because food, even more than sexual intimacy, is a basic human need; abstinence is not an option. But food can also so easily be misused through over-production, over-consumption, and as a means of war and oppression (through withholding access to food, for example). Food is also symbolic of our livelihood, our *parnassah*. Providing for our own material well-being and that of our family has been one of the core sources of anxiety throughout human history. Will we have enough to eat? The feeling of scarcity awakened by this question can lead to greed, violence and the worst aspects of human behavior. Thus, food is a *gashmi*— physical entity—the use of which reflects our spiritual state as individuals and as a human collective.

The *manna* test in the book of Exodus is the most explicit example of food production, distribution, and consumption as a means of spiritual development.[1] And to be sure, the *manna* test was carefully designed both as a diagnostic and also as a pathway for spiritual growth. Just days after the Israelites crossed the Reed Sea, God gives them a test to see if they internalized the faith they professed at the sea. God provides *manna*, a type of bread-like nourishment, but only allows the people to take exactly what they need and not save any for the next day. If they do save it, it rots:

> Then said God to Moshe, Behold, I will rain bread from heaven for you; and the people shall go out and gather a certain portion every day, that I may test them, whether they will follow my Torah, or no . . . . And Moshe said to them ... This is the thing which God has commanded, Gather of it every man according to his eating, an *'omer* for every man, according to the number of your persons shall you take it, every man for them who are in his tent. And the children of Israel did so, and gathered, some more, some less. And when they did measured it with an *'omer*, he that gathered much had nothing over, and he that gathered little had no lack ... Moshe said, Let no man leave of it till the morning. But they hearkened not to Moshe; but some of them left of it until the morning, and it bred worms, and stank ... (Exodus 16:4, 16–20)

The *manna* test was carefully crafted. God could have just given every household the amount of *manna* it needed to fulfill their daily nutritional requirements. Rather, they needed to work for their food by collecting the *manna* from the field. This requirement echoes the curse given to Adam in the Garden of Eden, "Cursed be the ground because of you; By toil shall you eat of it ... By the sweat of your brow shall you get bread to eat ... " (Genesis 3:17–19). Adam, and all humans, need to work for their food. It does not just come from heaven into to our doorsteps. But, the need to put in effort to earn our livelihood leads to another challenge. We feel pride in our labor and our ability to make things and support ourselves. The Torah warns us not to say: "My own power and the might of my own hand have won this wealth for me" (Deuteronomy 8:17). The Torah calls on us to do something quite counterintuitive and perhaps paradoxical. We need to use our capability to earn a livelihood (symbolized by collecting the *manna*) and, at the same time, recognize that it was not just our

---

1 This section about the *Manna* Test is taken from my book, *Changing the World from the Inside Out: A Jewish Approach to Personal and Social Change* (Boulder, CO: Trumpeter, 2016), 188–89.

own capabilities that earned us this livelihood (symbolized by the need to trust that more food will be there tomorrow) and thus, we don't get to do whatever we want with it (symbolized by the need to not hoard the leftover *manna*).

The *manna* test is a Biblical example of how food can be used for spiritual development. In this case, God wanted the Israelites to develop *bitahon*, or trust in God. The test called on the people to employ human effort but at the same time know that they were not ultimately in control. Trust is an essential counter-*middah* (character trait) to the fear and worry generated by the question, "Am I going to have enough (food, love, attention, success, etc.)?" But there is another *middah*—joy—that is also essential to develop in a culture of abundance, like the ones many Jews are privileged to live in Western Hemisphere, in the early years of the twenty-first century. It is well-documented that raw material abundance does not automatically correlate with a sense of well-being or happiness. Indeed, the richest country in the world, the United States, ranked sixteenth in the Sustainable Development Solutions Network's 2017 World Happiness Report.[2] What is the problem with being anxious, sad, and stressed? Beside the personal suffering associated with these emotional states, a society filled with sad and anxious people is not one that can tackle its immediate and long-term challenges with flexibility, creativity, and resilience. Its people are vulnerable to manipulation by leaders who offer quick, feel-good solutions. To develop real resilience and grit, as individuals and as a society, we need to be happy.

But how do we become more joyous? How do we cultivate happiness? I want to propose that the way we relate to food, if made into a spiritual practice, has the power to evoke joy, not just as a transitory emotion accompanying a good meal, but as a durable *middah* that permeates all of our lives. The Torah makes the connection between material abundance and lack of happiness towards the end of the book of Deuteronomy:

תַּחַת אֲשֶׁר לֹא־עָבַדְתָּ אֶת־יְהוָה אֱלֹהֶיךָ בְּשִׂמְחָה וּבְטוּב לֵבָב מֵרֹב כֹּל׃

Because you would not serve the LORD your God in joy and gladness over the abundance of everything …

וְעָבַדְתָּ אֶת־אֹיְבֶיךָ אֲשֶׁר יְשַׁלְּחֶנּוּ יְהוָה בָּךְ בְּרָעָב וּבְצָמָא וּבְעֵירֹם וּבְחֹסֶר כֹּל …

… you shall have to serve—in hunger and thirst, naked and lacking everything—the enemies whom the LORD will let loose against you.[3]

---

2 2017 World Happiness Report, Sustainable Development Solutions Network (funded by Ernesto Illy Foundation), http://worldhappiness.report/ed/2017/.

3 Deuteronomy 28:47.

While Psalms 100:2 exhorts us to "Serve God with joy," the verse here is the Biblical imperative for the emotion. It is curious that only time the Torah hints to serve God with joy, it is expressed in the negative, referring to the consequences of *not* serving with joy. And the context refers to a state of material abundance. Why is it so hard to feel deep *simha*—*joy*—in a state of material abundance? There are many reasons, including a desire to want more, feeling a relative lack in comparison to others who have even more abundance, and the fact that possessions can diminish attention to relationships, which are the core source of happiness for most people. No matter the reason, the Torah's assumption is that it is difficult to serve with joy in a state of abundance. The emphatic, and unusual last phrase in the verse (רב כל—much of everything) hints towards the challenges and spiritual opportunities of abundance.

רב כל—Much of Everything—alludes to an earlier interaction in the Torah between Jacob and his brother Esau in Genesis 33:9–11.[4] In this reconciliation scene, the two brothers meet for the first time in over twenty years since Jacob fled from his brother after stealing his birthright blessing. Jacob offers his brother many gifts and Esau demurs saying, "יש לי רב—I have many possessions." Jacob presses him to accept the gifts, describing his own state of material abundance as, "יש לי כל—I have all." Rashi, the eleventh-century Biblical commentator, explains these two words—רב and כל: "'I have all'—everything I need. While Esau's use of language connotes arrogance: 'I have many possessions,' meaning, way above and beyond what I need."[5] Putting aside the rabbinic and medieval inclination to always interpret Esau's words and actions in the most negative light, Rashi's comment points out an important difference in these two words.

Likewise, Rabbi Shlomo Wolbe, the twentieth-century Mussar master (d. 2005, Israel), picks up on Rashi's comment and explores the spiritual dimension of these two words. He writes that these words reveal a fundamentally different approach to the material world. One who says, *"Yesh Li Rav"* has a quantitative approach to possessions. More is better and so I am always striving for more. In contrast, one who says *Yesh li Kol*, has a qualitative approach to the material world: *What I have is all I need*. Rabbi Wolbe explains that this is the *middah* of *Histapkut*, which can be translated as "enoughness" or "being content with what one has." He is emphatic that this is not a post-facto *middah* where one says, "What can I do, this is all I have so I might as well be happy with

---

4 These following paragraphs about Rav and Kol are a paraphrase of Rabbi Shlomo Wolbe, *Aley Shur*, vol. 2 (Jerusalem: Beit HaMussar, 1986), 327–28.

5 Rashi Commentary to Genesis 33:11.

it." No, it is an attitude which one can bring to any state of material life. It takes reflecting deeply on what you have and your actual needs and seeing, whenever possible, that your basic needs are met. Rabbi Wolbe quotes the Talmud to demonstrate the spiritual impact of this *middah*:

> Our rabbis taught that God gave three people a taste of the next world in this world. They are Abraham, Isaac and Jacob. About Avraham it is written, "God blessed Abraham BaKol," about Isaac it is written, "And he ate *MiKol*," and about Jacob it is written, "I have *Kol*." There are three who were not governed by the Evil Inclination. These were Abraham, Isaac and Jacob about who it is written, "*Bakol, MiKol, Kol*."[6]

Careful cultivation of having enough opens up a world of spirituality. This takes calming the *yetzer hara*—that drive for more and more (literally: our evil inclination). With cultivation, one accepts and appreciates that one has enough. With this appreciation comes joy. Rabbi Wolbe calls this: "A taste of spirituality while enjoying the material world." The physical world can be the ground for such deep, lasting joy, but only if developed; joy is not an emotion that can be commanded.

In the remainder of the chapter, I propose a multi-step process for using food as a physical pathway for experiencing and cultivating deep, lasting joy. The three steps in this process are gratitude, generosity and joy. The starting point is with noticing that you have enough, or even more than enough. But for people in the top fifth of the income bracket (approximately $110,000 annual family income), what is known as the upper middle class, and where many North American Jews sit, truly acknowledging this can be a challenge. Richard Reeve, a Senior Fellow in Economic Studies at the Brookings Institute, describes this challenge in his 2017 book, *Dream Hoarders*:

> The upper middle class has been having it pretty good. It is about time those of us in the favored fifth recognized our privileged position. Some humility and generosity is required. But there is clearly some work to do in terms of raising awareness. Right now, there is something of a culture of entitlement among America's upper middle class. Partly this is because of a natural tendency to compare ourselves to those even better off than us. This is the "we are the 99 percent" problem.[7]

---

6   BT *Bava Batra* 16b.

7   Richard Reeves, *Dream Hoarders* (Washington, DC: The Brookings Institution, 2017), 4.

As Reeves describes, actually noticing the abundance and the privilege that comes with it is an essential step. We also see such an acknowledgement in the Torah's first instance of gratitude. Rabbi Wolbe writes:

> Rabbi Yehuda said in the name of Rabbi Shimon Bar Yehuda: Since the day God created the world, there hasn't been anyone who has thanked God until Leah and her thanks, as it says, "This time I thank God" (BT *Brakhot* 7b on Genesis 29:35)—Rashi: Because she saw with her holy spirit that Yaakov was going to establish 12 tribes from his four wives. Because she gave birth to her fourth son, she gave thanks for having a portion than was greater than she deserved." Rashi similarly writes on this line in the Bible (Genesis 29:35): "And she became pregnant again and gave birth to a son and said, this time I will thank God and call his name Yehuda, etc." Rashi: *This time I will thank*—that I took more than my portion, from now I need to give thanks.[8]

The matriarch Leah was able to notice that she was blessed with more than her portion. If evenly divided, each of the four wives should have given birth to three tribal founders. But she had four (indeed, she goes on to give birth to six tribal founders and one daughter). She calls her fourth son Yehuda, from the Hebrew root *L'hodot*, which means both to acknowledge and to give thanks. The Hebrew root emphasizes that to feel gratitude, one must first acknowledge what one has. Leah had plenty of reasons to ignore her bounty because of her status as the unloved wife. One can easily imagine her justifications for deserving more than her portion of children, spending a life watching her husband favor her younger sister. What justifications do we make for our privilege, to ignore the reality of abundance? As Leah demonstrates, acknowledgement of abundance precedes gratitude.

Here enters the role of food. A mindful trip to almost any major supermarket serving middle- and upper-middle class communities is an experience of almost obscene abundance. The next time you shop at the grocery store, gaze on the fresh produce area, or stand and face the wall of dried cereal boxes, with seventy different varieties of corn meal and sugar. When you are at a *bar mitzvah* or wedding, mindfully scan the buffet and acknowledge how much more sushi, roast beef, fish, or cholent there is than you could ever eat. Or just notice your table during a Shabbat meal. The abundance of food, beyond our

---

8 Wolbe, *Aley Shur*, vol. 2, 282–83.

portion, is so obvious that with a little mindfulness, gratitude will naturally arise. As Rashi says, paraphrasing Leah: "I took more than my portion, from now I need to give thanks."

Noticing our privilege and feeling grateful gives rise to the next step on the path towards sustainable *simha*. According to Rabbi Eliyahu Dessler (Israel, 1892–1953) gratitude with one's portion leads to a feeling a joy which, in turn, leads to a natural desire to give:

> The quality of giving inheres only in the person who is happy—not just satisfied—with his lot … In his happiness he resembles a river in flood whose life-giving waters overflow all its banks. We have already seen how the heart of one in a state of joy broadens to encompass all who are close to him; the more joyful the person the greater his desire that all his friends take part in his joy.[9]

Again, our relationship to food stimulates this type of giving. If we truly acknowledge how much of a surplus of food we have available to us, the natural inclination is not to hoard, but to share. To be honest, I sometimes experience my own personal abundance as guilt. I am self-conscious as I see the bags fill up and the bill get bigger as my organic celery, olive oil, free-range eggs, and cashew-milk ice cream pass through the check-out counter at the supermarket. As a result, I rarely put some of this bounty in the basket for the local food pantry on the way out of the market. I have been too busy justifying to myself why my family needs so much food for the week. By the time I finish my justifications I don't think I have a pack of cheese sticks to spare. Rabbi Wolbe and Rabbi Dessler suggest another way of dealing with the blessing of abundance. As I fill up my sizable shopping cart with items from around the world, I notice how readily available these goods are and how all my family's needs are being met.

It is important to notice that, with mindful intention, joy replaces guilt, and these feelings are followed by a natural generosity to share. Sometimes we think that people give to relieve guilt. This type of giving never makes a lasting impression on the soul. There may be temporary relief for the guilt of privilege, through giving *tzedakah* (donating money) or through *hesed* (an act of kindness), but if the motivation is guilt, it won't change you because you are

---

9 Rabbi Eliyahu Dessler (trans. Aryeh Carmell), *Strive For Truth* (New York, Feldheim, 1978), 140–43.

only giving to relieve yourself of discomfort. The giving that comes from joy is much more durable, as will be described in the final step in this process.

The third, and final, step is really the completion of a virtuous cycle. Acknowledgement leads to gratitude which leads to happiness which leads to giving which leads to more happiness. There are at least two ways that giving reinforces joy. The social sciences have taught us that meaningful human connection is one of the main sources of happiness, which in turn leads to better long-term health. Social isolation is a source of misery. Giving often puts us into contact with other human beings. The shot of joy we get from feeling grateful for abundance releases chemicals in the brain that encourage us in the direction of more human connection. We feel more gregarious and positively inclined towards humans around us. This openness and generosity of spirit towards others, even if transitory, can spark human connections that can develop into meaningful relationships. These relationships can then be the source of great, lasting joy.

Another way that giving reinforces joy is alluded to by Maimonides in his description of the *mitzvah* of *simhat yom tov*, the joy of the festivals:

כֵּיצַד. הַקְּטַנִּים נוֹתֵן לָהֶם קְלָיוֹת וֶאֱגוֹזִים וּמִגְדָּנוֹת. וְהַנָּשִׁים קוֹנֶה לָהֶן בְּגָדִים וְתַכְשִׁיטִין נָאִים כְּפִי מָמוֹנוֹ. וְהָאֲנָשִׁים אוֹכְלִין בָּשָׂר וְשׁוֹתִין יַיִן שֶׁאֵין שִׂמְחָה אֶלָּא בְּבָשָׂר וְאֵין שִׂמְחָה אֶלָּא בְּיַיִן. וּכְשֶׁהוּא אוֹכֵל וְשׁוֹתֶה חַיָּב לְהַאֲכִיל לַגֵּר לַיָּתוֹם וְלָאַלְמָנָה עִם שְׁאָר הָעֲנִיִּים הָאֻמְלָלִים. אֲבָל מִי שֶׁנּוֹעֵל דַּלְתוֹת חֲצֵרוֹ וְאוֹכֵל וְשׁוֹתֶה הוּא וּבָנָיו וְאִשְׁתּוֹ וְאֵינוֹ מַאֲכִיל וּמַשְׁקֶה לַעֲנִיִּים וּלְמָרֵי נָפֶשׁ אֵין זוֹ שִׂמְחַת מִצְוָה אֶלָּא שִׂמְחַת כְּרֵסוֹ. וְעַל אֵלּוּ נֶאֱמַר (הושע ט ד) "זִבְחֵיהֶם כְּלֶחֶם אוֹנִים לָהֶם כָּל אֹכְלָיו יִטַּמָּאוּ כִּי לַחְמָם לְנַפְשָׁם". וְשִׂמְחָה כָּזוֹ קָלוֹן הִיא לָהֶם שֶׁנֶּאֱמַר (מלאכי ב ג) "וְזֵרִיתִי פֶרֶשׁ עַל פְּנֵ3יכֶם פֶּרֶשׁ חַגֵּיכֶם":

How [does one make everyone happy appropriately]? Give the children nuts and candy and buy the women as much nice clothing and jewelry as he can afford. And the men eat meat and drink wine since there is no happiness without meat and wine. And when [the head of household] eats and drinks, he is obligated to feed strangers, orphans and widows as well as all other poor people. *However, if he locks his doors and eats and drinks with his family and does not feed the poor and others going through hard times, this is not the joy which was commanded, but [merely] satisfying his stomach [My emphasis].* About such people, it is said "Their sacrifices are like the bread of mourners, all who eat it will be contaminated for their bread is for their own appetites."

Such parties are disgraceful to those who participate in them as it says "I will spread dung on your faces, the dung of your festival [sacrificial meals]."[10]

According to Maimonides, the real joy of the festivals is sharing your abundance with others. It is easy, on a holiday, to want to hoard what you have for your own family, and maybe share just with friends. How often is this our instinct when we hear that a stranger in town is in need of a meal. Some righteous among us may respond immediately to open their homes, but many turn away, feeling like they've worked hard and deserve this time not to give. Maimonides comes to tell us that such an impulse undermines the spiritual opportunity presented by the holiday. We have a chance to participate in the virtuous cycle. By sharing your food, you are acting against your lower instincts to hoard your material and emotional resources. Acting on the higher instincts to give and share generates a feeling of joy. We feel joy when we act in integrity with our values. Overcoming a fear of scarcity and giving from our abundance is living out these values. By participating in this virtuous cycle, we can reinforce joy to the point that it becomes a durable, accessible attribute, available to us regularly in our lives.

Many contemporary Jewish communities around the world are blessed with unprecedented material wealth. While this abundance is certainly a blessing, it is also a spiritual challenge. On a full stomach, we get used to our physical comfort and forget our world-changing mission. But it doesn't have to be this way. If we can make the production, acquisition, and consumption of food into a spiritual practice of gratitude, giving, and joy, then this abundance can become an engine of connection and social change.

---

10 Maimonides, *Mishneh Torah*, Laws of Festivals 6:18 (Sefaria translation).

CHAPTER 1

Towards a Jewish Nutrition Ethic

The Theology, Law, and Ethics of Healthy Eating

Rabbi Daniel R. Goodman

"And You Shall Live By Them"
(Leviticus 18:5)

"Pour devenir un saint, il faut vivre." *["To become a saint, you need to live"]*
(Albert Camus, La Peste)[1]

INTRODUCTION

The imperative to eat healthily is a crucial religious, ethical, and *halakhah* precept that is implicit in the fundamental Jewish value *of u-vaharta ba-hayyim* ["choose life"]. It is only now, when the dangers of eating unhealthily are becoming more evident by the week, that the ethical, religious, and *halakhah* mandate to eat healthily must be made explicit. The ever-increasing information about the deleterious effects of obesity and poor nutritional lifestyles, combined with the growing public health crisis in the United States in particular,[2] are of immediate concern to all people, including Jews. We now know that one of the primary causes of obesity is the excess consumption of sugar:

> Consuming too much [sugar], especially in beverages, is linked to an
> increased risk of obesity, heart disease, diabetes, metabolic syndrome,

---

1   Albert Camus, *La peste* (Gallimard: 1947), 257; translation from The Plague (trans. Stuart Gilbert; New York: Vintage, 1948), 284.

2   Se, Andrew Pollack, "American Medical Association Recognizes Obesity as a Disease," *New York Times*, June 18, 2013.

gout, and tooth decay. And, of course, sugar provides "empty calories"—devoid of vitamins, minerals, protein, and other nutrients.[3]

Sugar consumption has not only been linked to an increased risk of Type 2 Diabetes (Type 1 Diabetes is hereditary; Type 2 is acquired and caused by an increased level of blood sugar), but has been linked to an increased likelihood of Alzheimer's disease and dementia as well.[4] The title alone of a recent *New England Journal of Medicine* article succinctly summed up the perils of sugar consumption: "Sugar Is Killing Us."[5] In 2015, the Dietary Guidelines Advisory Committee and other major health groups such as the American Heart Association advised people to "cut back on added sugars." The committee stated that Americans were "eating too much salt, sugar, and saturated fat, and not enough foods that fit a healthy dietary pattern, like fruits, vegetables, nuts, whole grains, fish, and moderate levels of alcohol." The committee "singled out added sugars as one of its major concerns," stating that "sugary drinks should be removed from schools."[6] "Research has linked unbalanced soda consumption to obesity, Type 2 diabetes, coronary artery disease, stroke, dental disease, bone disease, depression, gout, asthma, cancer and premature death."[7] James J. DiNocolantonio, a cardiovascular research scientist at Saint Luke's Mid America Heart Institute and Sean C. Lucan, an assistant professor at the Albert Einstein College of Medicine call sugar "dangerous"

---

3 Lisa Y. Lefferts and Michael F. Jacobson, "S-W-E-E-T! Your Guide to Sugar Substitutes," *Nutrition Action* 9, October 2014. Nutrition experts are urging new U.S. dietary guidelines that insist on "sharp new limits on the amount of added sugars that Americans should consume." See also Anahad O'Conner, "Nutrition Panel Calls for Less Sugar," *New York Times*, February 20, 2015.

4 Paul K. Crane, M.D., M.P.H., et al., "Glucose Levels and Risk of Dementia," *New England Journal of Medicine* 369:6 (2013): 540–48; Cristina M. Sena et al., "Type 2 Diabetes Aggravates Alzheimer's Disease-Associated Vascular Alterations of Aorta in Mice," *Journal of Alzheimer's Disease* (2014), and M. Suzanne and Jack R. Wands, "Alzheimer's Disease Is Type 3 Diabetes—Evidence Reviewed," *Journal of Diabetes Science and Technology* 2:6 (2008): 1101–13.

5 Loren Cordain, Live Well, et al., "Sugar Is Killing Us," *New England Journal of Medicine* 396:6 (2013): 540–48.

6 Anahad O'Connor, "Panel Calls for Less Sugar and Eases Cholesterol Restrictions," *New York Times*, February 20, 2015, A13, A17.

7 The health problems with soda are not limited to regular, sugar-laden soda; even diet sodas are dangerous. See Mark Schatzker, "Things Go Worse: Two Books Examine the Dire Health Consequences of Soda, and the Effort to Limit Them," *New York Times Book Review*, November 22, 2015, 15; Fred Barbarsh, "Study Links Diet Soda to Higher Risk of Stroke, Dementia," *Washington Post*, April 21, 2017.

and "addictive: we don't mean addictive in that way that people talk about delicious foods. We mean addictive, literally, in the same way as drugs … Cravings induced by sugar are comparable to those induced by addictive drugs like cocaine and nicotine."[8] A study they conducted demonstrated that "sugar, perhaps more than salt, contributes to the development of cardiovascular disease. Evidence is growing, too, that eating too much sugar can lead to fatty liver disease, hypertension, Type 2 diabetes, obesity, and kidney disease."[9]

In addition to the health problems specifically related to added sugar, there are a multitude of health maladies linked with poor nutrition in general, as detailed in many nutritional studies. The following represents just a sampling of these studies:

> **Saturated and trans-fat**: [L]imiting saturated fat remains important for heart health, according to Robert Eckel, MD, director of the Lipid Clinic at University of Colorado Hospital. The average American needs to cut saturated fat in half to meet the new American Heart Association recommendations of no more than five to six percent of calories daily … Trans fat, from partially hydrogenated oils in many processed snack and convenience foods, poses the greatest health risk. Amounts are dropping, but it still warrants checking nutrition labels to avoid trans-fat as much as possible.[10]
>
> **Weight**: Excess body fat, mainly around the waist, triggers inflammation and insulin resistance, posing a serious heart risk … According to guidelines from the American Heart Association in collaboration with other organizations, health risks decrease from a three to five percent weight loss—10 to 20 pounds or less for most people.[11] Health experts recommend, among other healthy eating strategies, replacing cheese with almonds or walnuts, and switching one meal a weak from red meat to fish.[12]
>
> **Benefits of a healthy lifestyle**: Major studies show that people who eat a healthy diet, don't smoke, get regular physical activity throughout the week, and maintain a healthy weight and waist size prevent about

---

8 James J. DiNocolantonio and Sean C. Lucan, "Sugar Season. It's Everywhere, and Addictive." *New York Times*, December 23, 2014, A25, adding that "functional M.R.I. tests involving milkshakes demonstrate that it's the sugar, not the fat, that people crave."

9 Ibid.

10 Ibid., recommending that whole and natural foods should be substituted for added sugars.

11 Karen Collins, MS, RDN, CDN, FAND, "The Latest Diet Strategies for Heart Health," *Environmental Nutrition*, February 2015, 4.

12 Ibid.

80 percent of heart attacks and 93 percent of type 2 diabetes, as well as substantially reducing their risk of stroke and cancer.[13]

The times call for a Jewish ethic of nutrition that demonstrates how eating healthily—and avoiding the excess consumption of sugar in particular—is not only a physical necessity but a religious obligation that is rooted in the ethic of choosing life [*u-vaharta ba-hayyim*], and for a Jewish theology of nutrition that guides conscientious religionists towards eating healthily. The purposes of this article are threefold: to articulate the theological, ethical, and *halakhah* bases on which a Jewish nutrition ethic can be built; to demonstrate how nutrition is a moral and religious issue and not an issue that can be demoted to a mere "lifestyle choice"; and to begin the construction of a contemporary nutrition ethic that integrates classical Jewish values with current medical, scientific, and physiological knowledge of the body, food, and nutrition.

HEALTHY EATING AS A RELIGIOUS OBLIGATION: THEOLOGICAL PREMISES

God is the God of Life

In order to understand how theology informs ethics, it behooves us to examine the Torah itself, which is the source for nearly all subsequent Jewish conceptions of God. From a theological perspective, Rabbi Dr. Irving Greenberg has consistently argued that the primary attribute of God is life. And from a biblical scholarship perspective, Jon Levenson has demonstrated that the Jewish God as seen in the Bible is the "God of Life": that is, the primary attributes for which YHWH is exalted is for giving life to his creations, for restraining the chaotic forces that threaten life, and for YHWH's hoped-for ultimate triumph over Death. Levenson's *Creation and the Persistence of Evil: The Jewish Drama of Divine Omnipotence*, brilliantly elucidates the Jewish view of God as life-giver and defeater of death:

> The adversary overcome in Isaiah 25:6-8 is not Leviathan under whatever name, but 'Death.' It is best to see in this term the name of a deity, because the same word (mt) denotes in Ugaritic the name of one of Baal's foes, Mot, the deadly son of El, who succeeds in swallowing Baal … In the biblical reflex of this myth in Isaiah 25:6-8, however, it is YHWH, like

---

13 Ibid.

Baal associated with natural abundance and enhanced vitality, who swallows Death ... Indeed, YHWH swallows Death 'forever' (*bila haMavet lanesah*): the life-sapping forces will at last be eliminated, as the living God celebrates his unqualified victory upon his Temple mount.

This resurrection (of 26:19, 'Oh, let your dead revive!') here is best seen as the logical consequence of the defeat of Death predicted in 25:8... The resurrection of the dead is to be distinguished, both in origin and implication, from the immortality of the soul, an idea attested poorly, if at all, in the biblical universe. The hoped-for resurrection originates in eschatology whose roots lie in the Canaanite tradition of the enthronement of the life-enhancing deity after his victory over the powers of chaos, disease, and sterility. Death, like the sea monster, must be defeated if life is to go on and the worshipping community is to survive. It is no wonder that the enthronement of YHWH stood at the center of that community's liturgical life.[14]

According to the biblical worldview, God's primary characteristic is life. Biblical scholar Gregory Mobley further articulated this biblical theological conception, writing that the "hidden foundation" of biblical theology—a theology which is reified through ritual—is that "the Creator desires life." This is most prominently seen in Second Isaiah's proclamation that the God who "created the heavens ... who formed the earth and made it—he did not create it to be chaos, *he formed it to be inhabited*" (Isa. 45:18).[15]

God as "God of Life" and "Defeater of Death" is not only a biblical theological trope, but a theological motif that persists in rabbinic theology as well:

---

14 Jon Levenson, *Creation and the Persistence of Evil: The Jewish Drama of Divine Omnipotence* (New York: Harper & Row, 1988), 30–31. Levenson expands on the significanc-e of life in biblical Jewish theology in *Resurrection: The Power of God for Christians and Jews*, with Kevin J. Madigan (New Haven: Yale University Press, 2008), and Jon D. Levenson, *Resurrection and the Restoration of Israel: The Ultimate Victory of the God of Life* (New Haven: Yale University Press, 2006).

15 Gregory Mobley, *The Return of the Chaos Monsters—and Other Backstories of the Bible* (Grand Rapids, MI: Erdmans, 2012), 92. The theological motif that the God of life desires us to choose life is also evident "within the Godhead itself": in Exodus 34:6–7, God's compassion overcomes His anger; or, "in Kabbalistic terms, hesed overpowers din." (Ibid.) Cf. Brent A. Strawn, "The Triumph of Life: Towards a Biblical Theology of Happiness," in *The Bible and the Pursuit of Happiness: What the Old and New Testaments Teach Us about the Good Life*, ed. Strawn. (New York: Oxford Univ. Press, 2012), 287–322.

> The fact is that Rabbinic midrash continues the tradition of eschatological combat and displays a greater interest in the figure of Leviathan than does the Hebrew Bible. In the future, the Leviathan is slaughtered, and eaten by the righteous, to teach that "Out of death—life."[16]

In the Middle Ages, Maimonides sought to purge Jewish theology of such anthropomorphic and graphic constructs and articulated a more sanitized, philosophically perfect image of God. But in the process of cleansing God from such belligerent imagery, something extremely valuable—and perennially Jewish—was lost: the depiction of God as the ultimate embodiment of life. With this theological understanding in mind, it is not hard to understand why God is praised as "the one who revives the dead" in the second paragraph of the centerpiece of Jewish liturgy, the Amidah. Jewish liturgy is often where the normative theological positions of Judaism of the various streams and denominations of Judaism have been embedded. Thus, if the Jewish view of God is that "He is the one who revives the dead"—the one who has such life-giving powers that He will even defeat death— Jewish theology posits that God is the God of life.[17]

The God of Life and Feminist Theology

The rise of feminist Jewish theology indicates that, at least in some circles, this biblical theology—according to which YHWH's primary characteristic is that of life—may be beginning to overtake Maimonidean theology. Jewish tradition is not wanting in metaphorical sobriquets for God, and feminist theology suggests that a return to emphasizing God's life-giving capacities (over, or instead of, God's monarchial and patriarchal characteristics) may be desirable. Both Marcia Falk[18] and Rachel Adler[19] illustrate how God has been (and still could be)

---

16 Jon Levenson, *Creation and the Persistence of Evil: The Jewish Drama of Divine Omnipotence* (New York: Harper & Row, 1988), 33–34.

17 See Neil Gillman, *The Death of Death: Resurrection and Immortality in Jewish Thought* (Woodstock, VT: Jewish Lights, 1997).

18 Rachel Adler, *Engendering Judaism: An Inclusive Theology and Ethics* (Philadelphia and Jerusalem: JPS, 1998), ch. 3, "And Not Be Silent." The other possible metaphors for God are foreclosed by the "totalized metaphor" of a monarchic God ("God as patriarchal male"), Adler notes. Ibid., 87.

19 In her liturgical compositions, Marcia Falk adapted the metaphors of creator, nurturer, and compassionate life-sustainer into divine appellations such as *ein ha-hayyim* and *nishmat ha-hayyim*; see Marcia Falk, "Notes on Composing New Blessings toward a Feminist-Jewish

portrayed as a nurturer, as a compassionate presence, and as a creator and sustainer of life, the *ruah Hayim* [Spirit of Life]. Though many of these divine depictions are indeed utilized from time to time (and thus are theoretically available for wider liturgical adaptation), the primary metaphor for the divine in classical rabbinic theology is that of kingship. "Accepting the yoke of heaven" (*kabbalat ol malkhut shamayim*) is the traditional analogical paradigm that is applied to the performance of *mitzvot*, most notably in reference to the recitation of the *Shema*.[20] Other masculine metaphors for God include "God as the Master of Nature, and "God who revealed the Torah."[21] That God is described as a law-giver—an authoritarian, masculine metaphor—nearly as often, if not more frequently, than as a life-giver—a generative, feminine metaphor—even though the Torah begins with Creation rather than legal Revelation (notwithstanding Rabbi Yitzchak's postulation that this alternative beginning should have preceded the Creation narrative[22]) is indicative of the extent to which the masculinization of the divine became embedded in Jewish liturgy.

Thus, since the monarchic image of God either resulted in or was indicative of the masculine image of God (at the least, the monarchic metaphor perpetuates the masculine image of God), feminist theologians addressed the problem of outmoded divine nomenclature through the power of naming: God needed to be ungendered, renamed, and endowed with new metaphors that are in consonance with modern sensibilities. Falk demonstrates that this may be done by discarding the metaphors rooted in authoritarian, patriarchal eras (kingship being the most prominent of such metaphors) and re-conceptualizing God with metaphors that speak to our own egalitarian, humanistic age.[23]

The new gender-neutral metaphors for God that feminists have used, such as *Shekhinah*, and especially *mekor ha-hayyim* ("Source of Life"), are theological metaphors that are primarily rooted in biblical theology, not medieval

---

Reconstruction of Prayer," 3 *Journal of Feminist Studies in Religion* 1 (1987): 39–53, and see Adler's discussion of these metaphors in *Engendering Judaism* (New York: Beacon Press, 1999), 91.

20 Solomon Schechter discusses this metaphor extensively *in Some Aspects of Rabbinic Theology* (Woodstock, VT: Jewish Lights, 1993), devoting three chapters to describing the usage of the "kingdom of God" metaphor in rabbinic sources, at 65–113.

21 Ibid.

22 See Rashi to Genesis 1:1, s.v. *b'reishit.*

23 Falk, "Notes on Composing New Blessings," 42, 43. Rethinking the monarchic image of God can eventually lead to "mutually supportive relationships between male and female, immanence and transcendence" in our "God-talk." Ibid.

philosophy.[24] Not only is *mekor ha-hayyim* a more inclusive image for God, but it is also more reflective of the traditional biblical Jewish conception of God as the Creator and Source of Life than many other appellations for the Divine. It is also in accord with a possible interpretation of one of the biblical names of God, *El Shaddai*. Often translated as "God Almighty" (explained by the rabbis as shorthand for the God who observed creation and uttered "enough," *she-amar dai*[25]), it may also mean "God of the Breasts," in the sense of Jacob's blessing to Joseph: "By the God of your father, who will help you, by *shaddai* who will bless you with blessings of heaven above, blessings of the deep that lies beneath, blessings of the breasts (*shadayim*) and of the womb" (Genesis 49:25). God is thus given feminine attributes[26] in order to stress the creative, life-giving, and life-sustaining capacities of the Divine, which are God's most important, recognizable, and perhaps only definitively knowable attributes.[27]

The basic theological premise of Judaism is that even though we have great difficulty saying what God is or what qualities God possesses, what we can say is that according to Rabbi Joseph Soloveitchik and Rabbi David Hartman, God's primary attribute is creativity—that is, God is the source of life, because God created life (the fundamental theological assumption of the Torah), and continues to nurture, sustain, and create life; as both Rabbi Shneur Zalman of Liadi (in the *Tanya*) and the Vilna Gaon explain, the basic biblical and rabbinic theological assumption is that God is not a watchmaker who absconded from the universe on completion of creation, but that God continues to sustain and create life: *mehadesh bekhol yom tamid ma'aseh b'reishit* [God renews the Creation each day], states the introductory blessing of the blessings prior to the morning recitation of the Shema in the *Shaharit* prayer service. The Talmud characterizes the Torah and Jewish legal discussions as the words of

---

24 See, for example, Neil Gillman, *The Way Into Encountering God in Judaism* (Woodstock, VT: Jewish Lights, 2000), 12. On "Shekhinah" as rooted in biblical rather than medieval theology, cf., however, Peter Schäfer *Mirror of His Beauty* (Princeton: Princeton University Press, 2002), and Arthur Green, "Shekhinah, the Virgin Mary, and the Song of Songs: Reflections on a Kabbalistic Symbol in Its Historical Context " *AJS Review* 26:1 (2002): 1–52, which complicates this claim.

25 BT *Hagigah* 12a.

26 See Douglas A. Knight and Amy-Jill Levine, *The Meaning of the Bible: What the Jewish Scriptures and Christian Old Testament Can Teach Us* (New York: Harper Collins, 2011), 140.

27 See also Levenson, *Creation and the Persistence of Evil*, 84, in which he links Bezalel's creativity—an attribute which is naturally linked to life—with God's creativity as a life-giver through the term *ruah elohim* that is used to describe attributes which they both possess.

the "living God," or "the God of life" [*elokim hayyim*][28]—that is, the words of the God who creates life, sustains it, and desires us to choose it as well. The biblical theological picture of God as the source of life[29] had ethical consequences for Jews even in biblical times. If God's primary quality was life, and if Jews were commanded to walk in God's ways, it was logical that Jews would need to choose between life and death (Jeremiah 21:8).

This chapter's next section discusses how this fundamental principle of prophetic ethics, with the theology that informed it, was ramified by the rabbinic tradition, transported into broader Jewish ethical thought, and carried into *halakhah* praxis.

ETHICAL PREMISES

The Primacy of Choosing Life in the Rabbinic Tradition

> "Who is the person who desires life?" (Psalms 34:12) There was once a merchant who frequented cities near Tzipori who would loudly proclaim, "Who would like to purchase a potion of life?" Crowds gathered around him. R. Yannai was sitting and studying in his house. Upon hearing this advertisement, he went to the merchant and said, "sell this [life-potion] to me." The merchant responded, "You do not need this, and it was not for those like you whom I exerted myself [in coming here]." [The merchant] took out a book of Tehillim (Psalms) and showed R. Yannai the verse, "Who is the person who desires life?," and [showed him] what is written in the next verse: "Guard your tongue from evil (34:13), distance yourself from evil and do good (34:14)" (*Leviticus Rabbah* 16:2).[30]

As Rabbi Dr. Irving Greenberg argued God's primary quality is life (see Rabbi Dr. Greenberg's contribution to this volume for a more thorough definition). God is the symbol and realization of infinite life and possesses the ability to bestow infinite life—and ethical mandates flow from this basic

---

28 BT *Eruvin* 13b

29 See, for example, Ezekiel 37:1–3 (the dry bones parable), Isaiah 25:6–8 (YHWH's swallowing of Death "forever"), Isaiah 26:19 ("Oh, let your dead revive!"), and Daniel 12:2: "And many of them that sleep in the dust of the earth shall awake, some to everlasting life, and some to shame and contempt" (KJV translation).

30 Vilna ed., vol. II, 22, author translation.

theological premise. One of the basic Jewish ethical imperatives lies in the principle of *imitatio Dei*, imitating God [*v'halakhta bid'rakhav*]. One of the highest Jewish values is to emulate God; this is traditionally fulfilled through acts of loving kindness, explain the rabbis: Just as God is merciful, so too must we be merciful.[31] A seemingly unrelated but equally (and perhaps more) important ethical imperative is the command to choose life, "*u-vaharta ba-hayyim.*" Though Deuteronomy 30:19 may not be a *mitzvah* in the legal sense, and though the verse can be read in a descriptive rather than proscriptive way, the rabbis interpreted "choose life" as a global, overarching, meta-*halakhah* principle that must inform all *halakhah* and ethical decision-making; one must even desecrate the Sabbath for the sake of life,[32] a striking law considering that Sabbath violators are compared to idolaters in rabbinic literature.

The concept of "desiring life" (with its accompanying psalmic ethical admonition) is "an encapsulation of the entire Torah," according to Rabbi David Luria's commentary on this midrash.[33] And the Talmud states in a number of places that the principle of choosing life overrides all but three biblical commandments.[34] The rabbis urge us to not simply accept sickness as an irrevocable divine decree, but—to the contrary—they implore us to fight sickness and ill-health with all the resources that we have at our disposal. In the prophetic and rabbinic age, without modern healthcare, the death-fighting resource they believed to be at their disposal was Torah study. Indeed, according to the Talmud, when King Hezekiah became ill, Isaiah went and established a yeshiva near Hezekiah, because, as Rashi explained, Torah study protects against death.[35]

Choosing life is such a fundamental principle of rabbinic theology, this article posits, because of theology: if God's most essential quality is life, and

---

31 On *imitatio Dei*, see Deuteronomy 28:9; cf. Deuteronomy 5:33, 8:6, 11:22, 13:5; BT *Shabbat* 133b, BT *Sotah* 14a, and *Sifrei* on Deuteronomy 11:22; cf. Maimonides, *Mishneh Torah*, "Laws of Character Traits" 1:5–6, and idem, *Guide of the Perplexed*, i. 54.

32 BT *Yoma* 85.

33 Chidushei Radal, ad loc., s.v. *"v'lo hayiti yode'a."*

34 BT *Sanhedrin* 74a; see also BT *Avodah Zarah* 27b, BT *Yoma* 85a–b, and BT *Avodah Zarah* 54b. See also BT *Eruvin* 45a (the Sabbath may be desecrated for military self-defense when life is at stake; furthermore, so sweeping is the legal permission to transgress the Sabbath to save life that those who go out to save lives may even violate the Sabbath in order to return ["kol ha'yotz'in l'hatzil hozrin limkoman … shehozrin bikhlei za'yin limkoman"], and on self-defense, cf. BT *Bava Metzia* 62a, BT *Sanhedrin* 72a, and Rashi to Exodus 22:1. On violating the Sabbath for the sake of preservation of life, cf. commentary of Ramban to Exodus 31:13.

35 BT *Eruvin* 26a, Rashi s.v. *l'hoshiv yeshiva.*

since we are commanded to imitate God, then choosing life in every area of behavior—including in the area of food choices—is self-evident. We are commanded to be like God by choosing life;[36] in the area of nutrition, this entails making food choices that increase our capacity for physical life, and distancing ourselves from consuming foods that have the potential to diminish life. The ethical mandate of *imitatio Dei* is not limited to emulating God's qualities of mercy. As Rabbi Greenberg has explained, if we say that God possesses infinite consciousness, power, and the capacity to love, we should increase our capacities in these areas by developing our consciousness, our scientific powers of apprehending the world, and our capacity for love.[37] Thus, if we say that God's preeminent quality is life, then we should increase our capacity for life by making nutritious choices in the area of food and drink. This is not to suggest that the sole basis for a nutrition ethic is *imitaito Dei*; it is only to suggest that *imitatio Dei* strongly suggests that we should be guided by ethics and theology when it comes to choosing what (and how) we eat.

Thus, in this area of Jewish life, theology and ethics function in a symbiotic relationship: The Jewish theological conception of God as the Source of Life informs how the ethical principle of imitating God [*v'halakhta bid'rakhav*] should be understood and practiced. At the same time, the ethical principle of "choose life" [*u-vaharta ba-hayyim*] can be best understood in a theological context: life is so precious in the Jewish tradition that it's said to be the single most important ethical principle in the tradition.[38]

---

36 The Hebrew Bible is teleological: it points its readers in the direction of life. The book of Chronicles ends on the upward, forward-looking note of the Jewish return to Israel after the Babylonian exile. On how the "triumph of life" is enshrined by the structural sequence of the Hebrew Bible, see Strawn, "The Triumph of Life: Towards a Biblical Theology of Happiness." Readers of the Hebrew Bible thus receive an implicit message directing them to follow this movement.

37 R. Soloveitchik also conceptualizes *imitatio Dei* in terms of agency, basing it on the Talmudic legal dictum of "*shluho shel adam k'moto*," a person's agent is like one's self; "Agency [Sh'li ut]," in *Yemei Zikaron* (Aliner Library; WZO, Dept. of Torah Education & Culture; Jerusalem: Orot, 1986), 9–28. If we are created in the image of God, then we are also agents of God—God endowed us with some of His capacities for the purposes of tikkun olam [perfection of the world], which is the teleology of *halakhah*, according to R. Soloveitchik (trans. Lawrence Kaplan), *Halakhah Man* (Philadelphia: Jewish Publication Society, 1983), 99.

38 The three cardinal sins, regarding which one must give up one's life rather than commit, are the exception that prove the rule, and even these sins are subject to casuistic readings that lead to exceptions: for example, married women may not be obligated to undergo martyrdom rather than subject themselves to rape (see BT *Sanhedrin* 74b); there may be no obligation to give up one's life rather than convert to Islam or other purely monotheistic

And precisely because God's primary attribute is Life, Jews are implored to "walk with God." If what we can definitively say about God is that God is the God of life, and if Jews are implored to emulate God, then "choose life" can be transformed from an overarching ethical maxim to a praxis that, through its fulfillment, manifests Jews' basic understanding about the nature of God.

EATING HEALTHILY AS A RELIGIOUS OBLIGATION: *HALAKHAH* (LEGAL) PREMISES

The Preservation of Life as the Greatest Value in Judaism

> For this reason, Adam was created alone: to teach you that destroying a single life is to destroy a whole world, just as to save a life is to save a whole world. And for the sake of the peace of creation, that no one should say to another, "My ancestor was greater than yours." And so that the heretics cannot say, "There are many powers in heaven." And to proclaim the greatness of the Holy One Blessed Be He, for when a person casts many coins from the same press, they all look alike, but the Holy One Blessed Be He stamps every human being with the press of the first Adam, and none resembles the other. For this reason, each and every person must declare, "For my sake the world was created" (Mishnah, *Sanhedrin* 4:5).
>
> If a building fell upon a person [on the Sabbath] and it is unknown as to whether he is there or not, whether he is alive or dead, or whether he is a Jew or a gentile—they clear away the debris that is on him [to save his life despite the ban on destroying a building on the Sabbath] … If they found him alive, they remove the remaining debris that is on him.
>
> If they found him alive they remove the remaining debris that is on him: Is that not obvious?! Actually, this statement comes to teach us an additional point, namely, that even if he has only a short time to live, they remove the remaining debris (Babylonian Talmud, *Yoma* 85a).

Traditionally, Judaism has not left important ethical values and theological concepts in the realm of thought but has instead consistently sought to translate them into practice. The ethics and theology of *u-vaharta ba-hayyim* [choose life] are no different: the fundamental theological and ethical concepts

---

religions; and one who nevertheless does not give up one's life in any of the circumstances of *yehareg v'al ya'avor* ["one must be killed rather than transgress"] may still not be liable for his or her choice.

encapsulated in the principle of choosing life were codified into normative law, thereby becoming reified in the minds and actions of Jews. In the case of *u-vaharta ba-hayyim*, Jewish legal authorities recognized that the logical consequences of a religion which valued life more than anything else would necessitate the codification of legal precepts that flow from this value; an obligation to care about one's own physical life became one such obligation. Thus, Rabbi Joseph Karo articulated this longstanding Jewish legal precept in the authoritative *Shulhan Arukh* when he wrote that: "It is a positive commandment to be very careful and guard oneself from any life-threatening object, as it is said, ". . . take utmost care and watch yourselves scrupulously" (Deuteronomy 4:9; *Hoshen Mishpat* 427:8).

The Talmud expanded the *mitzvah* of *hishamer lekha ushmor nafshekha me'od*, "take utmost care and watch yourselves scrupulously" (also derived from *v'nishmartem me'od le-nafshoteikhem*, "But you shall greatly beware for your souls" from Deuteronomy 4:15) into a fundamental principle of Jewish law, elevating the value of life to its preeminent position in the hierarchy of Jewish values. Although not self-evident in Torah, the Talmudic sages came to believe that life is the overriding value in Judaism, and that all of the Torah's commandments save three may be violated in order to preserve life. This applies even to the commandment to observe Shabbat—a commandment considered of equivalent importance to the rest of the Torah's commandments in totality. As Rabbi Eleazar ben Azarya explains in the Talmud:

> If circumcision, which pertains to only one of the two-hundred-and-forty-eight limbs of the body, takes precedence over the prohibitions of Shabbat, all the more so the saving of the entire body should take precedence over the prohibitions of Shabbat . . .
>
> Said Rav Yehudah in the name of Shmuel: "Had I been there, I would have presented an even better proof text, specifically, 'He shall live by them' (Leviticus 18:5) [that is to say, one should live by the commandments] and not die by them." (BTs *Yoma* 85b)

That the primacy of life is not only a basic ethical and theological precept but a fundamental legal concept in Jewish law is further evident in several other Talmudic passages which were later codified in Jewish law. In the Talmud, the principle of *hamirah sakanta me-isurah* [laws regarding danger to life are more grave than ritual laws (BT *Hullin* 10a)] came to be regarded as an important principle of Jewish law. Rabbi Moses Isserless, in his glosses to the *Shulhan Arukh*, elaborated on the codification of this principle:

> One should distance oneself from things that may lead to danger, for a danger to life is more serious than a [religious] prohibition—*and one should be more worried about a possible danger to life than a possible [transgression] of a prohibition (Yoreh De'ah* 116:5 [Rama], emphasis added). Therefore, the sages prohibited one to walk in a place of danger, such as close to a leaning (shaky) wall or alone at night. They also prohibited drinking water from streams at night or placing one's mouth on a flowing pipe of water to drink, for these things may lead to danger ... All of these things are intended to avoid danger, and one who is concerned with his health will avoid them. And it is prohibited to rely on a saving miracle, or to endanger oneself in a like way.[39]

Rabbi Akiva, perhaps the most influential rabbinic sage who more than any other was responsible for molding the law and thought of nascent rabbinic Judaism, succinctly stated the Jewish legal view on the matter when he said: "A person is not permitted to harm himself" (Misnhah, *Bava Kamma* 8:6; BT *Bava Kamma* 90b).[40]

> Anyone who transgresses these matters (health concerns), saying "I will endanger myself, what business is that of anyone else?" or "I'm not concerned with such things," prepare for him lashes. Anyone who is careful about such matters (health concerns), a blessing shall come to him (*Shulhan Arukh, Hoshen Mishpat* 427:10, Dorff and Newman translation).[41]

Halakhah establishes clear priorities regarding the imperative to care for one's health. At the same time, *halakhah* stresses the importance of empathy—that is, it

---

39 It is possible that the Rama added this last statement of *ein somchin al ha-Ness* as a prophylactic admonition directed toward pious Jews who mistakenly assume that their scrupulous ritual observance cosmically impels God to protect them from the health consequences of poor eating choices. One should not think, says the Rama, that one can simply rely on God's miraculous protection; because we do not rely on miracles—which is not only a theological concept but a legal precept as well— we are actively required to be just as scrupulous (if not more so) in matters of health as we are in matters of ritual.

40 The claim here is that self-harm, whether emotional or physical, is prohibited based on the Talmudic source even if Rabbi Akiva wasn't literally talking about physical self-harm.

41 Unless otherwise noted, all translations from Hebrew texts in this article are mine.

is insufficient to care about one's own health and well-being; one must also ensure that that the health and well-being of others are cared for as well:

- Do not stand idly by the blood of your neighbor (Leviticus 19:16).
- "To watch his death when you could have save him." For instance, if one is drowning in a river or if a wild beast or armed bandit is attacking him [this verse requires you to come to his rescue] (Rashi, op. cit.).
- When you build a new house, you shall make a parapet for your roof, so that you do not bring bloodguilt on your house if anyone should fall from it (Deuteronomy 22:8).
- The Rabbis are of the opinion that it is the responsibility of the owner of a hazard to remove it (BT *Bava Batra* 18b).
- Rabbi Natan said: How do we know that a person should not keep a vicious dog in his home, or keep an insecure ladder in his home? Because the Torah says, "You should not bring bloodguilt on your house" (Deuteronomy 22:8).

Considering the preexisting obligations to ensure that others do not persist in life-endangering activities, the thrust of these *mitzvot* and Talmudic statements strongly suggest that there may be an obligation to warn others about the dangers of unhealthy eating as well.

Toxic Foods and Sugar

"Many things are forbidden by the Sages because they are dangerous to life," wrote Maimonides. "If one disregards any of these and says, 'If I want to put myself in danger, what concern is it to others?' or 'I am not particular about such things,' disciplinary flogging is inflicted upon him."[42] And if one is called on to treasure life as a component of *imitatio Dei*—because God's primary characteristic is life, the imperative to imitate God is most demonstrably fulfilled when one engages in life-affirming activities and refrains from life-diminishing activities—the ineluctable *halakhah* conclusion is that not only are toxic foods (such as trans-fat) ethically problematic but that they should be prohibited (like smoking) by *halakhah*.

This ethico-legal position would have numerous applications: when certain substances become scientifically identified as particularly physically harmful (as hydrogenated oils and trans-fats were fifteen years ago, and as

---

42 Maimonides, M.T., Laws of Murder (*Hilkhot Rotze'ah*) 11:4.

sugar is slowly but surely becoming considered to be a toxic substance[43]), they should be prohibited as objects that endanger life. Dr. Robert Lustig, a specialist in childhood obesity at the University of California, San Francisco School of Medicine, has made the case that sugar (a category that includes high-fructose corn syrup) is a "toxin" or a "poison." "It's not about the calories," said Lustig. "It has nothing to do with the calories. It's a poison by itself." According to Lustig, sugar should be classified with cigarettes and alcohol as dangerous (and potentially lethal) substances.[44] Even artificial sweeteners are now being recognized as potentially just as harmful as sugar. According to recent scientific studies, artificial sweeteners "may disrupt the ability to regulate blood sugar, causing changes in metabolism that can be a precursor to diabetes."[45]

Furthermore, because of the *halakhah* principle of *hamira sakanta me-isurah*[46] [danger is a more serious prohibition than ritually prohibited foods], refraining from junk food (and especially from excess sugar, which is now considered "toxic" if consumed in high quantities) should be treated even more seriously than refraining from ritually unkosher food. The Talmud cares so much about preventing danger and safeguarding life that it even contemplates allowing one to heal oneself with idolatrous products.[47] As the Rama emphasized: "One should avoid all things that might lead to danger, because a danger to life is stricter than a (ritual) prohibition. One should be more concerned about a possible danger to life than a possible (ritual) prohibition."[48]

The prohibition against endangering oneself extends even to the realm of *mitzvot*. The Talmud states that one may not even endanger oneself in the performance of a *mitzvah*:

> One is not obligated to search in narrow crevices [when conducting *bedikat hametz* (the search for *hametz*) because of danger. What kind of

---

43 See Gary Taubes, "Is Sugar Toxic?" *New York Times Magazine*, April 13, 2011. Accessed January 15, 2015. http://www.nytimes.com/2011/04/17/magazine/mag-17Sugar-t.html?_r=0

44 "High-fructose corn syrup, sugar—no difference," said Lustig. "The point is they're each bad—equally bad, equally poisonous." Ibid.

45 Kenneth Chang, "Artificial Sweeteners May Disrupt the Body's Blood Sugar Controls," *New York Times*, September 17, 2014. http://well.blogs. nytimes.com/ 2014/09/17/artificial-sweeteners-may-disrupt-bodys-blood-sugar-controls/?_php=true&_type=blogs&emc=edit_th_20140918&nl=todaysheadlines&nlid=48898 062&_r=0

46 Rabbi Moses Isserless, *Shulhan Arukh, Yoreh De'ah* 116:5.

47 BT *Pesahim* 25a.

48 Rabbi Moses Isserless, *Shulhan Arukh, Yoreh De'ah* 116:5, translated in Abraham J. Twerski, "A Body of Laws": Traditional Texts Speak to Contemporary Problems," in Dorff and Newman, *Jewish Choices, Jewish Voices*: Body, 31 (emphasis in Twerski's translation).

danger? Because of the danger of scorpions [which are commonly found in such places—Rashi, ad loc., s.v. "d'nafal"] ... But did not R. Elazar say 'agents on their way to perform a mitzvah are not harmed?' Where harm is common, it is different (BT *Pesahim* 8a–8b, author translation).

Thus, overconsumption of harmful foods like sugar would not even be justified at weddings and other *se'udot mitzvah*, because the principle of not endangering oneself takes precedence. One may not say that excessive consumption of sugar, hydrogenated oils, or other foods that are considered nutritionally dangerous is permitted *at se'udot mitzvah* on the basis that those who are there are 'agents on their way to perform a *mitzvah*,' because excessive sugar consumption (like alcohol and cigarette smoking) is now considered to be in the category of *sh'khiah hezeikah* [danger is common and likely to occur].

Twerski and other legists applied the principle of *sh'khiah hezeikah* to cigarette smoking in order to postulate that cigarette smoking is biblically prohibited. Likewise, considering the growing evidence concerning the toxicity of sugar, the logical *halakhah* conclusion would result in excess sugar (viz., sugar not naturally found in foods like fruit, beets, and sweet potatoes) being prohibited by the Torah as well. Once it was discovered that smoking leads to numerous health problems, *halakhah* authorities were swift in deeming it a violation of Jewish law.[49] Since sugar, processed "junk foods," and hydrogenated oils are quickly reaching this point as well, ample room exists for rabbinic authorities to rule that consumption of these substances, in non-negligible quantities, is likewise a violation of Jewish law.

However, I would propose that sugar, salt, and fat should not and cannot be classified as either *issur* [prohibited foods] like meat-and-milk mixtures, or objects of *sakanta* [dangerous foods] like poison that harm life in any quantity of consumption, because no amount of sugar, salt, or fat, if consumed in a sufficiently minute amount, is harmful in and of itself; as many nutritionists have observed, it is the over-consumption of these foods, combined with a sedentary lifestyle, that leads to debilitating, life-endangering conditions like obesity, diabetes, and heart disease.

Instead, I propose, that sugar, salt, and fat be loosely placed in the category of *d'var sh'yesh lahem matirin*: food-items that are not absolutely prohibited, but only prohibited at certain times—for example, just as *hametz* is prohibited on Passover and permitted afterwards, each item of sugary or unhealthy

---

49 Ibid.

food may be permitted at certain times (e.g., at festive occasions like Shabbat, Yom Tov, and *se'udot mitzvah* such as weddings), but only in moderation. Alternatively, they can be said to be absolutely *asur* like forbidden mixtures, but just as forbidden mixtures and forbidden foods can be eaten if they become *batel* (nullified)—if there is a sufficient amount of permitted food corresponding to the prohibited food (usually assumed to be a ratio of 60:1), so too, sugar can become *batel* if its quantity in a food or drink is similarly sufficiently negligible.[50]

ANTHROPOLOGICAL PREMISES

God as Owner of the Human Body

The anthropological assumptions on which an obligation to safeguard one's own life rests are twofold. The first premise is that God, not the human being, is the true owner of each individual's physical body. The Torah articulated this anthropological premise in Deuteronomy 10:14: "Mark, the heavens to their uttermost reaches belong to the Lord your God, the earth and all that is on it!" Thus, a divine command to care for the body and to choose life are legitimate not only because they are ethically meritorious actions but because God can command the proper course of care and treatment of God's own possessions.

The sage Hillel explicitly based his practice of regular bathing on this anthropological premise:

> When he [Hillel] finished the lesson with his students, he accompanied them part of the way. They said to him, "Master, where are you going?" "To perform a religious duty [i.e., to take a bath]." "Which religious duty?" He answered them, "If somebody appointed to scrape and clean the statues of kings in the theaters and circuses is paid to do the work and furthermore is considered noble for doing so, how much more so should I, created in the divine image and likeness, take care of my body!" (*Leviticus Rabbah* 34:3).

---

50 Much nuanced, sophisticated *halakhah* and physiological analysis is required here. If one cigarette in and of itself is not toxic, but it is the cumulative effect of smoking that is dangerous and led to the prohibition of smoking, does that mean that any quantities of added sugar should be prohibited like all smoking, or is only habitual smoking prohibited, and likewise, only habitual consumption of sugar prohibited?

If God is the true owner of the human body, then one is ethically and legally obligated not only to obey God's commands concerning the body, but to care for the body in at least as good of a fashion as one would care for any other possession of a king. And accounting for ethico-anthropological precepts such as *tzelem Elokim*—that the human being is created in the image of God—only heightens the duty to care for one's body.

This anthropological premise is also implicit in the midrashic understanding of the drowning of Egyptian charioteers in the Sea of Reeds. According to the Midrash, after the Jews sang to God in praise, the angels also wished to sing, whereupon God refused them permission: "My creatures (lit., handiwork, *ma'aseh yadai*) are drowning in the sea, and you wish to sing songs?" (BT *Megillah* 10b). That God calls the Egyptians "*ma'aseh yadai*," "my handiwork," indicates that a basic Jewish assumption about the nature of man is that he is God's handiwork, and thus in God's possessory domain (which also serves to explain God's grieving over the destruction of the seemingly culpable Egyptian pursuers).[51]

---

51 Modern *halakhists* (legists) have used the anthropological premise of God's proprietary interest in the human body as a basis on wich to base decisions that assume healthy behavior is religiously obligatory, but some also use this same premise to delimit autonomy in biomedical ethics; see, for example, J. David Bleich, "Care of the Terminally Ill," in Jewish Values in Health and Medicine, ed. Levi Meier (Lanham, MD: Univ. Press of America), 146: "man does not have a proprietary interest in either his life or his body. If one looks for a legal category in order to explain man's rights and obligations with regard to his life and his person, it would be quite accurate to say that human life is a bailment, that man is a bailee, and that the Creator is the bailor. God has created man and entrusted him with this precious treasure called human life. Life has been entrusted to man for guardianship and safekeeping." Quoted in Abraham J. Twerski, "A Body of Laws": Traditional Texts Speak to Contemporary Problems, in Elliot N. Dorff and Louis E. Newman, Jewish Choices, *Jewish Voices: Body* (Philadelphia: JPS, 2008), 29.

See also Elliot N. Dorff, *Matters of Life and Death: A Jewish Approach to Medical Ethics* (Jewish Publication Society, Philadelphia and Jerusalem: 1998), 15: "For Judaism, God owns everything, including our bodies (referencing Exod. 19:15; Deuteronomy 10:14; Psalms 24:1; Genesis 14:19, 22, where God is described as the "Creator" [*koneh*], that is the "possessor," of everything in "heaven and earth"; Psalms 104:24, Exodus 20:11, Leviticus 25:23, 42, 55; Deuteronomy 4:35, 39, 32:6). God lends our bodies to us for the duration of our lives, and we return them to God when we die. Consequently, neither men nor women have the right to govern their bodies as they will; since God created our bodies and owns them, God can and does assert the right to restrict how we use our bodies according to the rules articulated in Jewish law." A central argument of this article is that God asserts the right to restrict how we use our bodies in the realm of food and drink (but this article argues that God does this out of love for us, in accord with *Avot* 3:14, and because God desires that we emulate Him by choosing life). Further, this article argues that the rules articulated by

Tzelem Elokim: The Human Being is Created in the Image of God

The second premise, but perhaps the one with the most far-reaching ethico-legal implications, is that the human being is created in the image of God. This is the *klal gadol baTorah*—the overriding meta-*halakhah* regulatory principle that informs the entire Jewish world-view.[52] Not only is it the "ground-norm" of Judaism, in Rabbi Dr. Yitz Greenberg's phrase—its fundamental religious criterion—but a principle that, if understood according to its original conception, means that the human body itself is Godly.[53] To be created in the "image" of God means that the human being is a *tzelem* (literally, an "icon") of God—while we cannot see God, the human being's image can give us a sense of what God is like. And if you look at a human being properly and observe his or her emotional, psychological, and intellectual capacities, one can glean a sense of God's presence, according to the rabbinic tradition.[54] The biblical tradition also views the human being as God-like: according to Psalms, the human being is like God in that she is "slightly less than the angels," is "crowned with soul and splendor," and is given "dominion over Your (God's) handiwork" (Psalms 8:6–7).

Jewish law demonstrate that human beings do not have the right to consume whatever foods and drinks they want in whatever quantities they want: Jewish law governs the domain of food choices as well.

Dorff draws forth legal and ethical consequences from this anthropological premise: "One of these rules requires us to take reasonable care of our bodies. Just as we would be obliged to take reasonable care of an apartment on loan to us, so too we have the duty to take care of our own bodies. Rules of good hygiene, sleep, exercise, and diet are not just words to the wise designed for our comfort and longevity but rather commanded acts that we owe God … Hillel regards bathing as a commandment (*mitzvah*) (based on *Leviticus Rabbah* 34:3), and Maimonides includes directives for good health in his code of law, considering them just as obligatory as other positive duties like caring for the poor" (referencing M.T. Laws of Ethics (*De'ot*), chaps. 3–5). Ibid., emphasis added

52 JT Nedarim 9:4, stating that Genesis 5:1 ("This is the account of the descendants of Adam—on the day that God created man, He made him in the likeness of God") contains the central principle (*k'lal gadol*) of Torah.

53 See Yair Loberbaum, *Image of God, Halakhah and Aggadah* (Tel Aviv: Schocken, 2004) (regarding the term *tzelem* [icon] in Mesopotamian contextual meanings of icons as representations of royal authority). For analyses of *tzelem elokim* (*imago dei*), see J. Richard Middleton, *The Liberating Image: The Imago Dei in Genesis I* (Grand Rapids: Brazos, 2005); and Brent A. Strawn, "Comparative Approaches: History, Theory, and the Image of God," in *Method Matters: Essays on the Interpretation of the Hebrew Bible in Honor of David L. Peterson* (eds. Joel M. LeMon and Kent Harold Richards; SBLRBS 56; Atlanta: Society of Biblical Literature, 2009), 117–42.

54 Ibid.

Recent scholarship illustrates that interpreting the concept of the image of God metaphorically—to mean that human beings are created with higher, God-like intellectual capacities—is a later innovation. Earlier understandings of *tzelem elokim* held it to mean that human beings were created with actual God-like bodies. Pre-Maimonidean theology (and a significant amount of post-Maimonidean theologians) never accepted the incorporeality of God as a Jewish dogma. As historian and Judaic Studies professor Rabbi Dr. Marc Shapiro has demonstrated, not only was there a widespread belief in divine corporeality during the rabbinic era,[55] but this belief persisted into the medieval period (despite Maimonides' best attempts to purge it)[56] as well. Not only laymen, but even scholars,[57] understood "God created man in His image" to mean that God has a human form, and that the human form is an approximation of God's physical image.[58] In rabbinic literature, the corporeality of God was not interpreted metaphorically by many Jews of that era; Jewish studies scholar and Elijah Interfaith Institute founder Rabbi Dr. Alon Goshen-Gottstein observed that many rabbinic texts can only be understood "if the correspondence between man's body and the divine body is understood to be exact."[59] After studying the relevant rabbinic and contemporary

---

55 Marc B. Shapiro, *The Limits of Orthodox Theology: Maimonides' Thirteen Principles Reappraised* (Littman, 2004), 45–70, at 49.

56 Ibid., 54.

57 See ibid., 55 and 59, for a list of medieval scholars who opposed Maimonides' doctrine of divine incorporeality; most notable is R. Abraham ben David (Rabad)'s gloss regarding this Maimonidean doctrine: "Why has he [i.e., Maimonides] called such a person a heretic? There are many people greater and superior to him who adhere to such a belief [in divine corporeality] ..." Gloss (*hasagah*) on Maimonides, *Mishneh Torah* "Hilkhot teshuvah," 3:7, ibid. According to Martin Lockshin, Rabbi Samuel Ben Meir's Commentary on Genesis (Lewiston, NY, 1989), 338, Rashi's grandson R. Samuel ben Meir (*Rashbam*) was a corporealist as well; ibid., 58.

58 Alon Goshen-Gottstein, "The Body as Image of God in Rabbinic Literature," *Harvard Theological Review* 87 (1994): 171–95: "'There is absolutely no objection in all of rabbinic literature' to the idea that man was created in the image of God's physical form." Shapiro, *Limits of Orthodox Theology*, 49, quoting Goshen-Gottstein, "The Body as Image of God," 172–3.

59 Ibid., 175, brought to my attention by Shapiro, *Limits of Orthodox Theology*. According to Goshen-Gottstein's analysis of the concept of tzelem elokim, "in all of rabbinic literature there is not a single statement that categorically denies that God has body or form." Goshen-Gottstein, 172–3. Other scholars also posit that rabbinic discussions of divine corporeality should be interpreted literally; S. Friedman, "Graven Images," *Graven Images*, I (1994), 233–8; cited in Shapiro, ibid.

  Elliot R. Wolfson, "Judaism and Incarnation: The Imaginal Body of God," in Frmyer-Kensky et al., eds., *Christianity in Jewish Terms* (Boulder, CO: 2000), 239–54, also reads rabbinic corporeal images literally, contending that "the evolution of the Christological

literature on the incorporeality of God in Jewish theology, Shapiro concluded that "it seems impossible to deny that a widespread rabbinic view was that God does, in fact, have a physical body."[60] And David R. Blumenthal explains the anthropological principle of *tzelem elokim* to imply the theological belief in God's corporeality:

> Since personhood is the core of our being and since we are created in God's image, God must also have personhood. In anthropopathic theology, God has a Face and a real Personal Presence or Personality. To put it formally: personhood, with its expressions as face, presence and personality, is God's, and we have that capacity because God has created us in God's image.[61]

---

doctrine of the incarnation of the Son is undoubtedly indebted to the scriptural tradition regarding the corporeality of God" (ibid., 240). Meir Sendor, "The Violence of the Neutral in Interfaith Relations," in Goshen- Gottstein and Korn (eds.), *Jewish Theology and World Religions*, 149–65, however, finds Wolfson's readings of rabbinic anthropomorphic imagery "unpersuasive" (ibid., 159), contending that "[n]ormative rabbinic authorities from the Talmudic period on tend to" interpret corporeal imagery of God "with nuance, complexity and delicacy (ibid.)." Other figurative interpretations of such rabbinic imagery include David Stern, "Imitatio Hominis: Anthropomorphism and the Character(s) of God in Rabbinic Literature," *Prooftexts*, 12 (1992), 151–74, and Elliot R. Wolfson, *Through a Speculum that Shines: Vision and Imagination in Medieval Jewish Mysticism* (Princeton, NJ: Princeton University Press, 1994) (challenging the assumption that Jewish mystics conceived of a corporeal God), 33 ff, referenced in Shapiro, *The Limits of Orthodox Theology*, 50. One can, though, simultaneously appreciate the nuance of rabbinic interpretation of divine anthropomorphic imagery (and the figurative interpretations of such imagery that have since become normative) while acknowledging the legitimacy (and arguably former normativity) of such readings. Meir Bar-Ilan, "The Hand of God: A Chapter in Rabbinic Anthropomorphism," in Rashi 1040–1990: Hommage à Ephraim E. Urbach (Paris, 1993), has argued that ascribing literal readings of anthropomorphic imagery to the Jews of the rabbinic era is persuasive, con- tending that "in the first centuries Jews in the Land of Israel and Babylon believed in an anthropomorphic God." Ibid., 331, quoted in Shapiro, *The Limits of Orthodox Theology*, 50. Bar-Ilan also believes that Rashi was a "corporealist."

Ibid., 326–27, based in part on Rashi's interpretation of Genesis 1:26—God created the human being in His 'image' [*tzelem*] to mean that "the form that was established for him [i.e., the human] is the form of the image of his Creator [*tzelem deyukan yotsro*]'), in Shapiro, ibid., 57. Shapiro further notes that Arthur Marmorstein likewise "concluded that there was 'a school in Judaism, and an important one too, that believed in a God who accompanies man in human form and shape.'" Ibid., quoting Marmorstein, *The Old Rabbinic Doctrine of God*, 2 vols. (London, 1927–37), ii. 52.

60 Marc Shapiro, *Limits of Orthodox Theology*, 52; n. 35, ibid., acknowledges the difficulty of parsing anthropomorphic imagery in Jewish mystical literature: "it is never clear when descriptions of God [in such literature] are to be taken literally and when they are only symbolic."

61 David R. Blumenthal, based on his "Tselem: Toward an Anthropopathic Theology," in

The ethico-legal implications of this view are profound: if the corporeal human body corresponds to the corporeal divine body, there are two basic reasons that the physical human body must be treated with the utmost respect, nourishment, and care. First, because of the imperatives of *u-vaharta ba-hayyim, imitatio Dei*, and *"ush'martem me'od lenafshoteichem* (the commandment to care for the physical wellbeing of one's body)," as discussed above; and secondly, as an outgrowth of another fundamental commandment: *"ve'ahavta et Hashem elokeikha"* (the commandment to love God) and *"et Hashem elokeikha tira"* (the commandment to fear God). In other words, the human body must be honored and respected because the physical human body itself is an "image" of God: to treat the body properly is thus to honor God, and to malnourish the body is to debase God. This anthropological understanding of *tzelem elokim* may well have informed Hillel's scrupulousness in his personal health and hygiene: as discussed above (*Leviticus Rabbah* 34:3), Hillel lent an ethico-theological rationale for this regular bathing: "If somebody appointed to scrape and clean the statues of kings in the theaters and circuses is paid to do the work and furthermore is considered noble for doing so, how much more so should I, created in the divine image [*tzelem*] and likeness [*demut*][of God], take care of my body!" According to Yair Loberbaum, the reason Hillel spoke in such terms was because Jews in the rabbinic era conceived of their bodies as *tz'lamim*, images of God, much in the same way that icons are images of a king, ruler, or a god.[62]

Christianity in Jewish Terms, Tikva Frymer-Kensky et al., eds. (Westview Press, Boulder, CO: 2000). Accessed at http://js.emory.edu/BLUMENTHAL/image2.html.

62 Yair Loberbaum, *Image of God, Halakhah and Aggadah* (Tel Aviv: Schocken, 2004). In his discussion of the corporeality and incorporeality of God in Jewish theology, Shapiro references Loberbaum's dissertation ("The Image of God: Rabbinic Literature, Maimonides, and Nahmanides" [*Tzelem elohim: Sifruit azal, arambam veharambam*] (Ph.D. diss., Hebrew University of Jerusalem, 1997)); shortly thereafter, Loberbaum's dissertation was published by Schocken under this title. Shapiro's *Limits of Orthodox Theology* bibliography also notes Loberbaum's "The Doctrine of the Corporeality of God Did Not Occur Even for a Single Day to the Sages, May their Memory be Blessed" (Guide of the Perplexed I, 46): Anthropomorphism in Early Rabbinic Literature—A Critical Review of Scholarly Research' (Heb.), *Mada'ei yahadut*, 40 (2000), 3–54. For a recent attempt to relate the historical-theological analyses of tzelem elokim to current ethical concerns, see Aaron L. Mackler (ed. Y. Tzvi Langermann), "Finding Common Ground Among Monotheists in Bioethics," *Monotheism and Ethics: Historical and Contemporary Intersections among Judaism, Christianity and Islam* (Brill, Boston: 2012), 219–31.

Additional contemporary scholarship on the concept of *tzelem elohim* is brought to readers' attention by Shapiro in *The Limits of Orthodox Theology*; such sources include Morton Smith, Studies in the Cult of Ya-hweh (Leiden, 1996), ch. II; Byron L. Sherwin, "The

Indeed, because the Jewish and rabbinic conception of *tzelem elokim* [*imago Dei*] is that the physical body of the human being (and not merely our intellect or spirit) is God-like, the imperative of choosing life (*u-vaharta ba-hayyim*) becomes a much more forceful *halakhah* obligation in the context of healthy eating, as does the admonition to safeguard oneself (*venishmartem me'od lenafshoteichem*) from any foods that, in sufficient and consistent levels of consumption, diminish life. If preserving the quantity and quality of the human body is a positive value because the human body is an icon of God, and if the physical body itself is precious in the eyes God[63] (as Rabbi Akiva said of the human being's overall "preciousness" in the eyes of God—"the human is beloved," or precious, "because he and she were created in the image of God," *Avot* 3:14[64]), nutrition is transformed from a lifestyle choice to a transcendent religious activity (much in the same way that Hillel transformed bathing and hygiene into religious practices).

Extrapolating from the meta-*halakhah*, ethico-theological principle of *tzelem elokim* to *halakhah* in order to reinforce and reinterpret pre-existing *halakhah* obligations is far from unprecedented. Loberbaum argues that this anthropological view had significant *halakhah* ramifications in the Talmud, particularly in the areas of life and death. For example, capital punishment (which is consistently advocated in the Torah) was minimized because killing a

---

Human Body and the Image of God," in Dan Cohn- Sherbock (ed.), A Traditional Quest (Sheffield, 1991), 75–85; Warren Zev Harvey, "The Incorporeality of God in Maimonides, Rabad, and Spinoza" (Heb.), in Sarah

O. Heller-Willensky and Moshe Idel (eds..), *Mehkarim behagut yehudit* (Jerusalem, 1989), 69–74; Martin Cohen, *The Shiur Qomah: Liturgy and Theurgy in Pre- Kabbalistic Jewish Mysticism* (Lanham, Md., 1983); 321–35, and David Aaron, "Shedding Light on God's Body in Rabbinic Midrashim: Reflections on the Theory of a Luminous Adam, Harvard Theological Review 90 (1997), 299–314.

63 See Joseph B. Soloveitchik (Michael S. Berger, ed.), *The Emergence of Ethical Man* (Jersey City, NJ: KTAV, 2005) (affirming the physical body as created in the image of God; thus, our instincts, living actions, and biological behaviors are also, in some respects, Godly).

64 The continuation of this *mishnah* is also critical: "Especially beloved is man because it was made known to him that he had been created in the image [of God], as it is said: 'for in the image of God He made man.'" (Gen 9:6). Because we are loved by God—and God loves us because there is no replacement for each and every one of us—we therefore should love others who are created in the image of God and should love ourselves (and take proper care of ourselves) as well. Showing love towards others and towards ourselves is thus showing love to God; loving others, and loving oneself, is a demonstration of our belief that we are created in the image of God. Mistreating the body by over-eating, under-eating, or denying it proper exercise, is thus to show contempt to the image of God in the body, and to show contempt to the human body is to show contempt of God.

human being is nearly equivalent to killing God. At the same time, the *mitzvah* of *p'ru ur'vu* [procreation] was maximized[65] and held to be a cardinal Jewish obligation,[66] despite the real uncertainty as to whether it was an explicit biblical *mitzvah* incumbent on Jews. (Genesis 1:28, "Be fruitful and multiply," could easily be interpreted as a divine blessing rather than a divine mandate; in fact, the verse begins in that language: "And God blessed them, and God said unto them, Be fruitful and multiply.")

The Ethics of Nutrition: Towards a Jewish Nutrition Ethic

The principles of nutrition ethics have been established on terra firma by the Talmud and other classical sources. These sources will be discussed momentarily, though ab initio, it should be noted that the crafting of a new ethic and the institution of updated *halakhot* to safeguard one's health would not be an entirely new phenomenon. The concept of *sakanah* (safeguarding oneself from bodily danger) has been used before in the crafting of Jewish laws; for example, as Rabbi Dov Linzer has observed, the *Shulhan Arukh*'s prohibition of mixing meat and fish is a prohibition that is grounded not in ritual, as is the prohibition of mixing meat and milk, but in bodily danger and health— it was once thought that eating meat with fish was a danger to one's health.

Additionally, the Talmud's enactment of *mayim aharonim* ('last waters' water poured on one's fingertips and lips after a meal), and its conceptualization of *mahim aharonim* as a *hovah* [obligation]—as opposed to *mayim rishonim* (['first waters'] *netilat yadayim*—ritual hand-washing prior to a meal)—is indicative of the fact that the sages support, and have in fact practiced, the crafting of laws of practices that are based on health concerns; the reason *mayim aharonim* is a *hovah*, states the Talmud, is because late-antiquity salt was so pungent that it could be dangerous if one wiped one's eyes with salt- tinged fingers (similar to how, nowadays, it is dangerous to touch one's eyes immediately after cutting jalapeño peppers with one's bare hands); thus, the rabbis decreed that one must wash one's hands and lips after a meal as a prophylactic measure to prevent oneself from incurring this bodily danger.[67] Furthermore, the Rabbis were wont to dispense nutritional advice—*sine pecunia*, of course: "Men who are still deprived of children [*hasukhei banim*] should not eat coriander," says a

---

65 Ibid.
66 See BT *Shabbat* 31a.
67 BT *Eruvin* 17b; See also ibid., Rashi, loc. cit., s.v. "*she'melah sedomit*," and Tosafot, s.v. "*mayim aharonim*."

baraita (BT *Eruvin* 28a), because coriander was believed to cause a reduction in sperm count;[68] neither should raw beets [*silka haya*] be eaten because they could "kill a living person" [*katil gavra haya*]— viz., they were believed to be unhealthy.[69] In our *mesorah*—in Jewish tradition—food is intimately linked to life; foods which may cause an enhancement of life should be eaten—"a dish of cooked beets [*tavshil shel t'radin*] is healthy for the heart and good for the eyes [*yafeh lalev v'tov la'einayim*], and certainly is good for the stomach [*v'khol sh'ken livnei mei'ayim*]"[70]— and foods which may cause a diminishment of life should be avoided.

Classical and rabbinic precedents are thus amply available to support the proposition that, just as new ethics and updated *halakhot* were once crafted for the purpose of safeguarding not merely the spiritual health but the physical health of human beings. It is therefore incumbent on us in our own time to be aware of the genuine health risks involved in unhealthy eating, and to craft a new nutrition ethic and to update traditional *halakhot* concerning health in a way which would be conducive to healthy lifestyles and in comportment with the overriding Jewish theurgic ethic to choose life.

As aforementioned, the ethico-theological foundation for principles of nutrition ethics is the *k'lal gadol* of *tzelem elokim*: if the idea of the human as made in the image of God is properly understood, every *mitzvah* should be understood as a logical outflow of this concept.[71] Through realizing that the human is created in the image of God, one should intuitively understand that taking proper care of one's being (Deuteronomy 4:9) is a religious obligation.[72] The foundation for these principles is also formed by the ethical imperative of *v'halakhta bidrakhav*, and the overriding *halakhah* obligation of *u-vaharta ba-hayyim* [choose life]. After having established the theological, ethical, and *halakhah* foundations for nutrition ethics, we can understand how the specifics of the Talmudic discussions of nutrition can help us begin to formulate a nutrition ethic for our times.

---

68 Ibid., 28a, Rashi, loc. cit., s.v. "*gud'gedaniot.*"

69 Ibid., 28b–29a.

70 Ibid., 29a.

71 P'nei Moshe on YT *Nedarim* 9:4, s.v. *zeh sefer.*

72 Understood properly, *tzelem elokim* means that if you treat your body improperly, you're treating God improperly, in that you are treating a representative (*tzelem*) of the divine improperly. And if one honors the body properly, one is showing respect for God, as Hillel realized. Thus, the logical outcome from a full understanding of *tzelem elokim* is that one should watch carefully over one's being (Deuteronomy 4:9); this *mitzvah*, then, is a behavioral response to the metaphysical conception of being created in the image of God.

The Talmud was not unaware of the importance of healthy eating; more significantly, its integration of nutrition into Jewish legal texts established an important precedent for the integration of current knowledge of healthy eating into contemporary *halakhah* guidelines. In the second to sixth centuries CE, despite limited knowledge of nutrition, basic nutritional principles were nevertheless known, such as the importance of eating green vegetables:

> Rav Huna said: Any city that does not have vegetables [available] in it, a Torah scholar may not reside in it ("because vegetables are beneficial for one's health, are inexpensive, and allow scholars to study Torah";[73] Rashi, ad loc.) (BT *Eruvin* 56a).

Additionally, the Talmud, based on its knowledge of proper nutrition (limited by today's standards, but still revelatory, and precedential for the integration of nutrition into normative Jewish thought and practice), discusses which foods are healthy and which should be avoided:

> Garlic and leek [are nutritious], as a *baraita* taught: Garlic is a vegetable [i.e., is healthy], and leeks are half-vegetables [i.e., are half as healthy as garlic]. If a radish appears, a medicine has appeared [i.e., radishes are healthy] ... the leaves [of a radish are not healthy], the roots [of the radish, though, are healthy] ... [radish roots are healthy] during the summer months, but even radish roots are unhealthy] during the winter months. (ibid.) A person should not eat an onion because of the poison [*nahash*] within (ibid., 29b).

The Talmud also discusses which foods should, for health reasons, be eaten:

> Abaye said: My mother told me that roasted grains are good for the heart [*ma'alu leliba*] and sooth one's worries [*u'mevatlei mahashavta*] (ibid.).

Moreover, both the Torah and Talmud advocate portion control and moderation. Rashi views the manna and *s'lav* (quail) narrative as a lesson in portion control. Based on the Talmud, Rashi interprets the statement of Moses—"When, in the evening, Hashem gives you meat to eat and bread to

---

73 Presumably because one must be in optimal physical condition in order to engage in Torah study at the highest level; as we now know (e.g., regarding the countless studies linking exercise to improved mental ability), one's physical health affects one's mental capacities.

satiety in the morning"—to mean that meat is given to be "eaten," but not for "satiety":

> The Torah teaches *derekh eretz* [proper behavior] (in the context of food and nutrition): that meat is not to be eaten to the point of satiety (BT *Yoma* 75a).[74]

We may quibble with Rashi's and the Talmud's nutritional guidelines; after all, many nutritionists teach that there are plentiful health-benefits in lean, non-fatty meat, which is a good source of heme-iron, vitamins B-6 and B-12, and protein. However, what is significant about this comment of Rashi is not the specific nutritional guideline he offers, but the fact that he (and the rabbis of the Talmud) believe that the Torah is instructive, and does have something to say, about the matter of health and nutrition—not only about what should be eaten, but how we should eat.

The Talmud further emphasizes the importance of portion control:

> One who eats as much as this measure [i.e., as the minimum quantity specified for *hallah*] is healthy (because one has eaten what his body needs; Rashi, ad loc., s.v. *"harei zeh bari"*) and blessed (because one has not eaten too much; Rashi, ibid., s.v. *"u'mvorakh"*); [if he eats] more than this, [he is considered] a glutton. If he eats [less than this, his innards (i.e., his digestive system) are defective[75] (BT *Eruvin* 83b).

What is significant about this passage is that the Talmud does not only condemn overeating but condemns under-eating as well. The body, the rabbis realized, must be given what it needs—not too much, and not too little. Also noteworthy is that the context in which this statement is found is within a discussion of the size of the daily portion of *manna* that fell for each person in the desert (see Exodus 16:36). That a proper portion fell from heaven for each person is indicative of a divine wish that humans practice portion control; to diminish or increase one's proper portion of food is to contravene the will

---

74 Rashi, commentary to Exodus 16:8, s.v. *basar le'ekhol*. On the notion of having fixed, daily, non-excessive portions of food as rooted in the *manna* narrative, cf. Nahum M. Sarna, *The JPS Torah Commentary: Exodus* (Philadelphia: Jewish Publication Society, 1991), 86, commentary to Exodus 16:4, s.v. *devar yom b'yomo*.

75 Translations from the Talmud are from the Artscroll-Schottenstein edition of the Talmud, *Eruvin* vol. II (Mesorah: Brooklyn, NY, 1991). Translations from Rashi's commentary are my own.

of heaven. Moreover, Rashi buttresses the grafting of religious values onto the practice of healthy eating by attaching a scriptural admonishment to gluttons. He cites a verse from Proverbs 13:25—the stomach of the wicked shall lack— to argue by implication that it is religiously improper to overeat or under-eat; the linking of wickedness with gluttony and with conscious under-eating indicates that the sages felt it proper to condemn unhealthy eating not only in nutritional terms but in ethico-religious terms as well. The utilization of religious discourse in the context of proper nutritional practices may be the most significant precedent for the utilization of religious discourse in the context of the current dialogue surrounding nutrition.

One must also be aware that eating whatever one wishes and counting on God to protect one from the negative health consequences of poor eating choices is not a pious attitude but is in fact inimical to traditional Judaism. As the Talmud states, *ki ha d'amar Rabbi Yannai: le'olam al ya'amod adam bimkom sakanah v'yomar osin li ness, shema ein osin lo ness, v'im timtzei lomar osin lo ness, m'makin lo miz'khuyotav* (Rabbi Yannai said: A person should never stand in a dangerous place and say, "A miracle will be performed for me to save me from the danger, because the miracle may not be performed for him. And even if you find your way to say that a miracle will be performed for him, it will be deducted from his merits") (BT *Taanit* 20b).

The seminal Jewish thinker and *halakhist* Maimonides not only wrote legal codes and philosophic texts, but ethical treatises (embedded in his legal code, *the Mishneh Torah*) as well. In his *Hilkhot De'ot*, sometimes translated as "Laws of Ethics" (lit., "opinions"), he expanded on the Talmudic illustrations of healthy eating by integrating the most advanced nutritional knowledge of his age into a medieval Jewish nutrition ethic:

> He who regulates his life in accordance with the laws of medicine with the sole motive of maintaining a sound and vigorous physique and begetting children to do his work and labor for his benefit is not following the right path. A man should maintain physical health and vigor in order that his soul may be upright, in a condition to know God ...
>
> Whoever throughout his life follows this course will be continually serving God, even while engaged in business and even during sexual relations, because his purpose in all that he does will be to satisfy his needs so as to have a sound body with which to serve God. Even when he sleeps and seeks repose to calm his mind and rest his body so as not to fall sick and be incapacitated from serving God, his sleep is his service to the Almighty (3:3).

Similarly, when one eats, drinks, and has sexual relations—it should not be done simply for the pleasure alone, for then [one might come to] eat and drink only sweet foods and have sexual relations only for pleasure. Rather, pay attention to eat and drink in order to keep the entire body healthy. Therefore, one should not eat anything the palate desires, like a dog or a donkey; rather, eat [also] things that are good for the body— whether they are sweet or bitter. Also, one should not eat things that are bad for the body, even if they are sweet to the palate … (ibid., 3:2).

Overeating is considered like poison to one's body—this is the essence of sickness. The majority of sicknesses that befall a person are from eating harmful foods, filling one's belly and overeating—even healthy foods (ibid., 4:15).

A crucial addendum to the ethics of eating is that just as overeating is a violation of the ethic of "choose life," so too is under-eating. The authoritative Jewish legal and philosophical sources are in consensus regarding the proposition that under-consumption is sinful:

A person may say, "Since jealousy, honor, and similar things are a bad path and remove people from this world, I will separate myself from them by doing the opposite." The person would not eat meat, not drink wine, not get married, not live in a nice home, not wear fine clothing; but rather this person would wear sackcloth and uncomfortable wool and the like … This is also a bad path down which one is forbidden to walk. The one who chooses this path is considered a sinner … Also, this category [of sinners] includes those who constantly fast. This is not a good path, for the Sages forbade us from afflicting ourselves with [constant] fasts.[76]

Maimonides' proposition that it is spiritually fulfilling to make sure one's belly is full (but not stuffed) should serve as encouragement to those afflicted with anorexia, bulimia, or other under-consumptive eating disorders. As Rabbi Judah Ha-Levi reminds us, taking care of the body and choosing life is essential to religious life; we should not be misled into thinking that religiosity is coterminous with denial:

The Divine law imposes no asceticism on us. It rather desires that we should keep the balance and grant every mental and physical faculty

---

76 Maimonides, *Mishneh* Torah, Laws of Ethics (*De'ot*) 3:1.

its due, without overburdening one faculty at the expense of another (Yehuda Ha-Levi, *The Kuzari*, Part 2, paragraph 50).

The servant of God does not withdraw himself from secular contact lest he be a burden to the world and the world to him. He does not hate life, which is one of God's bounties granted to him ... On the contrary, he loves this world and a long life because they afford him opportunities of deserving the world to come: the more good he does, the greater his claim on the world to come (ibid., Part 3, paragraph 1).

These ethical guidelines, written in the medieval era, serve as the preliminary foundations for a modern Jewish nutrition ethic. Maimonides, following Hillel's line of thought, transforms healthy eating, and maintaining a healthy lifestyle in general, into a theurgical pursuit: taking care of the body becomes not merely a physical activity but a means of serving God. Making sure to get enough sleep[77] and eating healthily are not to be taken lightly, for they are "service[s] to the Almighty."[78] It is now in the hands of this generation to carry forward the Talmudic, Maimonidean, and rabbinic precedents for contemporary nutrition ethics by crafting a twenty-first-century nutrition ethic that fully integrates the multitude of advanced knowledge of the body, food, and nutrition into *halakhah* praxis and normative Jewish life.

---

[77] Sleep is a crucial component of a healthy lifestyle as well and should not be overlooked. See, Jane Brody, "Cheating Ourselves of Sleep," *New York Times*, June 18, 2013: "Failure to get enough sleep night after night can compromise your health and even shorten your life. ... According to sleep specialists at the University of Pittsburgh School of Medicine and Western Psychiatric Institute and Clinic, among others, a number of bodily systems are negatively affected by inadequate sleep: the heart, lungs and kidneys ... and brain function. ... Several studies have linked insufficient sleep to weight gain. ... The risks of cardiovascular diseases and stroke are higher in people who sleep less than six hours a night. Even a single night of inadequate sleep can cause daylong elevations in blood pressure in people with hypertension. Inadequate sleep is also associated with calcification of coronary arteries and raised levels of inflammatory factors linked to heart disease." (emphasis added) And especially for yeshiva students and others focused on mental performance and intellectual endeavors, heed should be taken that "[s]ome of the insidious effects of too little sleep involve mental processes like learning, memory, judgment and problem solving. ... People who are well rested are better able to learn a task and more likely to remember what they learned ... Sleep duration and quality can be as important to your health as your blood pressure and cholesterol level." Adequate sleep is thus a key integument in any nutrition ethic.

[78] For many of the *halakhah* sources related to life, I am indebted to the helpful aggregation of these materials found in Elliot N. Dorff and Louis E. Newman (eds.) Jewish Choices, *Jewish Voices: Body* (Philadelphia: Jewish Publication Society, 2008), 4–25. Some of the translations of these sources are from *Jewish Choices*; others are my own.

CONCLUSION

The purpose of this chapter has been to adumbrate the theological, anthropological, *halakhah* (legal), and ethical premises that would form the theoretical and practical basis for a modern Jewish nutrition ethic. My purpose has been to demonstrate that the thrust of biblical, Talmudic, and post-Talmudic rabbinic writings favor a nutrition ethic. This article has done so by establishing that healthy eating, although not explicitly mandated by traditional Jewish sources, is a fundamental obligation that can be inferred from the basic theological, ethical, and *halakhah* postulates of Judaism. Biblical, Talmudic, and rabbinic precedents, this article has illustrated, broadly support the postulate that healthy, balanced, nutritious eating is a fundamental Jewish value that inexorably flows from the basic Jewish imperative to choose life. Hence, choices about what to eat and drink must be made based on an assessment of the particular food item's ability to increase or decrease the quantity and quality of one's life. Jewish tradition recognizes that there are no neutral choices; each life- decision implicates a religious, ethical, or legal value, and eating choices are no different. If making healthy choices in eating is as important as choosing to eat kosher and as important as reciting blessings over food—a position this article has sought to validate—then the same kind of religious rigor that is applied to kosher eating and to the recitation of blessings over food must be applied to healthy eating as well. In this way, placing the criteria of health, nutrition, and life on eating elevates healthy eating to the plane of a crucial ethical, spiritual, and religious activity. And, perhaps most significantly, the consideration of the sources on life, health, and the body clearly demonstrate that a Jewish ethic of nutrition is not a radical innovation, but merely an explication of the implicit religious obligation to eat healthily that is latent in Judaism's most fundamental precept: "choose life."

CHAPTER 2

Why Are We So Hungry? Our Betrayal of Eating, Being Satisfied and Blessing and The Way Back

Rabbi Daniel Landes

Have the poor and the deprived earned the right to be hungry? Their individual needs are quite modest. They can be met by any decent society that puts its mind to it and allows allocation of resources to run in a reasonable way. But the constant hunger of the well-off in the West should lead us to be overwhelmingly worried and, at least, questioning. But of what?

My question is: why are we, the ostensibly well fed, so hungry? In Israel, about thirty percent of Israeli children under the age of eighteen are overweight. In this, Israel is second only to the United States. Indeed, the data suggest that in eight years the rate will rise to fifty percent.[1] Eating disorders for women in the Israel Defense Forces, especially anorexia, have risen two hundred percent over the past decade.[2] And certainly one no longer notices ultra-thin or obese youth in the Orthodox world. Anecdotally, during a Passover vacation at a hotel, after a full, generous meal, the move to the snack room is an oft-experienced pilgrimage. This is especially curious. Rabbinic culture through the ages, while often working in times of scarcity, also had its times of abundance. Issues of what we term eating disorders do not seem to readily appear. It seems that our tradition had a recipe for hunger. Our real questions behind why are we so hungry are what is that recipe, how can it be applied now, and what is preventing us from putting it into action?

---

1   See Rotem Elizera. "Israel Leading Europe in Childhood Obesity." *Ynetnews*. October 4, 2016. Accessed March 28, 2018. https://www.ynetnews.com/articles/0,7340,L-4862813,00.html.

2   Marissa Lorusso. "The Newest Enemy of Female Soldiers in Israel? Eating Disorders." Public Radio International. June 16, 2015. Accessed March 28, 2018. https://www.pri.org/stories/2015-06-16/newest-enemy-female-soldiers-israel-eating-disorders.

The structure that can enable us to respond to this cluster of questions is the following verse: "And you shall eat and be satisfied, and you shall bless the Lord your God on the good Land that he has given you."[3] This verse is used rabbinically to create the number and structure to the blessings of the Grace After Meals.[4] Despite its seeming limitation to the Land of Israel, to bless God after a meal is considered to be a universal command,[5] not dependent on geography.[6]

The verse is understood as a unit, but each unit needs to be unpacked and contextualized. *Ve-Akhalta* ("And you shall eat") is itself a complex structure in Judaism. But, in brief, one does not merely "grab and graze." Indeed, for Maimonides, "[L]owlifes are invalid for witnessing according to the instructions of the rabbis. There are people who walk as they eat in the market place in front of all people … amongst all, [there are those] who have no shame. They are to be considered like a dog …"[7] While later authorities maintain that this statement does not apply to one who sits in the marketplace to eat, they consider it nonetheless a degradation for a scholar to do so in a public place.[8] In rabbinic practice, eating must be raised from an animalistic urge and fulfillment to a human level of restraint.

Thus, the emphasis in Jewish law that when eating, one is *kove'a seudah*—"establishes a meal." The legal requirements and particulars[9] involve the need for bread—the staff of life—of 1.9 fl. ounces (56 ml) within four minutes. The Ashkenazic tradition favors including the eating of sufficient cake or pizza as under that rubric, with the attendant, classic blessing of "Who brings bread from the earth," and would allow such eating for any of the three required Shabbat meals. The Sephardic tradition insists on bread itself as a non-negotiable requirement for that blessing and for a Shabbat meal. But for both sides, the idea of "establishing a meal" is a crucial aspect of "you shall eat."[10]

Establishing a meal is an essential element of human dignity. How one eats determines who one is—a dog or divinely endowed human, for example. Attendant to that dignity is the importance given to the food. Bread—no matter how we define it—is the key functioning symbol. The verse, "Not upon bread alone does man live, but upon all that proceeds out of the mouth of the

---

3 Deuteronomy 8:10.

4 BT *Berakhot* 48b; see Chizkuni commentary on this verse in standard *Mikraot Gedolot*.

5 Maimonides, *Book of Commandments*, Positive Laws 19.

6 Nachmanides' commentary on Deuteronomy 8:10.

7 *Mishneh Torah*, Book of Judges, Laws of Witnessing 11:5.

8 Joel Sirkes (known as the Bach), *Commentary on Shulhan Arukh, Choshen Mishpat*, 34.

9 *Tur Shulhan Arukh, Orach Chayim*. 165.

10 We should note that an important question of today is how do those who are on a gluten-free diet and cannot eat traditional bread made of the grains wheat, barley, oats, spelt, or rye establish a meal in accordance with *halakhah*?

Lord does man live"[11] does not negate but, rather, elevates its status. Indeed, the rabbis strove to align eating bread with the word of God: "One who does not state a word of Torah at his meal is as if he has eaten from the sacrifices of the dead."[12] This explains the custom to say a word of Torah with the breaking of bread. Such a practice in Jewish thought makes every meal into a holy sacrifice to the Lord. This democratic reenacted Temple-based ritual is everyone's obligation, and it is not limited to priests alone. It necessitates a purification of one's hands, which are considered as always "busy" and liable to impurity. A ritual water ablution of the hands is required once they have been cleaned of dirt, which necessitates the blessing "Who has commanded us upon the raising of hands [in washing]." And, as said, eating bread needs its own blessing while no other blessings over food are needed for the meal has been established. On the Sabbath, the importance of *Ve-Akhalta* goes into overdrive: the time of eating is long, the best food of the week is offered, the social aspect of having the family around the table along with friends is enhanced, and often the *mitzvah* of inviting guests who might not have a place to dine is brought into action. Along with song that combines spirituality with enjoyment—some of the songs extol food—the eating is profoundly real and is the focus of one's activity.

But this alone is not enough to capture what is offered by the tradition. The preparation of the food is also crucial. Preparation has great *halakhah* import. In cases of kitchen accidents in which the *kashrut* of a dish might be compromised, the authorities often allow for a lenient decision in a doubtful case, because of the loss involved if the food would be discarded, or if a Shabbat meal's enjoyment would be lessened.

We need to add to the notion the Jewish mystical ideal of *hakhanah*—preparation. The importance of preparation as a religious experience is seen in the old law of men being required to wear a *gartel*, belt, worn over one's clothes. This *halakhah* signified a dignified way of dress that was part of the look of a well-dressed man of antiquity. As such, one was required to wear that belt in prayer, for that would indicate a dignified way of encountering God. When wearing a belt fell out of general fashion, it also fell out generally Jewish practice.[13]

So too with food preparation, Western society embraced a takeout culture in which food preparation is assigned to another anonymous disconnected entity or food is bought already prepared except with the addition popping in

---

11 Deuteronomy 7:3.

12 BT *Avot* 3:1.

13 On a related note, the Hasidic movement, beginning in the eighteenth century through contemporary times, revived its practice and the *gartel* was worn with a flourish. It became a physical act of preparation to show the significance of prayer even before one actually prayed.

the microwave. All this has now had a counter-pull by food enthusiasts, the slow cooking movement, and the like, in which the investment of real time and one's personal effort in food preparation makes all the difference in the connection to the food, the resulting dish and its taste, its consequential enjoyment and for the people who prepare the meal. In my experience with *talmidim*, they experience Shabbat or holidays in a radically more profound manner when they have joined my wife and myself in the *hakhanah* of the feast.

Jewish legal sources indicate that Jews usually bought their food from people they knew who grew it, raised it, or prepared it.[14] That was, if they did not produce the food themselves. Indeed, it was not long ago that people (usually women) *kashered* their meat with salt to remove the blood, including more difficult processes utilizing fire, such as when *kashering* liver. In such cases they encountered the food itself and literally saw, smelled, and felt the blood of the animal to be eaten. It is hard to be more real than that experience, or therefore to feel more connected. And people lived near butcher shops wherein the chickens, at least, were slaughtered on the premises, in front of all. All of this is now almost gone. Most people buying into modernity's gods of efficiency and mass production, are happy with this departure. But with it has come an alienation from food itself. The abomination of advertisements, which imply or boldly state that food equals fuel, betrays a complete distance from experience. Eventually food might even become less than fuel, and eating only another virtualized reality, with pills supplying the "needed" sustenance.

Here, too, a counter-development in contemporary society could be helpful. The Local Food movement has sound ecological benefits but also connects people to the food they eat as it involves where they live and the workers neighbors who produce that food. In this light the attempts to create local non-assembly line *shekhitah* (in the United States and in Israel, where it is outlawed by the Chief Rabbinate, but nonetheless flourishes) needs to be supported. Even firm vegetarians and vegans have felt differently about *shekhitah* when they have viewed the connection and respect of the *shochet* for the animal. Certainly, meat eaters are often transformed when they see how *shekhitah* should be done—with respect for the animal, recognition of human needs (for flesh), and thus the act, with its own blessing, is a *mitzvah* as a divinely sanctioned, and well controlled, taking of life. To do it unsanctioned, would be a sin, not murder; a grievous waste of life.

Less dramatically, creating one's own produce gardens—even if only for herbs—would ensure food preparation with connectedness and the personal. Finally the use of personal or communal composters makes us conscious of waste and allows us to expand the avoidance of the sin of *Bal Tashhit* rooted

---

14 See, for example, *Shulhan Arukh*: Chapter 254; Rashi on Esther 2:9; BT *Megillah* 13a.

in the prohibition of cutting down fruit trees in a time of siege[15] and extended to wasting the oil of lamps, needless tearing of clothing, using furniture for kindling, and hunting of animals.[16] Now *Bal Tashhit* can be further broadened so that even supposed waste has organic utility.

Let's review the promise of *halakhah* to ending our hunger. A connected life, that brings us close to production in both a spiritual and physical way—and in Israel we have the added benefit of the agricultural laws—can make our food truly ours and at the same time God's. our insistence on cooking and preparing this food in a real personal, familial, and communal and spiritual way raises the *hakhanah* to great heights culinary, interpersonal, and holy. The *keviut seudah* roots us both in time and space with the transcendence of Torah learned and blessings made. Such eating is real and *ve-savata* "and you will be satisfied."

All this explains why we have remained so hungry even if we are in compliance with the usual and popularly-observed kosher laws. We eat without any connection to the land and its fruit. It all comes wrapped in plastic, and it might as well be plastic that we eat. We usually don't prepare food at all, and if so, then only minimally and without focus. We are not *koveah seudah*; we graze, or we multitask as we consume. And alternatively, we compulsively binge on store-bought ice cream or pig-out on buffalo wings. This not a dignified *akhilah* and of course we are hungry. We never arrive to *ve-savata*; we are just never satisfied. And even if we did things better, there are still two stumbling blocks to satisfaction. The foods we consume prevent achieving satisfaction—the unconscionable terrific amounts of sugar and salt—the nicotine and opioids of the food world—that are routinely and abundantly placed in our food guarantee that we remain hungry. They are addicting substances that break down our will, strength, and focus.

The second stumbling block is the reaction that many have to these health concerns over sugar and salt as well as food that have been genetically modified (known as GMOs). One can well argue that health concerns are not "Jewish" issues, per se. But it is crucial to argue the opposite. The *Shulhan Arukh*[17] states the issue of fish cooked alongside meat and whether the scent of the meat renders the fish impermissible to be eaten later on with a dairy product. An often-introduced issue is that of *sakanah* (danger) of eating fish and meat in that it was claimed that it caused leprosy.[18] As current medicine no longer

---

15 Deuteronomy 20:19–20.

16 BT *Shabbat* 67b; BT *Hullin* 7b; BT *Kiddushin* 32a.

17 *Yoreh De'ah* 97:3; 116:2.

18 Rashi Commentary on BT *Pesahim* 76b.

supports this assessment, those who support this ban[19] are thrown into a difficult position of defending its continuation. One rabbi writes: "Even if modern
medicine does not recognize these health concerns, we can never be sure that
the concerns are outdated."[20] Those who favor getting rid of the ban follow
the *Magen Avraham*;[21] who wrote that this natural phenomenon no longer
exists and the ban is voided, as it no longer applies. Much ink has been spilled
by those defending, awkwardly, the ban, and those calling, somewhat shame-
facedly for its termination. But the real point is missed by current advocates of
both sides: the *halakhah* is concerned with health issues, especially those that
pose a *sakanah* even if the latter eventually proves doubtful, and it doesn't hesi-
tate to incorporate these concerns into the laws of *kashrut*. This being the case,
there is a clear precedent and a clearer mandate to incorporate safeguards to
well proven health dangers into the *halakhah* of what we eat. And that is really
a Torah-derived obligation: "And you shall zealously guard your life."[22] Indeed,
this prohibition means that a *sakanah* must be treated with greater stringency
than a ritual prohibition.[23] Maimonides writes as law "many things were forbidden by the sages because they are a danger to life. Whoso transgresses
stating 'I endanger myself and it should be of no matter to anyone else' or
'I don't really care,' he is to be struck with blows of rebellion."[24] (Interestingly,
Maimonides lists some of those prohibited dangerous activities and doesn't
include cooking and eating meat with fish.) The point is that from the side of
halakhah, obvious health concerns are not a voluntary or whimsical matter, but
are rather fully covered by Jewish law, and as we have seen have also a place in
the laws of *kashrut*. Finding these dangers and making them explicit becomes
a major concern. A contemporary and largely successful example is smoking,
which was rife in the Orthodox community, especially the yeshiva world. The
houses of study were known by the haze of smoke. The initial attempts to curb
this practice were met with derision, as not being a *halakhah* issue; but today,
while not eliminated, the incidence of smoking has gone down tremendously,
and it is forbidden to smoke in almost all houses of study.

Certainly we need to build in a proper shelf life for prohibitions that ends
when research conclusions change; we also need to act with restrain in what we

---

19   *Yad Efraim* 116, Rabbi Efraim Zalman Margalios, 1760–1828, Brody, Western Ukraine.
20   See Aryeh Lebowitz. "Eating Fish and Meat Together." YUTorah Online. Accessed March
     28, 2018. http://www.yutorah.org/lectures/lecture.cfm/735391/rabbi-aryeh-lebowitz/
     eating-fish-and-meat-together/.
21   *Orach Chayim* 173, R. Avraham Gombiner, 1635–1682, Poland.
22   Deuteronomy 4:9,15.
23   BT *Hullin* 9a.
24   Maimonides, "Laws of a Murder and of Guarding Life" 11:5.

can realistically prohibit (again, actually such "dangerous activities" are already implicitly forbidden) realistically. But to observe a prohibition of fish and meat—which I do adhere to—and to ignore a health crisis is morally absurd. To merge our genuine health needs with an integrated *ve-akhala* (eating) program for life would guarantee a genuine *ve-savata* (satisfaction).

The final triad of our verse is *uveirachta*: "And you shall bless the Lord thy God." The act of blessing, which is thankfulness, transcends physical satisfaction, while raising it to a noble level. *Hakarat HaTov* (recognizing the good which one has received) is a *halakhah* necessity, which makes a man into a mensch. In so doing one finds the source or root /*shoresh* of true satiation in what he has been granted by God. The spiritual and physical practice of *ve-akhalta* "you shall eat" and *ve-savata* "you shall be satisfied" lies in not resisting the blessings that God has granted us. It means not succumbing to the stumbling blocks of a life, which is potentially fragmented by separating the mind from the body from the spirit. One can be satisfied only when one knows that he has been taken care of, that indeed he is loved.

Only one step remains: the verse concludes—"upon the good land, which the Lord God has given you." The Land—most importantly, Israel—but also true of all Jewish communities—must be truly good. This *Tovah* (feminine) or *Tov* (masculine) is the moral quality that is associated with God. "God is Tov to all; His mercies are upon all creation."[25] Rav Kook actually defined God with this quality, applying it also to His People "the essential desire to be *tov* to all without any limitation, whether in the number of applications or in the quality of the *tov*—this is the inner core of the soul of the community of Israel, its inheritance and its patrimony."[26] "On the good land" must be defined as a society, which is able to manifest the divine quality of Good/*tov* to all without limit. Satisfying ourselves is not the final end-goal. We need, from our own self-definition of *tov*, to worry about the other.

At this point we have gone a full circle. We can only lose our modernity derived constant hunger when we regain our connectedness to food production and preparation, and eat in a mindful, spiritual, social, and moral way. Then we can be truly satisfied by locating and naming the source of blessing in the Divine. At that point we turn our focus to the truly hungry and know that our only real hunger and need should be to nourish, feed, and sustain them. Conscious of love granted by God, we are fully drawn to love and sustain others.

---

25 Psalms 145:9.
26 *Orot Yisrael* I:4.

CHAPTER 3

Your Grains, Your Grape Juice, and Your Oil

Coming to Terms with Unhealthy Foods Venerated by Jewish Tradition

Rabbi Asher Lopatin

The rabbis prescribed many different types of foods for us to eat that allow us to lead a healthy life. Further, they discouraged other foods and even feared for danger from eating some foods that, today, we know from observation and nutritional science are not dangerous at all. Some of the foods the rabbis recommend—such as eating garlic on Friday nights—do indeed seem to have some health benefits. Others are more questionable. If we disagree with the rabbis about these foods, we can either say that their science was limited and that they had incorrect information. In any case, we can read all these writing as merely suggestions and not binding *halakhah*, so disagreeing with the rabbis does not result in a practical problem for the law-observant Jew.

Alternatively, if we take an approach that gives the rabbis respect even in the realm of the sciences, then we can say that human beings of the modern era are simply physically different than human beings that existed a millennium or two ago. And not simply physically different, but also living in an environment that affected eating certain foods in ways different from the modern perspective. For example, some explain the seemingly great prevalence of food allergies to a change in our environment.[1] Rav Moshe Sofer—known as the Chatam

---

1 K. Reinmuth-Selzle, C. J. Kampf, K. Lucas, N. Lang-Yona, J. Fröhlich-Nowoisky, M. Shiraiwa, P. S. J. Lakey, S. Lai, F. Liu, A. T. Kunert, K. Ziegler, F. Shen, R. Sgarbanti, B. Weber, M. G. Weller, I. Bellinghausen, J. Saloga, A. Duschl, D. Schuppan and U. Pöschl, "Air Pollution and Climate Change Effects on Allergies in the Anthropocene: Abundance, Interaction, and Modification of Allergens and Adjuvants," *Environmental Science & Technology*, 2017, 51 (8), 4119–41.

Sofer (1762–1839)—who ruled against any innovation in the holy law—says that human nature changed regarding the danger of eating fish with meat[2] while the rabbis seem to say it causes a form of leprosy and therefore was much more lenient in his rulings regarding mixing the two.

In this chapter, I will outline the theological and *halakhah* struggle with foods that are regarded today, by many experts, as dangerous or unhealthy, yet which seem to venerated beyond specific rabbinic writings, but by long-standing Jewish tradition and which are required to be eaten by accepted Jewish law. What do we do with the praise found in the Torah and beyond for foods that should be avoided? How do we navigate seeming requirements to each such foods?

It is difficult to adopt the approach that in the days of the Bible, when traditions of eating foods that modern observers consider unhealthy started, these foods were healthy and wonderful for the human condition but not anymore. First, it is hard, as someone who venerates the Holy Bible as the word of God, to maintain a diet which recommends against eating sugary foods—even natural sugars—or foods high in carbohydrates; the Bible seems to venerate such foods. It is an uphill battle anyway to resist unhealthy foods. Having the Torah speak so glowingly of them, even if they were healthy at one time but not anymore, makes maintaining a healthy to a diet a challenge.

A second reason it is hard to claim that such foods were at one time healthy and are not anymore is that nutritional science is constantly changing and there is much we still do not know and cannot be certain of. Much of the ambiguity of recent science is based not on how these foods react to our bodies, nor the suggestion that human beings used to be any different thousands of years ago. If anything, they feel that we never ate these unhealthy foods in the past, and now the problem is that we eat them all the time. If these foods were never healthy, in the understanding of today's science, that challenges our loyalty to a Scripture and to certain age-old customs that both seem to direct us to eat unhealthy foods. To dismiss the notion that certain foods—a delicious donut, let's say (which even seems to fit the description of *Manna*)—requires me to believe it was never good for anyone. How would I accept the wonder of the *Manna* as something good if it is described as *Ketzapichit bidvash*—a food fried and soaked in honey—which, anecdotally, the majority of nutritionists today would argue is unhealthy and to be avoided as much as possible? Yet, the Torah says that the Israelites ate this food in the wilderness of Sinai for forty years.

---

2 *Yoreh De'ah* 101.

I will try to face this challenge in two ways: First, by showing that the Torah and midrashim actually have quite an ambivalent attitude toward sugar-laden products, considered unhealthy today by many, and perhaps even carbohydrates. Secondly, I will attempt to show a manner of embracing *halakhah* requirements for eating sugar and carbohydrates even within a healthy, low carb diet.

On the surface, the words "A Land Flowing with Milk and Honey," which is repeated sixteen times in the Torah, seem to extol the Land of Israel"s for its bounty of rich and delicious foods. Ehud Rost, Dean of Students at Herzog College in Alon Shvut, published a convincing piece arguing that the "milk" featured in this quote is not talking about animal milk *per se* but, rather, refers to the milk of fruit and vegetables that oozes from the produce of the Promised Land.[3] He argues, as many other have over the years based on certain midrashim and Talmudic statements, that "honey" does not mean bee's honey, but, as with milk, refers to the sweetness of the fruit of Israel.[4] As Rashi comments on Exodus 13:5: "The honey oozes out from the dates and the figs." Thus, the Torah in this passage is not intending to praise specific produce of the Holy Land that comes from animals; nor does it mean to praise any sugary product, whether from a bee or from a fruit. Rather, the verse intends to praise the Land of Israel and its products in general through the lens of metaphor. Sweetness and creaminess evoke an image and a taste, but are not meant to refer to a specific substance. The joys and bounties of Israel are not about any specific fruit or vegetable. Rather, they are about an attitude, a frame of mind, and a way of life. This framework allows us to enjoy the wonderful gifts that God promises through ethical and righteous living in the destined land of the Jewish people.

Honey and sweetness coming from fruit, especially figs, as Rashi adds, are, in a sense, praise regarding Israel.[5] Yet, they may also be seen in these verses not as items that are recommended for actually eating—certainly not on a regular basis—but those conjured up as a temptation to get the Israelites to crave going into the Holy Land. When Datan and Aviram use this promise pejoratively (Numbers 16:23), they are portrayed as mocking the way God and Moses tempt the Israelites and try to lure them to this incredible land with sweets and ubiquitous creamy, fatty substances. God knows human weaknesses and knows

---

3 Ehud Rost, "Towards Understanding the Term 'Land Flowing with Milk and Honey.'" *The Journal of the Land of Israel in the Bible* 6 (February 2000).

4 Although in contradiction to Rabbi Akiva in *Mekhilta* 13:5.

5 The *Mekhilta* only mentions dates.

how alluring sugar and sweets are. Imagine a land filled with milk chocolate, ice cream, and lollypops. Indeed, according to the rabbis, the forbidden fruit in the Garden of Eden, the ultimate symbol of temptation, was not apples but, rather, might have been three other items: grapes, wheat, or figs.[6] The Talmud sees these products as either problematic (wine), or both poisonous and curative (figs—i.e., sugar), and challenging (wheat—i.e., causing children to get smart and call out their parents). Through these Talmudic explications, we are able to conjure a different image of sweetness: tempting, potentially dangerous, and certainly something to be careful with. Even carbohydrates and gluten (in the form of wheat) are not spared. One can interpret the Talmud seeing wheat as potentially giving children their first positive bolt of knowledge as a reflection of the "knowledge of good and evil" part of the Forbidden tree.[7]

Therefore, the image of the Torah regarding sweets and other questionable foods seems not to venerate the foods unconditionally. Instead, we are tasked recognize how enjoyable these foods are to humankind and to view them with caution. Just as *hametz* is permissible year-round but forbidden on Passover and on the altar and most sacrifices, wine, sweets, fats, and even carbohydrates likewise have value but should be viewed with a certain amount of suspicion. Rost points to many midrashim that link "milk and honey" to wine as well, but perhaps God thought that tempting the Israelites explicitly with wine went too far.[8]

Nevertheless, we traditionally mention God's promise to the Jewish people if we fulfill the commandments in terms of grape juice, grain, and oil twice daily during the Sh'ma prayer.[9] Here, again, we see sweets—in the form of grape juice—carbohydrates and fats. Are we meant to eat these in an unrestricted way? Wouldn't this imply that a blessed life is one filled with these products which nutritionists have shown need to be eaten in restricted quantities? Yet, here, too, I believe we have to view the notion of "And you will gather" in a more metaphorical and abstract manner. We will be blessed, as America is today, with an abundance of sugars, of carbs, and of dairy and vegetable fats. Whatever the health challenges of these products in a First World nation like America,

---

6 BT *Sanhedrin* 70a–b.

7 These notions also reflect an awareness that can be dangerous as well, especially in interpretations that the tree represented an awareness of sexual knowledge and the sexual dangers represented by the serpent.

8 Ehud Rost, "Towards Understanding the Term 'Land Flowing with Milk and Honey.'" *The Journal of the Land of Israel in the Bible* 6 (February 2000).

9 Deuteronomy 11:14.

these are important products of basic nutrition that can and do sustain billions of people worldwide today, and have done so for thousands if not millions of years. The Torah tells us, however, that God only enables us to grow them and to gather them. What we do with them, how much we consume of them is a different challenge and a different question. After we feed our animals, the Torah utilizes more general language: "You shall eat and you shall be satisfied."[10] The Torah seems to make a distinction of the supply of produce—some of it healthier, some less healthy—and then the decision of how one actually eats and how one finds fulfillment and satisfaction in eating. Feeding one's animals, as the rabbi's acknowledge, is part of this sense of satisfaction even before we eat at all.[11] When we do eat, we need to make choices: simply having the food in front of us, having gathered it, does not mean what we should eat or how much we should eat; some people may cope with a certain food better than others.

Gathering all the food groups presents us with a blessed choice of abundance, just like the presence of the tree of knowledge in the Garden of Eden presented Adam and Eve with a choice. On its own, eating (ve-akhalta) needs to be done carefully, realizing the trade-offs that are present with the health consequences. Moreover, an abundance of grape juice and wine (tirosh) does not mean we have to get drunk with those beverages—as the Torah is critical of Noah for doing when he exited the Ark—nor does the presence of grains mean that humans have to eat them or that anyone has to eat them— they could become fuel or some other product. Satisfaction (ve-savata) requires us to make decisions and not just to accept the temptations that come with abundance. The book of Deuteronomy warns us: "lest you eat and become [too] satisfied … "[12] The Torah warns of the dangers of satisfaction, as well as the dangers of mindless consumption. Yet, the aisles in any American grocery store burst with sugar-filled products. The cheapest, most available, most colorful products are usually the least healthy. We can easily be filled up and complacent, even drunk. The challenge is: are we filling ourselves up with the products that lead to a healthier physical, spiritual, and ethical life, or are we merely consuming what we "gather" without conscious thought?

It is with this mindfulness and the imperative from Torah thought that I would like to turn to the struggle with legal rulings requiring eating foods that the diet that I have chosen—low sugar and low carbs—discourages.

---

10 Ibid., 11:15.

11 BT Gitin 62a.

12 Deuteronomy 8:12.

The conflict between personal health the general *halakhah* eating require-ments is an ancient problem. The Talmud deals with cases where fasting on Yom Kippur would be dangerous (a woman who has just given birth, for exam-ple) and, thus, should not be observed.[13] In general, there is a clear law of pre-serving life which precludes doing anything that might cause immediate harm to your life—any danger of death. Rabbis have ruled that those allergic to any grains may avoid *matzah* altogether if this will endanger their digestive system. Alcoholics should never have wine, even for Kiddush, and there are ways of avoiding grape juice—excess sugar—for Friday night Kiddush by saying Kiddush on the challah, and even on Saturday morning Kiddush is frequently said on any *chamar medina*—established drink, such as whiskey or scotch—with much less sugar than grape juice or sweet wine.

Even when there is no actual danger, there are frequently *halakhah* ways of avoiding the unwanted requirement.[14] The law of eating meat on a holiday based on the Talmudic phrase *ein simha ela b'basar vayayin*—"There is no joy with-out meat and wine"—merely means eating delicious foods and nice drinks on the holiday, as Rabbi Yosef Karo explains in his interpretation of the Talmudic passage which rejects Maimonides' more literal interpretation.[15] Salt on challah, or honey (a sugar) is not even necessary *halakhically* unless the challah is real black bread, which is a rare exception.[16] The custom on Shavuot to consume dairy is not about literally *eating* dairy but, rather, according to reasoning of Rav Moshe Isserless's gloss on the *Shulhan Arukh*, it is about serving dairy at one meal and meat at a different meal.[17]

Yet, what happens when the general direction of a specific diet calls for low sugar and low carbs, and that goes in the opposite direction of *halakhot*? Unlike the verses of the Torah and the midrashim we quoted *supra*, *halakhah* is not tra-ditionally understood as a metaphor—*halakhah* tells us what we actually have to do, not just imagine in our own way. Moreover, the approach we took with those sources, one focusing on making the right choices within an environ-ment of plenty and blessing, cannot work within a *halakhah* system. Perhaps the starkest illustration of this is the requirement to eat three meals on Shabbat, each with at least an olive's worth of bread. The *Aruch HaShulhan* rules that it

---

13   BT *Yoma*: 82a–83a.
14   There may also be moral reasons why someone may not want to eat a traditional food.
15   BT *Pesahim*,109a; Maimonides, *Yad Hachazaka, Hilchot Yom Tov*, 6:17–18, Kesef Mishneh, ad loc.
16   *Shulhan Arukh*: OH 167:5.
17   Ibid., 494:3.

is preferable to eat an egg's worth of bread at each of these meals—double an olive's worth.[18] If someone wants to limit their carb intake, how can they possibly feel good about eating an egg's worth of bread three times? On holidays the requirement is only two meals with bread, but that is also a demand that goes against a low carb diet.

I would suggest that for a person on a careful low sugar and low carb diet, not because of a medical condition but because of a desire to eat healthy or even lose weight, our tradition wanted to extend its classic efforts to make Shabbat stand out from the week—including foods—even more pronounced. On weekdays, Jewish law gives the individual the responsibility of choosing what to eat—within the general constraints of the laws of *kashrut*. But on Shabbat and holidays, the rabbis wanted the individual to feel some guilty pleasures. Bread, carbs, even sweet things—*mamtakim*, as one of the classic Shabbat songs specifically mentions—are what tempted us to come to the Holy Land, what tempted us in the Garden of Eden, and what made the *manna* so compelling. During the week, we are open to challenging whether these are healthy for us, depending on which nutritional approach our understanding of the current science dictates. On Shabbat and holidays, however, the rabbis did not want us to fast or deprive ourselves of the pleasures of this world. Indeed, sex, wine, fine drinks, and fine foods all play a role in creating the pleasurable, even tempting, atmosphere of Shabbat and holidays.

Bread, and usually sweeter traditional bread known as *challah*, thus, should not be seen as sending a message against any particular diet. We can still believe sugars and sweetened foods are unhealthy, but we can indulge with them on these special days. In fact, when I avoid cakes and cookies on Shabbat or holidays, I feel guilty. I feel like I am violating the law of *oneg Shabbat* or *oneg Yom Tov*. I feel that enjoying and getting physical pleasure from the special days is imbued with the day. Conversely, when I do indulge in these treats, I need to say to my body and my diet that it is not a violation of the nutritional path I have taken, but, rather, it is distinguishing between my weekday routine and these special days. If there would be an issue of an immediate danger eating sugars or carbs, then legally there would be no issue eliminating them. Yet, since it is only a general guideline for healthy eating, Shabbat and holiday pleasure pushes away the strictest standards of healthy eating.

Humans are omnivores, and while I cannot prove it, I feel it: I can fill up on any number of savory foods, and even fatty foods, but I will still have a craving

---

18 274:7.

for a donut if I see one. Normally, that is a craving that has to be dismissed. Yet on Shabbat and holidays, which represent a world without the need to deprive ourselves, proper behavior, is to indulge. Of course even on Shabbat and holidays, disgusting, over-indulgent eating—*achila gasa*—is still prohibited. So a little bit of indulgence in foods I avoid during the week is permitted, but even that must be controlled based even on the laws of holiday and Shabbat eating. Enjoy, even more than during the week, but still, satisfaction must be something beyond gluttony and total disregard for nutrition and the physical body. Even the *Manna* had limitations: one *Omer* per person, enjoying the miraculous food, but never over-indulging in it.

The struggle to eat in a healthy way lingers. In America, we live in a society which presents many temptations and challenges. Can we look to the Torah, the writings of the rabbis, and the laws for re-enforcement of a low sugar or even a low-carbohydrate diet? I believe if we step back away from overly literal interpretations and understand the broader message of the Torah, we see that we are asked to always make choices. We are promised a life filled with delights and temptations, sometimes pulling us towards the promised land but sometimes pulling us out of the Garden of Eden: it is our responsibility to make the right choices and to respond to abundance—in our supermarkets, in our food courts, and in our homes—with the ability that God gave Adam and Eve to choose wisely, and to select the amount and the type of foods that work for our bodies, based on the best understanding we have of our nutritional needs. And then, we have to loosen up a bit on Shabbat and holidays and eat in a way that lets us dream of a world with no limitations: no poverty, no inequality, where everyone can gather all of God's bounty for this world and everyone can partake from all the blessings that they need. If we make these choices properly and we allow our special days and times to shake up our regular routine, then, may we merit the blessings from our world and on high to provide our bodies with the healthy nutrition they need to live a meaningful and satisfied life.

Section 5   Worker Rights, Equality, and Hunger

CHAPTER 1

The Divine Image

Theological Reflections on Jewish Labor Law

Rabbi Dr. Ariel Evan Mayse

> *Rabbi Akiva said, "Beloved is the human being, created in the image of God. Yet an even greater love was shown in making it known that one is created in the divine image"*—m. Avot 3:14
>
> *"Just as the Torah was given in a covenant, so was work given in a covenant, as it says, 'Six days you shall labor and do all of your work, and the seventh day is a Sabbath to Y-H-V-H your God'"*—Avot de-Rabbi Natan

Hasidic tradition tells of Rabbi Yehudah Aryeh Leib Alter of Ger (d. 1905), better known as the *Sefat Emet*, entering the *beit midrash* shortly before the prayers were to begin one morning. The master gazed on his Hasidim for a few minutes and then offered a few cryptic words of guidance. It was a festival day, and the assembled community was preparing to recite *Hallel*, a liturgy filled with praise and thanksgiving. Rabbi Alter charged his Hasidim as follows: "This morning you must have extra *kavvanah*, additional focus and intention, when you recite the words *ana Hashem*." He then walked out of the *beit midrash*, leaving his Hasidim to ponder his words. This poignant phrase appears several times in *Hallel*. Which of them did he mean?

Some of Rabbi Alter's disciples argued that he was referring to *ana Hashem hoshia na* ("Please, Y-H-V-H, deliver us"), but others felt that their teacher must have meant *ana Hashem hatzlihah na* ("Please, Y-H-V-H, make us succeed"). The students continued to disagree until Rabbi Alter returned to the *beit midrash* and gave ear to their bickering. "No," he said sharply, "You've totally misunderstood. I really meant *ana Hashem ki ani avadekha*—please, Y-H-V-H, for I am your servant." The deepest prayer, suggests Rabbi Alter, is expressed in our longing to become a servant of the One.

Focusing the entirety of *Hallel* on this single liturgical refrain suggests a profound truth: the greatest acclamation of the Divine is a lifetime of humble service. We accomplish this goal through religious rituals such as study and worship, of course, but Hasidism emphasizes that the service of God is equally manifest through works of kindness and compassion for other human beings. Martin Buber, the highly perceptive interpreter of Hasidic spirituality, offered the following summary:

> You cannot really love God if you do not love men, and you cannot really love men if you do not love God. This is the stage that Hasidism reached, even if the new life established by it remained fragmentary and fleeting. One shall, says Kierkegaard, have to do essentially only with God. One cannot, says Hasidism, have to do essentially with God if one does not have to do essentially with man.
>
> The uniqueness and irreplaceability of each human soul is a basic teaching of Hasidism. God intends in His creation an infinity of unique individuals, and within it he intends each single one without exception as having a quality, a special capacity, a value that no other possesses; each has in His eyes an importance peculiar to him in which none other can compete with him, and He is devoted to each with an especial love because of this precious value hidden in him.
>
> Hasidism is one of the great movements of faith that shows directly that the human soul can live as a whole, united in itself in communication with the wholeness of being, and indeed not merely individual souls, but a multitude of souls bound into a community … [1]

Hasidic piety understands, as has much of Jewish spirituality from the time of the Hebrew Bible, that the realms of ritual and ethics are fundamentally intertwined. The Hasidic masters teach that the keys to the life of the spirit are found in cultivating a posture of humility and open-heartedness toward the

---

1 Martin Buber, "Love of God and Love of Neighbor," *Hasidism & Modern Man* (Princeton and Oxford: Princeton University Press, 2016), 112, 125, 128.

human beings around us. Such moments of compassion allow the Divine to irrupt into our lives:

> An explanation of the verse, "And I shall behold Your face in righteousness" (*tsedek*; Ps. 17:15). When a person gives a coin to a pauper, he effects a heavenly unification (*yihud*) [of Y-H-V-H, God's sacred name]. The coin is [the letter] *yod*, the giver's five fingers are *heh*, the outstretched arm is *vav*, and the five fingers of the poor person are the final *heh* … This draws forth a flow of compassion.[2]

Attentiveness to the needs of others enables the seeker or worshiper to lovingly embrace the immeasurable worth of each human being, seeing an imagine of the Divine manifest in every person.

This posture of kindness, compassion, and respect should apply equally to our engagement with the economy, informing our relationship to the human beings at the heart of every financial and industrial system.[3] The Jewish tradition has much wisdom to share on the dignity of work, the fundamental importance of workers' rights and their obligations to their employers, and specific complexities of labor law. These themes are treated at great length in the sixth and seventh chapters of the Talmudic tractate *Bava Metzia*. There we find discussions about contract negotiations, setting wages, different categories of workers, the reciprocal obligations of the employees and employer to one another, what steps must be taken when one side—or both sides—wishes to change or dissolve the agreement, and so forth. Like much of *Seder Nezikin* (the Mishnaic order of "damages"), these chapters are complicated and quite intricate. This complexity makes these laws exciting to study. But this conceptual dexterity and thrilling focus makes it all too easy to become ensnared in the minutiae of Talmudic reasoning and to forget about the enduring theological, legal, and moral questions that should be the foundation of any economic discussion from a Jewish perspective.

The issues in the modern economy that confront those fighting for progressive values are legion: insufferable working conditions, unequal pay for women, terrible discrimination against people of color, ethnic minorities or LGBTQ status, lack of freedom to organize, and systematic degradation

---

2 *Mevasser Tsedek* (Tsefat: 2010), *re'eh*, 221.

3 This essay began as a course offered at the Rabbinical School of Hebrew College in 2017. I wish to thank the students for our many stimulating, insightful, and thoughtful discussions, and for constantly pushing me to refine my thinking and deepen my reading of the sources.

and exploitation of disenfranchised or powerless workers. Many contemporary thinkers and scholars have explored how the resources of Jewish labor law for helping to speak to these and other contemporary issues, plumbing its wisdom as well as exploring instances in which the answers of classical *halakhah* has proven insufficient.[4] My aim in this chapter is to demonstrate that careful attention to the interstices of law and theology grant us another important lens for exploring and navigating the question of labor law and workers' rights.

Halakhah and the Duties of Intimacy

I understand *halakhah* to be a quest for the Divine that is full of motion and movement. It is a trail of deeds (from the word *halikhah*, or "walking" along the path), a religious journey of disciplined, constant journey of striving for the One with courage, integrity, and compassion.[5] Our religious rituals and obligations should lead us to construct a life of devotion. This is the purpose of *halakhah*, for the ultimate goal of our religious quest is to stand in the presence of the One. The rites, commitments, and responsibilities of *halakhah* must shape our journey toward the ultimate goal of *devekut*, a moment of radical awareness and awakening to the Divine. "Religion begins," wrote Rabbi Abraham Joshua Heschel, "with a consciousness that something is asked of us. It is that tense, eternal asking in which the soul is caught and in which man's answer is elicited."[6] Our answer to God's enduring and ever-present beckoning comes in the form of sacred deeds, specific actions shaped by the covenant that have the power to bring us into the presence of the Infinite. Our duties may be lovingly performed, but devotion to a beloved is not simply supererogatory; obligations are part and parcel of the mutual vows that bind us evermore; meaningful intimate relationships must also entail responsibility, and it is no different for those who long to experience the Divine.

At the heart to this devotional understanding of Jewish practice is the full integration of *halakhah* and *aggadah*, between the discourse of law and the

---

4 The most comprehensive and accessible reading of Jewish legal sources and their importance of contemporary issues is Jill Jacobs, *There Shall be No Needy: Pursuing Social Justice through Jewish Law & Tradition* (Woodstock, VT: Jewish Lights, 2009).

5 For a fuller exploration of this, see my "Neo-Hasidism and the Theology of *Halakhah*: The Duties of Intimacy and the Law of the Heart," *A New Hasidism: Branches*, ed. Arthur Green and Ariel Evan Mayse (Philadelphia: Jewish Publication Society and University of Nebraska Press, forthcoming 2018).

6 Abraham Joshua Heschel, *God in Search of Man: A Philosophy of Judaism* (New York: Farrar, Straus and Giroux, 1955), 162.

theological, spiritual, and philosophical narratives that shape practice and give it meaning.[7] I suggest that this interweaving takes place on two interrelated fronts. The first is that each point of *halakhah* be understood as making a theological claim. In other words, every legal formulation or decision may be interpreted as revealing something regarding a person's (or a community's) beliefs about God and the divine Will. The second claim, perhaps the more audacious of the two, is that inner awakenings, ethical intuition, moral reflection, and spiritual illumination may lead one to alter his or her own religious practice. Law is driven forward by values, which are ethical, theological, and cultural, as well as jurisprudential. It seeks to express these values and is in concern—sometimes in tension—with them.

What are the theological principles that should drive forward the contemporary formulation of Jewish labor law? Like all ideals, they are easy to enumerate and frustratingly difficult to realize: the inherent dignity of all human beings; the creation of each individual in the image of God; the belief in the utter primacy of our fundamental servitude to God rather than to social conformity and to the most powerful of people. Of course, our framing of economic policy needs to maintain a sense of balance and fairness, and equity. We know that cheating and dishonesty can—and does—happen in both directions. *Halakhah* clearly demands much from both employers and employees; these obligations are reciprocal, if not necessarily coterminous. And yet, together with this well-placed rabbinic pragmatism, a brooding voice of the prophets is carried forward in Jewish literature as well.

Labors of Love

Jewish reflections on labor law are expansive and sprawling, well beyond the confines of the present chapter, but some mention should be made of the fundamental or core precepts.[8] The Hebrew Bible demands that an employer

---

7 Here, I am inspired by the grand vision of Rabbi Abraham Isaac Kook. For example, see *Abraham Isaac Kook: The Lights of Penitence, the Moral Principles, Lights of Holiness, Essays, Letters and Poems*, trans. and ed. Ben Zion Bokser (New York: Paulist Press, 1978), 196–98; Avinoam Rosenak, *The Prophetic Halakhah: Rabbi A. I. H. Kook's Philosophy of Halakhah* (Jerusalem: Magnes Press, 2007) [Hebrew]; and Yehudah Mirsky, *Rav Kook: Mystic in a Time of Revolution* (New Haven and London: Yale University Press, 2014), esp. 31–35,127–40, 183; See also Robert Cover, "The Supreme Court 1982 Term—Foreword: Nomos and Narrative," *Harvard Law Review* 97 (1983–1984): 4–68; and Hayyim Nahman Bialik, "Halachah and Aggadah," *Revealment and Concealment: Five Essays* (trans. Zali Gurevitc) (Jerusalem: Ibis Editions, 2000), 45–87.

8 In addition to Rabbi Jacobs' book, see Michael S. Perry, "Labor Rights in the Jewish

pay day-laborers in a timely fashion,[9] a religio-ethical obligation which emerges from the awareness that such hired-hands may be in moral peril if they do not receive payment immediately on completing their work. Rabbinic law builds on this biblical command—and the later prophetic voices of concern that greed may lead to its transgression—emphasizing that an employer or owner must pay his workers and treat them in accord with the ethical and financial norms of their community. This standard, called variously *minhag ha-medinah* or *minhag ha-makom*, is the minimum for working conditions and remuneration, though it need not—and should not—function as a glass ceiling.[10] Workers, in turn, are obligated by Jewish law to work with focus, concentration, and discipline, toiling to the fullest extent of their ability, taking care of the property entrusted to them, and demonstrating concern for the ways in which their labor impacts the financial wellbeing of the employer.[11] The right of workers to organize— and strike—has been debated by modern *poskim* precisely because of the economic loss that such actions may entail.[12]

The Talmudic explorations and formulations of Jewish labor law should be read as an exploration of *halakhah* seeking to construct the workings

---

Tradition," (Jewish Labor Committee, 1994); David J. Schnall, *By the Sweat of Your Brow: Reflections on Work and the Workplace in Classic Jewish Thought* (New York and Hoboken: Michael Scharf Publication Trust of Yeshiva University Press and KTAV Publishing House, 2001); and Shillem Wahrhaftig, *Dinei Avodah be-Mishpat Ivri* (Tel Aviv: 1969), vol. 2.

9 Leviticus 19:9–13 and 25:39–55; Deuteronomy 24:14–15 and 23:25–26. Cf. Amos 4:1–3; Malachi 3:5; Job 31:13–15; Isaiah 1; and, on the looming specter of corvée or forced labor, see Judges 1:27–33 and Lamentations 1:3.

10 See mishnah *Bava Metzia* 7:1–7; BT *Kiddushin* 22a; BT *Taanit* 24a; BT *Bava Metzia* 112a; *Mishneh Torah, Hilkhot Sekhirut* 11:1–2; and cf. ibid., *Hilkhot Shekalim* 4:7, which may suggest that the community is responsible for paying a living wage to public-sector employees. See also *Shulhan Arukh, Hoshen Mishpat* 331:1–3, and 339:1–3,10; *Sefer ha-Hinukh*, nos. 230 and 588. On payment for wages in with goods other than money, see *Shulhan Arukh, Hoshen Mishpat* 336:1–2, and cf. the ShaKH ad loc., no. 2–4;

11 Mishnah *Bava Metzia* 6 and 7:8–11; JT *Bava Metzia* 8:2–4; *Mishneh Torah, Hilkhot Sekhirut* 13:6–7; *Shulhan Arukh, Hoshen Mishpat* 333:3–5 and 337:1–2, 19–20; and BT *Berakhot* 16a; BT *Taanit* 23a–b.

12 See the sources discussed in Benjamin Brown, "Trade Unions, Strikes, and the Renewal of *Halakhah* Labor Law: Ideologies in the Rulings of Rabbis Kook, Uziel and Feinstein," *Contention, Controversy and Change: Evolutions and Revolutions in the Jewish Experience*, vol. 2, ed. Simcha Fishbane and Eric Levine (New York: Touro College Press, 2016), 82–118; and David J. Schnall, "Ba'alei Umanut: Organized Labor and the Jewish Tradition," *Hazon Nahum: Studies in Jewish Law, Thought, and History Presented to Dr. Norman Lamm on the Occasion of his Seventieth Birthday*, ed. Yaakov Elman and Jeffrey S. Gurock (New York: Yeshiva University Press, 1997), 627–42.

of a moral economy infused with God's presence.[13] The Torah tells us that: "The Israelites have become servants unto me; they are my servants, whom I have taken out of the land of Egypt—I am Y-H-V-H your God" (Lev. 25:55). Rashi's comment on this verse, reflecting the classical midrash, is repercussive: "If one enslaves them below, it is as if I have been enslaved on high." The Talmud affirms that to indenture an Israelite indefinitely, and with a spirit of cruelty, is an abject violation of God's covenant. Lest one be tempted into thinking that this is no more than a clever homily or fanciful exegesis, this concept appears in the Gemara as the reason that a day-laborer (*sekhir yom* or *po'el*) may quit the job halfway through—otherwise, the employment is a kind of unconscionable servitude.[14] The flexibility of human contracts (which invariably protect the party with less power) is therefore preceded by and predicated on an inviolable foundation: the loving bond between Israel and the Divine.[15]

This framing brings us to the questions that dwell at the heart of these Talmudic chapters: What does it mean to be a servant of the Divine, working to create a world more in keeping with God's vision? And how does my constant awareness of this role, cultivated through engagement with the Talmudic text and the later sources of *halakhah*, inform my moral obligations to other human beings? Consider the following tradition recorded by one of the students of Rabbi Yitzhak Luria, the great Kabbalist of Safed (1534–1572) widely known by the acronym of "the ARI":

> With respect to the wages owed a hired laborer, my teacher, may his memory be for an everlasting blessing, used to be exceedingly careful. He would sometimes delay in praying the afternoon service until he had paid someone his wages. And on occasion, he would not pray the afternoon service until after sundown when he did not have the money with which to pay what he owed; he would request money from this one and that one until he could pay what he owed to a hired laborer. Only afterwards would he pray the Afternoon Service. He would say: "How can I pray to God, may He be exalted, when I have an obligation such as this to fulfill and I have not yet done so? And how can I lift up my countenance to pray?"[16]

---

13 See the fourteenth-century Rabbi Yaakov ben Asher's introduction to the *Hoshen Mishpat* section of his magnum opus, the *Arba'ah Turim*.

14 BT *Bava Metzia* 77a; BT *Bava Kamma* 116b. Cf. BT *Kiddushin* 22b.

15 This verse is so central that it is even quoted in the *Shulhan Arukh*. See *Shulhan Arukh*, *hoshen mihpat* 333:3.

16 Ariel Evan Mayse, *From the Depth of the Well: An Anthology of Jewish Mysticism* (New York: Paulist Press, 2014), 91.

One might be tempted to offer a purely formalistic explanation for Luria's behavior. Because it is a biblical commandment to pay a laborer on the day he completes his work (Deuteronomy 24:14–15), and only a rabbinic enactment to pray at a certain time, the former takes precedent over the latter. Yet closer inspection of this source reveals that there is a deeper competition of values afoot, especially given that the sages determined that the obligation to pay a worker *only* applies if the employee actively requests his recompense.[17] Our identity as servants of God is expressed through our worship, but it is equally manifest in our religious obligations directed to other human beings.

Expanding the category only slightly, we may argue that becoming a servant of God means acting as an agent of grace and compassion toward all those in need. Rabbi Yisrael Meir Kagan (1839–1933), best known as the author of the *Hafetz Hayyim* and the *Mishnah Berurah*, also authored a small book called *Ahavat Hesed* on commandments rooted in kindness and love for others. The fact that he devotes several lengthy chapters of this work to the *mitzvah* of paying one's workers in a timely fashion reveals his understanding of labor law as rooted in concern and love for others.[18] Throughout this volume, Rabbi Kagan asserts that each day of one's life, and indeed, one's existence, reveals God's benevolence and blessing. Folded into our being is the obligation to pay forward that divine love toward others.

Rabbi Sarra Lev recently argued that the genre of the Talmud is best understood as "summons."[19] The Gemara is a literature that calls its readers to a sense of holiness and a greater degree of self-actualization, a transformation sparked through study and engagement with the text. Lev explains that this approach, "requires us to see the struggles, decisions, opinions, and behaviors of those in the texts as connecting with and relevant to our own lives, even when those behaviors do not seem to reflect our own."[20] Thus construed, these central chapters of *Bava Metzia* provide a "summon" us by challenging the reader to confront the following questions: How are we obligated, morally and theologically, to treat our workers? And, more broadly, does the contemporary

---

17 BT *Bava Metzia* 112a.

18 *Ahavat Hesed* (Jerusalem: 2014), pt. 2, 8–9. See also the link between compassion, love and prayer drawn in BT *Berakhot* 20a-b.

19 See Sarra Lev, "Talmud that Works Your Heart: New Approaches to Reading," in *Learning to Read Talmud: What it Looks Like and How It Happens*, eds. Jane L. Kanarek and Marjorie Lehman (Boston: Academic Studies Press, 2016), 175–202.

20 Ibid., 194.

economy represent God's hope for a world founded in justice, mercy, and compassion? One of my students recently pointed out that such essential questions are rarely—if ever—voiced in contemporary boardrooms. Commerce must function, of course, but the divine scales invariably incline to favor the poor, the workers, the disenfranchised, and widow and the orphan.

Boundaries, Borders, and Slavery

Our contemporary world presents many challenges to the classical sources of Jewish law, which were formulated to address the salient issues in pre-globalized (and often pre-industrial) economies. Among these is how modern Jews are to reconcile our understanding of a unique covenant between Israel and God, with the notion that *all* human beings are created in the image of God? The particularism of the covenant, a bond that undergirds much of Jewish labor law, is specific and by nature quite exclusionary. In the modern world we must work to preserve the dignity of this special relationship between God and the Jewish people, without in any way compromising the dignity of others and our ethical, moral and religious obligations to them as our workers as well as our employers.

Hillel Zeitlin, the leading figure of philosophical neo-Hasidism among Eastern European Jews in the pre-Holocaust era, dreamt of bringing about a new revival of Judaism that would bear within it much of the spiritual energy and enthusiasm that had characterized Hasidism in its early heyday.[21] Crucial to his project was assembling an elite Jewish spiritual fellowship to be called *Yavneh*. The values of socialism, including supporting oneself by the dignity of one's own labor and disdain for commerce as a form of exploitation are part of the rules he composed for the community he sought to create. This idealistic religious community was to serve as a beacon for alienated Jewish youth, presenting Judaism to them at once as both as a highly moral and profoundly spiritual way of life. This stood in sharp contrast to the petty and divisive squabbling, as well as to the questionable ethical standards, that he saw in the existing Orthodox and Hasidic communities of his day.[22]

---

21 See Hillel Zeitlin, *Hasidic Spirituality for a New Era: The Religious Writings of Hillel Zeitlin*, trans. and ed. Arthur Green (New York: Paulist Press, 2012); and Arthur Green and Ariel Evan Mayse, "'The Great Call of the Hour': Hillel Zeitlin's Yiddish Writings on *Yavneh*," *Geveb: A Journal of Yiddish Studies* (Spring, 2016).

22 Zeitlin, an active and sharp-tongued polemicist, was bitterly attacked by the leadership of Agudat Yisrael, the party that dominated Orthodox Jewish life in central Poland and was

In 1924, Zeitlin published a small pamphlet that included the piece "What Does Yavneh Want?" This piece was an imagined interview with himself in which he described the new society of Yavneh as a renewed and more universalized version of the Baal Shem Tov's spiritual path. He wrote that the latter's theology was founded in three interwoven expressions of love: the love of God, the love of Torah, and the love of Israel. Each of these core values, said Zeitlin, must be reinterpreted and pushed farther, broader, and deeper in the contemporary world:

> In the time of the Baal Shem Tov, it was enough for Israel to shine a light for itself. In these times, in a time when a world has been destroyed and a new one is being built, Israel has to be a light for itself and for all peoples, as in the verse: "I the Lord call you in righteousness and hold fast to your hand, making you as a covenantal people, a light to the nations" (Isaiah 42:6) . . .
>
> In the time of the Baal Shem Tov the class conflicts among people were not yet so sharply defined. The demand for social justice had not yet been articulated with full seriousness and honesty. Today we are undergoing horrible evils that are taking place in the world. But these are leading us to a more just and honorable relationship with those who work with sweat on their brows. The "Hasidism of the future" will incorporate all that is healthy, pure, and honorable in Socialism. But it will with great bitterness cast aside all in Socialism that is petty, egotistical, merchant-like in its materialism, unjust, jealous, or vengeful. It will reject the dark and wild tyranny of the masses and of those adventurers who climb up on the backs of the masses . . .
>
> In the Hasidism of the future the love of God will shine forth and burn even more brightly than it did in the days of the BeSHT. The "Love of Israel" will be transformed into a great worldwide "Love of Humanity."[23]

Zeitlin's remarkable vision of spiritual fellowship that extends to all human beings, while still acknowledging the central place of the Jewish people, had a crucial ethical component as well. His dream was deeply infused with the ethical voice of the prophets and Jewish literature, demanding justice in God's name, as well as the moral philosophy of modern social and economic thought.

---

represented in the Polish parliament by leading followers of the rebbe of Ger (Gora Kalwarja), the chief Hasidic group in the Warsaw region. For one of Zeitlin's many responses to his Orthodox critics, see his "*Mayn Apikorses,*" *Der Moment* 149, July 27, 1924, 4.

23 Zeitlin, *Hasidic Spirituality*, 41–42.

In a set of admonitions for the imagined Yavneh community published in the same pamphlet, he wrote:

> Do not exploit anyone! If you support yourself solely by the work of your hands, the length of your days will be surrounded by modesty, calm, and humility, by abstention from indulgence, luxury, and pleasure seeking. It will simplify your task if you fulfill the great and holy commandment to every pure mortal: do not exploit anyone! Do not "use" people, seeking your own benefit without their agreement, or even with their agreement, if a full exchange of value is not received. Every person is a complete world. From the standpoint of morality and pure religion, every business abuse, in any form whatsoever, is robbery and murder.
>
> A factory boss or supervisor who takes advantage of workers by paying them the lowest wage acceptable on the market, and not the full and proper sum for value received, is exploiting those workers. The merchant who takes unfair advantage in buying or selling exploits the people that merchant is dealing with.[24]

Zeitlin's words lead us to consider another defining aspect of the modern economy, one that is even more troubling and unsettling than issues of particularism and universalism. In today's globalized world, we are moving away from the small-scale models of workers and artisan contractors (*poalim, sekhirei yom,* and *kablanim*) that undergird these Talmudic sections. Unfortunately, it seems that we are returning to a socio-economic model close to that of slavery. Our modern economies—and we as the consumers who drive them—are unfortunately responsible for the outrages of poverty wages, horrific working conditions, an ever-widening income gap, systemic reliance on foreign workers without offering them rights or freedoms, and reinforcing the cycles of poverty among the disenfranchised while reaping untoward benefits.

There is, I believe, an indigenous language in Jewish law and theology that aptly describes this one-sided, extractive vision of labor and human relationships: the foreign slave (*eved kenaani*) vis-à-vis the Israelite slave (*eved ivri*). The latter, the Hebrew bondsman, is never forced to surrender his place in the community.[25] His or her term of service is delimited, and the rabbis offer clear definitions of what sorts of labors the Israelite slave may—and may not—be

---

24 Ibid., 44.
25 See Exodus 21; Leviticus 25; and Deuteronomy 15.

forced to do.[26] These ethical and temporal boundaries ensure aim to ensure neither the slave's master nor the community at large come to see the individual as an outsider. Safeguarded by these laws, the Hebrew bondsman returns after a period of temporary servitude that never effaces their membership.

The foreign slave, by contrast, remains fundamentally other and alien.[27] Offered little protection and few rights, he or she has a position in the community that is liminal at best. The foreign slave is like chattel: his labors are nearly unrestricted, his servitude is held by the master in perpetuity, and such an individual has few chances to achieve freedom. This bondage gives rise to a unidirectional vector of benefit: the master takes all, and the slave contents himself with nothing.

We need not look far to glimpse the contemporary correlate of the *eved kenaani*. Modern slaves come in many different forms.[28] One example are the many foreign workers in the United States, especially those who have entered a country illegally. With no recourse and no clear path beyond their current status, these workers live on the margins of society and, though they are a pillar of the agricultural economy, they are denied access to the basic rights and social services available to those born on our shores. They live in constant fear of deportation, often laboring in difficult circumstances and performing menial, thankless jobs without receiving the respect and social support to which they are entailed as human beings and as employees.

Yet, the boundaries of slavery stretch include American citizens as well. In the United States, endemic racism and Jim Crow policies, including the so-called "War on Drugs" and the phenomenon of mass incarceration, shunted people of color into a virtually inescapable marginal position. And, turning the telescope around, what are we to do about the hidden laborers who work in factories and industries across the ocean, who receive poverty wages (perhaps even by their own standards) and toil in disgraceful working conditions? Such labor supports our standard of living, at least for the time being, but it exacts a terrible human price and sullies our hands.

---

26 See Maimonides' restatement in *Mishneh Torah, hilkhot 'avadim* 1:6, and cf. *Shulhan Arukh, Yoreh De'ah*, 267:16–17, 79.

27 See Leviticus 25:44–46. Attitudes toward the *'eved kena'ani* in the rabbinic imagination are complicated. See *M. Berakhot* 2:7; and cf. *M. Bava Kamma* 8:3, *JT Bava Metzia* 6:1.

28 It is worth noting that the possibility of holding such slaves exists in rabbinic law into the medieval and modern periods, long after the practice of the *eved ivri* had been abandoned. See Tur and *Shulhan Arukh, Yoreh De'ah* 267.

Emmanuel Levinas developed a philosophy in which the Other becomes a figure to whom we owe a higher level of moral and ethical obligation. Hasidism, taking a different tack, understands our responsibility to other human beings as grounded in our shared connection to the Divine; every individual is sustained by God's mercy, and each person represents a unique manifestation of the Divine. But the modern slaves that surround us have become an Other that is disenfranchised, pushed down, and ignored. They embody the subaltern, a class of people of lower socio-economic status from whom those higher up take *everything*. They have no way to advance or to escape the cycles of poverty and servitude.

Here, I wish to turn to the carefully measured words of Maimonides (also known as Rambam). His formulation tracing the contours of one's obligations to the *eved ivri* rests on many layers of rabbinic exegesis, but his crystalline expression allows the moral voice to resound with utmost clarity. Rambam comments as follows:

> It is forbidden to work a Hebrew slave with rigor. What is working him with rigor? Any labor without clear limit, or labor of which he has no need other than the intent to subjugate him, lest he stop working ...
>
> It is forbidden for an Israelite who buys any Hebrew slave to make him do menial tasks which are assigned to slaves only, such as to make him carry his clothes after him to the bathhouse or take off his shoes, for it is said: "You shall not make him serve as a bondservant" (Lev. 25:39) ... This applies only to a Hebrew bondman who feels humiliated because he was sold into servitude. It is permitted, however, to make an Israelite who was not sold do the work of a slave inasmuch as he does that work of his own volition.[29]

Hebrew slaves must be treated with dignity, honor, and respect. The determinative factor, suggests Maimonides, is maintaining some semblance of the worker's freedom of choice. This mirrors a rabbinic law declaring that a day-laborer may quit in the midst of a task, since his foremost allegiance—i.e., our ultimate debt of servitude—is to God alone. Workers and Hebrew slaves are full-members of our covenant with God, and thus participate in to this

---

29 *Mishneh Torah, hilkhot 'avadim* 1:7; See Isadore Twersky, *A Maimonides Reader* (Springfield, NJ: Behrman House, Inc., 1972), 175.

intractable and equalizing bond. Rambam continued to lay out his vision for Hebrew bondsman in the next *halakhah*:

> ... The master must treat his Hebrew male and female slave as equals in regard to food, drink, clothing, and shelter, as it is said: "because he is well with you" (Deut. 15:16); i.e., you should not eat white bread and the slave black bread, you drink old wine and he new wine, you sleep on down feathers and he on straw, you reside in the city and he in the country, or you reside in the country and he dwell in the city, for it is further said: "He shall go out from you" (Lev. 25:41) ... [30]

Such law makes it clear that discrimination—and segregation—are intolerable. The master and the slave must dwell in the same conditions, enjoying the same kinds of food and sharing a standard of living that is commensurate in every way. Were it not for the biblical proof text, we might be tempted to translate this message into something akin to "separate but equal" (all too often a smoke-screen for institutionalized segregation). But the unmistakable emphasis of the slave's proximity, found in words like "with you" and "he shall go out from you," suggest that *halakhah* demands something far beyond the conveniences of segregation.

But Maimonides, accenting a particular voice in classical rabbinic *halakhah*, also provided an inspiring voice of moral clarity when it comes to the way we are meant to treat the *eved kenaani*—the indentured or enslaved Other. He admitted that while *halakhah* permits one to deal with such workers harshly, the Torah demands that we extend ourselves beyond the letter of the law:

> It is permitted to work a heathen slave with rigor. Though such is the rule, it is the quality of piety and the way of wisdom that a man be merciful and pursue justice and not make his yoke heavy upon the slave or distress him, but give him to eat and to drink of all foods and drinks.
>
> The sages of old were wont to let the slave partake of every dish that they themselves ate of and to give the meal of the cattle and of the slaves precedence over their own. Is it not said: "As the eyes of slaves to the hand of their master, as the eyes of the female servant to the hand of her mistress?" (Psalms 123:2)

---

30 Ibid., 176.

Thus also the master should not disgrace them by hand or by word, because Scriptural law has delivered them only to slavery and not to disgrace. Nor should he heap upon the slave oral abuse and anger, but should rather speak to him softly and listen to his claims. So it is also explained in the good paths of Job, in which he prided himself:

> "If I did despise the cause of my manservant,
> Or of my maidservant, when they contended with me ...
> Did not He that made me in the womb make him?
> And did not One fashion us in the womb?" (Job 31:13, 15).

Cruelty and effrontery are not frequent except with heathen who worship idols. The children of our father Abraham, however, i.e., the Israelites, upon whom the Holy One, blessed be He, bestowed the favor of the Law and laid upon them statues and judgments, are merciful people who have mercy upon all.

Thus also it is declared by the attributes of the Holy One, blessed be He, which we are enjoined to imitate: "And His mercies are over all His works" (Ps. 145:9)

Furthermore, however has compassion will receive compassion, as it is said: "And He will show you mercy, and have compassion upon you, and multiply you" (Deut. 13:18).[31]

Rather than exploiting and ignoring those with less power, Maimonides' vision demanded that the employer (or master) must pay careful attention to those in his care. The worker is a human being, an individual deserving of the consideration, compassion, love. Laborers are an organic part of our community, and employers and employees are bound together by a knot of shared humanity. As Jews we must shy away from anything that smacks of cruelty (*akhzariyyut*), effrontery (*azut*), and moral insipidity, all of which are anathema to the Jewish tradition. We should note that Maimonides' claim that the favor of the Law (*tovat ha-Torah*), a gift bestowed on us from God, has transformed us into agents of mercy responsible for sharing our illumination with others. We must, said Rambam, embody compassion and mercy rather than strident judgment, revealing these qualities through our treatment of *all* other human beings.

---

31 Ibid., 177.

This compassion for others is a direct outgrowth of our relationship with God. The next part of the verse (Psalms 123:2), which includes the second half of the parallelism, reveals that our ethical concern for the Other is founded in religious commitment: "so do our eyes look upon Y-H-V-H our God, that He be gracious unto us." We express compassion to others because, as the *Hafetz Hayyim* reminds us, we are the recipients of infinite kindness. That is the fiber of our existence.

This passage concludes Rambam's restatement of the laws of slavery, but it is also the final *halakhah* in *Sefer Kinyan*, the section of *Mishneh Torah* dealing with acquisitions of property. The ethos may thus be understood as in some way undergirding the entire book. We have power over other things, expressed as ownership over possessions and relationships with other human beings, but hiding behind the letter of the law is not enough. We are called to something greater. Injustice is an unfortunate part of our world. True economic and social equality may not be attainable in the present reality. This is compounded by the fact that communities have boundaries and limits, which have beneficial as well as exclusionary roles. But rather than admit this and then say that we can do anything we want to other people lower on the economic food chain, Rambam's words should galvanize us to treat people in a way that reflects the "quality of piety and the way of wisdom."

This fundamental insight of refusing to treat foreign workers as the Other, as outsiders to be exploited and then forgotten, may be formulated even more sharply. Our religious tradition demands that we see an image of God whenever we step into the presence of another human being. This is equally true on all sides of the economic equation; whether this person is our worker or our employer, the individual must be treated with dignity, compassion and empathy. Rabbi Abraham Joshua Heschel, well known for his role as a social prophet and critic as well as a theologian, wrote as follows:

> There is no insight more disclosing; *God is One, and humanity is one.* There is no possibility more frightening: God's name may be desecrated … The image of God is in either every man or in no man …
>
> You shall not make yourself a graven image or any likeness of God. The making and worshiping of images is considered an abomination, vehemently condemned in the Bible. The world and God are not of the same essence. There can be no man-made symbols of God.
>
> And yet there is something in the world that the Bible does regard as a symbol of God. It is not a temple or a tree, it is not a stature or a star.

> *The symbol of God is man,* every man ... [who] must be treated with the honor due to a likeness representing the King of kings.[32]

The only fitting representation of the blessed Holy One is that of the human being, whose worth and capacity for growth are indeed immeasurable. Though it does not appear in every Talmudic discussion of inter-personal obligations, this spiritual ethos must be allowed to drive forward our reading of these texts and thus challenge our contemporary patterns of life as potentially immoral and complicit in desecrating God's sacred name.

Taking the message of Zeitlin and Heschel seriously means understanding that the project of Judaism is bigger than about a single people. As full participants in the modern economy, we must be careful in evaluating the way that categories inherited from antiquity and medieval times are to be applied. Indeed, our industrialized (and post-industrial) and increasingly globalized economies do not easily square with the economic systems found in classical rabbinic discourse from the Mishnah into the early modern period.

Rambam's ethical framing is helpful for reminding us that we are left with a clear choice, one that confronts us each and every day. Do we exploit people who have been forced by our consumer-driven economy into the modern equivalent of slavery? Our responsibility is not necessarily linked to active exploitation. Simply tolerating systematic injustices and complicity in the face of suffering is bad enough.

Do we strive to treat all people, including workers and laborers, as full members of our community, expansively defined, with dignity, honor, and compassion? Furthermore, do we have the courage to draft economic policies in light of these values? Have we the mettle to make choices, as consumers, to drive them forward? An excellent first step is to encourage our families and communities to purchase items under the auspices of organizations like Fair Trade, supporting movements and groups that help workers enforce their rights, and so forth. Buying organic produce and other sustainable agricultural goods is important, of course, but stamps that help us avoid environmental degradation do not necessarily help alleviate the profound human cost of our decisions. On a daily basis, we make choices, directly and indirectly, that force us to ask the question: are we treating each member of our global society as an *'eved 'ivri*, as a dignified worker to whom we are bound with covenantal regulations?

---

32 Abraham Joshua Heschel, *The Insecurity of Freedom: Essays on Human Existence* (New York: Farrar, Straus & Giroux, 1966), 95. Italics in the original.

Or have we allowed him or her to become like *'eved kena'ani*, nothing more than a de-humanized tool for satisfying our consumer hungers?

Beyond the Bottom Line

The Hasidic master Rabbi Nachman of Breslov was gravely concerned with the way that human beings are easily controlled by their lust for money. Such anxiety lies at the heart of one of his famous tales, which were remarkable in their ability to speak to the imagination and the heart. The story known as the "Tale of the Master of Prayer" includes a striking caricature of a rich but feckless country that is has been corrupted by their obsession with money.[33] The land is a place of great wealth—indeed, it is the source of money—but the inhabitants behavior is bizarre and their mannerisms peculiar. As the tale continues we learn that these oddities stem from their craven system of values. Anticipating the objectivist philosophy of Ayn Rand by over century, Rabbi Nachman's fictional kingdom measures the worth of an individual by their richness and fortune alone. The wealthiest of all, of course, is the king, but he is also the most depraved. This Hasidic tale is a tale of greed run amok to the point of absurdity, yet at the same time it is a chilling tale that has proven to be an unfortunate portend of modern economic realities.

Rabbi Nachman was gravely concerned about the human lust for money and the ethical collapse that inevitably follows the un-tempered quest for riches. In his collection of sermons, he offers a fascinating bit of exegesis about the power of the commandment to free us from fixating upon profit as an ultimate, self-standing goal:

> "I have commanded the ravens to sustain you" (1 Kings 17:4). This is like the aspect of *tzedakah*. When one begins to give alms, he must shatter the innate cruelty (*akhzariyyut*) and transform it into compassion. This is the essence of service of *tzedakah* (*avodat ha-tzedakah*). One may be compassionate by nature, giving tzedakah because of this innate compassion, but this is not such a great service. There are many kinds of compassionate animals. The essence of the service is the break through the callousness and transform it into compassion. This is "I have commanded the ravens to sustain you"—the raven is naturally a cruel bird, but it is transformed [through the divine command] into compassion to sustain Elijah. So too we must accomplish with *tzedakah*. It is thus for all those who poses a

33 Arnold J. Band, *Nahman of Bratslav: The Stories* (New York: Paulist Press, 1978), 211–50.

giving heart. A giver must, at the very beginning of the path, stride forward and overcome this level.[34]

Our natural impulse is to keep things to ourselves, protecting the self at the expense of the other. To erect boundaries and keep what is mine, mine. But a *mitzvah* has the power to open us up to helping others. These sacred deeds open the heart and allow us give with a sense of purpose. The precipitating commandment behind Rabbi Nachman's exegesis may have been distributing alms, but it applies equally to paying our workers and creating a moral economy more broadly. One must break the yearning for money as an end goal, or even the highest priority. The human life is so much more than that. We must shatter the idea that one's financial holdings or material possessions should provide a rubric for worth or value.

Hasidic sources often interpret the word *mitzvah* as related to the Aramaic *tzavta*, or "connection." The commandments effect the bond between the worshiper and the Divine, and performing these sacred deeds makes it possible to step beyond one's ordinary consciousness and into the dimension of the holy. But this moment of connectivity that links us to God also has the power to bind us to other people. The commandments allow us to transcend our ordinary consciousness, to rise above our concern and to look toward others. Giving alms is one expression of this. Treating our workers with a sense of respect, compassion, dignity is another.

In his vision of the rebuilt Jerusalem, the prophet Zechariah offers the following dream: "So says the Lord of Hosts—old men and women will once again dwell in the streets of Jerusalem; each person with staff in hand, because of their [lengthy] days. The streets of the city will be filled with boy and girls playing in its squares" (Zechariah 8:4–5). Rabbi Meir Leibush ben Yehiel Mikhel Weiser, better known by his acronym MaLBIM (1809–1879), seemed to have been troubled by the mundanity of this prediction. Other biblical prophets refer to redemption in far grander and more magnificent terms, so why should the simple fact that youthful and aged people once again inhabit the holy city herald the dawn of a new era? The remarkable beauty of Zechariah's vision, suggests the MaLBIM, is precisely in the ordinariness: "Addressing the concern that Darius might exile them from the land a second time, [Zechariah] explains that "old men and women will once again dwell in the streets of Jerusalem," promising a peace so enduring and great

---

34 *Likkutei Moharan, Tinyana*, no. 4.

that even the weak—the elderly and the children—will walk in the streets without fear."[35]

We are called to envision a time in which the disempowered and disenfranchised can walk in the middle of the road. In some cases, frailness stems from old age or youth, but in our contemporary society "the weak" have been made so—vulnerable and defenseless, they have been abused—because of predatory economics and apathetic lack of concern for those in need. Zechariah's vision calls us to task and reminds us to fight for those who have been pushed to the margins, vulnerable workers who toil out of sight and out of mind. The dream of redemption is rooted in our ability to grant them dignity, confidence, and peace.

---

35 My thanks to Rabbi Yonatan Cohen for drawing this source to my attention.

CHAPTER 2

Judaism and The Crisis of the Rural Village in the Global South

Rabbi Micha Odenheimer

Torah as a Guide for the World

For many of us nourished and inspired by the integrity and spiritual depth of the Orthodox tradition, how to apply Torah to meta-issues which are not obviously legislated by *halakhah* and codified in the *Shulhan Arukh* is a burning, urgent question, for if the Torah can no longer inspire us and guide us in transforming the human future, it means that we have lost our connection with its ethical core.

The subject of this chapter—developing a Jewish ethical stance towards poor farmers in the Global South—evokes this question in two ways: First, can specific legislation from the Torah, directed as it was to an agrarian society in a remote historical era, help us think through contemporary issues of poverty and the environment? And second, can *mitzvot* which were, at their origin, meant only for Israelite society guide us in the universal human arena?

Exploring these questions in this chapter is a worthwhile, but fully exploring them would take volumes. Nonetheless, it is important to acknowledge these questions as they are hiding in clear sight waiting to be discovered. There are ample sources in the Jewish tradition, both ancient and contemporary, to support the notion that the Jewish ethical imagination includes all of humanity in its vision and embrace. For example, Rabbi Yehuda Ashlag, perhaps the twentieth century's most influential Kabbalist, makes the extension of "Love your neighbor as yourself" to include all of the peoples of the world a cornerstone of his philosophy.[1] Also pertinent is the Baal Shem Tov's statement that the principle of *arvut*—mutual responsibility (as in "All if Israel are responsible

---

1   See Baal HaSulam, "Introduction to the *Book of Zohar*," item 19.

for one another")—and its application to non-Jews in regards to the Seven Noahide commandments.[2] One of the Noachide commandments is to build a fair and righteous system of justice and governance. In an increasingly globalizing world, our responsibility is thus to do our part to ensure that humanity's governing structures and conceptions are fair and just. Echoing Rav Kook's admonishment to listen to our own inner moral compass, means that even if these sources and authorities did not exist, our enmeshment and power in a globalized world means that we must apply our ethical tradition in the broadest possible way. If we are global in everything we do, from the food we eat to the gas we put in the car, from the clothes we wear to the stocks we own, our ethics must also be global in scope or our Judaism stands to lose something critical of its soul.

The working thesis of this chapter is that Torah contains a vision for human life that can and should help guide us in thinking through contemporary challenges and issues even though circumstances have drastically changed. The biblical scholar Norman K. Gottwald rendered it this way: "So we are left with the logically perplexing but morally empowering paradox that the Bible is both grossly irrelevant in direct application to current economic problems and incredibly relevant in *vision* and *principle* for grasping opportunities to make the whole earth and its bounty serve the welfare of the entire human family."[3] Our task is thus two-fold: understanding the contemporary situation in the Global South, and teasing out of our tradition, Biblical and Rabbinic, the "incredibly relevant' vision and principles that can guide us in choosing an ethical path.

Why Small Farmers Matter

I became aware of the centrality and significance of small farmers in the contemporary human story in Kathmandu, where the organization I founded in 2007, Tevel b'Tzedek, was first situated. Contemplating the various forms of poverty and enslavement in Kathmandu, from slums to street children to trafficked women, I came to realize that everything led back to the rural village. All over Nepal—in fact, all over the Global South—the rural village, where seventy percent of the population still lived, was in crisis. The most acute symptom was that many villages were not growing enough food to feed their population

---

2 See Yitzhak Buxbaum, *The Light and Fire of the Baal Shem Tov* (New York: Continuum, 2006), 301–2.

3 Norman K. Gottwald, *The Hebrew Bible in its Social World and in Ours* (Atlanta, GA: Society of Biblical Literature, 1993), 364.

year-round. The result was a cycle of temporary, then permanent, migration: either to slums, to factories where the work and living conditions were injurious to human health and dignity, or to menial jobs abroad, separated from family for years at a time, deprived of civil and political rights. Leaving villages meant abandoning community and culture for anonymity. Exile from community, for the rural Nepalese and many others, meant leaving a place where you had some voice in local and regional politics for a situation where you were completely powerless.

The crisis of the rural village, I came to realize, was arguably *the* root cause of poverty in the Global South. There are 1.5 billion people who are part of small farming families, and another billion depend on these farms for food; the majority of the population in Asia and Africa.[4] The international definition of small farmers refers to those who own ten hectares (about twenty-five acres) of land or less, but most small farmers work much smaller plots—often less even than an acre. The profound sadness of exile is, of course, one of the enduring themes of the Torah and the Jewish people throughout history, from the expulsion of Adam and Eve from the Garden of Eden to Jeremiah's lament for the people of Judea. Is this enough of a reason to care about the massive exile of small farmers from their land? Don't most small farmers *want* to leave their farms for the big city? Aren't cities in any case the wave of the future? And aren't large, mechanized, monoculture farms more effective in feeding the world than small farms?

The fate of small farming communities has huge significance beyond the lives of the farmers themselves—economic, political and ecological. In a shifting, volatile world, the food security of the poorest nations still depends on small farmers. Indeed, eighty percent of the food in Sub-Saharan Africa and Asia is grown by small farmers Although many contemporary "Green Revolution" agronomists argue that large mechanized farms produce more food per acre then small farms, that is the case only when one looks one year at a time. Over the long term, mechanized farms, with their mono-culture, dependence on fossil fuel fertilizers and chemical pesticides, deplete soil fertility. Small farms, according to United Nation reports, produce substantially more food in the long term than large farms. According to the Factsheet on Smallholders Food and Agriculture Organization of the United Nations while seventy-five percent

---

4 Sarah K. Lowder, Jakob Skoet, and Terri Raney, "The Number, Size, and Distribution of Farms, Smallholder Farms, and Family Farms Worldwide," *World Development* 87,16–29, https://doi.org/10.1016/j.worlddev.2015.10.041.

of the world's food is produced through twelve plant and five animal species,[5] making the world food supply "highly vulnerable to shocks." This means that small farmers are one of the key guardians of our biodiversity, storing seeds from hundreds of species and thousands of subspecies, including climate and pest resilient strains.

Large-scale, corporate farming produces many calories per acre of corn or soy, but always at enormous environmental cost. In contrast to small farms, these farms are monoculture, and need copious amounts of chemical fertilizer, herbicides, and pesticides that do great harm to the biosphere. A handful of giant firms now control seventy-five percent of the world's grain trade, chemical inputs (pesticide and herbicide), and seeds.[6] An extensive study by the *New York Times* showed conclusively that genetically modified (GM) seeds did not increase yields overall.[7] Instead, GM products were being used primarily in order to sell herbicide made by the company Monsanto by tweaking corn and other crops so that they would be immune to these poisons, which could then be used to destroy competing plants. Of course, the rest of the natural world is not immune to Monsanto's herbicides; their increased use has led to wide scale poisoning of the earth and water, with potentially disastrous results for human health. Even more fundamentally, how much power over our food system is safe to place in the hands of giant corporations, whose sole focus is continued and expanded profit?

Environmentally, small farmers have an intense and intimate relationship with soil, water, and forests, and their presence on the land often prevents erosion and desertification. Small farmers rely on a magic triangle between the health of farmland, domestic animals and surrounding forests or wilderness: Villagers need the forests to bring fodder for their animals and need the animals to fertilize the farms. In Nepal, when forests were the property of the government, they were exploited for timber by private individuals and companies and often almost completely denuded, causing erosion and soil degradation. Thirty years or so ago, communities were put in charge of regulating the usage of community

---

5 See Antony Joseph Raj and S. B. Lal, *Agroforestry: Theory and Practices* (New Dehli: Scientific Publishers, 2014), 627.

6 For more information, see James M. MacDonald. "Mergers and Competition in Seed and Agricultural Chemical Markets." USDA ERS - Mergers and Competition in Seed and Agricultural Chemical Markets. April 03, 2017. Accessed March 28, 2018. https://www.ers. usda.gov/amber-waves/2017/april/mergers-and-competition-in-seed-and-agricultural-chemical-markets/.

7 Danny Hakim, "Doubts About the Promised Bounty of Genetically Modified Crops," *New York Times*, October 29, 2016, page A1.

forests; the forests have miraculously rebounded. Sometimes, when well protected by strong government, wilderness thrives better in pristine isolation from man, but often, it is the presence of sustainable human community that prevents the wholesale ravaging of the wild.

The exodus of small farmers from their farms is also a major cause of instability and potential violence in Asia and in Africa. The genocides in Sudan (Darfur) and Syria, for example, would likely not have happened without the prior displacement of hundreds of thousands of small farmers because of climate change. In Sudan, the expulsion of farmers from their land by elites catalyzed the creation of the Janjaweed militias, who carried out the massacres against the people of Darfur. In Syria, small farmers pouring into the cities were a significant trigger of the initial non-violent demonstrations, to which government forces loyal to President Bashar al-Assad responded with murderous force, sparking the broader civil war. For all of these reasons—the fate of the farmer's themselves, the impact on environment and the food system, and the connection between floods of internal refugees and civil war, the fate of small farming communities is an issue that deserves our attention and thought.

Why are Farming Villages in Crisis?

In order to understand how ethical guidance from the Torah might be relevant in shaping our thinking on small farmers, we first have to understand why villages are in crisis today. The answer is multi-dimensional, but it's important to say at the outset that much has to do with policies and practices, which could, with political will and wisdom, be corrected or ameliorated. The list of challenges facing farming villages are all tied to climate change. While urban-dwelling Westerners may already be alarmed by shifts in the weather, for the world's 1.5 billion small farmers these changes make their life impossible. When weather becomes less predictable or more extreme, crops fail. In Nepal, during the monsoon season, the same amount of rain falls as once did, but in short violent bursts which the saturated earth cannot absorb. For the hill villages, this means that the springs the villages relied on for water throughout the dry season now go dry with months to go until the next big rain. Downhill, in the flat-lands, the villages, homes and crops alike, are devastated by flooding. In East Africa, drought is moving millions of pastoralists and farmers from their ancestral homes, in search of food, water and grazing land.

Other environmental factors in our ecologically challenged age have been negatively influencing small farmers for the last half-century. Moses tells us that the Land of Israel is not like Egypt, where the earth is watered by the Nile River (Deuteronomy 11:10–12). Instead, it is a land of micro-environments, which must be tended to constantly and sensitively—something small farmers do. As new technologies, trade routes, and agreements have opened the hinterland to both local businessmen and international corporations, the logging, mining and fishing industries, as well as factories and dams built to provide electricity, have stripped hillsides from forests, causing erosion and desertification, and poisoned and diverted water systems. During the Green Revolution, from the mid-1960s onward, governments and producers pushed chemical fertilizers and pesticides to small farmers, without providing them with enough instruction on its safe use. Fertilizers and pesticides both poisoned the land, and also weakened ancient agriculture practices. All these factors together have reduced soil fertility by as much as thirty percent in even remote farming villages.

Two other major factors in the crisis are population growth and international economic policy. Perhaps the most effective international humanitarian project of the last half century has been the World Health Organization's vaccination program. Many of the diseases that used to kill children no longer do; this has resulted in population growth in many regions and thus further fragmentation of land. Awareness and availability of family planning, however, is now reducing population growth, especially in Asia. If villages were aided in becoming more prosperous, other jobs, in teaching, solar energy, agricultural inputs, and much more could absorb much of the increase in population.

International economic policy and trade agreements have deeply affected small farmers as well. After aggressively seeking to lend money to developing countries in the 1970s, offering low interest and the promise of large returns on investment in industry and infrastructure, the United States raised interest rates precipitously in 1980. That year also marked the rise of three Western leaders—Ronald Reagan in the United States, Margaret Thatcher in Britain, and Helmut Kohl in Germany—who were all adherents of neo-liberal economic theory, as taught by Fredric Hayek and Milton Friedman. These leaders placed the International Monetary Fund (IMF) and the World Bank in the hands of neo-liberal economists while also promoting general trade agreements which eventually morphed into the World Trade Organization.

When countries all over the Global South began to default on their loans, because of the high interest and much lower returns on investment than had been predicted, the IMF bailed the countries out in return for their agreement to accept draconian Structural Adjustment Programs, which followed the economic ideas of what became known as the "Washington

Consensus." These programs required governments to cut taxes and their budgets, especially for social services such as education, health services, and agricultural extension (more on agricultural extension in a moment). SAPs imposed a variety of measures, including the devaluation of local money, that would ensure the ease of foreign investment. One of the goals of the Washington Consensus was to integrate the Global South into the global economy, specifically by moving these countries from an emphasis on food self-reliance, which had marked policy in the post-colonial age, to growing specialty items—coffee, tropical fruits, spices—for the United States and the European market. At the same time, the United States and Europe continued their long-held policies of providing billions of dollars of subsidies to their farmers, exporting their grain and rice subsidies to developing countries at cut-rate prices, and increasing what Richard E. Bell, US Undersecretary of Agriculture called "agri-power, which, along with military might, is a major bulwark of the United States' position in the world."[8]

The accrued result of these policies has been devastating for small farmers in the Global South. Agricultural extension—meaning expertise, seeds and other inputs provided by the government—is crucial if small farmers are to grow enough from small plots of land. The downsizing or elimination of these programs, because neo-liberal economists believed that government must be downsized to make way for private enterprise, crippled small farmers. Often, so did the increased presence of corporate agricultural conglomerates, which bought up land, sucked up water, and used their influence with the government to take over the very areas once cultivated by small farmers. Reliance on specialty items like coffee meant extreme vulnerability to fluctuations in the global market. The high cost of seeds and other inputs controlled by giant corporations has caused millions of farmers to fall into debt; over 200,000 small farmers have committed suicide in India alone since 1997, largely because of debt, and often, ironically, by swallowing pesticide.[9]

Wholesale devastation was also caused by the influx of cheap grain and other products from the West. President Bill Clinton's remarkable confession in this regard relates to Haiti but is valid for several dozen other countries and crops as well, from Jamaica to Malawi, from Mexico to Bangladesh:

---

8   National Crimes Record Bureau of India, as quoted in, Suvojit Bagchi, "Punjab Suicides Cast Shadow on Polls." BBC News. April 12, 2009. Accessed March 3, 2017. http://news.bbc.co.uk/2/hi/south_asia/7992327.stm.

9   Ibid.

Since 1981, the United States has followed a policy which we are now rethinking, that we rich countries that produce a lot of food should sell it to poor countries and relieve them of the burden of producing their own food, so that thank goodness they can leap directly into the industrial era. It has not worked. It may have been good for some of my rice farmers in Arkansas, but it has not worked. It was a mistake. It was a mistake that I was party to, I'm not pointing the finger at anybody. I did it. I have to live every day with the consequences of the loss of capacity to produce a rice crop in Haiti to feed those people.[10]

The Torah on Food, Land, and Basic Human Needs

In building a Torah perspective on issues of agriculture and economics, I begin with the following premise: Basic human need, according to the Torah, transcends considerations of ownership, profit, or market. A passage in Exodus makes this quite clear, in talking about the collateral—a blanket or night-garment—given for a loan by a poor person. The lender is required to return it each night because: "It is his covering, his garment for his skin. With what shall he sleep? This passage is moving in its simplicity, telling in the fact that all the Torah needs to do is to evoke the feeling of the blanket on bare skin and to ask: "With what shall he sleep?"[11] A basic human need is more important than the right to possession of the blanket which was transferred in order to pressure the borrower into returning his loan. With what shall he sleep? How will she eat? How will they be healed? Whose heart can fail to resonate with what is obvious to the Torah: basic human needs are their own argument, with no need to justify beyond a question which doubles as an outcry.

Earlier, in a key part of its pedagogical narrative, the Torah contrasted the economy of Egypt with what might be called God's economy. The economy of Egypt is based on the centralized hoarding of food. Food serves in Egypt as capital—in fact, Joseph uses it to buy out all the remaining cattle, land and even the persons of the starving Egyptians. The Israelites—whose slavery is a consequence, it seems clear, of the centralization of power in Pharaoh's hand that Joseph helped engineer—make bricks for gigantic food storage silos. After Moses appears, Pharaoh punishes the Israelites with a kind of hyper-slavery,

---

10 See Mats Lundahl, *The Political Economy of Disaster: Destitution, Plunder and Earthquake in Haiti* (New York: Routledge, 2013), 274.

11 Exodus 5.

where they have to produce their quota of bricks without the straw they were once provided. This is an image of labor alienated not only from the laborer's needs, but also from his capabilities.[12]

Then comes the *manna*, and its main characteristic: no matter what you do, you can't gather more than what each family member needs that day—an *omer* (about 2.3 liters) per person. If you try to store it, it rots.[13] The command is given to place a jar with an *omer* of *manna* in the holy of holies, along with the Tablets, broken and whole, of the Ten Commandments. Thus the amount each person needs to eat each day, *the fact* that each person needs to eat each day, becomes a religious symbol par excellence. Over and above all else, to me this means that keeping in mind the basic human need to eat must be at the center of our religious consciousness.

The economic program which the Torah commands on entry into the land integrates the values emphasized in the *manna* story with a society of small farmers, each with their own relatively small plot of land. There is much to say about the radical stance towards economics that emerges from the Torah's social justice legislation—the equitable redistribution of land every fifty years, which means that harvests, not land, are all that is ever owned, the sabbatical year with its periodic repudiation of ownership, the absolute prohibition against interest, debt forgiveness every seven years, and other commandments Remembering again Gottwald's distinction between "direct application" to current economic problems and "vision and principle" one significant take away from the Torah's narrative and laws is that economic power, and especially food power, should be widely distributed, not concentrated in the hands of the few. Pharaoh's food power equals slavery, while the *Manna*, which can't be hoarded or stored, is produced and collected in absolute equity. The Jubilee and the prohibition against interest are aimed at preventing the kind of massive control over food and livelihood that the giant monopolies that threaten to make small farmers history would have us embrace. If, in fact, a Jubilee-like reform that gave land to the tiller, along with micro-credit schemes that gave small farmers access to cash at low or no interest were instituted, much of the poverty in the Global South could be overcome.

The Talmud, and in its wake the *Shulhan Arukh*, absorbed and even sharpen the Torah's natural aversion to the control and manipulation of

---

12 Genesis 47:13–20.
13 Exodus 16: 15–34.

agricultural products for profit.[14] The Talmud (in tractate *Megillah*), explores the meaning of the ninth blessing in the Amidah prayer, the blessing for rain and thus an abundant year, takes the interpretation in an unexpected direction. One might think that the prayer for rain would be one of the most straightforwardly vertical of requests. After all, rain (along with birth and the revival of the dead) is one of the three elements whose keys remain in God's hands alone. But the blessing for rain, says Rav Alexandrai, the only sage who weighs in, is aimed at foiling speculators in basic foodstuffs. These speculators, who are called "wicked," "ambush the poor" by taking advantage of a year of poor rainfall to create even more scarcity by buying and hoarding food. The prayer for rain is aimed at stopping the speculators before they can begin. Fifteen hundred years or so before Nobel Prize-winning economist and Harvard University Amartya Sen, whose book *Poverty and Famine* demonstrated the political and economic nature of famine, the Talmud was deeply aware that the hunger of the poor was connected at least as much to human greed as to nature's failures.[15]

A thousand years later, the *Shulhan Arukh* codifies the Talmud's insight into a series of quite astounding laws:

- "It is forbidden to deal commercially in the Land of Israel with (food) products that are essential for life but instead this farmer should bring from his storehouse [i.e., bring directly from what they have grown and stored to sell to the consumer, with no middleman] and sell and this farmer should bring from his storehouse and sell, in order that prices remain cheap."

- It is forbidden to store agricultural produce that is essential for life in the Land of Israel or in any place where the majority are Jews. When is this said? When one is storing foodstuffs from the marketplace, but if one stores from one's own field that is permissible. But when there is a famine, one must not store more than enough to feed your family for one year.

- Whosoever raises prices through speculation or stores essential foodstuffs in the Land of Israel is considered (as bad) as one who lends with interest.

---

14 *Shulhan Arukh* 231; 23–26.

15 See Amartya Sen, *Poverty and Famines: An Essay on Entitlement and Deprivation* (New York: Oxford University Press, 1981).

One must not export essential food products out of the Land of Israel, or to a place that is a majority Jewish outside the Land of Israel, including to Syria. And not from one kingdom to another in the Land of Israel.[16]

The phrase "In the Land of Israel or any place where the majority are Jews" is a practical restriction, not a mandate to confine our ethnicize our ethics: These are laws that demand communal adherence; individual observance will not have the desired effect of keeping the price of essential foods low, thus they are relevant only in a place where Jews have majority power.

From these remarkable *halakhot* one learns, first of all that keeping food cheap enough for everyone to enjoy in abundance is a basic Jewish value, and that, in the eyes of the *Shulhan Arukh* (echoing the Talmud's deep suspicion of middlemen), this means creating a direct line from local farmers to the local population. This is reinforced with by the law against exporting basic foodstuffs even to an adjacent Jewish kingdom. The dictates of the free market have their place, but not when it comes to basic human needs—there, the commercial must be circumscribed.

Much thinking still needs to be done, but, to this writer at least, it is clear that the vision and principles of the Torah favor keeping in place a local and de-centralized food system, safe from the manipulations that are the inevitable result of large-scale commercialization and the profit motive. This means that, as Jews, we should seek to support those environmental and economic measures which protect and enable small farmers. Battling climate change, deforestation, poisonous pesticides and herbicides is a must, as is encouraging food self-reliance by allowing global south countries to limit food imports, which usually begin cheaply to undercut local farmers and put them out of business but are expensive and unreliable in the long run.

Although small farmers are in crisis, climate change and other challenges can be mitigated by a wide array of techniques. Governments and international organizations should be encouraged to make agricultural instruction and aid, specifically for small farmers, a priority. Peaceful land reform, such as that which took place in South Korea and Taiwan in the 1940s and 1950s and helped establish their economies, should be supported, as should micro-credit and micro-savings schemes that allow small farmers to access cash to invest in their land, and make them less vulnerable to market forces.

---

16 *Hoshen Mishpat* 231; 23–26.

In her book, *Scripture, Culture and Agriculture*, Ellen F. Davis, a professor at Duke Divinity School, writes on the prophetic concern with cities, where the political and financial elite were concentrated:

> What is often overlooked is the extent to which the prophetic judgment of the city's righteousness (or unrighteousness) reflects a central agrarian concern. Righteousness is a question of who controls the land that feeds the city and fuels the royal trade economy, and who works that land; A question of who has plenty to eat and drink and who does not; a question of who reaps the profits from the land's fruitfulness.[17]

In our day and age, replacing "royal" with corporate, these prophetic questions remain as penetrating as ever.

Conclusion: The Inside of the Soup

Although I have focused this chapter primarily on the economic, political, and environmental reasons to support small farmers within our food system, I wish to end by adding that there are spiritual reasons to preserve a place for the production of food which is human and intimate rather than industrial and alienated. In *Avot of Rabbi Nathan*, we find this striking statement:

> Rabbi Ahai ben Josiah says: He who purchases grain in the market place, to what may he be likened? To an infant whose mother died, although he is taken door to door to other wet nurses, he is not satisfied.
>
> He who buys bread in the market place, what is he like? He is as good as dead and buried.
>
> He who eats of his own is like an infant raised at his mother's breast.[18]

In addition, Rabbi Shlomo Carlebach (my teacher) put it this way:

> You know the difference between eating soup in a restaurant or eating soup ... I'm coming to somebody she made soup for me with so much love and [she gives] it to me. We've learned it a thousand times. It's very simple. The deepest question is: Are you receiving the outside of the soup or the inside of the soup? Is it **your** soup or just soup? If I go to a

---

17 Ellen F. Davis, *Scripture, Culture and Agriculture: An Agrarian Reading of the Bible* (New York: Cambridge University Press, 2009), 156.

18 *Avot d'Rabbi Natan* 1:30–B.

restaurant and I pay five dollars for a plate of soup, it's not really my soup. I ate it and I paid for it. If someone loves me very much and they are giving me soup, it is my soup. And you know, friends, when someone gives me soup, and it's my soup, basically then I don't need anything anymore. It's so good. It's so good." [19]

Are we raised at our mother's breast or are we orphans? Food is not only calories and molecules. The ethics, intention, and emotions that go into producing our food are the inside story of the food, and they affect us and determine what kind of world we are living in. Standing idly by while small farmers are forced from their land into slums and factories is not an option, not if we want our human civilization to receive "the inside of the soup" that we so desperately need.

---

19 From tape transcribed by Rabbi Shlomo Katz.

CHAPTER 3

Let Them Have a Little Bread

Rabbi Marc Gitler

In the fourth year of the reign of Darius the Great, with the building of the Second Temple well underway, the prophet Zechariah receives a prophecy regarding fasting. The prophecy pertains to a question posed by the Jews in the Diaspora: "Shall I weep in the fifth month, separating myself as I have done these past years?"[1] Since the Temple's rebuilding was nearing completion, the Jewish community wanted to know if it was necessary, or even appropriate to continue fasting on the ninth of Av.[2] The question is understood in a variety of different ways,[3] but it is God's remarkable answer that is most striking and instructive: "When you fasted and lamented in the fifth and seventh month these 70 years, did you fast for My benefit?"[4]

According to the medieval commentator Ibn Ezra, Zechariah is supposed to tell the people that God never commanded the Jewish people to fast. Rather, they need to absorb and practice the messages delivered by the earlier prophets when the first temple still stood. Messages that Zechariah succinctly summarizes as "Execute true justice, act kindly and compassionately with each other. Do not oppress the widow, the orphan, the stranger or the poor."[5] The message of creating a just and kind society was ignored by the Jews during the First Temple period, and as a result, the temple was destroyed, and Israel was left as a wasteland. At the outset of the Second Temple period, God tries once again to

---

1 Zechariah 7:2. According to the majority of commentators, Rashi, Radak, Ibn Ezra, etc., the question was sent from Babylon. Ibn Ezra records the view of the Karaite commentator Yefet Ben Ali that the question was posed by Judean officers.

2 Av is the fifth month of the Jewish calendar. When God responds in verse 5, He also mentions the fast of the seventh month. This refers to the fast of Gedaliah.

3 Some examples of the different ways to understand the question include: 1. Are those in the Diaspora still obligated, but not the Jews in Judea? 2. Do we need to fast now, since the temple is not yet fully built, but when it is fully built we will not? 3. Is this temple as great as the first? If not perhaps we still need to fast.

4 Zechariah 7:5.

5 Ibid., 7:9–10.

impress on the people that if Jerusalem is to become the *ir ha'emet* (city of truth) then it must, first and foremost, be a place of kindness, compassion, and justice.

Two and a half thousand years later, God's response remains relevant to all areas of Jewish life and tradition. Yet, this chapter explores only the original issue raised: fasting. What can we do to make the six yearly fast days not just days that we are hungry on, but also an opportunity to improve our communities?

The prophet Isaiah relays the ineffectiveness of fasting as a means to receive divine favor some two hundred years earlier.[6] In the fifty-eighth chapter of the book of Isaiah, Isaiah gives voice to the Jewish people's surprise, and disappointment, that their fasts have not brought about divine protection. He records their questions: "Why when we fasted did You not see? We afflicted ourselves and You didn't take notice?"[7] Isaiah's answer is immediate: even on fast days you exploit your workers. Your fasting results in more strife and struggle and is thus ignored in the heavens. Isaiah then describes the fast that God wants: the unlocking of wickedness and the untying of the yoke of the oppressed. In addition to the general statements of social justice, Isaiah refers to one specific deed, sharing your food with the hungry, three times in the verses that follow the discussion referenced *supra* in Chapter 58. God's message is straightforward: abstaining from food will get you nowhere but sharing food with those who face hunger will result in the Divine mercy that you seek.

Presumably Isaiah's message was not heeded by the inhabitants of Jerusalem during his lifetime. We do not know whether the Jewish people heeded Zechariah's advice to build a just society, but the Rabbis of the Talmud thought enough of Zechariah's idea to make it the *haftorah* on Yom Kippur morning.[8] It seemed obvious to them that, at the time of our most intense fasting and prayer, we needed a blatant reminder that at all times, we must act with compassion to those in need.

Fast-forwarding a number of centuries, the Talmud revisits the idea of feeding the hungry as a necessary aspect and outcome of fast days. In *Mesechet Sanhedrin*, Rabbi Elazar reports a teaching he heard from Rabbi Yitzchak: "Any fast day on which the distribution of charity is delayed [overnight] it

---

6 Yeshayah was an eighth-century BCE prophet who prophesied during the reign of four Judean kings Uziah, Yotam, Achaz, and Chizkiyahu. According to the Talmud in BT *Yevamot* 49B, he was killed by Chizkiyahu's son Menashe.

7 Isaiah 58:3.

8 BT *Megillah* 31a. This is one of the rare instances when the customs of various different communities Ashkenazim, Sephardim, Romanite, and Yemenite align.

is as if blood was spilled."[9] The implication of the frightening statement is actually wonderful; the Jewish community was following Isaiah's charge and sharing their bread with the hungry. Isaiah's charge was now an accepted practice. Another statement in the Talmud further demonstrates the centrality of the custom: In the opening chapter of *Mesekhet Berakhot*, the Talmud records a number of different *mitzvot* where the reward for the *mitzvah* is not given for simply performing the *mitzvah*, but rather for an associated action. Included in the list is "the reward from fasting derives from the charity dispensed."[10] Rashi, referencing the aforementioned notion in *Mesechet Sanhedrin*, explains that it was customary to distribute food to the hungry in the evening after the fast. The connection between the pieces, I believe, is much stronger. Providing for the hungry is not just an appropriate and natural outcome of a fast day, but rather the central and essential outcome of the fast day. This statement is a repackaging of Isaiah and Zechariah's messages. Indeed, God doesn't care whether one has eaten or not, but He really cares that one takes care of those in need. Share bread with the hungry, then the merits from fasting will come.

Rabbi Shmuel Eidels (Krakow, 1555–1631, known as Maharsha), in his commentary on the piece in *Mesekhet Berakhot*, raises a question regarding fasting. The Talmud asserts that *mitzvot lav lehanot nitnu*—one is not allowed to attain a benefit from the performance of a commandment.[11] Fast days, he argues, present a problem, because those who fast benefit by saving money that they would have otherwise spent on food and drink. Rav Eidels opines that this is the reason why the Talmud orders us to donate to charity on fast days. In order not to attain even a scintilla of benefit, he suggests that one calculate the costs of food saved when fasting, and to donate those monies to charity.

Despite Isaiah and Zechariah's charges, despite the Talmud's repackaging of the idea and the frightening warning, despite the codification of the idea by

---

9 BT *Sanhedrin* 35a. The Talmud continues by explaining that the need for same day delivery only applies in a place where ready to eat products, such as figs and dates, were delivered to the hungry, but in places where money, or ingredients are given, the distribution can take place the next day. Either way, clearly the Talmud is advocating that hunger relief must be part and parcel of the fasting experience. Despite the fact that this line is presented as *Aggadic*, Maimonides codifies it as law *Mishneh Torah: Matanot Aniyim* 9:4

10 BT *Berakhot* 6b. Other examples include attending a *shiva* house, where the merit is garnered due to silence, and the merit of repeating a lesson learned is improving its understanding.

11 BT *Rosh Hashanah* 28a.

the Rambam[12], and the *halakhah* underpinning of the law by the Maharsha,[13] the idea is no longer well known. In 2015, in order to both raise needed funds for the hungry, and to restore the centrality of charity to the fasting experience, I founded Fast for Feast. The mission of Fast for Feast is to raise money for the hungry and bring meaning to fast days by reclaiming the ancient custom of donating the dollars saved by fasting. All donated funds are divided, with half sent to local hunger relief organizations, and the other half sent to feed the hungry in Israel.

In founding Fast for Feast, I was attempting to both give individuals a tangible benefit of a fast day, and also create a charity that everyone can participate in. I hope and pray that it is one of many such initiatives that heed the challenges of the great prophets of the past *lehachzir Atarah Leyoshnah* (to return the crown to its glory), to restore the crown of our bygone days, when the leaders of our people pushed for a Judaism that was not about preservation of the past, but rather the creation of a just society in the present. If we are able to create such a society, one that is concerned with the hungry and homeless, those abused and those neglected, then the utopian answer of Zechariah to the Jews of Babylon will come true: "The fast of the fourth month, and the fast of the fifth month, and the fast of the seventh month, and the fast of the tenth month shall become for the house of Judah times of joy and happiness and holidays."[14]

---

12 Rambam *Mishneh Torah: Hilchot Matanot Aniyim* 9:4.
13 Maharsha: Commentary on *Mesekhet Berakhot* 6b.
14 Zechariah 8:19. The verse ends with the words *Haemet Vehashalom Ahavu* ("But you must love honesty and integrity"). The Radak, Metzudat Zion, and others explain that these words are conditional, if we love and act with honesty and integrity, then these fast days will serve as joyous times.

CHAPTER 1

תשובה בעניני צער בעלי חיים

Rabbi David Bigman

שאלה

לכבוד הרב ביגמן,

אני עובד כשוחט בבית מטבחיים. נהוג פה להשתמש בשיטת "כבילה והנפה"
(shackle and hoist). בשיטה זו, לפני השחיטה קושרים את הבהמה מרגליה ומניפים
אותה באוויר כשראשה כלפי מטה. השיטה נועדה לייעל את תהליך השחיטה, אך
במהלכה נגרם לבהמה סבל רב. האם שיטה זו מותרת על פי ההלכה? ואם לא, האם עליי
להתפטר מעבודתי בגין האיסור?

בברכה,

תשובה

עיקר שאלתך נוגע בגדרי איסור צער בעלי חיים. בשאלה זו דן הגאון רבי ישראל
איסרליין, בעל תרומת הדשן, באחת מתשובותיו. אמנם הוא נשאל שאלה אחרת לגמרי
אך תשובתו נוגעת גם בשאלה שלך.[1] מפאת חשיבות התשובה אצטט אותה במלואה
ואסבירה בקצרה, ולאחר מכן אדון בדבריו. כך הוא נוסח השאלה:[2]

אם למרוט נוצות לאווזות חיים, אי דומה לגיזת כבשים או אי הוו צער בעלי חיים?

---

[1] ולא זו בלבד, יש לזכור שהשאלות בספר תרומת הדשן הן שאלות שעלו בתקופתו ובמקומו של המהרא"י,
אך הוא ניסח את השאלות בלשונו, בין אם נשאל על ידי אדם בקהילתו בין אם לאו. גם השאלה כאן
מנוסחת בלשון וכרשימה של מקרים שונים ביחס לבעלי חיים. ועל כן ברור שתשובתו היא תשובה
עקרונית לשאלה ואינה נוגעת רק למקרה פרטי זה או אחר.

[2] תרומת הדשן, פסקים וכתבים, סימן קה.

גם לחתוך לשון העוף כדי שידבר, ואזנים וזנב מכלב כדי ליפותו.

כך היא תשובתו של המהרא"י:

נראין הדברים דאין אסור משום צער בעלי חיים אם הוא עושה לצורכיו ולתשמישיו.

ומביא המהרא"י ארבע ראיות לשיטתו:

1. דלא נבראו כל הבריות רק לשמש את האדם, כדאיתא פרק בתרא דקידושין.

2. ותדע דבפ' ב' דב"מ חשיב פריקה צער בעלי חיים, וא"כ היאך מותר משא כבד על בהמתו להוליכו ממקום למקום הא איכא צער בעלי חיים? וכ"ת אין הכי נמי, הא אמרינן התם דרבנן דר"י הגלילי סברו דאפילו תחת משאו שאין יכול לעמוד בו חייב לפרוק, וכי ברשיעי עסקינן?

3. ואמרינן נמי פ' שמונה שרצים דאמר ר' יוסי הרוצה שיסתרס תרנגולו יטול לכרבלתו, והשתא תיפוק ליה דאסור משום צער בעלי חיים.

4. ואמרינן נמי פ' אין דורשין אמרו ליה לבן זומא מהו לסרוסי כלבא? משמע הלשון דלכתחילה קבעו, והשתא תוכל לומר דמשום צער בעלי חיים מותר.

ומקשה המהרא"י על שיטתו:

ואל תשיבני מהא דאמרינן פ"ק דחולין מהא דר' פנחס בן יאיר עקרינא להו איכא צער בעלי חיים.

דהתם לא קעבד לתשמישו וליפותו אלא כדי שלא יזיקו, וההיא היזיקא לא שכיחא כ"כ, דמסתמא רבינו הקדוש לא הוה מגדל מזיק תוך ביתו כדתניא שילהי פ"ק דב"ק /דף טו:/ מנין שלא יגדל אדם כלב כו' ת"ל לא תשים דמים בביתך.

אלא דרבי פנחס בן יאיר מתוך רוב חסידותו הוה קפיד.

מכל מקום הכרעתו של המהרא"י לגבי המקרים המיוחדים שהציג בשאלתו, שבהם צער בעלי חיים אינו נצרך אלא לצורך קלוש של האדם, אינה נחרצת:

ומתוך הלין ראיות הוה **נראה קצת דליכא איסור** בכה"ג.

ומוסיף את ההערה המרתקת הבאה:

אלא שהעולם נזהרים ונמנעים, ואפשר הטעם לפי שאינו רוצה העולם [לנהוג] מדות אכזריות נגד הבריות, שיראים דילמא יקבלו עונש על ככה. כדאשכחן פ' הפועלים גבי רבינו הקדוש בההוא עגלא דתלא לרישה בכנפיה, דרבי אמר זיל לכך נוצרת. ואף על גב דהיתר גמור הוא לשחוט העגל לאכילתו, אפ"ה נענש וקבל יסורין על ככה.

אח"כ הגידו לי שנמצא כן בפסקי ר"י בפ"ק, ועוד דליכא איסור צער בעלי חיים אא"כ דאין לו ריווח והיינו דלעיל.

כלומר, אף על פי שיש מקום להתיר על פי ההלכה, נהגו ישראל להימנע מאכזריות כלפי בעלי חיים!

גם תלמידו של תרומת הדשן, האיסור והיתר הארוך, פסק להתיר צער בעלי חיים במקום של תועלת לאדם:

[. . .] וכתב התו' בעבודה זרה אף על פי שצער בע"ח דאורייתא אם יועיל לאיזו דבר מותר עכ"ל. פי' לרפואה אפילו אין בו סכנה.[3]

הרמ"א מביא את פסקו של תרומת הדשן בצורה חדה ובהירה בהגהה לשולחן ערוך, אבן העזר ה, יד:

כל דבר הצריך לרפואה או לשאר דברים, לית ביה משום איסור צער בעלי חיים (איסור והיתר הארוך סימן נט).

ולכן מותר למרוט נוצות מאווזות חיות, וליכא למיחש משום צער בעלי חיים (מהרא"י סימן קה). ומ"מ העולם נמנעים דהוי אכזריות.

לכאורה נסתם הגולל על כל ערעור הלכתי על צורת השחיטה שנהוגה במקום עבודתך, שהרי היא נועדה לתועלת האדם, במטרה לייעל את תהליך השחיטה, אף על פי שנגרם בה צער לבהמות. מאידך, ברור שאתה צריך להימנע מכל פעולה שמצערת את הבהמות סתם ואינה נצרכת לצורך הגידול הרווחי, שהרי לא הותר צער בעלי חיים אלא לצורך. מכל מקום, כבני תורה אין אנו פטורים מלדון בראיותיו של תרומת הדשן ובשיטות הראשונים בנידון.

בחינת הראיות

בשלב ראשון נבדוק את ראיותיו של תרומת הדשן לפסיקתו שאין איסור צער בעלי חיים במקרה של תועלת לאדם.

הראיה הראשונה היא מהגמרא בקידושין (פב ע"א):

ספר איסור והיתר הארוך, שער נט, סימן לו. אך מהתוספות המודפסים אצלנו משתמע שהפוך מדברי   3
האיסור והיתר, וכבר העיר על כך הנודע ביהודה בתשובותיו, מהדורא תניינא, יורה דעה סימן י: "ובאמת
בתוס' בע"ז דף י"א ע"א בד"ה עוקרין משמע היפך. וז"ל התוס' שם: וא"ת אמאי לא פריך והא איכא
צער"ב בשלמא משום בל תשחית ליכא כיון דלכבודו של מלך עושין כן אין כאן השחתה והוי כמו תכריכין
של מאה מנה אלא צער"ח היאך הותר ויל"ל דשאני כבוד המלך שהוא כבוד לכל ישראל ואתי כבוד דברים
ודחי צער"ח עכ"ל התוס'. וא"כ משמע מדבריהם דצער"ח חמיר מבל תשחית ואינו מותר אפילו לצורך
רק משום כבוד רבים". עיינו שם היטב גם בהמשך דבריו ועיין עוד שו"ת נודע ביהודה מהדורא תניינא -
יורה דעה סימן יג.

רבי שמעון בן אלעזר אומר: ראית מימיך חיה ועוף שיש להם אומנות? והן מתפרנסין שלא בצער, **והלא לא נבראו אלא לשמשני**, ואני נבראתי לשמש את קוני – אינו דין שאתפרנס שלא בצער! אלא שהורעתי מעשי, וקפחתי את פרנסתי.

ראיה זו נראית קלושה, שהרי אינה אלא דברי אגדתא, ואין הכרח לראותם כמחייבים להלכה. אך גם אם נקבל את העמדה שכל בעלי החיים נבראו רק כדי לשרת את האדם, אי אפשר להסיק מכך שמותר **לצער אותם** לכל הקשר של צורך האדם.

הראיה השניה היא ממחלוקת התנאים במסכת בבא מציעא (לב ע"א–ע"ב) אם יש חובה לפרוק כאשר יש משא יתר על הבהמה. המהרא"י טוען שלא ייתכן שהמשנה, המדברת בהווה, עוסקת ברשעים שעוברים על איסור צער בעלי חיים, ולכן נראה שאין איסור בהעמסת יתר על הבהמה. דא עקא, מהסוגיה משתמע הפוך. לדברי הגמרא, אפשר שתנא קמא סבר שיש לעזור משום שסבור שצער בעלי חיים הוא דאורייתא (אמנם יש לציין שהגמרא מתלבטת בשאלת הנימוק לקביעתו של תנא קמא):

. . . תדע דצער בעלי חיים דאורייתא, דקתני סיפא, רבי יוסי הגלילי אומר: אם היה עליו יתר [על] משאו – אין זקוק לו, שנאמר תחת משאו – משאוי שיכול לעמוד בו. לאו מכלל דתנא קמא סבר זקוק לו?

מאי טעמא – לאו **משום דצער בעלי חיים דאורייתא?** – דלמא בתחת משאו פליגי, דרבי יוסי סבר: דרשינן תחת משאו – משאוי שיכול לעמוד בו, ורבנן סברי: לא דרשינן תחת משאו . . .

ומסביר רש"י שם:

זקוק לו – ואמאי זקוק לו, אי משום מצות עזוב תעזב – הא כתיב משאו הראוי לו, אלא משום צער בעלי חיים.

כלומר, כאשר המשא מוגזם, לבעלים לא מגיעה עזרה בפריקה שהרי הוא העמיס על הבהמה מעל יכולת הנשיאה הנורמלית שלה, אך לבהמה מגיעה עזרה מדין צער בעלי חיים. כלומר יש אפשרות שהבעלים מעמיס על הבהמה יתר על המידה ועובר על איסור של צער בעלי חיים. אמנם אין זו ראיה מובהקת נגד תרומת הדשן, שכן אפשר לטעון שיש מצווה עשה לעזור בפריקה משום צער בעלי חיים אך אין איסור להעמיס יתר על המידה. מכל מקום הגמרא חושבת שיש בני אדם המעמיסים בהמותיהם יתר על המידה בצורה שאינה ראויה, ומוזר לטעון שאותם בני אדם שנוהגים שלא כהוגן אינם עוברים על איסור פורמלי, רק משום הטיעון הכוללני "וכי ברשיעי עסיקינן?".[4]

---

4 הטיעון "אטו ברשיעי עסיקינן" מופיע חמש פעמים בבבלי (יומא ו ע"א, יבמות לג ע"ב, כתובות קה ע"א, גיטין ל ע"ב, קידושין לג ע"א). השימושים שונים ומגוונים, ובמקרים הנידונים בסוגיות אלו קושיה ראויה, ומולידה או מאפשרת שינוי פרשני בסגנון האוקימתא. אין אף שימוש בקושיה "אטו ברשיעי עסיקינן" כדי להתיר את המעשה שנראה על פניו אסור, אלא להפך – מטרת הקושיה להעמיד את המקרה במעשה מותר, או לפחות בפחות "רשעות". השימוש של תרומת הדשן בטיעון הזה קשה ואינו הולם את הגמרות, שהרי על פי שימושו אין ספור איסורי תורה היו ניתרים.

הראיה השלישית של המהרא"י מיוחדת במינה:

[. . .] דאמר רבי יוחנן: הרוצה שיסרס תרנגול, יטול כרבלתו, ומסתרס מאליו. והאמר רב אשי: רמות רוחא הוא דנקיטא ליה!

שני משפטים אלו מופיעים בגמרא בשבת (קי ע"ב) בשקלא וטריא בנושא איסור סירוס, כאשר האמירה של רבי יוחנן היא הצעה איך לעקוף את האיסור. נטילת הכרבולת מצערת את התרנגול פעמים. ה"ניתוח" בעצמו כואב, וגם התרנגול "עצוב" כאשר אין לו כרבולת כפי שמעידים הדברים של רבי יוחנן – ואף על פי כן רבי יוחנן מורה כך, ואם כן נראה שלצורך כך הותר צער בעלי חיים. ראיה זו אכן נראית חזקה.[5]

גם הראיה האחרונה דומה לשלישית ונראית חזקה:

שאלו את בן זומא: מהו לסרוסי כלבא? אמר להם: ובארצכם לא תעשו – כל שבארצכם לא תעשו.[6]

וכך פירש רש"י במקום: "שאלו את בן זומא מהו לסרוסי כלבא – הואיל וסירוס כתיב אצל מומי קרבן, וכלב אפילו חליפיו אסור למזבח משום מחיר כלב, אסור לסרסו או לא". כלומר בן זומא אסר לסרס כלב רק משום שכלב נכלל באיסור לסרס בהמה, וחידושו הוא שגם כלב, שאינו קרב על המזבח, כלול באיסור סירוס. מכאן דייק המהרא"י: לולא איסור מיוחד של סירוס לא היתה שום בעיה של צער של בעל חיים. ראיה זו נראית על פניה כחזקה, אך צריך לזכור שהיא רק ראיה מהשואלים, ותשובת בן זומא שאוסרת סירוס כלב משום פסוק אינה שוללת נימוק אחר לאסור, מסיני או מדברי חכמים.

לאיזה צורך הותר צער בעלי חיים?

כאמור, פסיקתו של תרומת הדשן התקבלה להלכה, והרמ"א הביאה בהגהה על השולחן ערוך. בעקבות הכרעה זו דנו הפוסקים בעיקר בשאלה האם כל צורך מתיר איסור צער בעלי חיים.

הגאון הרב אליהו קלצקין חידש בספרו אמרי שפר (סימן לד) שכוונת האיסור והיתר שציטט הרמ"א היה לצורך רפואה בלבד, ולא סתם לרווח כללי. הוא הביא ראיה לשיטתו משקלא וטריא בגמרא בבבא בתרא (כ ע"א) על דברים שממעטים בחלון. הגמרא דנה שם בסתימת החלון על ידי בהמה כחושה, וזה לשונה: "בכחושה. פסיק שדי לה לכלבים! כיון דאיכא צער בעלי חיים לא עביד". הגר"א קלצקין טוען שהגמרא מניחה

5   וכן כתב גם הרב מרדכי יעקב בריש חלקת יעקב בשו"ת חלקת יעקב, חושן משפט, סימן לד: "המובחר שבראיות הוא מגמרא שבת קי"י ב' שציין הגר"א, הרוצה שיסרס תרנגול יטול כרבלתו ומסתרס מאליו הרי דבצורך מותר צעב"ח, דודאי יש צעב"ח בנוטל כרבלתו וכמבואר שם ברש"י דמשניטל הודו הוא מתאבל."

6   תלמוד בבלי מסכת חגיגה דף יד עמוד ב

שיש תמיד איסור צער בעלי חיים במקרה כזה, למרות שייתכן שהאדם מאכיל כלבים שברשותו שהוא חייב להאכילן, ולכן הוא מרוויח מהשימוש בבהמה הכחושה.

לראיה זו נחזור בהמשך. בינתיים חשוב לציין שפוסקים רבים חלקו עליו[7] ואף טענו שראייתו אינה חד משמעית כי מספיק **שלא נהגו** משום צער בעלי חיים ואין ראיה שזה איסור הלכתי ממש. וכן מוכח מלשון הרמ"א שאינו אוסר נטילת נוצה מאווזה היה משום צער בעלי חיים, אלא משום מנהג לא לנהוג באכזריות.[8] כלומר ברור שנטילת נוצה אינה לצורך רפואה אלא לצורך כתיבה, ותרומת הדשן והרמ"א לא אסרו זאת מעיקר הדין.

מכל מקום אי אפשר להמשיך בדיון בלי לציין אבחנות שהציעו רבותינו הראשונים בהקשרים שונים.

הראשונים נתקלו בסתירה פנימית בתוך סוגיית טעינה ופריקה שהוזכרה לעיל (בבא מציעא לא ע"א–ע"ב). בתוך אותו קטע של שקלא וטריא הגמרא טוענת בתחילה שעזרה בטעינה אינה מונעת צער בעלי חיים אלא רק עוזרת לבעלים, וכמה שורות אחר כך היא טוענת שבעזרה לבעל הבהמה לטעון יש גם יתרון שמשום צער בעלי חיים:

ולמה ליה למכתב פריקה ולמה ליה למיכתב טעינה? צריכי דאי כתב רחמנא פריקה הוה אמינא משום דאיכא צער בעלי חיים ואיכא חסרון כיס אבל **טעינה דלאו צער בעלי חיים** איכא ולא חסרון כיס איכא אימא לא; ואי אשמעינן טעינה משום דבשכר אבל פריקה דבחנם אימא לא; צריכא. [...]

למה לי למכתב הני תרתי ולמה לי למכתב אבידה? צריכי דאי כתב רחמנא הני תרתי משום דצערא דמרה **צערא דידה איתא** אבל אבידה דצערא דמרה איתא וצערא דידה ליתא אימא לא; ואי אשמעינן אבידה משום דליתא למרה בהדה אבל הני תרתי דאיתא למרה בהדה אימא לא; צריכא.

הריטב"א על אתר מסביר שיש דרגות שונות בצער בעלי חיים:

אבל טעינה דליכא צער בעלי חיים. פי' דליכא צערא כולי האי כמו בפריקה, אבל צער קצת איכא אף בטעינה וכדאמרינן בסמוך. ואי אמר הני תרתי משום דאיכא צערא דידה וצערא דמרה, והטעם כי הבהמה מצטערת כשטוענין אותה הבעלים לבדם ולא כשטוענין אותה שנים.

כלומר, עיקר מצוות פריקה הוא מניעת צער מהבהמה הכורעת תחת משאה. במצוות טעינה, מניעת הצער אינה עיקר המצווה ואף מדובר בצער פחות, אך בכל אופן כאשר טוענים בשניים מקלים על הבהמה, כפי שמסביר הרא"ש בתוספותיו על אתר:

---

7 ט"ז אבן העזר סימן ה, ח; שו"ת רב פעלים חלק א, יורה דעה, סימן א ד"ה והשתא מ"ש; שו"ת משנה הלכות חלק ד, סימן רלט, ד"ה משמע דס"ל; שו"ת עטרת פז חלק א, כרך ג, חושן משפט, סימן ט, ד"ה ונמצא לפי"ז.

8 שו"ת חלקת יעקב, חושן משפט, סימן לד. עיין שם בראיה היפה שלו מביאור הגר"א.

בהני תרתי דאיכא צערא דידה. ואף בטעינה איכא צער לבהמה כשאחד טוען לבדו טפי משנים שטוענין יחד, שמגביהין המשוי בקל על הבהמה.

את העיקרון של רמות שונות של צער מנצל הריטב"א להסביר עוד סוגיה תמוהה. בסוגיית "שורפים על המלכים" במסכת עבודה זרה (י"א ע"א) מביאה הגמרא ברייתא: "עיקור שיש בה טריפה – אסור, ושאין בה טריפה – מותר. ואיזהו עיקור שאין בה טריפה? המנשר פרסותיה מן הארכובה ולמטה". הריטב"א על אתר מסביר את ההבדל בין שני סוגי העיקור: "ואפשר דטעמא משום דהוי צער בעלי חיים טפי כשעוקרה במקום שעושה אותה טריפה", כלומר ההבדל בין העיקור המותר והאסור הוא בשאלה האם נגרם בגינו צער בעלי חיים.[9]

שנינו בשבת בסוגיה שעוסקת בביטול כלי מהיכנו (קנד ע"ב):

חמורו של רבן גמליאל היתה טעונה דבש ולא רצה לפורקה עד מוצאי שבת, למוצאי שבת מתה. והאנן תנן: נוטל כלים הניטלין! – כשהדביש. – הדביש למאי חזי? – לכתיתא דגמלי. – ויתיר חבלים ויפלו שקין! – מיצטרו זיקי. – ויביא כרים וכסתות ויניח תחתיהן! – מטנפי, וקמבטל כלי מהיכנו. – **והאיכא צער בעלי חיים!** – קסבר: **צער בעלי חיים דרבנן.**

ופירש רש"י שם:

והא איכא צער בעלי חיים – וליתי דאורייתא ולידחי דרבנן, ביטול כלי מהיכנו.

קסבר – רבן גמליאל צער בעלי חיים דרבנן, ופלוגתא היא באלו מציאות.

אך הרמב"ן דן בפירוש זה של רש"י וחולק עליו:

אלא ש"מ דהכי פירושא כדאמרן והא איכא צער בעלי חיים [וקא עבר אדאורייתא ופריק קסבר צער בעלי חיים] דרבנן ובמקום פסידא לא גזור.[10]

כלומר הרמב"ן סבור שהקושיה אינה מול האפשרות של ביטול כלי מיהכנו, אלא שאם צער בעלי חיים דאורייתא, הוא מחייב גם הפסד ממון. אלא שלפי הגמרא רבן גמליאל סבור – שלא כהלכה – שצער בעלי חיים אינו אלא דרבנן, ולכן אינו חושב שחובה לפרוק מעל הבהמה את הסחורה.

הר"ן דחה את עמדת הרמב"ן, ושיטתו מקבילה לשיטת תרומת הדשן שפסק הרמ"א:

ולי נראין דברי רש"י ז"ל עיקר, משום דאפי' דמ"ד צער ב"ח דאורייתא – ה"מ שלא לצורך תשמישו של אדם אבל לצורך תשמישו ושמירת ממונו ודאי שרי, שאם לא תאמר כן אסור להטחין חמור ברחים מפני צער בעלי חיים. אלא ודאי לצורך

---

9   אך עיינו שם היטב בהצעותיו האחרות לפרש את ההבדל בין סוגי העיקור.

10 חידושי הרמב"ן, שבת קנד ע"ב. ועיינו עוד ברשב"א ובריטב"א שם.

תשמיש של אדם לא חייישינן לצער בעלי חיים כלל, וכיון שכן היכי מקשינן והא איכא צער בעלי חיים? וכי משום צער בהמתו יפסיד דבשו ומדותיו? הא ודאי לא!

בסוף דבריו מציין הר"ן שנראה שהרמב"ם סבר כשיטת הרמב"ן, וזו לשון הרמב"ם בהלכות שבת (כא, ט–י):

עלה באילן בשבת – בשוגג מותר לירד, במזיד אסור לירד. בבהמה – אפילו במזיד ירד משום צער בעלי חיים. וכן פורקין המשאוי מעל הבהמה בשבת משום צער בעלי חיים. כיצד, היתה בהמתו טעונה שליף של תבואה מכניס ראשו תחתיו ומסלקו לצד אחר והוא נופל מאליו; היה בא מן הדרך בליל שבת ובהמתו טעונה [...] היו השקים גדולים ומלאים כלי זכוכית וכיוצא בהם פורק בנחת, ומכל מקום לא יניחן שם על גבי בהמה משום צער בעלי חיים.

החזון איש (שבת, סימן מח, ז) תירץ את קושיית הר"ן על הרמב"ן ודעימיה:

נראה דס"ל לרמב"ן ורשב"א אף על גב דליכא משום צער בעלי חיים בדרך עבודת הבהמה, אבל צער מרובה שלא כדרך עבודתה אלא צערא בעלמא אסור, והלכך חייב להשליך משאה אף בהפסד ...

דברים אלו הולמים את הסיפור של רבן גמליאל, שכן הבהמה מתה מרוב מעמסה, ומתאימים גם לפירוש רש"י בסוגיא פריקה וטעינה. וידוע שרש"י מפרש כל סוגיה בצורה ההולמת אותה ואינו נוהג להצליב סוגיה מול סוגיה.

סיכום הלכה למעשה

מצאנו שהראשונים חלוקים בגדרי צער בעלי חיים. לר"ן ולתרומת הדשן יש הגדרה מחמירה וחדה של צער בעלי חיים – כל צער במשמע. דא עקא, מאחר שבסוגיות שונות הותר לצער את בעלי החיים, ההגדרה החדה של צער גורמת לראשונים אלו להקל ולהתיר צער בעלי חיים בכל מקום של צורך בני אדם.

לעומתם חשבו הרמב"ן ודעימיה שמשא הראוי לבהמה אינו בגדר צער בעלי חיים ולכן מותר, ובכלל אין להגדיר כל מאמץ המוטל על הבהמה כצער בעלי חיים. כלומר לשיטתם גם לצורך האדם לא הותר צער בעלי חיים, אלא שלא כל שימוש בבעלי חיים מוגדר צער. וקשה עליהם הסוגיות עיקור הבהמה וסוגיית נטילת הכרבולת,[11] שם מדובר במובהק בצער בעלי חיים ומותר.

אין ברירה וצריך לומר שהריטב"א, שאף הוא סבור כמו הרמב"ן, השלים את התמונה באמרו: "ואפשר דטעמא [לאסור עיקור שיש בו טריפה] משום דהוי צער בעלי חיים טפי כשעושה במקום שעושקרה אותה טריפה". כלומר יצאנו עם הגדרה מדורגת: משא

---

11 אף על פי שטענתי שהדיוק של תרומת הדשן מסוגיית סירוס כלב אינו חד-משמעי, דברי הריטב"א המוצעים להלן יכולים לשמש הסבר גם לסוגיה זו, אם כי אפשר להניח שסירוס כואב יותר מנטילת כרבולת.

שהבהמה מורגלת בה אינו אסור משום צער בעלי חיים, ואילו משא כבד שעלול לסכן את הבהמה או להזיק לה נחשב צער בעלי חיים ואסור. גם ב"ניתוחים" חד פעמיים האיסור תלוי במידת הסבל בטווח הקצר ובטווח הארוך.

והנה הגענו למקרה שלך. שיטת השחיטה שתיארת תלויה לכאורה במחלוקת הראשונים. העינוי של הבהמה גדול ומסתבר שלפי שיטת הרמב"ן ודעימיה שיטת ה"כבילה והנפה" אסורה משום איסור דאורייתא[12] של צער בעלי חיים. אך לפי שיטת הר"ן ותרומת הדשן שנתקבלה להלכה כל מה שהוא צורך האדם מותר, וכך גם שיטת השחיטה הנדונה.

אזכיר בהזדמנות זו את שיטת הגר"א קלצקין שנזכרה לעיל, שאף לשיטת המקלים אוסר אם לא נעשה לצורך רפואה.[13] כמו כן ראוי להזכיר את מחלוקת הפוסקים על מריטת נוצות לצורך שחיטה,[14] וכן את הדיון על גדרי צורך האדם שבא לידי ביטוי במקרה של עז שקרניו עקומות ואינן מאפשרות שחיטה אלא בצורה שתהיה כשרה בדיעבד, ונחלקו הפוסקים אם מותר לחתוך את הקרניים כדי לאפשר שחיטה כשרה לכתחילה.[15]

למעשה, משורת הדין, אין אתה חייב להתפטר מעבודתך שכן יש למשחטה על מי לסמוך והיא הלכה פסוקה; אך ראוי לבן תורה להחמיר בדין תורה, וראוי שתחפש עבודה שאינה תלויה במחלוקת הראשונים במצווה דאורייתא.

משום אכזריות

מכל מקום אין אנו פטורים מלדון בהמשך הדברים של תרומת הדשן, שנותן עוגן למנהג שלא ליטול נוצות מאווזות חיות משום אכזריות. ואמנם יש מי שטוען שהמנהג הוא רק לעניין הזה ואין להרחיבו לשום עניין אחר,[16] אך דעתי אינה נוחה מעמדה זו שנסמכת בעיקר על התקציר של הרמ"א במפה ואינה יורדת לעומק דעתו של תרומת הדשן. נצטט שוב את דבריו ונדון בהם:

אלא שהעולם נזהרים ונמנעים, ואפשר הטעם לפי שאינו רוצה העולם [לנהוג] מדות אכזריות נגד הבריות, שיראים דילמא דתלא עגלא דתלא לרישה בכנפיה, דרבי אמר זיל לכך נוצרת. ואף על גב דהיתר גמור הוא לשחוט העגל לאכילתו, אפ"ה נענש וקבל יסורין על ככה.

12 ומצאנו מי שסבור אחרת. עיינו בספר יראים, סימן קמב [דפוס ישן: שנב]: "וצער בעלי חיים דרבנן ואתי דרבנן ומבטל דרבנן . . . "

13 אמרי שפר, סימן לד; ועיינו גם שו"ת שבות יעקב חלק ג, סימן עא.

14 שולחן ערוך, יורה דעה כד, ח, ועיינו פתחי תשובה שם. עיינו גם בשו"ת עטרת פז חלק א, כרך ג – חושן משפט, סימן ט, שדן על בסיס זה בשאלת ניסויים רפואיים בבעלי חיים.

15 עיינו בשו"ת רב פעלים, יורה דעה חלק א, סימן א, ובהערת הגר"ע יוסף, שו"ת יביע אומר חלק י – יורה דעה, סימן נח.

16 ילקוט יוסף, שבת ד הערות, סימן שכד – דיני הכנת מאכל לבהמה בשבת.

כלומר, העולם נזהר בצדק להימנע מדבר שהוא היתר גמור שמא יענשו על כך. דברים אלו נראים תמוהים: אם ההנהגות הללו מוגדרות כמותרות, היאך סבר המהרא"י שהחשש של העולם להיענש בגינן הוא חשש מוצדק?

כדי להבין את דברי המהרא"י עלינו לחזור על הדברים המפורסמים של הרמב"ן על "קדושים תהיו" (ויקרא י"ט, ב):

וזה דרך התורה לפרוט ולכלול בכיוצא בזה, כי אחרי אזהרת פרטי הדינין בכל משא ומתן שבין בני אדם, לא תגנוב ולא תגזול ולא תונו ושאר האזהרות, אמר בכלל "ועשית הישר והטוב", שיכניס בעשה היושר וההשויה וכל לפנים משורת הדין לרצון חבריו, כאשר אפרש בהגיעי למקומו ברצון הקדוש ברוך הוא. וכן בענין השבת, אסר המלאכות בלאו והטרחים בעשה כללי שנאמר "תשבות", ועוד אפרש זה בע"ה.

ובמקום אחר, על "ועשית הישר והטוב" (דברים ו', יח):

וזה ענין גדול, לפי שאי אפשר להזכיר בתורה כל הנהגות האדם עם שכניו ורעיו וכל משאו ומתנו ותקוני הישוב והמדיניות כלם, אבל אחרי שהזכיר מהם הרבה, כגון "לא תלך רכיל", "לא תקום ולא תטור", ו"לא תעמוד על דם רעך" "לא תקלל חרש", "מפני שיבה תקום", וכיוצא בהן, חזר לומר בדרך כלל שיעשה הטוב והישר בכל דבר, עד שיכנס בזה הפשרה ולפנים משורת הדין, וכגון מה שהזכירו בדינא דבר מצרא, ואפילו מה שאמרו "פרקו נאה ודבורו בנחת עם הבריות", עד שיקרא בכל ענין תם וישר.

למרות המסורת הרחבה של תורה שבעל פה, שדנה ברבות הימים על הרבה מבוכות שונות שהזמן גרמן, אין ההלכה מכסה כל מכלול ההתנהגויות הרצויות. היא משאירה מרחב פתוח לפרט ולכלל לעלות במעלות תיקון המידות ובמעלות הקודש מעבר לדרישות של ההלכה. כך נוצרים מנהגים יפים שאין להם ביסוס בהלכה מסוימת, אך הם ביטוי נאמן ל"דרך ה' לעשות צדקה ומשפט", וכדברי הרמב"ם בהלכות דעות (א, ה–ו):

ומצווין אנו ללכת בדרכים האלו הבינונים והם הדרכים הטובים והישרים שנאמר "והלכת בדרכיו". כך למדו בפירוש מצוה זו, מה הוא נקרא חנון אף אתה היה חנון, מה הוא נקרא רחום אף אתה היה רחום, מה הוא נקרא קדוש אף אתה היה קדוש.

אמנם אדם ששומר קלה כחמורה אינו ראוי לעונש, אך צאן קדשיו מבינים באינטואיציה עמוקה את המשמעות של שמירת ההלכה היבשה בלי הרוח המחיה שלה, וחשים ראויים לעונש אם אינם מתעלים בשעת מבחן.

לפי הרא"י"ה קוק, ההבחנה זו בין ההלכה לבין לפנים משורת הדין אינו נובע רק מקושי טכני לכסות את כל המקרים, אלא מעקרון מקודש. כך כותב הרב באגרת פט:

ודע עוד, שההחזיון של הכחות המתפתחים לטובה ולאורה מצד כח התורה הוא הולך במערכה, עד כמה ראוי שיהיה נובע מכח הדין והמשפט ועד כמה ראוי

שיהיה נובע דוקא מטוב הלב ומהסכמה פנימית בלא שום מעיק כלל, אפילו מועקה מוסרית. וזהו היסוד שאנו מחברים תמיד אבות ברית עם כל הדברים היותר עקריים, וברית ארץ ישראל היא מחוברת מחזקת ירושת אבות וקבלת התורה.

אמנם האבות קיימו את התורה מהכרה פנימית וחפשית, וזה היתרון ראוי שלא יחסר על חלק גדול מהמציאות המוסרית, וזהו יסוד החלקים הגנוזים שהמה יוצאים דוקא בתור מדות חסידות ולפנים משורת הדין, שאם היו באים בתור הלכה הכרחית היו מטשטשים את ההדרכה הקבועה, להיות הולכת הלוך ואור לדורות עולם ולהיות לאור גויים ועמים רבים לפי מעלות רוחם השונה מאד. כי הצד המוסרי שצריך להימצא בתור נדבה ואהבת חסד הוא צריך לעולם להיות לו משקל נודע לפי הערך המוסרי הכללי החיובי, כערך האויר החופשי לעומת הבניינים והמעשים הקולטוריים הממלאים אותו, שאי אפשר שלא ישאירו בעבורו מקום רחב מאד. ומה שצריך להסתפח על פי נדבת הרוח וחופש הרצון הטוב חייב להרשם בתור מדת חסידות. ואין לשער גודל ההפסד, שהיתה התרבות האנושית סובלת, אם אלה המדות הנעלות היו נקבעות בקבע חיובי. כי רק מה שהוא יותר הכרחי לחיים החמריים והמוסריים בהווה, ופוגע אם יחלש להשרשת העתיד, זה נכנס באזהרה, וגדול המצווה ועושה, אבל מה מה שקולע לעומק הטוב בהיותו עומד ומתפשט בתור טל של תחיה לימים יוצרו, מבלי לפגוע ברכותו וספוגיותו את כל מטרת העילוי העתידי, זכה להקבע בתור נדבה ואהבת חסד. זהו גורל ה"לפנים משורת הדין", שמאד יפעל לטובה לעת אשר יהפך לב האבן אשר לבני אדם ללב בשר. על כן אותו החלק הנשאר לפנים משורת הדין מוכרח להישאר במדתו, וכל אשר תתרומם האנושיות יצאו מדות-החסידות מרשות היחיד לרשות הרבים, ויהיו קנין כל העם, "וכל בניך לימודי ד'".

במילים פשוטות: העובדה שההלכה אינה מכסה חלק ניכר מהההתנהגויות הרצויות היא חשובה וראויה. חשוב שנהיה מודעים לכך שיש מרחב עצום בעולם לפעול לטובה גם מעבר לחובות המוטלות עלינו על פי ההלכה. כל אדם מסוגל, על פי נטיותיו וכישרונותיו ובהתאם לנסיבות חייו, לפעול להיטיב עם בריותיו יתברך גם במקום שאין התייחסות מפורשת בש"ס ובפוסקים.

לסיכום

ראוי לבית מטבחיים להימנע משימוש בשיטת "כבילה והנפה", שתלויה במחלוקת הראשונים. אף לשיטת תרומת הדשן שנפסקה להלכה, שמותר לצער בעלי חיים גם לצורך מועט, ראוי להימנע מכך כי יש בשיטה זו משום אכזריות. הרגישות שלך היא במקום, ויש מקום לשכנע את בעלי המשחטה לנהוג אחרת. מכל מקום, כל עוד פרנסתך תלויה בכך אין צורך שתתפטר שכן יש לנוהגים בשיטה זו על מי לסמוך.

CHAPTER 2

Animal Suffering and the Rhetoric of Values and *Halakhah*

Rabbi Dov Linzer

INTRODUCTION AND SYNOPSIS

In the discourse of factory-farmed meat and the Jewish tradition, a recurring theme is whether the Talmudic concern for animal suffering, or *tza'ar ba'alei hayyim* (hereafter, *tbh*), should deem the practice of producing such meat a violation of Jewish law and whether those who consume such meat should be deemed *misayei li'dei ovrei aveirah*, accessories to those who are engaged in a sinful activity. At the core of this question is whether, and to what degree, *halakhah* (Jewish law) permits one to cause animal suffering if it is for the purpose of satisfying a human need or desire.

The purpose of this chapter is not to make a *halakhah* argument for or against eating factory-farmed meat. It is rather to look at the arguments employed by *poskim* (decisors of Jewish law) when giving *halakhah* rulings on the question of whether one is permitted to cause animal suffering when done to serve human needs. More specifically, we will see how *poskim* use rhetoric to dissuade or prohibit certain behavior that they deem morally offensive or in violation of Torah values but which is not forbidden as a matter of Jewish law.

In Jewish tradition, the primary arena of one's religious obligations is the observance of *halakhah*, a highly technical and rule-based system. Within this system, a *posek's* role is to give *halakhah* rulings; the questioner wants to know if a certain behavior is permitted or forbidden, and it is assumed that she will act in accordance with the ruling that she receives. In contrast, it is quite possible that a statement about the morality of a particular act will be not be attended to since it lacks binding legal force. In such a case, it is not enough to state the moral claim. The *posek* must persuade the questioner why she should care about acting in accordance with Torah values not embodied in *halakhah* rules.

In doing so, the *posek* must engage in a rhetoric that is absent from more standard *halakhah* rulings. While our focus will be on the rhetoric that is employed, we will also take note of the substance of the argument. On what basis does the *posek* argue that such extra-*halakhah* concerns be followed?[1]

In addition to making a persuasive argument why one must act in accordance with Torah values, the *posek* must also demonstrate why a particular case is indeed a violation of such values. This is similar to the *posek's* need to argue compellingly that a certain behavior is a violation of Jewish law. When it comes to Jewish law, however, the authoritative texts are well-known; a *halakhah* argument is based on the Talmud, the codes, the commentators, previous responsa and accepted practice. But what are the "texts" (written or otherwise) on which to base an argument about the nature and scope of a Torah value? In the writings of the first two *poskim* we consider, we will see a number of different genres of texts that are used to serve as the basis for determining what is and what is not a Torah-based value.

We start with a brief overview of the Talmud's approach to animal suffering and then analyze three responsa, one by Rabbi Israel Isserlein (fifteenth century), one by Rabbi Yehezkel Landau (eighteenth century) and one by Rabbi Moshe Feinstein (twentieth century). These three responsa by major Ashkenazic *poskim* are central to contemporary *halakhah* discussions on the topic of causing animal suffering. All three responsa grapple with the challenges that emerge when there is a gap between Torah values, which in their understanding dictate that one must refrain from certain actions that cause animal suffering, and *halakhah* which permits such actions. Of particular interest to us, all three also operate with an implicit understanding that *halakhah*

---

1 Both primary and secondary sources address the question of whether an obligation exists to act in accordance with Torah values and what the nature of that obligation is. The most relevant primary source is Ramban, *Commentary on the Torah,* Leviticus 19:2, Deuteronomy 6:18 and Deuteronomy 23:24. Classic articles addressing this question are: Saul Berman, "Law and Morality," *Encyclopedia Judaica* 10 (1971) 1480–84; Yeshayahu Leibowitz, "Religious Praxis," *Judaism, Human Values, and the Jewish State,* Cambridge: Harvard University Press (1992), 12–21; Aharon Lichtenstein, "Does Jewish Tradition Recognize An Ethic Independent of Halakha," *Modern Jewish Ethics,* ed. Marvin Fox, Ohio: Ohio State University Press (1975), 62–88, Saul Berman, "*Lifnim Mishurat Hadin,*" *Journal of Jewish Studies* 26, no. 1 (1975): 86–104; 28, no. 2 (1977): 181–193, Walter Wurzberger, "Covenantal Imperatives," in *Samuel K. Mirsky Memorial Volume,* Jerusalem: Sura Institute for Research; New York: Yeshiva University (1970), 3–12 and his collection of essays in *Covenental Imperatives,* Jerusalem: Urim (2008). To some degree, the entire enterprise of *ta'amei hamitzvot*—to the degree that it is not a purely academic enterprise in theology—can be said to be based on the assumption that the underlying values of the *mitzvot* are relevant to how we live our lives.

rulings will always achieve greater compliance than values-based dicta. As we will see, each one these *poskim* responds to this challenge differently.

Tza'ar Ba'alei Hayyim: Permission, Obligation, Prohibition

The Talmud rules that concern for the suffering of animals is a Torah-based principle and that a person may violate Rabbinic restrictions in order to allevi-ate such suffering.[2] One application of this principle is that a person may have a gentile milk his cows for him on Shabbat since the cows will be in pain if they are not milked.[3] This principle, as articulated, gives the person the right to violate a Rabbinic prohibition in order to alleviate an animal's suffering but does not *obli-gate* the person to act to alleviate such suffering if she has no interest in doing so.

The principle of *tbh* could demand action; *tbh*, as understood by the Talmud,[4] lies at the core of the Biblical commandment to remove burdens from an animal struggling beneath its load (Exodus 23:5). One could reasonably argue that the Biblical concern for *tbh* translates into a general obligation to alleviate animal suffering when one sees it. This general obligation, however, is not found in either the Talmud or *Shulhan Arukh* and is debated by the *poskim*.[5]

It is generally agreed that one may not actively inflict pain and suffering on an animal, although this is also never stated explicitly in the Talmud. The question that arose in the post-Talmud period was whether the prohibition of causing or inflicting suffering applies even when the purpose of doing so is to serve human needs. The fact that the Torah permits eating meat was not seen as sufficient evidence to answer this question since it is possible to slaughter an animal without inflicting pain. Similarly, use of beasts of burden, which is permit-ted, was also not dispositive, since that exertion does not necessarily entail pain.[6]

The Responsum of *Trumat Ha'deshen*

The question of inflicting animal pain for the sake of human benefit received extensive treatment by Rabbi Israel Isserlein (1390–1460, Germany-Austria)

---

2 BT *Shabbat* 128b.
3 *Shulhan Arukh, OH* 305:1.
4 BT *Bava Metzia* 32a–b.
5 These *poskim* include: *Shulhan Arukh Ha'Rav*, Laws of Animal Suffering, 4; *Minhat Hinukh.* 80:1; *Maharam Shik*, 80.
6 See *Tosafot, Avodah Zarah* 11a, *s.v. okrin*, who state that one may not inflict suffering on ani-mals to serve human needs except in special cases. In contrast, Ramban, *Avodah Zarah* 13b, *s.v. u'li'divrei*, and *Piskei Tosafot, Avodah Zarah* 11a, assert that it is always permitted when done for the sake of human benefit.

in his work, *Trumat Ha'deshen*.[7] *Trumat Ha'deshen* is written as a collection of responsa, but it is well-known that the author composed the questions to which he was responding. In this responsum, the author discusses the gap between *halakhah* obligation and Torah values in cases of *tbh*; this requires him to articulate the reason why extra-*halakhah* Torah values should be followed. Here is the responsum (I have subdivided it; the translation is mine):

[א] אם למרוט נוצות לאווזות חיים, אי דומה לגיזת כבשים או אי הוו צער בעלי חיים? גם לחתוך לשון העוף כדי שידבר, ואזנים וזנב מכלב כדי ליפותו,

[ב] נראין הדברים דאין אסור משום צער בעלי חיים אם הוא עושה לצורכיו ולתשמישיו. דלא נבראו כל הבריות רק לשמש את האדם, כדאיתא פרק בתרא דקידושין)דף פ"ב ע"א(.

[ג] ותדע דבפ' ב' דב"מ)לו ע"א(. . .

[ד] ומתוך הלין ראיות הוה נראה קצת דליכא איסור בכה"ג

[ה] אלא שהעולם נזהרים ונמנעים, ואפשר הטעם לפי שאינו רוצה העולם [לנהוג] מדות אכזריות נגד הבריות, שיראים דילמא יקבלו עונש על ככה. כדאשכחן פ' הפועלים [ב"מ פה ע"א] גבי רבינו הקדוש בההוא עגלא דתלא לרישיה בכנפיה, דרבי אמר זיל לכך נוצרת. ואע"ג דהיתר גמור הוא לשחוט העגל לאכילתו, אפ"ה נענש וקבל יסורין על ככה.

[ו] אח"כ הגידו לי שנמצא כן בפסקי ר"י בפ"ק, ועוד דליכא איסור צער בעלי חיים אא"כ דאין לו ריוח והיינו דלעיל.

[A] Is it permitted to remove the feathers of geese while they are alive? Is this similar to sheering sheep [which is permitted] or is [it forbidden for reasons of] animal suffering? Similarly, is it permissible to cut the tongue of a bird to enable it to speak, or the ears and tail of a dog to make it look attractive?

[B] It appears that there is no prohibition regarding pain to animals if one is doing it for his needs and his various uses for all creatures were created only to serve man (BT *Kiddushin* 82a).

[C] A proof to this may be found in BT *Bava Metzia* (36a) ...

[D] From all these proofs it would seem, at least somewhat, that there is no prohibition in these types of cases.

[E] Nevertheless, people are scrupulous and they refrain [from doing this]. And it is possible that the reason is that the people do not want to act in a cruel way against living creatures, for they are afraid

---

7 *Trumat HaDeshen* 2:105.

lest they be punished as a result. As we find in BT *Bava Metzia* 85a regarding Rabbi Yehudah *HaNasi* and the calf [which hid in its cloak to avoid being slaughtered and] to whom he said, "Go, for it was for this that you were created." Although it was totally permissible for him to slaughter the calf to eat it, nonetheless, he was punished and he endured suffering as a result (i.e., due to his callousness).

[F] After I wrote this, I was told that it is written in *Piskei R"I,* first chapter [of *Avodah Zarah*], that there is no prohibition of causing pain to animals except in the case where there is no resulting benefit—as I have written above.

Rabbi Isserlein begins by presenting three cases of animal suffering and asks if causing suffering is permitted in these cases as they bring some benefit to humans (section A). In terms of the degree of benefit, the three cases are not the same. The first case—plucking goose feathers—provides a potential source of income. The second and third cases are ones of more trivial benefits—owning a talking bird or an attractive looking dog. By including these last cases, the author explores the limits of permissibility: is causing *tbh* permitted when it serves human benefit and, if so, does that benefit have to be *significant* or may it even be a trivial one?

The answer begins in section B. Before presenting the relevant proof texts from the Talmud, Rabbi Isserlein begins by outlining a religious-philosophical justification for permitting such behavior. Since animals were created to serve humans, humans are free to do with them as they wish; this argument is flawed. The fact that the Torah grants humans the use of animals, and even the right to kill animals for meat, does not mean that it does so without any restrictions attached. After all, land is given to humans as well and was created to serve their needs, and yet the Torah puts limits on land use, stating that the Israelites are to work the land only six years and let it lay fallow on the seventh. Similarly, the Creation story tells us the first human was placed in the Garden of Eden: "[In order] to work the land and to protect it."[8] While Rabbi Isserlein's opening statement is not a proof or a conclusion, it is significant as it indicates the author's general orientation towards the issue at hand. If a *halakhah* decisor believes that animals exist only to serve humans, he will look to prove that humans can use them without restriction.

---

8   Genesis 2:15.

(In section C, the author presents Talmudic passages to argue that the acts under question are permitted. I have cut out this section as it is not relevant for our purposes.)

In section D, Rabbi Isserlein arrives at his legal conclusion. He states that he has demonstrated to some degree that these acts are permitted, implicitly acknowledging that he has not proven his case definitely. This ruling is then surprising given the Biblical nature of the concern for animal suffering. Rabbi Isserlein's permissive position is consistent with his original religious-philosophical orientation that such acts should be permitted, and this orientation likely informed his final ruling.

The moral values are treated in section E. Here, Rabbi Isserlein states that while these behaviors are permissible, the practice is to refrain from doing them. In other words, people sense that there is something wrong with inflicting pain on animals in these cases even if *halakhah* permits it. What motivates them to do so, in the author's estimation, is that they know, from a passage in the Talmud, that acting cruelly to animals incurs Divine punishment.

The author is not an anthropologist nor a sociologist; he is a *posek*, and his task in this responsum is to address a matter of law. Why, then, does he discuss people's behavior and explore their motivation? The answer is obvious: the author is uncomfortable allowing the behavior to be determined purely by legal considerations. Since he ruled that there are no legal restrictions to causing *tbh* when done for even the most trivial human benefit, were one to be guided only by the demands of *halakhah*, one would be free to inflict enormous pain on an animal in gross disproportion to the benefit derived. Such a conclusion is unacceptable to Rabbi Isserlein from a moral-religious perspective.

Since Rabbi Isserlein wished to proscribe certain behavior on moral-religious values, and not on legal grounds, he had to lay down the proper foundation. To do so, he had to first identify the value or values at stake and show that these values matter, that is, that they are rooted in the Torah or the tradition. In addition, he must show that there is a religious responsibility to act in accordance with these values even when one is not required to do so as a matter of *halakhah*, and he had to persuade his audience to actually do so.

Identifying the Value

Rabbi Isserlein writes:

> And it is possible that the reason is that the people do not want to act in a cruel way against the creatures ...

The author identifies the relevant value as not acting in a cruel manner towards living creatures. This is not the same as the Talmudic value of concern for animal suffering. Concern for animal suffering means that animal suffering is inherently bad; the author's concern for not acting cruelly is a concern for humans, not for animals. The reason why animal suffering is bad, according to this line of thought, is that it may lead to callousness towards suffering in general and that inflicting suffering, even on animals, inculcates bad character traits in a person.[9]

There is a good reason why the author does not identify the relevant value as that of concern for animal suffering. To do so raises an obvious question—if concern for animal suffering is the reason for refraining from such behavior, why does *halakhah* permit a person to cause animal suffering in such a case? One answer to this question is that *halakhah* addresses the minimum standard; it is a floor. But a moral, religious system does not dictate only minimally acceptable behavior but also articulates the ideal—a ceiling. It is then conceivable that the value inherent in a certain *halakhah* would call on a person to strive to act in ways that go beyond what *halakhah* demands.[10]

---

9 This shift from a concern for animal suffering *per se* to a concern for human acts of cruelty may be seen in Ramban's *Commentary on Torah*, Deuteronomy 22:6, regarding the *mitzvah* to send away the mother bird when one takes the eggs from the nest (*shiluah ha'ken*). In explaining the Talmudic statement (BT *Berakhot* 33b) that this *mitzvah* is not an expression of Divine compassion but rather a Divine edict, he states: . . . לומר שלא חס האל על קן צפור שאין רחמיו מגיעין בבעלי הנפש הבהמית למנוע אותנו מלעשות בהם צרכנו. שאם כן היה אוסר השחיטה, אבל טעם המניעה ללמד אותנו מדת הרחמנות ושלא נתאכזר, "The intent of this statement is that God does not have compassion on the bird's nest ... for His compassion does not extend to living creatures that have only an animalistic soul to the extent that it would prevent us from using them for our benefit, for had this been the case, God should have forbidden us to slaughter them for meat. Rather, the reason to prevent us [from taking the mother bird with the eggs], is to teach us the character trait of compassion, and that we should not [act in ways that] make us cruel and callous." This is also consistent with Ramban's *halakhah* position in his commentary to BT *Avodah Zarah* 13b, *s.v. u'li'divrei*: דבעלי חיים לצורך אדם שחיטתם וצערן מותר, "When it comes to using animals for human benefit, it is permitted to slaughter them and it is permitted to cause them to suffer."

10 Directly on this point, see the two-part article by Saul Berman "*Lifnim Mishurat Hadin*," *Journal of Jewish Studies* 26, no. 1 (1975): 86–104; 28, no. 2 (1977): 181–93 and Korn, Eugene, "*Legal Floors and Moral Ceilings: A Jewish Understanding Of Law and Ethics*," *Edah Journal* 2, no. 2 (2002): 1–19. For further discussion on *lifnim mi'shurat hadin* see, among others, Aharon Lichtenstein, "*Does Jewish Tradition Recognize An Ethic Independent of Halakha*," *Modern Jewish Ethics*, ed. Marvin Fox, Ohio: Ohio State University Press (1975); Shilo, Shmuel,"On One Aspect of Law and Morals in Jewish Law: *Lifnim Mishurat Hadin*," (1978). 13 Isr. L. Rev. 359 (1978); Aaron Kirschenbaum, *Equity in Jewish Law* (Hoboken, N.J:KTAV Pub. House, 1991), 109–36; Lewis E. Newman, "*Law, Virtue and Supererogation in the Halakha: The Problem of 'Lifnim Mishurat Hadin' Reconsidered*," *Journal of Jewish Studies* 40, no. 1 (Spring 1989): 61–88.

This is not the path Rabbi Isserlein chooses. It is easier to discourage acting cruelly than it is to advocate adhering to the value underlying *tbh* when it requires one to go beyond actual *halakhah* demands. In addition, the author has already given a religious-philosophical reason why inflicting pain on animals is permitted for human benefit, namely, all animals were created to serve humans. As such, it would be hard to argue that the value underlying the prohibition of *tbh* requires people to curtail their own benefit for the sake of animals. To do so would upend the hierarchy that the author has articulated, one he believes is rooted in the structure of creation. If the issue at stake is human cruelty, however, then humans must sometimes restrain their behavior, not for the sake of animals but for their own sake, to avoid acts of cruelty and callousness.

The Value is Rooted in our Tradition

Rabbi Isserlein proceeds to demonstrate that avoiding cruelty is a Torah-based value:

> ... As we find in [BT] *Bava Metzia* (85a) regarding Rabbi Yehudah *HaNasi* and the calf [which hid in its cloak to avoid being slaughtered and] to whom he said, "Go, for it was for that that you were created ... although it was totally permissible for him to slaughter the calf to eat it, nonetheless he was punished and he endured suffering as a result.

In the Talmudic story cited here, Rabbi Yehudah *HaNasi* showed callousness towards the calf and endured many years of Divinely-ordained suffering as a result. This story demonstrates that, for the Talmud, to act without compassion, even towards animals, is to act against our religious values.

Rabbi Isserlein underscores that Rabbi Yehudah *HaNasi's* behavior was fully in keeping with *halakhah*. That he was Divinely punished nonetheless, makes it clear that Jewish religious obligations do not end with satisfying our *halakhah* responsibilities. Torah values matter, even when not mandated by *halakhah*. They are not merely "extra credit"; to act in a way that compromises or violates these values is deserving of punishment.

This selection from the responsum also answers the question: which types of texts qualify for determining a Torah-based value? The legal sections of the Talmud serve as the prime corpus for *halakhah* rulings; we see in this selection that, for Rabbi Isserlein, the *aggadic*, or narrative and philosophical, sections of the Talmud are excellent sources for identifying the values that are prized or shunned by the tradition.

The Religious Obligation to Adopt the Value

Now that the author has demonstrated the religious importance of this value, he must persuade the reader to act accordingly. He does this by presenting his understanding of how this Talmudic story has influenced people's practice:

> ... for they (people) are afraid (to act cruelly towards animals) lest they be punished as a result ...

In offering his interpretation, Rabbi Isserlein is not engaging in idle, armchair anthropology. He is attempting to persuade his audience that they should act in accordance with these values. He does not make a philosophical or religious argument, e.g., God cares about values, not just *halakhah*, and these values constitute part of our religious obligation. Rather, his argument plays to people's fears and emotions. If they don't act in accordance with this value, they will suffer the same punishment that Rabbi Yehudah HaNasi did. Such an assertion could be met with skepticism: Must we take the Talmudic story literally? Would the same fate befall an ordinary person? Consequently, Rabbi Isserlein points to the practice of the people rather than arguing for the relevance of the Talmudic story. People's practice shows that they believe that a similar punishment would befall them if they were to act in a cruel manner towards animals. Noting this practice and framing it the way he does, makes the threat real and present—if everyone around you feels the reality of this danger, then it must be real and it would be foolhardy to disregard it.

There is another implicit emotional appeal in Rabbi Isserlein's statement. If "people" refrain from such behavior, then to act otherwise is to act against commonly held morals. Regardless of one's personal moral convictions, it is rare for someone to act in a way that will be perceived as immoral by his peers.

It should be noted that Rabbi Isserlein does not only offer an interpretation of people's motivation, he offers an interpretation of the facts. Rabbi Isserlein did not collect data to determine whether most or all people actually did restrain from acting cruelly towards animals. By reading the facts in a certain way, and by offering his interpretation of these facts, Rabbi Isserlein presents his audience with a strong, emotionally persuasive argument not to engage in cruelty to animals: to do so would violate a commonly held moral behavior and would invite Divine punishment on oneself.

Rabbi Isserlein chose to appeal to people's fears: fear of Divine punishment and fear of violating communal norms. That he did not find it sufficient to label such behaviors immoral and against Torah values, and assume that his readers would act accordingly, demonstrates that value statements are not assumed to be met with the same level of compliance as *halakhah* rulings. A *posek* who wishes to achieve compliance with Torah values must engage in rhetoric, persuasion, and possibly even scare tactics to convince his audience to act in accordance with these values.

Why Not Forbid the Behavior?

One final question remains: If Rabbi Isserlein wanted people to avoid inflicting suffering on animals even for the sake of human benefit, why did he not rule that such behavior was *halakhically* forbidden? One possible answer is that he had no choice: he believed that the Talmudic sources unambiguously dictated that such behavior was *halakhically* permissible. But by his own admission, this was not the case. He stated that the sources "prove, to some degree," that the behavior is legally permissible. Since the proofs are not definitive, he could have ruled restrictively following the general principle that when there is a doubt about Biblical matters, we rule strictly. Why did he not do this?

There are two possible answers to this question, a religious-philosophical one and a practical one. The religious-philosophical answer is based on Rabbi Isserlein's opening statement that he is inclined to permit inducing animal suffering since he believes that animals were created solely to serve humans. From this statement, it may then be reasonably assumed that the same may be said of animal suffering. Just as a person may do what he wants with an inanimate object that he has fashioned, he can do what he wants with an animate object that God created for his benefit. Within such a religious system, there would be no basis to proscribe behavior due to a concern for the animal and its suffering. The only way behavior may be proscribed would be out of concern for the person and how such behavior would impact his character. Such concerns are, by their nature, not the province of *halakhah*. Rabbi Isserlein finds himself unable to prohibit causing *tbh* as a matter of *halakhah*, and contents himself with dissuading such practice as a violation of Torah values.

It is also possible that Rabbi Isserlein did not forbid these behaviors for practical reasons. Simply stated, it would be impractical to demand that people never cause animals to suffer when using them to serve human ends. A horse or donkey driver will inevitably hit his animal harder than necessary from time to time, and, to take his own example, a feather seller will find it necessary to pluck feathers from his geese and not wait for them to molt.

Of course, one could rule that there is neither blanket permission nor blanket prohibition and that animals can be made to suffer only when the benefit sufficiently justifies it. But it is hard to imagine what such a cost-benefit calculus would look like and even harder to base such a calculus on Talmudic sources. Thus, if the only options available to him are either blanket permission or blanket prohibition, it is understandable why Rabbi Isserlein did not choose to issue a blanket prohibition. As the Talmud states in an analogous case: One does not issue an edict on the community unless the majority of the community can live up to it.[11]

As stated above, *halakhah* sets a floor for people's behavior; it must provide a minimal standard that can be observed by all. The ceiling is set based on the Torah value to encourage people to strive for more ideal behavior, something that is achieved to different degrees by individual people. Rabbi Isserlein allows a gap between law and values, allowing for people to choose to abide strictly to the letter of the law, and at the same time encouraging them—even scaring them—to live a life guided by these higher values, not just by the law.

We now move forward three centuries to see a similar dynamic at work in a responsum of Rabbi Yehezkel Landau addressing the question whether a person is permitted to hunt for sport.

The Responsum of *Noda Bi'Yehudah*

Rabbi Yehezkel Landau (1713–1793) was Chief Rabbi of Prague and Bohemia was perhaps the greatest *posek* of his day and certainly one of the greatest *poskim* of all time. His collection of responsa is called *Noda Bi'Yehudah*. In the undated responsum featured here,[12] he responds to a question from a wealthy man who wanted to know whether it was permitted to hunt wild game for sport. Here are the relevant parts of the responsum; I have divided it into sections for easier reference:

[א] ושורש שאלתו איש אחד אשר זכהו השם בנחלה רחבה ויש לו כפרים ויערות
אשר ביערות תרמוש כל חיתו יער אם מותר לו לילך בעצמו לירות בקנה שריפה
לצוד ציד או אם אסור לישראל לעשות דבר זה אי משום צער בעלי חיים אי משום
בל תשחית . . .

---

11 BT Avodah Zarah 36a.
12 Noda Bi'Yehudah, Tinyana, Yoreh De'ah 10.

[ב] ובאמת בתוס' בע"ז דף י"א ע"ג בד"ה עוקרין . . . משמע מדבריהם
דצעב"ח חמיר מבל תשחית ואינו מותר אפילו לצורך רק משום כבוד רבים . . .
וא"כ איך נימא שיהיה מותר לצורך דבר הרשות. אבל בפסקי תוס' שם כתבו
צעב"ח אינו אסור אלא כשמצטערה בלי ריוח עכ"ל

[ג] ואמנם אין לנו להאריך בזה כי כבר האריך מהרא"י בפסקים וכתבים סימן
ק"ה שכל דבר שיש בו צורך להאדם לית ביה משום צעב"ח וגם לא שייך צעב"ח
אלא לצערו ולהניחו בחיים אבל להמית בהמה וחיות וכל מיני בעלי חיים לית ביה
משום צעב"ח . . . וא"כ אין בנדון שאלתו משום צעב"ח, ומשום בל תשחית ודאי
ליכא דהרי נהנה בעור וגם אינו עושה דרך השחתה . . .

[ד] ואמנם מאד אני תמה על גוף הדבר ולא מצינו איש ציד רק בנמרוד
ובעשו ואין זה דרכי בני אברהם יצחק ויעקב . . . ופוק חזי לומר תבלה ותחדש
כתב מהרי"ו בפסקיו הביאו רמ"א בא"ח סוף סימן רכ"ג שאין לומר כן על הנעשה
מעורות בהמה משום רחמיו על כל מעשיו . . . ואיך ימית איש ישראלי בידים בעלי
חיים בלי שום צורך רק לגמור חמדת זמנו להתעסק . . .

[ה] אבל לרדוף אחריהם ביערות מקום מעונתן כשאין רגילין לבוא לישוב
אין כאן מצוה ואין כאן רק לרדוף אחר תאות לבו ועצת הנדמה כטביא. ומי שהוא
איש הצריך לזה ופרנסתו מצידה כזו בזה לא שייך אכזריות והרי שוחטין בהמה
וחיות ועופות וממיתים דגים לצורך האדם ומה לי טהורים שיאכל מבשרם ומה
לי טמאים שיאכל ויפרנס עצמו מדמי עורותיהן וכל בעלי חיים ניתנו לאדם לכל
צרכיו, אבל מי שאין זה לצורך פרנסתו ואין עיקר כוונתו כלל בשביל פרנסתו
הוא אכזריות . . .

[ו] ועד כאן דברתי מצד יושר ההנהגה שראוי לאדם להרחיק מזה ועכשיו אני
אומר אפילו איסורא איכא שהרי כל העוסקים בזה צריכין להכנס ביערות ולהכניס
עצמם בסכנות גדולות במקום גדודי חיות ורחמנא אמר ונשמרתם מאד לנפשותיכם
. . . ומעתה איך יכניס עצמו איש יהודי למקום גדודי חיות רעות ואף גם בזה מי
שהוא עני ועושה זו למחייתו לזה התורה התירה . . . אבל מי שאין עיקר כוונתו
למחייתו ומתאות ומתאות לבו הוא הולך אל מקום גדודי חיות ומכניס עצמו בסכנה הרי זה
'עובר על ונשמרתם מאד כו.

[ז] ומעתה אני אומר שיש בדבר זה איסור וגם סכנה, ועוד בו שלישיה שעכ"פ
מזכירין עונותיו . . . וממילא הקדוש ברוך הוא מתמלא עליו עברה . . . אבל מי
שעושה כן בשאט נפש איך תקובל תפלתו . . .

[ח] ולכן יש בדבר זה מדה מגונה דהיינו אכזריות וגם איסורא וסכנתא וגם
הזכרת עונותיו ולכן השומע לי ישכון בטח השקט ושאנן בביתו ולא יאבד זמנו
בדברים כאלה. . . .

[A] And the essence of your question is that there is a certain man that
God has blessed with vast property. He owns villages and forests, and

in his forests roam all types of wild animals. Is it permissible for him to go on his own and to hunt with a rifle or is it forbidden for a Jew to do so, either because of the prohibition of [causing] *tbh* or of *bal tashhit* (wanton destruction) ...

[B] In fact, *Tosafot*, BT *Avodah Zarah* (11a) indicate ... that causing pain to animals is a more severe prohibition than *bal tashhit* and it is not permissible even when serving a need; it is only allowed [in special cases where it must be done to protect] the dignity of the community ... and if so, how can we say that [according to *Tosafot*] it [*tbh*] should be permitted when it does not serve a purpose? However, in *Piskei Tosafot* they write that *tbh* is forbidden only if one receives no benefit.

[C] In truth, it does not pay to go on at length about this because Rabbi Isserlein already wrote at length in his rulings, no. 105, that anything that serves a human need does not fall under the prohibition of [causing] pain to animals. Furthermore, [the prohibition of causing] animal suffering only applies when one causes it pain while it is still living, but killing animals is not included in the prohibition ... And therefore, in our case there is no concern of animal suffering, and regarding *bal tashhit,* there certainly is no problem, for he benefits from the hide and he is not doing it in a destructive manner ...

[D] Nevertheless, I am greatly astounded about this matter for we have never found a hunter [in our literature] except for Nimrod and Esau, and this is not the way of the children of Abraham, Isaac, and Jacob ... And regarding saying "You should wear it out and get a new one," Rabbi Isserlein wrote—and it is quoted in Rema (*OH*, 223)—that one should not say this over items made from leather since the verse says: His compassion is on all his creatures (Ps. 145:9) ... And how could a Jewish person kill an animal with his own hands for no purpose at all except to amuse himself? ...

[E] [Although it is permissible and a *mitzvah* to kill dangerous animals, that is when they come into an inhabited area, but] it is not a *mitzvah* to chase after them in the forests where they are living when they do not regularly come into inhabited areas. Such an act is nothing other than chasing after them to satisfy one's heart's desire [i.e., for fun and entertainment] ... Now, for a person who needs to do this, and whose livelihood is earned from hunting, it would not be considered to be an act of cruelty [to hunt wild animals]. In fact, we slaughter domestic and wild animals and birds and kill fish for the benefit of humans. And it makes no difference if a person is slaughtering kosher animals to eat from their flesh or if he is killing non-kosher animals so that he can make a living from selling their hides; all animals have been given to human beings [to use and dispose of] for any need that they may have. But when this hunting is not serving the benefit of earning a living, and a person is not doing it for this purpose, then it is nothing more than an act of cruelty...

[F] So far I have been addressing the issue from the perspective of proper behavior, that it is fitting that a person should distance himself from this. But I will now go further and assert that there exists a prohibition. For all who hunt, enter the forests and expose themselves to great dangers in these places of wild animals, and the Torah says, "And you must take great heed for yourselves" [i.e., for your safety] (Deuteronomy 4:15)... Given this, how may a Jewish person enter into a place of wild animals? Despite this [obligation to protect one's wellbeing], the Torah allows someone who is poor and does this for his living [to expose himself to danger] ... But, someone who is not entering into places of wild animals and endangering himself for his livelihood but rather in order to satisfy his desires, behold such a person transgresses the verse: 'And you shall take great heed for yourselves.'

[G] Based on this, it is my position that this matter involves both a prohibition [exposing oneself needlessly to danger] and a danger. There is also a third problem, for when one exposes himself to danger, his sins are recalled [in Heaven] ... and as a result God is filled with anger against him ... and one who exposes himself to danger needlessly, how can we imagine that his prayers [to be saved from harm] will be answered?

[H] Therefore, there lies in this matter a despicable trait, i.e., cruelty, as well as a prohibition, and a danger, and also causing one's sins to be remembered. And one who listens to me will rest tranquilly at home and not waste his time in such pursuits...

In section A, Rabbi Landau frames the question, and identifies two possible *halakhah* concerns with hunting for sport: inflicting pain on animals (causing *tbh*) and wanton destruction (*bal tashhit*). In section B, he makes the argument that according to Tosafot (twelfth- and thirteenth-century Franco-German Talmudic commentators), it is *halakhically* forbidden to cause animal suffering even when it serves human needs. However, he quickly abandons this position in section C on the basis of Rabbi Isserlein's responsum which permits one to inflict pain on animals when it is done for human benefit. [Although in our case the benefit is merely one of entertainment, it will be remembered that Rabbi Isserlein allowed a person to cause *tbh* even for a trivial benefit, such as cutting a parrot's tongue so it could talk or a dog's ears and tails so that it would look nice.]

It is not immediately clear why Rabbi Landau favored the position of Rabbi Isserlein over that of Tosafot,[13] although it is likely that this is due to the fact that Rema (Rabbi Moshe Isserles, 1520–1572, Krakow), author of the Ashkenazic glosses to *Shulhan Arukh* (Code of Jewish Law), ruled in accordance with Rabbi Isserlein.[14] Of interest to us, is that Rabbi Landau demonstrates here a desire to forbid such activity on a *halakhah* basis, an approach that he returns to in a different form at the end of his responsum.

Rabbi Landau adds a new reason why *tbh* is not a concern here: The animal is killed instantly and is not subject to any suffering (assuming the person is a good shot). He also dismisses the concern of wanton destruction since the animal is being killed for a purpose—namely for sport—the destruction is not wasteful and is, therefore, not forbidden.

Rabbi Landau finds himself in the same position as Rabbi Isserlein. He has concluded that the behavior is *halakhically* permissible, but he cannot condone this behavior as it runs counter to his sense of Torah values and proper character traits. If he wants to dissuade people or forbid them to hunt for sport, then, as we saw with Rabbi Isserlein, he has two tasks. He must: (1) identify the values at stake and show that these are values are rooted in our tradition; (2) show that there is a religious responsibility to act in accordance with these values and persuade his audience to do so. Let us see how he accomplishes these two tasks.

---

13 In contrast to *Tosafot Avodah Zarah*, *Piskei Tosafot*, authored by one of the Tosafists, permits causing animal suffering when done for human benefit. This work does not carry the same legal weight as Tosafot.

14 *Shulhan Arukh*, EH 5:14.

Identifying the Values

Rabbi Landau, like his predecessor, Rabbi Isserlein, identifies the relevant value here as the need to avoid acting cruelly (sections E and H). That is to say, a concern with humans and not a concern with animals per se. While Rabbi Isserlein uses the aggadic sections of the Talmud to demonstrate that the tradition censures cruelty, Rabbi Landau references Biblical verses as they have been interpreted by the Rabbis. He notes that the only hunters in our tradition are Nimrod (Genesis 10:9) and Esau (Genesis 25:27). Both of these figures are traditionally understood—in the Midrash and in the Talmud—as wicked men, although this is not explicit in the verses.[15] These Biblical stories teach, according to Rabbi Landau, that being a hunter is a profession fitting only for wicked people.

Rabbi Landau then states: "This is not the way of the children of Abraham, Isaac and Jacob." On one level, he reiterates his previous point: based on stories in the Torah, we see that treating animals in such a manner was never the way that our forefathers acted. But he is deepening his argument as well. He is implicitly stating that these are not just traits or professions that are shunned by the Torah, but also that such behavior is decidedly not Jewish. This is based partially on Biblical stories, but it is also based on Jewish history and cultural memory. There is no tradition of Jewish hunters. Jewish cultural memory reflects values that Jews valorize and would like to believe distinguish them This belief is not just an additional source for this value but also a different framing of the problem. To act in this way is to act in a decidedly non-Jewish fashion; it is to betray one's Jewish identity.

Finally, Rabbi Landau adds one more facet to his argument. He points to a minhag, a custom, to wish prosperity to someone who purchases a new item by saying: "May you wear out this item and be able to purchase a replacement." Over time, it became customary to refrain from extending this blessing when the new item was made of leather since purchasing this item requires more leather and the death of another animal. This is based on the Biblical verse: "God's compassion is on all of His creatures" (Psalms 145:9), presumably including animals. Rabbi Landau points out that refraining from giving this blessing over a leather item expresses a worthy sensitivity. Were we to take such sensitivity seriously, we would never slaughter animals for meat or for leather. Nevertheless, or perhaps specifically because of this, this custom may be seen

---

15 See Ramban, *Commentary to the Torah*, Genesis 10:9.

as a good basis for inculcating values that are important to us even when not required by *halakhah* and even when we do not practice them in their ideal expression. Our religious, not our *halakhically* required, practice reflects and reinforces values that are central to us as a religious community, values that are rooted in the Torah.

Gaining Compliance

There is powerful persuasive force in the claim (section D) that hunting for sport undermines one's identity as a true descendent of Jewish forbearers. It labels one an outsider, one of "them," not one of "us." This echoes Rabbi Isserlein's statement that "people" don't act cruelly to animals, a statement which implicitly labeled the person who acts cruelly towards animals an outsider, violating the norms of the community. Such a person is not just acting immorally, he is showing that he is not a true Jew, raising questions as to his very identity and membership in the group.[16]

Another (subtle) tool of persuasion used in this section is the opening phrase: "I am greatly astounded about this matter." If the response to someone's questions is, "I can't believe you are asking such a question!" or "I can't believe you are even thinking of doing such a thing!" this has the effect of shaming the questioner and making him doubt the possible legitimacy of what he was suggesting.

Later in the responsum, Rabbi Landau states that going hunting exposes one to danger (section F). As we have seen, Rabbi Isserlein used the fear of Divine punishment to convince people to heed the concerns he articulated. In a similar fashion, Rabbi Landau plays on people's fears to persuade them to avoid going hunting: it's dangerous and you might get killed! This argument is unpersuasive when hunting for sport is widespread activity and the presumed risk is small. Consequently, Rabbi Landau adds a metaphysical concern, one that parallels the "Divine punishment" argument expressed by Rabbi Isserlein, namely,

---

16 The argument that acting cruelly betrays one's Jewish identity may be found in a number of Talmudic statements. The Talmud states: "Whoever has compassion on God's creatures, it is known that he is a descendent of Abraham our father, and whoever does not have compassion on the creatures, it is known that he is not a descendent of Abraham our father" (BT Beitzah 32a). Similarly, the Talmud states: "There are three distinguishing character traits of this nation: they are compassionate, they have shame and they do acts of loving-kindness" (BT Yevamot 79a). While these statements refer, specifically, to compassion towards other people, they may easily have been extended to treatment of animals, and it is curious that Rabbi Landau does not reference these statements directly.

exposing oneself to danger without justifiable reason brings the memory of one's sins before God. As a result, God might choose to bring harm to the person and, certainly, will not be receptive to one's prayers for protection (section G). In short, Rabbi Landau argues, if you won't avoid this behavior because it runs counter to Torah values, you should at least avoid it as an act of self-preservation. To go hunting is to ask God to punish you.

Finally, Rabbi Landau bolsters his argument in a way we do not see in Rabbi Isserlein's responsum; he makes a *halakhah* argument against this behavior. In section B, Rabbi Landau attempted to forbid hunting on the basis of the *halakhah* restrictions against *tbh* but was unable to do so. Now, in section F, he attacks this problem from a new *halakhah* angle. He states that hunting is a violation of the Biblical mandate to protect one's health and well-being since, in doing so, the person exposes himself to danger. Such an argument is far from obvious. First, many of our activities involve a certain degree of risk, consequently, the prohibition of exposing oneself to risk must be limited to cases of significant risk. Second, it is a general understood by the Talmud that when a behavior is widely practiced by people, even when it involves risk, it cannot be prohibited.[17] (Of course, it might be different if this practice is not yet being practiced within the Jewish community and it is possible to prevent it from starting.) Third, there are many activities, particularly those associated with making a living, that *halakhah* permits although they involve a degree of risk. Rabbi Landau addresses this last point and states that when the risk is undertaken for a good, justifiable reason, then the risky activity is permitted but not when undertaken for a trivial purpose. He offers no proof texts or evidence to support this claim.

It seems clear that that Rabbi Landau was aware that this *halakhah* claim— that such activity was a violation of the obligation to protect one's health—was a weak one. In his closing paragraph (section H), he lists a number of reasons why a person should refrain from hunting: it is dangerous, it causes God to recall one's sins, it is indicative of bad character and it is associated with a *halakhah* prohibition. But it seems like he is protesting a bit too much. If this activity were truly a *halakhah* violation, he would not need a long list of reasons; all he would need to say is: "It is forbidden because it violates law X." Rabbi Landau's need to bolster his claim, and to even underplay the prohibition argument by

---

17   BT Shabbat 129b; BT Yevamot 72a: The masses have already trodden down that path; BT Yevamot 12b: Heaven will have mercy.

burying it in the middle of the list, indicates that this is not a real *halakhah* violation.

The phraseology is indicative of this. Rabbi Landau states: "There is in this matter … a prohibition." Saying that a prohibition exists is not the same as saying that it is *halakhically* forbidden to act in a certain way.[18] It is also worth noting, that nowhere else in his extensive responsa does Rabbi Landau ever reference the prohibition to engage in actions that expose oneself to danger. It seems that Rabbi Landau, like other *poskim*, believed that *halakhah* does not actually forbid a person from engaging in these activities in the absence of a clear and present danger.[19] The plea at the close of the responsum to refrain from hunting and spend the time more productively at home, again indicates Rabbi Landau's awareness that he has not made an actual *halakhah* argument to forbid this behavior.

---

18   Elsewhere, Rabbi Landau uses the same phrase, "a prohibition exists," to describe an act that is not strictly forbidden. See *Noda Bi'Yehudah Kamma, EH* 54, אף אלא אפילו לגבי דידיה שפטור משום שאינו בר עונשין אבל עכ"פ איסורא איכא ודומה לקטן אוכל נבילות דעכ"פ מקרי נבילה אלא שאינו חייב, "But even in regards to him (the minor), although he would be exempt (if he engaged in a forbidden sexual relationship), because he is not of the age of majority and not deserving of punishment, nevertheless, a prohibition still exists; it is similar to a case of a minor eating meat that has not been ritually slaughtered—the meat is still considered to be forbidden although the minor is not liable for eating it."

19   The reluctance to forbid an activity based on a concern for self-injury can be seen in the responsum of Rabbi Moshe Feinstein, *Iggrot Moshe, HM* 2:76, where he discusses the issue of eating unhealthy foods: נראה פשוט דבדבר דאיכא הרבה הרבה שלא קשה להו לבריאותם כלום כגון הרבה מיני אוכלין שהאינשי נהנין מהם ביותר כבשרא שמנא ודברים חריפים ביותר אבל קשה זה לבריאותן של כמה אינשי, ליכא בזה איסור מלאוכלן מצד חשש סכנה, מאחר דהרוב אינשי לא מסתכנין מזה. ועיין ברמב"ם פ"ד מדעות שנקט שם עניני אוכלין ומשקין הטובים לבריאות הגוף והרעים לבריאות הגוף ולא כתב בלשון איסור לא מדאורייתא ולא מדרבנן שאסרו חכמים, "It seems obvious that when it comes to something that for many people is not at all injurious to their health—such as many types of food in which people get great pleasure in eating, like fatty meat or sharp foods, but are injurious to the health of some people—there would be no prohibition to eat such foods out of a concern that they may prove injurious, since this is not the case for most people. See Rambam, *Hilkhot De'ot,* 4:1, where he discusses the foods that are good for a person's health and those which are injurious to one's health, and he never uses the term "forbidden," indicating that it is neither forbidden Biblically nor rabbinically [to eat such foods]." [This is presented in contrast to Rambam, *Hilkhot Rotzeiah U'Shmirat Ha'nefesh,* 11:5-6, where Rambam forbids practices that present a serious danger.] Somewhat surprisingly, Rabbi Feinstein states that smoking cigarettes is similar to eating unhealthy foods, and cannot be forbidden as a matter of *halakhah*. He claims that the risks of cancer from smoking cigarettes are "extremely small." [This responsum is undated, however, he issued a similar ruling in responsa dated December 1963 (*YD* 2:49) and dated October 1984 (*OH* 5:34)]. Rabbi Feinstein's position is representative of most *poskim* who do not, as a rule, forbid behavior that is potentially dangerous to oneself except in extreme situations.

The attempt to produce any *halakhah* argument, even a weak one, reflects the challenge in persuading one's audience to adhere to a value when it is not mandated by *halakhah*. The easier path to compliance is through issuing *halakhah* rulings. There is always a temptation for a posek faced with a values or policy issue to make a *halakhah* argument no matter how weak or forced it might be.

In the responsa of Rabbi Isserlein and Rabbi Landau we have seen two approaches to dealing with the gap between *halakhah* and values:

1. Arguing for the importance of values and employing a range of strategies to gain compliance.
2. Making a *halakhah*, or quasi-*halakhah*, argument which seeks to prohibit the behavior based on a secondary aspect of the case (e.g., the danger involved in hunting).

We now turn to a contemporary ruling of Rabbi Moshe Feinstein regarding the raising and eating of veal. In a notable departure from the previous two responsa, Rabbi Feinstein does not seek develop a moral or Torah values argument (approach 1). In abandoning the first approach, Rabbi Feinstein limits himself to *halakhah* arguments, the traditional purview of a *posek*. He begins his *halakhah* argument by prohibiting veal based on a concern unrelated to animal suffering (approach 2) and then introduces a third approach:

3. Bringing the values into direct dialogue with the *halakhah* and reworking the *halakhah* parameters to narrow the gap between *halakhah* and values.

The Responsum of Rabbi Moshe Feinstein

Rabbi Moshe Feinstein (1895–1986), was born in Eastern Europe and lived most of his life on the Lower East Side of New York. He was considered the authoritative *posek* for American Jewry. In the following responsum from 1982 (*Iggrot Moshe, EH* 4:92), he addresses the question of whether it is permissible to eat or raise veal:

[א] ב' דר"ח תמוז תשמ"ב. מע"כ חתני כבני אהוב וחביב ויקר כש"ת הרב הגאון משה דוד טענדלער שליט"א . . . בענין עגלים שמפטמין אותם באופן שבשרם יקבל מראה לבן.

[ב] ובדבר העגלים שנתחדש זה לא כבר שמפטמין אותן כל עגל במקום מיוחד לבד צר מאד שאין להם מקום אף לילך איזה פסיעות, ואין מאכילין אותן כלום ממאכלי בהמות הראוים לעגלים ולא טעמו חלב אמם כלל, אלא מפטמין אותן במשקין שמנים מאד שאין הבהמות נהנים מזה . . . . וגם נעשים חולים מזה וצריכים למיני רפואות

[ג] וכפי שאומרים שוחטים מובהקים לא נכשרו מהם אלא ט"ו עגלים ממאה, ולשוחטים המקילים הוא ערך מ"ד או מ"ה עגלים כשרים למאה, והכל מודים שרובן טרפות היפוך מחזקת בהמות שהן כשרות . . . אבל אפשר איכא עוד טרפות בבני מעים, שפשוט שצריך נמי לבודקם שמסתבר שיש לחוש לזה מאד. שלכן מהראוי היה לאסור מלעשות זה ובעלי נפש אין להו לאכול כלל מעגלים כאלו אף אם יבדקו גם הבני מעים. . . . ובלא בדיקת הבני מעים אין להכשירם.

[ד] והנה לאלו שעושין זה איכא ודאי איסור דצער בע"ח דאף שהותר לצורך האדם הוא כשאיכא צורך, כהא דלשוחטם לאכילה ולעבוד בהם לחרישה ולהובלת משאות וכדומה. אבל לא לצערם בעלמא שזה אסור אף אם יהיה לאחד הרוחה בזה כגון שנכרי אחד רוצה להרוג או לחבול באיזו בהמה שכעס עליה שודאי אסור אף שמשלם לו שכר בעד מעשה הרע הזה . . . וחבלת בע"ח אסור אף שהוא להרוחה לצורך האדם דוקא בדבר שדרכן דאינשי בכך.

[ה] עכ"פ חזינן שלא כל דבר רשאי האדם לעשות לבהמות שמצער אותם אף שהוא להרויח מזה, אלא דבר שהוא הנאת האדם ממש כשחיטת הבהמות לאכילה ולעבוד בהם וכדומה. וכן היה מותר לזונם בדברים שיותר טוב להמתיק את בשרו ולהשמין את בשרו באופן שהאינשי שיאכלו את בשרו יהנו יותר מכפי שהיתה אוכלת שחת.

אבל לא בדבר שהוא רק לרמות ולהטעות את האינשי שיאכילום בדבר שגם לאינשי אינו כלום ורק לרמותם להאינשי שמזה שיראו מראה הבשר שהוא לבן ולא במראה אודם קצת שיטעו מזה שהוא בשר יותר טוב לבריאות ולהנאה וישלמו בשביל זה יותר . . .

מ"מ אסור לצער את הבהמה להאכילה דברים שאין לה הנאה מהן שהיא מצטערת באכילה, וגם הם נחלות מזה וסובלין יסורין מהחולי, שבשביל הנאה זו דיכול לרמות להאינשי אסור לעשות כן מאיסור צער בע"ח מדאורייתא שלא הותר זה להאינשי לצער בע"ח.

[A] The second day of *Rosh Hodesh Tamuz*, 5742 (June 22, 1982). To my son-in-law ... Rabbi Moshe David Tendler ... Regarding calves which are fattened to make their flesh have a white appearance.

[B] Regarding calves [being raised for veal]. [The procedure for doing so that] was recently innovated is to fatten each calf in its own narrow pen in which they are unable to move even a few steps; they are not fed food that is fit for calves and they have never even tasted their mother's milk; rather, they are fattened with very fatty liquids, from which they derive no pleasure ... and they even become quite sick from this diet, and require various forms of medications.

[C] Based on what expert ritual slaughterers report, no more than 15 out of every 100 of such animals are kosher and for ritual slaughterers who are more lenient, approximately 44–45 percent are kosher. All [ritual slaughterers] agree that the majority [of such animals] are *treifot* (not-kosher due to an internal injury), unlike most animals which are presumed kosher.[20] [This is only as far as injuries of the lung, which are the most common, are concerned.] It is possible that there are additional *treifot* (injuries or holes) in the intestinal tract and one must check these as well [to ensure that they are free from injuries], for it stands to reason that the likelihood [of some injury in these organs] is very great.

Thus, it would be appropriate to forbid one to do this (i.e., fatten the calves in this manner) and a righteously-minded individual should not eat from such meat at all, even if the intestinal tract is checked ... and without checking the intestinal tract one cannot declare such meat to be kosher.

[D] Now, regarding those who produce veal in this manner, there is definitely a prohibition of [causing] suffering to animals. Although causing *tbh* is permissible when done to serve human needs, that is only when there is a true need, for example, to slaughter animals for food, or use them to plow and to carry burdens and so on. But to cause them pain for no good reason, is prohibited even when someone will make some profit from this. For example, if a Gentile [who is not obligated to follow *halakhah's* requirements regarding animal suffering] wanted to kill or wound an animal with which he was angry, it would certainly be prohibited for a person to receive payment and allow this evil act [to be done to his animal] ... The injuring of animals is forbidden, even when done for profit which serves

---

20 The term *treifah* (pl., *treifot*) refers to an animal that has adhesions on the lung or holes in any of the internal organs. This term is also used to refer to the injuries; an animal may be said to be a *treifah* or may have *treifot* in its organs.

a human need, unless it produces a recognizable, common benefit.

[E] In any case, we see that a person does not have blanket permission to cause pain to animals even when making a profit, except when the benefit is considered a true human benefit, such as slaughtering them for food, or working them and the like. Similarly, he may feed them food that is best for improving the taste of the meat and make it more fatty if the people who eat the meat will derive greater pleasure that had the animal been fed fodder.

But it is not allowed [to inflict pain on animals] if the result is merely to deceive and mislead people and feed them something from which they derive no real benefit. The fact that the meat now has a white appearance, and not one that is a little reddish, will lead them to believe, in error, that it is healthier tastier meat and they will then pay more for this meat ...

It is thus forbidden to cause pain to an animal to feed it food from which it derives no benefit and which causes it pain in the process of eating and brings about diseases from which the animal endures more pain. It is Biblically forbidden to [cause] animal suffering [merely] for the sake of a benefit based on deceiving people [and profiting by doing so].

Rabbi Feinstein begins by outlining, in some detail, the conditions under which calves are raised for veal (section B). The description of these conditions signals his sympathy for the suffering the calves are forced to endure, and tips off the reader to the fact that Rabbi Feinstein will be looking for a way to forbid or restrict such a practice.

Halakhah Argument no. 1—The Meat Isn't Kosher

The first *halakhah* argument Rabbi Feinstein makes (section C) is reminiscent of Rabbi Landau's argument prohibiting hunting on the grounds that is a dangerous activity prohibited by the injunction of *vi'nishmartem me'od li'nafshoteikhem*: to protect oneself from danger. Rabbi Feinstein argues, in a similar fashion, that it is forbidden to eat veal, not because of how the animals are treated, but because so many of them are not kosher.

Rabbi Feinstein states that based on the facts as they have been reported to him, a much higher percentage of calves raised for veal have injuries of the lungs, and, likely, injuries in the intestinal tract. Based on this concern, Rabbi Feinstein concludes that it would be forbidden to eat this meat unless the entire intestinal tract was checked and determined to be problem-free. What Rabbi Feinstein does not say, but what would have been understood by the reader, is that a requirement to check the entire intestinal tract of every animal would raise the cost prohibitively, effectively destroying the market for kosher veal. This argument, however, is based on an inaccurate assumption; the majority of calves raised for veal are free of internal injuries.[21] As we saw earlier in our discussion of Rabbi Isserlein's statement, "People don't act this way," a *posek* not only determines matters of law, but also assesses and interprets the relevant facts. Rabbi Moshe's determination of the frequency of these problems of *treifot*, served as the basis for his *halakhah* argument and freed him from the need to make an argument based on values. However, as his interpretation of the facts were not born out, the intestinal tracts of the calves are not checked by the ritual slaughterers and American Orthodox Jews continued to eat veal.

Rabbi Feinstein did not issue a dictum regarding the ethical issues involved and focuses solely on formulating *halakhah* ruling, despite the fact that it appears, certainly in hindsight, that the ruling is built on a shaky foundation. A similar approach can be found in other of his responsa that involve Torah values; Rabbi Feinstein chooses to make *halakhah* rulings, albeit forced ones, even while acknowledging that the issue at stake is primarily one of values.[22]

---

21 See Ezra Schwartz & Josh Flug, "The Other White Meat," *RJJ Journal of Halacha and Contemporary Society* 45 (2002): 6, "Despite Rav Moshe's position, common practice in the Orthodox community is that veal is consumed, even by *ba'alei nefesh* [religiously scrupulous people] although all the innards are not checked for *treifot* as per Rav Moshe's specifications. The justification for this practice is that research done by *kashrut* organizations subsequent to the writing of the *teshuva* [responsum] has shown that, although there is an extraordinarily high percentage of *treifot* in the lungs of calves, there is no higher incidence of *treifot* in the *b'nei mei'ayim* [intestinal tract] of calves than in mature cows. Therefore, even Jews who abide by the most exacting standards of *halacha* consume veal, relying on the fact that the lungs were adequately examined and no *treifot* were found in the veal sold as kosher."

22 See *Iggrot Moshe*, OH 4:60, where Rabbi Feinstein rules that it is forbidden to use timers on Shabbat to turn on electrical appliances. He bases this first on the argument that it should be included as an extension of the Rabbinic prohibition to have a non-Jew do an act on Shabbat that is forbidden for a Jew to perform. He then concedes that the use of timers might not be formally prohibited on this basis, but it *should be* prohibited: אבל אף אם נימא שאין לאסור אלא מה שתיקנו חכמים . . . מ"מ אין להתיר זה כיון שהוא דבר הראוי ליאסר, "Even if we say that we can only forbid what the Rabbis instituted (which would not include timers) ... nevertheless, the [use of these timers] should not be permitted, since it is a matter that deserves to . be forbidden (and would have been forbidden by the Rabbis had such timers existed in their time)."

Halakhah Argument no. 2—It Is Not Always Permitted to Cause Animal Suffering to Serve Human Needs

Rabbi Feinstein continues to make *halakhah* arguments in the final part of his responsum (sections D and E), where he shifts his attention to the veal farmers. Raising veal causes needless animal suffering and, he argues, violates the *halakhot* relating to *tza'ar ba'alei hayyim*. In section D, Rabbi Feinstein argues that although it is permissible to cause suffering to animals for the sake of human benefit, this benefit must be deemed a common one; making a profit is not sufficient if what was done to the animal did not produce a recognizable, common benefit. For example, a person may not rent out his dog to someone who gets pleasure from torturing animals. Although the owner benefits by making money, the pleasure derived from torturing an animal is not a commonly recognized benefit and the owner may not be a party to such acts.

In section E, Rabbi Feinstein argues that this is relevant to the production of veal. Although it would seem that raising of veal produces a real benefit—better tasting meat—Rabbi Feinstein argues that this is an illusion. He states that veal raised under these conditions does not result in tastier or healthier meat, and people's impression that this is the case is due to misleading advertising. In his assessment, raising veal does not confer a benefit. Consequently, in this case, *tbh* is not permitted even if the owners can make a profit.

Rabbi Feinstein's argument is based on his assumptions of the relevant facts. It is possible that his assertion is correct, and that veal raised under more humane conditions is healthier and tastier.[23] At the same time, Rabbi Feinstein chooses to ignore the likely possibility that there are people who are not being deceived by marketing, who genuinely prefer the taste of veal

---

Rabbi Feinstein then argues that the use of timers should be forbidden on the basis of זילותא דשבת, a disparaging of the sanctity of Shabbat: אף שלא אסרו זה ביחוד דכל ענין זילותא הוא האיסור, "[this is forbidden] even if they (the Rabbis) didn't forbid this specifically, for any act of disparaging [the sanctity of Shabbat] is in itself prohibited." Rabbi Feinstein, however, does not leave it at that. Since there is no actual *halakhah* rule that a person cannot disparage the sanctity of Shabbat, he proceeds to argue that to impinge on the spirit of Shabbat is a formal *halakhah* violation of the positive Biblical or Rabbinic obligation to honor Shabbat: וממילא מובן דהדברים שעשייתן הוא זילותא לשבת הוא ג"כ עובר על מצוה זו.. במעשה, שלכן אף שנימא שאינו בכלל הגזירות דחכמים, אבל גם בלא צורך הוא עובר במעשה על חיוב כבוד השבת, "What emerges is that when it comes to acts whose performance would be a disparaging of [the sanctity of] Shabbat, [one who does them] would actively transgress this mitzvah of honoring the Shabbat ... Therefore, even if we concede that this is not included in the Rabbinic edict, nevertheless, in the absence of a [justifying] need, a person [who used such a timer] would transgress the obligation to honor the Shabbat."

23 See Marian Burros, "Veal to Love, Without the Guilt," *New York Times*, April 18, 2007.

produced under the current harsh conditions, and for whom this process produces real benefit.

In terms of the substantive legal issues regarding *tbh*, Rabbi Feinstein's ruling is quite significant. As far as we can tell, it is the first ruling since *Trumat Ha'deshen's* responsum that does not give blanket *halakhah* permission to inflict animal suffering when done for the sake of human benefit. Rabbi Feinstein does not bring any textual evidence to support his innovative *halakhah* ruling; his position is based on claims he considers self-evident.[24] This is a good indication that it is the intrinsic values behind the prohibition against causing *tbh* that are motivating Rabbi Feinstein. For Rabbi Feinstein, absent authoritative texts, it is obvious that *halakhah's* concern for animal suffering must put some limits on how we treat animals, even though it allows us to use them to serve our needs.

This portion of the responsum regarding raising veal is meaningful theoretically but has no significant practical import—there are not many *halakhically*—observant veal farmers. Nevertheless, Rabbi Feinstein's limitation of the parameters of "human need and benefit" has significant application in other cases where the possible benefits accrued by performing procedures on animals that increase their suffering are of highly questionable value. That said, Rabbi Feinstein's ruling would not mandate costly protocols to minimize animal suffering so long as the enterprise produces real benefit to humans (e.g., scientific studies and factory-farming.)

Rabbi Feinstein's first ruling did not succeed in changing the Orthodox community's practice; people continue to eat of veal. At the same time, his second ruling led to a reworking of the *halakhah* parameters of *tbh* and a narrowing of the gap that had opened up between *halakhah* and the pertinent Torah values. Rabbi Feinstein's approach stands in marked contrast to the responsa of Rabbi Isserlein and Rabbi Landau.

---

24 His one passing reference to *Rashi, Shabbat* 105b, and the Talmud's discussion there, is not relevant. The Talmud does not prohibit the activity in question—tearing a garment to give vent to one's anger—because of *bal tashhit* but because the Talmud considers it detrimental to one's character to give such vent to anger. This type of argument might lead to restricting raising veal because it is an act of human cruelty, parallel to the arguments offered by Rabbis Isserlein and Landau. It is not an effective argument for prohibiting raising veal under cruel conditions based on *tbh* as Rabbi Feinstein seeks to do.

Conclusion

We have seen how two important *poskim,* Rabbi Isserlein and Rabbi Landau, addressed an issue that they believed violated Torah values but was not *halakhically* prohibited. To argue that these values are important to the tradition, they turned to a range of sources—Biblical narratives, Talmudic *aggadot,* customs and the community's self-identity. These sources stand in contrast to the usual authoritative sources for *halakhah* argumentation— Biblical laws, *halakhah* sections of the Talmud, rulings in the legal codes and responsa literature. Because the first set of sources does not speak with *halakhah* authority, these two *poskim* knew that their audience would not automatically adhere to the religious values rooted in these sources and would need to persuaded and motivated to do so. They used a range of different strategies to accomplish this including scare tactics and shaming. We also saw Rabbi Landau make a rather forced *halakhah* argument to prohibit the activity, implicitly recognizing that *halakhah* rulings are far more powerful in achieving compliance.

In contrast to these two *poskim,* Rabbi Feinstein engaged solely in *halakhah* argumentation. His ruling prohibiting raising and eating veal may also be seen as somewhat forced and, in fact, it is not followed in practice. Nonetheless, when it came to veal farming, Rabbi Feinstein's focus on *halakhah* considerations led to a narrowing of the gap between *halakhah* and values, as well as an important revising of the parameters of *tbh.*

It is, at times, possible to narrow the gap between *halakhah* and Torah values, as Rabbi Feinstein did, but often this goal will remain elusive. The alternative, developing compelling language rooted in Torah values that creates a religious obligation, as seen in the first two responsa we examined, is quite challenging and continues to be so in contemporary discussions around factory-farmed meat. A community that cares about religious values, not just *halakhah,* must continue to work towards creating a discourse of values rooted in Torah sources carrying obligatory or, at least, persuasive force. To avoid doing so is to limit our tradition to purely legalistic concerns, which is a disservice both to the tradition and to the fullness of what a religious life can and should be.

The Commandments Were Only Given for the Purpose of Refining People

Rabbi Dr. David Rosen

Behold I have taught you statutes and ordinances as the Lord my God commanded me …. Keep them and do them, for it (the Torah) is your wisdom and understanding in the sight of the peoples who, when they hear all these statutes will say 'surely this great nation is a wise and understanding people.'[1]

The above verses make it clear that the Jewish people's observance of God's commandments is meant to inspire the world to acknowledge their wisdom and values. In addition, the Torah makes it clear that the observance of the *mitzvot* is for our own benefit[2]; *Chazal* describe the commandments as beautifying us.[3] In the following passage, they portray the *mitzvot* as having the goal of refining our characters:

What does God care whether a man kills an animal in the proper Jewish way and eats it, or whether he strangles an animal and then eats it? Will the one benefit Him or the other injure Him? What does God care whether a man eats kosher or non-kosher animals? Doesn't it say: "If you are wise, you are wise for yourself, but if you scorn, you alone shall bear it."[4] So you learn that the commandments were given only to refine God's creatures,

---

1 Deuteronomy 4:6.
2 Deuteronomy 30:15–2.
3 *Song of Songs Rabbah* 1:1.
4 Proverbs 9:12.

as it says:[5] "God's word is refined. It is a protection to those who trust in Him".[6]

In keeping with this text, the Ramban emphasized the purpose of the *mitzvot* as improving human character. Concerning the *mitzvah* of *shiluah haken* (driving away the mother bird from its nest before taking the eggs), he explained the commandment is not out of compassion for the bird but in order to educate *us* to be compassionate.[7] Ramban took issue with Rambam on the latter's claim that the commandments relating to kindness to animals are for the latter's benefit. Nevertheless, Rambam already explained the goal of the laws of *shehitah* as having the purpose which Ramban sees as behind the former *mitzvot*:

> The object of the prohibition against causing an animal pain is in order to perfect us so that we should not acquire habits of cruelty and should not inflict pain gratuitously without any utility, but we should be kind and merciful to all living creatures, except in case of need … We must not kill animals out of cruelty or for sport.[8]

Furthermore, Rambam writes that: "Every single one of the 613 *mitzvot* serves to inculcate an authentic philosophy of life, to repudiate a pernicious ideology, to promote justice and eradicate injustice, to cultivate morality and avoid evil conduct."[9] And in his *Code of Jewish Law*[10] he stated: "Most laws of the Torah are but good guidance from the Greatest Guide, in order to improve traits and direct all actions with integrity."[11] These lines of thought reflect the views within *Chazal* and the later *rishonim* who saw the limitations under which the killing of animals is permitted for human needs, *shehitah*, and precepts related to *kashrut*, as having the purpose of minimizing animal pain and

---

5 2 Samuel 22:31.

6 *Midrash Tanhuma, Parshat Shmini* 15b; Similarly, *Genesis Rabbah, Lech Lecha* 44:1; *Leviticus Rabbah, Shmini* 13:3.

7 Deuteronomy 22:6.

8 *Guide for the Perplexed* 111:17.

9 Ibid., 3:31.

10 *Mishneh Torah, Hilchot Temurah* 4:17.

11 See also the *Magid Mishneh* at the end of his commentary on *Yad Hahazakah, Hilchot Shchenim*

promoting compassion[12] in consonance with the prohibitions of *tza'ar ba'alei hayyim*.[13]

In modernity, Rabbi Avraham Yitzhak Ha-Cohen Kook expanded extensively on this theme.[14] Compassion is portrayed by our sages as a defining Jewish character trait, so much so that they declare[15] that it is compassion that proves one is an authentic descendent of Abraham (thus questioning the provenance of one lacking in compassion), in keeping with the *Torah*'s portrayal of compassion as the determining quality that makes Rebecca[16] suitable for the family of Abraham.[17] It is similar compassion towards animals that is portrayed as the quality that made Moses fit for leadership of the Jewish people, and the same with *King* David.[18]

Compassion is at the heart of the key mitzvah to cleave to/emulate the Divine "His mercies are upon all His creatures"[19]; thus we are told: "Just as He is compassionate and merciful, so you be compassionate and merciful."[20] Accordingly, Chazal declared that by showing compassion towards living creatures that we elicit God's compassion towards us.[21] Indeed, it would appear that our sages urge us to go even beyond the letter of the law regarding compassion for animals, as indicated in the famous story of Rabbi Yehudah HaNasi,[22] who received Divine punishment for refusing to protect a frightened calf that sought his refuge while being taken to slaughter.[23]

The tension between the Torah's permissive mandate to use animals and even take animal life for our human needs versus our obligations to care for and be compassionate towards animal life raises the question of determining what and when is a legitimate human need.

---

12 See *Sefer ha-Hinuch* 451.
13 BT *Bava Metzia* 32b; *Sefer ha-Hinuch*, 148, 284, 452, 550, 596.
14 *Hazon hatzimhonut vehashalom*, ed. David HaCohen, first published in HaPeles, 1903.
15 BT *Beitzah* 32b.
16 Genesis 24:10–15.
17 See Malbim, *Hatorah Vhamitzvot*.
18 *Exodus Rabbah* 2:2; See also *Midrash Tanhuma, Noah*, 4.
19 Psalms 145:9.
20 BT *Shabbat* 133b; JT *Pe'ah* 3; Sofrim 3:17.
21 Ibid., 151b; *See Sefer Hasidim*, 87.
22 BT *Bava Metzia* 85a.
23 See Maharsha, loc. cit.; *Imrei Shefer* No. 34, 10–12; *Ma'archei Lev* no. 110.

Rabbi Israel Isserlein—known as the *Trumat Hadeshen* (basing himself on *Piskei ha-Tosafot, Avodah Zarah*, 1:11)[24]—commented that it is permitted to cause pain to animals for human benefit, referring to plucking feathers off a live goose. Yet, he indicated that we should refrain from doing so because of the inherent cruelty in the act.[25] However, Rabbi Yitzhak Dov Halevi Bamberger (*Yad HaLevi*, known as the Würzburger Rav, 1807–1878)[26] contests this permission on principle as contravening the prohibition of *tza'ar ba'alei hayyim*. And according to Rabbi Yeruham Yehudah Leib Perlman (*Or Gadol*, also known as the "Gadol of Minsk," 1835–1896),[27] the matter of permitting *tza'ar ba'alei hayyim* for human material benefit is a matter of debate among *rishonim*, with Rashi permitting but Ramban and Rashba both forbidding.

These deliberations have contemporary practical ramifications, notably in relation to the production of goose liver through force feeding. This was prohibited by a number of authorities both because of damage to the internal organs as well as contravening the prohibition of *tza'ar ba'alei hayim*, notably Rabbi Yoel ben Shmuel Sirkis (*Bayit Hadash*, 1561–1640[28]; see also *Hokhmat Adam*, Rabbi Avraham Danzig, 1748–1829).[29] More recently, Rabbi Eliezer Yehudah Waldenberg (*Tzitz Eliezer*, 1915–2006) [30] and Rabbi Ovadiah Yosef (1920–2013)[31] have reaffirmed this position. Similarly, Rabbi Moshe Feinstein (1895–1986) ruled against the production of veal as transgressing on these accounts.[32]

Rabbi Jacob Ettlinger (*Binyan Tziyon*, 1798–1871) used the term *to'elet muhletet*[33]—i.e., "categorical advantage"—as the only basis for justifying cruelty to animals, and even then, as long as it does not cause "great pain." While *Yad Halevi* referred to above and Rabbi Eliyahu Klatzkin (*Imrei Shefer*, 1852–1932)[34] are of the opinion that only clear human medical benefit can justify cruelty to animals.

24 *Piskei ha-Tosafot*, Avodah Zarah, 1:11.
25 *Shulhan Arukh, Even HaEzer* 5:14. Similarly, the Rema, loc. cit.
26 *Yoreh De'ah* 196.
27 BT *Shabbat* 24a.
28 *Yoreh De'ah* 33:9.
29 *Hilchot Treifot* 16:10.
30 Vol. 11, no. 49, 55.
31 *Yehaveh Daat* 3:66.
32 *Igarot Moshe, Even Ha'ezer* 4:92.
33 *Binyan Zion* 108.
34 *Imrei Shefer* 34.

The modern world in which we live, however, poses new challenges, even for the position of those authorities who gave restricted permission justifying animal pain for human benefit. While there is universal *halakhah* consensus regarding the use of animals for direct health benefits for humans, strong *halakhah* objections have been raised regarding cruelty for cosmetic purposes and in particular regarding the fur trade. In his *responsum*[35] prohibiting killing animals for their fur, the late Rabbi Hayim David Halevi (1924–1998) insisted that causing pain to animals can only be justified for "essential need" (*tzorekh hiyuni*).

What may have been an "essential need" in the past or in a different location (for example due to limited resources) may not be such in other time periods and places. These questions arise today in particular in relation to the livestock trade. In the past, animals slaughtered for consumption typically were raised on private farms, under relatively humane conditions. Nevertheless, in modern society, this has changed, and "factory farms" produce beef cattle by the millions and fowl by the billions every year for human consumption. And because factory farming is a business, its goal is to maximize production and, consequently, profit. Since the animals are seen as mere commodities, they are bred, fed, confined, and drugged to lay more eggs, birth more offspring, and die with more meat on their bones. Farmers cut costs by keeping animals in extremely confined and segregated conditions. As a result, animals experience intense stress that leads to unnatural aggression. To curb this aggression and prevent animals from damaging one another they are de-horned, typically without anesthetic. To protect the animals from the bacteria-full air in their confines and to stimulate aberrant growth, farmers routinely administer drugs and hormones to animals, which are passed on to the meat-eating public.

The consequences of agribusiness are institutionalized animal cruelty, environmental destruction, resource depletion, and health dangers. Dairy cows live in crowded pens or barns with concrete floors. They are forced to produce ten times more milk than they would produce in nature and as a result, experience numerous health problems. After dairy cows give birth, their calves are immediately separated from them, a practice which causes great distress (cows can be heard bellowing for their young.) They are then milked, re-inseminated, their calves taken away again and milked continuously until they are exhausted. Cows normally live twenty to twenty-five

---

35 *Aseh lcha rav*, vol. 3, no. 54.

years or more; dairy cows are slaughtered when they are three or five years old. Male calves are raised for both beef and veal. Veal calves live in particularly small confines and are often chained. They are fed a milk substitute deficient in iron and fiber. In other words, they are deliberately kept anemic and their muscles are atrophied so that their flesh will be pale and tender. They never see the sun or have contact with the natural vegetation. Ten percent of veal cows die in confinement.[36] Furthermore, farmers get more money for chickens with enlarged thighs and breasts. As a result, they breed the animals to be so heavy that their bones cannot support their weight. Consequently, the chickens have difficulty standing, and their legs often break. Like other factory-farmed animals, broiler chickens are raised in such overcrowded enclosures that they become aggressive. To stop them from fighting with one another, their beaks and toes are cut off *without* anesthetic, a painful practice that involves slicing through bone, cartilage, and soft tissue. Some cannot eat after being "de-beaked" and starve to death.

In the case of egg-producing chickens, newborn chicks are placed on a conveyor belt where a worker picks each one up to see if it is male or female. Newborn males are placed in trash bags and suffocated, crushed, or ground up alive. Newborn females are placed back on the belt. The next worker then picks up the female chick, holds her up to a machine's hot iron which cuts off her beak, and then places her back on the belt. Approximately one in five dies of stress and disease. Others are ground up and turned into animal feed on site. Layer hens are exposed to light constantly so that they will lay more eggs. At the end of their laying cycle, they are killed or subjected to "forced molting," a process that entails withholding food and water for up to eighteen days and keeping them in darkness so that their bodies are shocked into another laying cycle; many of these birds die from fatigue. Layer hens are slaughtered when they are one to two years old; hens normally live fifteen to twenty years. [37]

One might also note, as a means to buttress the main thesis of this chapter, that human health dangers that have arisen from such intensive animal

---

36 While there has been progress in veal calf confinement techniques, the quality of life improvement has still been poor. See Lawrence M. Hinman, *Contemporary Moral Issues: Diversity and Consensus* (New York: Routledge, 2016 [fourth edition]), 407; Linda Elkin McDaniel (Lisa Kemmerer, ed.), "Here I Stand by Faith" in *Speaking Up for Animals: An Anthology of Women's Voices* (New York: Routledge, 2012), 88.

37 See Peter R. Cheeke, *Contemporary Issues in Animal Agriculture* (Danville, IL: Interstate Publishers, 1999).

farming,[38] as well as the fact that intensive factory farming has grown to become the biggest threat to the global environment through deforestation for animal feed production; unsustainable use of water for feed-crops, including groundwater extraction; pollution of soil, water and air by nitrogen and phosphorus from fertilizer used for feed-crops and from manure; land degradation (reduced fertility, soil compaction, increased salinity, desertification); and loss of biodiversity due to eutrophication (the presence of excessive nutrients primarily in bodies of water due to effluent and other run off from the land), acidification, pesticides and herbicides.[39]

This wholescale transgression of Jewish values relating to animal life in industrial livestock production led the late Rabbi Aryeh Carmell to state that: "It seems doubtful that the Torah would sanction factory farming, which treats animals as machines, with apparent insensitivity to their natural needs and instincts."[40] Technical *halakhah* problems also result from this intensive farming as it leads to widespread distortions of animal organs.[41] The result is that commercially-produced milk contains the product of a significant number of deformed cows which may well disqualify the *kashrut* of the milk.[42]

Given the economic realities of today's food industry, the Jewish community has been enlisted inexorably into this system. It is not commercially feasible for kosher food suppliers to raise their own livestock. Even for argument's sake, one does not question the actual *kashrut* of the foodstuffs concerned; as the products of such wholescale transgressions of *halakhah* prohibitions, there is surely a serious *halakhah* question as to whether one can be party to such

---

38 See "Factory Farming: The Impact of Animal Feeding Operations on the Environment and Health of Local Communities" *Schneider K, Garrett L, June 19, 2009*; https://www.organic-consumers.org/news/hidden-link-between-factory-farms-toxic-chemicals-and-human-illness; "The Hidden Link Between Factory Farms, Toxic Chemicals and Human Illness," 2017. https://www.organicconsumers.org/news/hidden-link-between-factory-farms-toxic-chemicals-and-human-illness.

39 See "Environmental Impact of Industrial Farm Animal Production." *A Report of the Pew Commission on Industrial Farm Animal Production. Accessed July 2017.* https://www.ncifap.org/.

40 Aryeh Carmell, *Masterplan: Judaism, Its Programs, Meaning, Goals* (Jerusalem: Jerusalem Academy Publications, 1991), 69.

41 See Peter R. Cheeke, *Contemporary Issues in Animal Agriculture* (Danville, IL: Interstate Publishers, 1999).

42 See J. David Bleich," Is the Milk We Drink Kosher?" *Tradition: Contemporary Halakhah Problems*, vol. 6, Rabbinical Council of America, 2008, 55–70. Accessed March 26, 2018. http://traditionarchive.org/news/_pdfs/55-70%20Bleich.pdf.

desecration let alone aid and abet it. But this is precisely what we are doing when we buy these products.

As Rabbi David Sears writes:

> In light of the importance of proper animal treatment in Jewish law and tradition, we must not implicitly condone such practices by taking advantage of them without protest, rationalizing that we have not directly violated the laws of *tzaar baalei haim*. The establishment of higher humane standards in our society as a whole is a moral undertaking for which we, as willing participants in the system, must take responsibility. While the political issue of "animal welfare" may be new to many Jews, our concern about proper treatment of animals is clearly called for by traditional Jewish values. [43]

Indeed, if the hallmark of the Jew is their quality of compassion, including compassion for animals; and if the *raison d'être* of Jewish existence as a people is to observe the *mitzvot* as a testimony to higher Divine wisdom and beauty, then the purpose of the *mitzvot* is to refine us and make us more compassionate human beings, one must surely question how it is possible for those who seek to live in the fullness of both the letter and the spirit of Torah to be party to such terrible exploitation and cruelty.

Kashrut must be seen as more than purely the technicalities of *shehitah*, *bedikah*, and the *halakhically* required processing of the product. Judaism makes moral demands of us concerning our whole relationship with the animal world (and with the environment as a whole.) Even if the *halakhah* requirements at point "Z" concerning the termination of animal life are fulfilled; if in the process the obligations towards such life from point A to Y have been ignored and desecrated, it is not just a matter of what Ramban describes as *naval birshut ha-Torah*—observing the letter of the law while desecrating its spirit. It involves a massive *hillul ha-Shem* in which the Torah is not seen as a refinement of the human character, but as something that can legitimately collaborate with such cruelty and danger to humans and the environment.

---

43 David Sears. "Tsa'ar Baalei Chaim: Animal Welfare." Green Zionist Alliance: The Grassroots Campaign for a Sustainable Israel. Accessed July 27, 2018. http://aytzim.org/resources/articles/237.

The *mitzvah* of *Kiddush Ha-Shem* is not only an internal one, but an external one in relation to the nations of the world as the opening quotation in this article affirms (it is also the basis of Moses' intervention to prevent Divine extermination of Israel after the sins of the Golden Calf and the Evil Report of the Spies.) The inevitable conclusion should be that it is our sacred duty to refrain from being a party to a barbaric industry. Only animal products that come from humane farming should be considered as truly kosher, and a plant based diet should be upheld as the greatest guarantee that we are not party to the desecration of the Divine Name.

CHAPTER 4

The Case for Limiting Meat Consumption to Shabbat, Holidays, and Celebrations

Rabbi Aaron Potek

The Torah has an ambivalent relationship with meat-eating.[1] Although eating meat is clearly permitted, it is also highly regulated: only certain animals,[2] ritually slaughtered,[3] drained of blood,[4] with certain parts removed,[5] and prepared separate from any dairy.[6] Considering these many restrictions, the Torah's seemingly laissez-faire approach regarding when we can eat meat is surprising: "You may eat meat whenever you desire."[7] Perhaps it was taken for granted that meat would not be taken for granted. Prior to entering the Land of Israel, the Israelites could only eat meat that was brought as a sacrifice,[8] imbuing every

---

1 For this chapter, I will be using the rabbinic definition of meat—animals and fowl, but not fish. Individuals may choose to define meat more broadly (including fish) or narrowly (excluding fowl) for their own practice. Furthermore, the translations contained in this essay are a combination of scholarly sources combined with some emendations where I found it appropriate to the best of my ability.

2 See chapters Leviticus 11 and Deuteronomy 14. For example: Leviticus 11:3—"You may eat any animal that has a split hoof and that chews its cud."

3 Known as *shehitah*. While this process is explicitly defined in the Torah, it is alluded to in Deuteronomy 12:21. Rashi on the verse explains: "'You may slaughter any of the cattle or sheep that the LORD gives you, *as I have instructed you*.' This teaches us that there was already a commandment regarding the slaughtering of animals—as to how one should slaughter; it is not written in the Torah but it comprises the traditional regulations regarding the slaughter of animals that were given orally to Moses on Mount Sinai."

4 Deuteronomy 12:23.

5 See Leviticus 7:23: "You shall eat no fat of ox or sheep or goat."

6 This restriction is also not explicit in the Torah, though it is learned out from the verse "You shall not cook a kid in its mother's milk," which occurs three times in the Torah (Exodus 23:19; Exodus 34:26; Deuteronomy 14:21). The school of Rabbi Ishmael learns from this repetition: "One is a prohibition against eating it, one a prohibition against deriving benefit from it, and one a prohibition against cooking it" (BT *Hullin* 115b).

7 Deuteronomy 12:20.

8 See BT *Hullin* 16b.

act of eating meat with sanctity.[9] This sense of reverence toward eating meat would surely have continued after they entered the Land of Israel, where a Temple centered around animal sacrifices both reflected and perpetuated people's proximity to animals.

Today, we live in a vastly different reality. The dramatic rise of concentrated animal feeding operations (CAFOs) in just the last forty years has made meat significantly more affordable and more available. Meat consumption is at an all-time high—the average person now consumes over seventy-five pounds of meat per year.[10] Meat is also much more dissociated from its living source. "Factory farming now accounts for more than 99 percent of all farmed animals raised and slaughtered in the United States."[11]

Cheaper meat comes with serious costs. Large amounts of meat consumption can have negative health consequences.[12] The high demand for meat production has led to the mistreatment of both animals and workers in factory farms.[13] On a more global scale, the large quantity of animals raised to meet the high demand of consumers is a significant contributor to greenhouse gases and climate change, and the inefficient use of resources needed to raise these animals has contributed to global hunger.[14] These issues could be mitigated, even eliminated, with a substantial reduction in meat consumption.

Jews alone cannot drastically curb the negative effects of mass meat consumption; our consumption of meat represents only a small fraction of the world's total meat consumption. Nevertheless, while there is no data on meat consumption by Jews, it's fair to assume—based on where most Jews live—that we consume far more than the world average; the average American consumes

9 See Rashi on Deuteronomy 12:20, s.v. "As all the desire of your soul." See also Nehama Leibowitz, *Studies in Devarim (Deuteronomy)* (Jerusalem: World Zionist Organization, 1993), 135.

10 Meat consumption (indicator). doi: 10.1787/fa290fd0-en. Accessed on 30 July 2017.

11 "Ending Factory Farming." Farm Forward. November 3, 2017. Accessed March 26, 2018. https://farmforward.com/ending-factory-farming/.

12 See A. Pan, Q. Sun, A.M. Bernstein, et al. "Red Meat Consumption and Risk of Type 2 Diabetes 3 Cohorts of US Adults and an Updated Meta-analysis." *Am J Clin Nutr.* 94, no. 4 (2011):1088–1096. Conclusion: "Red meat consumption is associated with an increased risk of total, CVD, and cancer mortality."

13 See Technical Report no. 2: *Occupational and Community Public Health Impacts of Industrial Farm Animal Production,* and Technical Report no. 4: *The Welfare of Animals in Concentrated Animal Feeding Operations,* "Putting Meat on the Table: Industrial Farm Animal Production in America," A Report of the Pew Commission on Industrial Farm Animal Production, 2008.

14 See "The Importance of Reducing Animal Product Consumption and Wasted Food in Mitigating Catastrophic Climate Change," Brent Kim, MHS; Roni Neff, PhD, SM; Raychel Santo; and Juliana Vigorito, December 2015.

over two hundred pounds of meat per year, and Israel consumes more poultry (especially turkey) per capita than any other country.[15] We still have the opportunity, maybe even the responsibility, to model a more mindful, ethical meat-eating practice. Together, we are able to contribute to an important paradigm shift. After all, our influence as "a treasured people" stems not from our size but from our ability to serve as pioneers.[16]

While an in-depth analysis of the consequences of modern-day meat consumption is outside the scope of this chapter, the possibility that any, let alone all, of them are as dire as some claim should inspire some self-reflection. As Jews, we must take seriously the prohibitions against animal cruelty,[17] worker abuse,[18] and wasting resources.[19] We must also take seriously the injunctions to ensure and protect our health[20] and the health of our planet.[21] Surely, we should factor in these considerations when deciding how much meat we should eat.

Still, these aspects of Jewish law are hard to quantify. A direct cause-and-effect relationship between eating meat and these negative consequences is hard to prove, so arguments for meat reduction based on these reasons are easy to dismiss or ignore. I'll therefore focus my case for reducing meat consumption from within the realm of Jewish thought as it relates to meat consumption itself. Those who value a more holistic approach to Judaism and the broader impact of our actions can benefit from a richer, more comprehensive foundation on which to base a practice of meat reduction.

Limiting Meat Production

Within the laws of *kashrut*, eating meat is rarely explicitly prohibited.[22] One might conclude, then, that kosher meat-eating can be, with a few exceptions,

---

15 See Chris Mayda, *A Regional Geography of the United States and Canada: Toward a Sustainable Future* (New York: Rowman & Littlefield Publishers, 2013), 372; OCED. "OECD Review of Agricultural Policies: Israel 2010." *OECD Review of Agricultural Policies*, June 2010. doi:10.1787/9789264079397-en, 59.

16 See Ibn Ezra on Deuteronomy 7:6–7: "'Of all the peoples on earth the Lord chose you to be His treasured people. It is not because you are the most numerous of peoples that God desired you and chose you—indeed, you are the smallest of peoples.' Treasured denotes something beautiful, the like of which can be found nowhere else."

17 See BT *Shabbat* 128b.

18 See Deuteronomy 24:14.

19 Known as *Bal Tashhit*. See Maimonides, *Sefer ha-Mitzvot*, Negative Laws, no. 57.

20 See Maimonides, *Mishneh Torah, Hilchot De'ot* 4:1.

21 See *Ecclesiastes Rabbah* 7:13: "Be careful that you do not ruin and destroy My world; for if you destroy it there is no one to repair it after you."

22 The two obvious examples are 1) An *onen* 2) During the Nine Days, from Rosh Chodesh Av through Tisha B'Av.

unlimited. Yet, before uncovering our tradition's specific unease regarding meat-eating, this conclusion is at odds with a more general Jewish value of moderation. Aware of the spiritual danger inherent in unregulated pleasure, which includes meat-eating, the medieval scholar Rabbi Moses ben Nachman (1194–1270)—Nachmanides—comments on the commandment "You shall be holy":

> The Torah has admonished us against immorality and forbidden foods, but permitted sexual intercourse between husband and wife and the eating of [kosher] meat and wine. If so, a man of desire could consider this to be permission to be passionately addicted to relations with his wife … and "be among winebibbers and gluttonous eaters of flesh"[23] … since this prohibition has not been mentioned in the Torah, and thus will be an abomination with the permission of the Torah. Therefore, after listing matters altogether prohibited, the Torah in general terms commands us to practice moderation even in matters which are permitted.[24]

Even permitted desire must be checked by the overall command to "be holy"; restraint and holiness are interconnected. According to Rabbi Avraham Yishaya Karelitz—known as the Hazon Ish (Belarus 1878–1953)—the most important attribute for a Jew to possess is self-control.[25] Rabbi Joseph Hertz, the Chief Rabbi of the United Kingdom in the early part of the twentieth century, frames this idea nicely: "The highest artist, in the eyes of Jewish teachers of all generations, is not the greatest master in self-expression, but in self-control."[26] Or, as it says in Proverbs: "It's not good to eat a lot of honey." [27]

But there is a particular concern around excess meat-eating. A defining characteristic of the wayward and rebellious son[28] is being "a glutton and a guzzler."[29] The Talmud,[30] drawing on the Proverbs verse cited by Nachmanides, defines "glutton" as someone who eats an excessive amount of meat. Elsewhere

---

23 Proverbs 23:20.
24 Nachmanides, Commentary on Leviticus 19:2.
25 *Sefer Emunah v'Bitahon*, 4:1–6, cited by Aharon Hersch Fried, "Is there a Disconnect between Torah Learning and Torah Living?" *Flatbush Journal of Jewish Law and Thought*, fn. 16.
26 J.H. Hertz, *The Pentateuch & Haftorahs: Hebrew Text, English Translation and Commentary* (London: Soncino Press, 1996 [Second Edition]), 376.
27 Proverbs 25:27.
28 Deuteronomy 21:18.
29 Ibid., 21:20.
30 BT *Sanhedrin* 70a.

it states that parents should not accustom their children to meat.[31] Excess meat consumption seems to be indicative of, or a cause of, rebelliousness.

The correlation between meat-eating and rebellion is highlighted in another story in the Torah: when the "riffraff"[32] who are wandering with the Israelites in the desert desire meat. That desire is inherently problematic, which we learn from God's response, in both words and action:

> "Purify yourselves,[33] for tomorrow you will eat meat, for you have kept whining before the Lord, saying: 'If only we had meat to eat! Indeed, we were better off in Egypt.' The Lord will give you meat and you shall eat. You shall eat not one day, not two, not even five days or ten or twenty, but a whole month, until it comes out of your nostrils and becomes loathsome to you. For you have rejected the Lord who is among you" ... While the flesh was still between their teeth, not yet chewed, the anger of the Lord was kindled against the people, and the Lord struck the people with a very severe plague. That place was named *Kivrot ha-Ta'avah*, because the people who had the craving (*ta'avah*) were buried (*kavru*) there.[34]

God interprets their desire for meat as a desire to rebel;[35] allowing them to eat meat here seems more sarcastic than authentic.[36] The desire for meat is yet again associated with serious spiritual danger. Rabbi Nachman Goldstein of Tcherin (d. 1894) sums up this sentiment: "One must be particularly careful about eating meat, for its potential for spiritual harm is far greater than other foods."[37] Other Jewish thinkers, like Spanish philosopher Rabbi Yosef Albo

---

31 BT *Hullin* 84a.

32 Numbers 11:4. In Hebrew: *asafsuf*. According to Rashi this group is connected to the *erav rav*, the crowd that accompanied the Israelites leaving Egypt.

33 Interestingly, this may be an indication that even non-sacrificial meat was intended to be imbued with a level of sanctity. Alternatively, as Rabbi Naftali Zvi Yehuda Berlin—known as Haamek Hadavar—writes, it could be meant to convey the importance of a meal involving meat—"for there is no preparation for a meal without meat."

34 Numbers 11:18–20; 33–34.

35 See *Harchev Davar* 11:4.

36 According to Nachmanides: God gave them meat for a full month "to such a great extent that they will become sick of it, and they will consider it detestable and like a strange inedible food" (Numbers 11:19).

37 *Nachas Hashulhan, Hilchot Shehitah*, 1; For a more comprehensive analysis, see David Sears, *The Vision of Eden: Animal Welfare and Vegetarianism in Jewish Law and Mysticism* (CreateSpace Independent Publishing Platform, 2014 [Second Edition]), 308–10.

(1380–1444), went a step further, understanding the many harmful spiritual side-effects of eating meat less as a possibility and more as an inevitability:

> For in addition to the cruelty, rage, and the accustoming of oneself to the evil habit of shedding innocent blood, the eating of meat from certain animals also gives rise to thickness, gloom, and opacity of the soul ... And even with regard to those animals the Torah permitted, the Torah only spoke to the evil impulse.[38]

In light of these negative consequences, regardless of their probability, it's no surprise that God's original plan was for humans to be vegetarian. "Meat was not permitted to the first human for consumption ... But when the children of Noah came, God permitted them to eat meat."[39] Still, the prohibition from eating the blood[40] served as a reminder that the divine concession to eat meat was only out of necessity.[41] Indeed, "This partial prohibition was designed to call to mind the previously total one."[42]

Within this critical context, we can now better understand the Torah's strangely-worded permission to eat meat:

> When the Lord your God has enlarged your territory as He has promised you, and you say, 'I shall eat meat,' for you have the desire to eat meat, then you may eat meat whenever you desire. If the place where the Lord your God chooses to establish His name is too far from you, you may slaughter from your herds and flocks that the Lord has given you, as I have commanded you, and in your own towns you may eat meat whenever you desire ... But be sure you do not eat the blood, because the blood is the life, and you must not eat the life with the meat. You must not eat it; pour it out on the ground like water. Do not eat it, so that it may go well with you and your children after you, because you will be doing what is right in the eyes of the Lord.[43]

---

38 *Sefer ha-Ikkarim,* Book 3, chapter 15.
39 BT *Sanhedrin* 59b.
40 Genesis 9:4.
41 Rabbi Yosef Albo, *Sefer ha-Ikkarim,* Book 3, chapter 15.
42 See Umberto (Moses) Cassuto, *From Adam to Noah: A Commentary on the Book of Genesis, Part 1* (Jerusalem: Magnes Press, 1978) on Genesis 1:27; See also Nehama Leibowitz, New Studies in Bereshit (Genesis) (Jerusalem: World Zionist Organization, 1981), 76–77.
43 Deuteronomy 12:20–25.

The language of this permission—with its emphasis on desire and blood—is ambivalent at best. As biblical scholar Nehama Leibowitz (1905–1997) points out: "How grudgingly is such permission granted! 'If you cannot resist the temptation and must eat meat, then do so' seems to be the tenor of this barely tolerated dispensation."[44] Modern scholar Samuel H. Dresner (1923–2000) connects this dispensation given to the Israelites with the similar dispensation given to Noah:

> The permission to eat meat is thus understood as a compromise, a divine concession to human weakness and human need. The Torah, as it were, says: 'I would prefer that you abstain from eating meat altogether, that you subsist on that which springs forth from the earth, for to eat meat the life of an animal must be taken, and that is a fearful act. But since you are not perfect humans, and your world is neither a Garden of Eden nor the Kingdom of Heaven; since your desires cannot be halted nor your nutritional requirements altered, they must at least be controlled; since you will eat meat and since, perhaps, you need to eat meat, you may eat it, but with one restriction—that you have reverence for the life that you take.' 'The flesh with the soul thereof, which is the blood thereof, shall you not eat' (Genesis 9:4).[45]

The restriction on consuming blood is a reminder to control our desire for meat by reminding us that it involves the taking of a life. Rabbi Abraham Isaac Kook (1865–1935), the first Ashkenazi Chief Rabbi of Palestine, also noticed a "hidden reprimand between the lines of the Torah in the sanction to eat meat."[46] He writes:

> When you say 'I shall eat meat,' for you have the desire to eat meat, then you may eat meat whenever you desire (Deuteronomy 12:20) ... [this is] as long as your inner morality does not abhor the eating of animal flesh, as you already abhor the eating of human flesh ... but when the time comes for the human condition to abhor [eating] the flesh of animals, because of

---

44 Nehama Leibowitz, *Studies in Devarim (Deuteronomy)* (Jerusalem: World Zionist Organization, 1993), 136.

45 Samuel H. Dresner, "Keeping Kosher: A Diet for the Soul (New York: United Synagogue Commission on Jewish Education, 2000 [Revised Edition]), 15.

46 Rabbi Abraham Isaac Kook, *Talelei Orot*, 318 (trans. Ben Zion Bokser).

the moral loathing inherent in that act, you surely will **not** 'have the desire to eat meat,' and you will not eat it.[47]

According to Rabbi Kook, Jews will come to embrace vegetarianism "through a moral struggle, but the time for this conquest is not yet … What prepares the ground for this state is the commandments, those intended specifically for this area of concern … [which] came to regulate the eating of meat, in steps that will take us to the higher purpose."[48] For Rav Kook, all Torah laws relating to animals are intended as a constant "reminder that we are not dealing with things outside the law, that they are not automatons, devoid of life, but with living things."[49] Similarly, Rabbi Dresner writes: "Reverence for life, teaching an awareness of what we are about when we engage in the simple act of eating flesh, is the constant lesson of the laws of Kashrut."[50] This sensitivity will inevitably lead to a reduction in meat consumption and, eventually, to its elimination.

It should be no surprise, then, that we find the sages limiting the permissibility of meat consumption in a variety of extra-*halakhah* statements. Here are seven examples:

1. "The Torah teaches etiquette (lit. *derech eretz*), that one should only eat meat at night [as Moses said to the children of Israel: 'This shall be, when the Lord will give you in the evening meat to eat' (Exodus 16:8)]."[51]
2. "The Torah teaches etiquette, that one should only eat meat with this preparation [of catching the animal himself]."[52]

---

47 Rabbi Abraham Isaac Kook (ed. David Cohen; trans. Jonathan Rubenstein) *A Vision of Vegetarianism and Peace*. A version of this text is accessible at https://archive.org/stream/AVisionOfVegetarianismAndPeace/AVisionOfVegetarianismAndPeace_djvu.txt

48 Rabbi Abraham Isaac Kook (trans. Ben Zion Bokser), *Talelei Orot*, 318–19.

49 Ibid., 319.

50 Samuel H. Dresner, "Keeping Kosher: A Diet for the Soul (New York: United Synagogue Commission on Jewish Education, 2000 [Revised Edition]), 27.

51 BT *Yoma* 75b.

52 BT *Hullin* 84a. This seems to be the simple understanding of the Talmud. Rashi, however, has a different interpretation. He understands the Talmud to mean "*as if* he himself had caught it, and that it wasn't prepared for him"—that is only the amount that he could have caught himself. Interestingly, the Rif has an alternative version of the Talmud: " … that a person should only eat meat that is not with this preparation." According to this *girsa*, the "preparation" is not referring to the hunting of the animal but to its domestication. This, then, leads to a similar conclusion, as explained by *HaHagot HaBach*: "If the meat was prepared for him (domesticated), he should not eat it. Rather he can only eat it if it was not prepared (domesticated) and he needs to catch it himself."

3. "When the Lord your God has enlarged your territory [as He has promised you, and you say, "I shall eat meat," for you have the desire to eat meat ...]" (Deuteronomy 12:20). The Torah teaches etiquette, that one should only eat meat when one has a special craving for it."[53]

4. "'You might think you can purchase meat at a marketplace and eat it. [This is not so, as it teaches:] " ... you may slaughter from your herds and flocks.'" (Deuteronomy 12:21). If one owns a flock of [animals], one may take from it. But if not, one may not buy [meat] from the marketplace."[54]

5. "The Torah teaches etiquette, that one should not desire to eat meat unless one lives in abundance and wealth."[55]

6. "It is prohibited for an ignoramus to eat meat, as it is stated: 'This is the law (lit. *torah*) of the beast and of the fowl.'[56] Anyone who engages in Torah study is permitted to eat the meat of animals and fowl, and anyone who does not engage in Torah study is prohibited to eat the meat of animals or fowl."[57]

7. "It is enough for a healthy person to eat meat once a week, on Friday night."[58]

Clearly, significantly reducing meat consumption is a Torah value, upheld and expanded by the rabbis.

Eliminating Meat Consumption

Given the Torah's serious unease with meat-eating, why not take this sentiment to its logical conclusion: Why not become a vegetarian? Rabbi Kook deals with this question explicitly. He believes that the moral energy spent on vegetarianism will distract from more important and urgent moral crises. There is a certain hypocrisy, he argues, in focusing that energy on being a vegetarian:

> . . . as if the rule of evil and falsehood had been banished; as if hatred between peoples, national rivalries, racial animosity, and family strife, which cause so many mortal casualties and spill so much blood—as if

---

53 Ibid.
54 Ibid.
55 Rashi on Deuteronomy 12:20, s.v. "When the Lord expands your border." Based on BT *Hullin* 84a.
56 Leviticus 11:46.
57 BT *Pesahim* 49b.
58 Maimonides, *Mishneh Torah, Hilchot De'ot* 5:10. Based on BT *Hullin* 84a.

all these had already disappeared from the earth, and the only way left in which to elevate human piety was to attend to the establishment of a moral foundation in regard to animals. Therefore, this is not a fitting standard for humanity in general as long as humanity remains in its state of moral baseness, except insofar as it does not overtax the capacity which is possible for the force of human morality, in its weakened state, to sustain.[59]

Some may be able to take on vegetarianism without feeling morally "overtaxed." But Rabbi Kook is concerned, rightly so, "that there ought to be a proper ordering of priorities."[60] Alleviating human suffering must take precedence over animal welfare. But beyond its establishing of a moral hierarchy with humans at the top, eating meat is also valuable as a source of joy. As it says in the Talmud: "When the Temple is standing, there is only rejoicing through meat, as it is stated[61]: 'And you shall sacrifice peace-offerings and you shall eat there and you shall rejoice before the Lord your God.'"[62] According to some commentators,[63] although the Temple is no longer standing, one still must fulfill the commandment to rejoice on holidays by eating meat.[64]

The status of the obligation to eat meat on holidays notwithstanding, our tradition certainly appreciates the joy associated with meat consumption.[65] Completely denying ourselves this joy, or any permitted joy, is not what the Torah wants us to do. As Maimonides explains:

Our Sages directed man to abstain only from those things which the Torah denies him and not to forbid himself permitted things by vows and oaths [of abstention]. Thus, our Sages stated: "Are not those things which the Torah has prohibited sufficient for you that you must forbid additional

---

59 Rabbi Abraham Isaac Kook (David Cohen, ed.; Jonathan Rubenstein, trans). *A Vision of Vegetarianism and Peace.*

60 J. David Bleich, "Vegetarianism and Judaism," *Tradition*, vol. 2–3, no. 1 (Summer, 1987), 86.

61 Deuteronomy 27:7.

62 BT *Pesahim* 109a.

63 Maimonides, *Mishneh Torah, Hilchot Yom Tov* 6:18; *Tur Shulhan Arukh*, OH 529; and *Magen Avraham*, OH 529:3.

64 Others disagree. See Bleich's, "Vegetarianism and Judaism," 87–89, for a more comprehensive analysis.

65 Of course, this does not apply to someone for whom eating meat is not joyous, for reasons of palate, health or otherwise. See Rabbi Hayyim David HaLevi, *Aseh Lekha Rav* 5:47 and *Shulhan Arukh HaRav* 242:1–2.

things to yourself?" ... So King Solomon says[66]: "Do not be overly righteous and do not be overly clever; why make yourself desolate?"[67]

The holiness of moderation goes both ways.[68] Just as we should not overindulge permitted pleasures, we also should not refuse them. As Rabbi Shlomo Prager of Hungary (1887–1944) beautifully describes:

> It is fitting for Jews to enjoy from G-d's creations and to give praise and thanks to the G-d who created them, as it says in the Ethics of Our Fathers, "Everything that the Holy One created was for His glory."[69]

Or, as it was written in Ecclesiastes over two thousand years earlier:

> There is nothing better for a man than that he should eat and drink, and make his soul enjoy pleasure for his labor. This also I saw, that it is from the hand of God. For who will eat, or who will enjoy, if not I?[70]

If Not Now, When?

How then do we realize this goal of limiting, without eliminating, meat consumption? Without a set practice, our meat-eating would be unintentional, irregular, and reactive, defined by fickle desires. This is not the model of control that the laws relating to meat-eating are meant to instill.[71] And without a clear definition of when to eat meat, it is difficult to check ourselves from excess meat-eating.

---

66 Ecclesiastes 7:16.
67 Maimonides, *Mishneh Torah, Hilchot De'ot* 3:1.
68 Nachmanides, Leviticus 19:2, referenced above.
69 *Shu"t Sheilat Yaakov* 1:93.
70 Ecclesiastes 2:24–25.
71 Interestingly, Shlomo Ephraim Luntschitz (1550–1619, Prague)—the *Kli Yakar*—based on his commentary of Genesis 27:3, believes an irregular meat-eating practice is the intension of Torah's dispensation. "A person should not become accustomed to eating meat, as it is written, 'You shall eat meat with all your desire. Eat it, however, as you eat the gazelle and the deer ...' (Deuteronomy 12:21–22) This means that you should eat meat by circumstance rather than in a set way. For the gazelle and the deer are not easily found around human dwellings." Still, he agrees that the ultimate goal is reducing our meat consumption: "Consequently, since one eats of them rarely, one will not come to habituate oneself to eating ordinary meat since it gives birth to cruelty and other bad qualities in the body of a person."

By limiting our meat consumption to Shabbat, holidays, and celebrations, we not only resolve these challenges, but we also add to the joy of these days/occasions.

As we've already seen in the context of festivals,[72] food is a way to express and enhance the celebration of important moments in the Jewish calendar. The Talmud relates that Shabbat delight (*oneg*) is experienced through food.[73] And the existence of religiously commanded meals (*seudot mitzvah*), which have a special status because they are linked to a celebration like a circumcision, bar/bat *mitzvah*, or wedding, underscores the connection between food and joy.[74]

But for the food to truly add to the celebration of the day, the meal itself needs to be special. Regarding Shabbat (and, by association, holidays),[75] Maimonides writes:

> "One needs to prepare extra fatty meat and quality wine for Shabbat, all according to one's financial abilities, and anyone who adds to what is brought out on Shabbat and who prepares lots of good food is praised ... "[76]

We see a similar idea regarding a new month:

> "It is a commandment to add to meals eaten on the first day of each month."—one who brings out lots of food during the *Rosh Chodesh* meal and eats and drinks well—this is praiseworthy.[77]

"Adding" to an ordinary meal could be understood in terms of quantity and/or quality. But it could also be understood as adding a different type of food in order to make the meal special. According to Maimonides, the Shabbat

---

72 BT *Pesahim* 109a, referenced *supra*.

73 See BT *Shabbat* 118b.

74 I intentionally do not wish to objectively define the terms "holidays" and "celebrations." These could be any days that are Jewishly significant. They could be any meals that are considered a *seudat mitzvah*—for example, *brit milah, pidyon haben, bar/bat mitzvah, siyum masechet*, wedding, etc. They could be any meals eaten on a day when *hallel* is said. They could be any meals eaten on a day when we *daven mussaf*, corresponding to special sacrifices that were brought in the Temple. Analyzing which days/occasions fall into each category and the practical differences between these different definitions is beyond the scope of this chapter.

75 He makes clear that what is true for Shabbat is equally true for all the holidays. See *Mishneh Torah, Hilchot Yom Tov* 6:16.

76 Maimonides, *Mishneh Torah*, Laws of Shabbat 30:7.

77 *Shulhan Arukh* 419:1.

meal should be different not only in quantity and/or quality, but in the content of what is being served:

> One who is delighted and rich so that all his days are like Shabbat needs to change his food on Shabbat from what he eats during the week.[78]

This idea of adding something unique to Shabbat provides a nice counterbalance to the many negative restrictions of the day. After all, the laws of Shabbat have two dimensions: not doing (*shamor*—observe[79]) and doing (*zachor*—remember[80]). Given meat's association with joy within the Jewish tradition,[81] limiting it to only joyous meals would be fitting. As Rabbi Eliezer Melamed, Rosh Yeshiva of Yeshivat Har Bracha, explains: "When one eats meat at Shabbat and *Yom Tov* meals, or at *seudot mitzvah*, then the meat becomes joined with the happiness of the commandment [to eat a joyous meal] and helps with its fulfillment."[82] Eating meat on only Shabbat, holidays, and celebrations is an easy way to make these days feel special while substantially limiting our overall meat consumption.

Additional Benefits

Just as eating meat enhances the experience of day, the day enhances the experience of eating meat. This happens in two ways. First, the day itself spiritually transforms the food eaten during it, imbuing the food with holiness.[83] "On Shabbat and festivals the day revolves around *seudot* [meals] which are necessary and intrinsic to its observance."[84] Since the food is part of a religiously-commanded meal, it attains an elevated status. This helps "elevate the holy sparks and the divine life-force garbed within food and drink,"[85] a kabbalistic idea that holy eating is an important part of *tikkun olam*, repairing the world.[86] As Rabbi Nachman of Breslov explains: "The eating of the Sabbath is entirely

---

78 Maimonides, *Mishneh Torah*, Laws of Shabbat 30:8.
79 Deuteronomy 5:12.
80 Exodus 20:8.
81 Maimonides explicitly mentions meat as a form of Shabbat *oneg*. See *Mishneh Torah*, Laws of Shabbat 30:10.
82 *Peninei Halacha*, "Pious Customs Regarding the Eating of Meat," *Likutim* 3:9:4.
83 See *Minhag Yisrael* Torah O.C. 274:1.
84 Susan Schneider, *Eating As Tikkun* (Jerusalem: A Still Small Voice, 1996), 44.
85 Rabbi Nachum of Chernobyl, *Me'or Einayim, Emor*, s.v. *v'hinei noda*, 246.
86 See Schneider's *Eating As Tikkun* for a more comprehensive analysis.

spiritual, entirely holy, and it ascends to a completely different place than the eating of the ordinary days of the week."[87]

By reserving our meat-eating for only the days that are spiritually significant, we make the act of eating meat more spiritually significant. Rav Tzadok Ha-Cohen of Lublin[88] notes that the paschal offering[89] is the only instance of biblically commanded meat-eating. He explains that after "the Temple's destruction we no longer eat a portion of the Pesach sacrifice at our seder, which means there is no longer a moment in the year when the meat that we have eaten has an opportunity to elevate through *mitzvah* [commandment]. For this reason, he implies that one should be a vegetarian except on Shabbat and Yom Tov, where the *mitzvah*-like status of those meals protects the soul from damage."[90]

Rabbi Melamed describes a similar practice:

> With optional meals [meals that do not have the category of *seudot mitzvah*], the sages of the kabbalah said that this elevation (lit. *tikkun*) does not always happen ... therefore the pious ones refrained from eating meat during these optional meals. Their goal was that all their eating would be only for a commandment. Any time when it wasn't completely clear that the meat would be elevated through their eating, it de facto returned to the ethical challenge that eating meat requires the killing of a bird or animal.[91]

A second way that holy days elevate meat-eating is by creating elevating our mindfulness. "'[One should eat meat] from one Sabbath evening to the next,'[92] for then divine mercy prevails, and one's intent is perfect."[93] The expanded consciousness that we achieve on these holy days can help us more deeply appreciate the meat we consume during it.

According to Rabbi Mordechai Yosef Leiner—the Ishbitzer Rebbe—this "expanded consciousness" is actually a necessary precondition to eating meat.

---

87 Rabbi Nachman of Breslov, *Likkutei Moharan* II, 17.

88 *Pri HaTzadik*, vol. 1, A Treatise on the Time of Eating, section 10.

89 Exodus 12:3–13.

90 Susan Schneider, *Eating As* Tikkun (Jerusalem: A Still Small Voice, 1996), 47, fn. 21.

91 *Peninei Halacha*, "Pious Customs Regarding the Eating of Meat," *Likutim* 3:9:4.

92 BT *Pesahim* 49b.

93 *Sefer ha-Peliach*, s.v. U'r'ei v'havain, 282.

He comments on the opening phrase to the Torah's permission to eat meat, "When the Lord expands your borders ... ":

> When the Torah was given to the Israelites, this is called "when the Lord expands your borders" because this is the fundamental great expansion, the expansion of knowledge to understand that this is a living (*nefesh*) animal, and this is why the verse says "you may eat whenever you desire" (lit. whenever your soul (*nefesh*) desires).[94]

Eating meat during holy moments, then, should help us be optimally present and mindful, which some see as a requirement for eating meat. As Rabbi Yitzchak of Vorka writes: "In order to eat meat one must not do so in a state of distraction ... rather, the desire of one's entire being for God must be present."[95] Consequently, this would imbue the act of eating meat with a sense of gravitas. This practice has an added benefit: in addition to elevating the happy occasions themselves, it also helps to create an anticipation leading up to them. This isn't simply a nice idea. Indeed, according to some commentators like Nachmanides, the commandment to remember the Sabbath day[59] applies every day, not just on Shabbat.[96] He cites an example from the Talmud where this commandment can be fulfilled through an eating practice:

> It was said of Shammai the Elder that all his days he would eat in order to honor Shabbat. If he would find a nice cow he would say, 'This will be for Shabbat.' If he found one that was nicer, he would set aside the second one and then eat the first one.'[97]

By saving the best food for Shabbat, Shammai not only believes meat adds joy to the day but also anticipates it during the whole week leading up to it. Though his eating habits, Shammai embodies a yearning for Shabbat, the culmination of each week. As Rabbi Abraham Joshua Heschel writes:

> Judaism tries to foster the vision of life as a pilgrimage to the seventh day; the longing for the sabbath all days of the week, which is a form of longing

---

94 Rabbi Mordechai Yosef Leiner, "Mei Hashiloach" Part 2, 115.
95 *Beis Yitzchak, R'eh*, 91.
96 See Nachmanides on Exodus 20:8.
97 BT *Beitza* 16a. Hillel did not share in this practice, "For all his deeds were for the sake of heaven."

for the eternal sabbath all the days of our lives. It seeks to displace the coveting of things in space for coveting of things in time, teaching man to covet the seventh day all days of the week.[98]

A slight adaptation to Shammai's practice—eating meat on only Shabbat, holidays, and celebrations—allows us to experience this daily yearning for these special days, like one who anticipates seeing a lover.[99] And since we must enter Shabbat with an appetite as a visceral expression of that yearning,[100] this way we can also ensure we are eating meat with the proper, necessary desire.

Precedent

Hopefully, by now, I have made a compelling case that the practice of eating meat on Shabbat, holidays, and celebrations will help reduce our meat consumption, sanctify the meat we do eat, and elevate the days on which we do it. But Jews, a people of tradition, are traditionally skeptical of new ideas. Is this practice an innovation or does it have its roots in the past? We have already seen some allusions to this practice.[101] Rabbi Yechial Epstein of Lithuania (1829–1908), in his discussion on the status of the *seudah hamafseket* [the meal eaten before the Yom Kippur fast], mentions the practice of vowing to eat meat on only Shabbat and holidays.[102] And, not surprisingly, Rabbi Kook also ate meat only once a week, on Shabbat.[103]

Many others who did not have this explicit practice still strongly urged the refraining of meat during the week. Rabbi Moses Cordovero taught thirty-six rules "which if a man practices, he shall live by them."[104] One of them was: "One should be sparing with meat and wine during the weekdays [i.e., not Shabbat]."[105] Another early Kabbalist, Rabbi Abraham Berukhim, reported that "there are certain especially pious scholars of Torah who neither eat meat nor

---

98 Abraham Joshua Heschel, *The Sabbath* (New York: Farrar, Strauss and Giroux, 1951), 90–91.

99 Rabbi Israel ben Joseph Al-Nakawa (fourteenth century), *Menorat Hamaor*, ch. 8, 575.

100 Maimonides, *Mishneh Torah*, Laws of Shabbat 30:4.

101 See Rabbi Tzadok Ha-Kohen, Rabbi Eliezer Melamed, and *Sefer ha-Peliach*, supra.

102 *Orech Hashulhan*, O.C. 604:11.

103 While I am not aware of any written source confirming this, I have heard from reliable sources that this is a true statement.

104 Leviticus 18:5.

105 See Lawrence Fine (ed.), *Safed Spirituality: Rules of Mystical Piety, the Beginning of Wisdom* (Mahwah, NJ: Paulist Press, 1984), 35.

drink wine during the entire week."[106] Similarly, Rabbi Yehudah Ashkenazi of Poland (d. 1723) wrote: "Praiseworthy is the one who can separate from meat and wine during the week."[107]

Even without explicit precedent, this practice may be a closer realization of the Torah's goal as it relates to meat-eating. As Maimonides writes in the *Guide of the Perplexed*, God does not always lead us by a "direct path," refraining "from prescribing what the people by their natural disposition would be incapable of obeying."[108] As we have discussed, the dispensation to eat meat may not reflect the Torah's ultimate intention. As Rabbi Kook explains: "Through general, moral and intellectual advancement ... shall the latent aspiration of justice for the animal kingdom come out into the open, when the time is ripe."[109] Even if the time for complete vegetarianism is not "ripe," perhaps adopting this practice is an important next step of our "general, moral and intellectual advancement."

Conclusion

In this essay, I attempted to demonstrate that limiting meat consumption to Shabbat, *Yom Tov*, and celebrations is an idea that is deeply rooted in traditional Judaism. While this practice is certainly not an obligation, it has many benefits—physical and spiritual—and demonstrates the elevated consciousness that the Torah intended when it comes to meat-eating. "Just as a wise man is distinct in his wisdom and his character traits, and he stands apart from others regarding them, so too he must be distinct ... in his eating."[110] I believe this distinct eating practice reflects a distinct Jewish wisdom, and I hope it will help people to further embody Torah values.

---

106 Ibid., 12.
107 *Ba'er Heitiv* on O.C. 134:3.
108 Maimonides, *Guide to the Perplexed*, 3:32.
109 Rabbi Abraham Isaac Kook, *Talelei Orot*: See "A Vision of Vegetarianism and Peace."
110 Maimonides, *Mishneh Torah, Hilchot De'ot* 5:1

Section 7   Environmentalism, Conservation, and GMOs

CHAPTER 1

Ethical Eating and the Impact on Our Environment

Rabbi Dr. Mel Gottlieb

As living beings in the twenty-first century, we are confronted with increasing threats to our environment. As caretakers of the Earth, it is incumbent on us to consider alterations to our lifestyle to protect the environment. When we consider the threats to our land, water, and air, the proliferation of pesticides and other chemical pollutants, resource scarcities, and the perils awaiting our climate, we have a special obligation to sustain our world. With the Torah as our guide, I would like to make some suggestions that relate to our eating habits, particularly to our heavy animal ingestion.

The Torah teaches us that, though human beings are given the mandate to rule the Earth, we are also instructed to serve and care for it. While everything belongs to God, the earth has been given to the human family.[1] We are the stewards of the Earth to see that its bounty is available for all of God's children and distribute part of our produce for the poor and needy (e.g., *Leket, Shickcha, Peah, Shmita*) (Leviticus 25:1–7, 18–22). We are to be co-workers with God in helping to preserve and improve the world. An oft-paraphrased quote, based on the Gemara, illuminates this ethos: "We are to be co-workers with God in the work of creation."[2]

At the beginning of the Torah narrative we are told: "And God took the human being, and placed him in the Garden of Eden, to work it and to guard it."[3] And as the Midrash relates: "When the Almighty created Adam He led him around the Garden of Eden. 'Look at my works,' He said, 'See how beautiful

---

1   Psalms 24; 115.
2   See BT *Shabbat* 10a. While the literal meaning of quote is in reference to judges, it works well here as reminder that we are also obligated to shape the world around us.
3   Genesis 2:15.

they are; how excellent! I created them all for your sake. See to it that you do not spoil and destroy my world; for if you do, there is no one to put it right.'"[4] The Midrash places on human beings the responsibility for preserving the well-being and health of the environment. The results of our failure to adhere to these warnings are becoming unfortunately obvious. The world is becoming a place that is less fit for life as a whole.

A shift in our eating habits, including reducing our meat intake, has the ability to ameliorate some of the damage that an animal-based diet does to the environment. If we look carefully at the creation story, we see that God's first dietary law given to human beings was vegetarian. The Torah states: "I have given you every herb yielding seed which is on the face of the earth, and every tree which is yielding seed—to you it shall be for food. And to every beast of the earth, and to every fowl of the air, and to every living thing that creeps on the earth wherein there is a living soul, every green herb for food."[5] As Rashi states: God did not permit Adam and his wife to kill a creature and eat its flesh,[6] for it states that *only every green herbs shall they all eat together*.[7] A Gemara in the name of Rav states that:

> Meat was not permitted to Adam, the first man, for consumption, as it is written: "And God said: Behold, I have given you every herb that brings forth seed, which is upon the face of all the earth, and every tree, in which is the fruit of a tree that gives forth seed; for you it shall be for food, and for every animal of the earth, and for every fowl of the air, and for everything that creeps upon the earth, in which there is a living soul, every green herb for food. And it was so" (Genesis 1:29–30). It is derived God told Adam: Eating vegetation is permitted to people and animals, but eating the animals of the earth is not permitted to you.[8]

It is only later after the Flood and Noah's redemption of the world when violence and instinctual behavior runs rampant that a change in eating patterns is introduced in the Torah. The Torah states after the Flood: "Be fruitful and multiply and replenish the earth. And the fear of you shall be upon every beast of the earth, and upon every fowl in the air and upon all fish in the sea; into

---

4 *Ecclesiastes Rabbah*, 7.
5 Genesis 1:28–30.
6 Commentary on Genesis 1:28–30.
7 Ibid., 1:29.
8 BT *Sanhedrin* 59b.

your hand they are delivered. Every moving thing that lives shall be for food for you; as the green herb I have given to you."[9] According to Rabbi Abraham Isaac Kook, this permission was only a temporary concession to human weakness, which will be changed during the coming of the Messianic era.[10] Rav Kook felt that God—who is merciful to *all* creatures—would never institute an everlasting law which permits the killing of animals for food or, indeed, for any reason. Only in this period of a reduced moral standard, when one could not resist the temptation to eat meat, is the human being permitted to do so.

A categorical prohibition of meat during the time of moral depravity would never have been observed, nor would it have cultivated compassion to animals. Rather, it would have driven humanity to its unexplored and uncontrolled depths of depravity, as the appetite to shed blood indiscriminately became all the more heightened in the mind. Thus, a concession to slaughter animals—a controlled outlet for his heightened passion—and the permission to eat meat was thought sufficient enough to satisfy his lust for blood and aggression and, thus, to prevent him from releasing this drive on to human beings.

When violence was prevalent and when humankind had given reign to its worst instincts, the human being was no longer required to make the supreme moral exertion required to forego the slaughter of animals. It was far more important that humanity should utilize what moral fiber it had in refraining from killing its own kind (at the least) and respecting the life of his neighbor. Yet, according to Rav Kook, during the ushering in of the Messianic era, one will forgo the concession made by the Torah in allowing the slaughter of animals.[11] Through general moral and intellectual advancement, the sensitivity to all of God's creatures will be revivified; he will only eat plants again. During the interim period (in deference to moral frailty when the power of an evolved moral self-control had not yet arrived), it was better for people to fulfill minimal demands rather than become sinful in not being able to achieve the higher demand of refraining from animal meat. But as consciousness and sensitivity evolve and creates greater moral strength, humanity (writ large) will begin to be able to see that all creation is to be respected and not harmed. This will be the time when "all of them shall know Me.'"[12] Now, in the years of the preceding of the Messiah—*ikveta D'Meshicha*—we may take it on ourselves to hasten his coming by reducing our meat intake and thereby protect our environment.

---

9   Ibid., 9:1–3.
10 *Talelei Orot.*
11 *Olat Reiyah*, 292.
12 Micah, 7: 15–18; Jeremiah, 31:33; Isaiah, 2:4

Rav Kook, furthermore, regarded all the biblical dietary laws—ritual slaughter and covering the blood, for instance—as designed to arouse man to the injustice committed against the animal kingdom, even to the extent of making him ashamed of his actions. At a point in future, Rav Kook surmised that a greater consciousness would arise and the moral fiber that is present in all people would lose the need for meat.[13]

In the same vein, Italian rabbi and scholar Umberto (Moshe) Cassuto (1883–1951) wrote that: "The natural diet is vegetarian. The Torah was in principle opposed to the eating of meat in the beginning. When Noah and his descendants were permitted to eat meat-that was a concession conditional on the prohibition of the blood. This prohibition implied respect for the principle of life ('for the blood is the life') and an allusion to the fact that in reality all meat should have been prohibited. This partial prohibition was designed to call to mind the previously total one."[14]

Dr. Richard Schwartz, a prominent pioneer in the Jewish vegetarian movement and an expert on Judaism and the environment, supports this line of thinking by illustrating examples of how the divine instructions regulating the consumption of meat all lead gradually to the desired spiritual goal of reducing desire for meat. The permission given to eat meat is contingent on following specific rules: Only limited species of animals are permitted. In the desert they could only eat meat as a part of the sacrificial service in the Sanctuary.[15] No "unconsecrated meat" for private consumption was allowed. Then in Deuteronomy 12:20, God allows it only as a concession to their lust.

The concept of covering the blood of fowl and venison creates a consciousness of shame, which is the beginning of moral improvement. The nature of the principles of ritual slaughter with their specific rules designed to reduce pain, create the atmosphere that you are dealing with a living being, and creates sensitivity. There is a prohibition towards eating blood,[16] for the Torah identifies blood with life,[17] so the Gemara elaborates the process of

---

13 Nehama Leibowitz, *Studies in Devarim (Deuteronomy)* (Jerusalem: World Zionist Organization, 1993), 136.
14 Umberto (Moses) Cassuto, *From Adam to Noah: A Commentary on the Book of Genesis, Part 1* (Jerusalem: Magnes Press, 1978), 58.
15 Leviticus 17: 3–5.
16 Genesis 9:4.
17 Deuteronomy 12:23.

removing blood from the animal. The *Kli Yakar* expressed the same idea. He writes:

> What was the necessity for the entire procedure of ritual slaughter? For the sake of self-discipline, it is far more appropriate for man not to eat meat; only if one has a strong desire for meat does the Torah permit it, and even then only after the trouble and inconvenience necessary in order to satisfy his desire. Perhaps because of the bother and annoyance of the whole procedure he will be restrained from such a strong and uncontrollable desire for meat (Deuteronomy 12:21).

As a matter of course, even if meat is allowed, Jews are called on to arrange humane living conditions for animals and meriful slaughter. Some of the modern treatments of livestock in preparation for slaughter, such as "shackle and hoist" procedures, are not humane. Because of the proclivity for material gain, greed and the neglect of spiritual values animals are often raised to ensure the highest profit possible without consideration of the pain caused to the animals. The value of *Tza'ar Ba'alei Hayyim* would prohibit animal cruelty and the consumption of flesh when it involves raising animals under cruel conditions in crowded cells, in which they are denied fresh air, exercise and clean conditions.

The Torah, in numerous passages, speaks against maltreatment of animals. Rabbi Samson Raphael Hirsch, in his work *Horeb: A Philosophy of Jewish Laws and Observances*, points out that not only are we to refrain from inflicting unnecessary pain on an animal, but to help to lessen the pain whenever you can even if it is not through any fault of yours. Even if the owner does not do anything to reduce the pain of the animal one has the obligation towards the animal to release it of its burden.[18] The law also sets a suffering animal on the same level as a non-seriously ill person as far as customs on Shabbat and holidays are concerned, in that *melachot derabbanan* (rulings of the rabbis) are permitted in order to help them.[19] Furthermore, one may not burden the animal with excessive loads, or make it work constantly without rest, or deny it the food that it needs.[20]

To be sure, the most egregious implication of a meat-heavy diet is that raising cattle involves a heavy burden on the environment. The dynamics at

---

18 *Choshen Mishpat*, 272.
19 *Or Chaim*, 305:19–20.
20 Samson Raphael Hirsch (trans. Isidore Grunfeld), *Horeb: A Philosophy of Jewish Laws and Observances* (London: Soncino Press, 1962), 292–93.

play should one want to eat a steak or a hamburger are many: there are issues of extensive soil depletion and erosion of soil due to overgrazing, air and water pollution related to the widespread production and use of pesticides to increase grain to feed the cattle, fertilizer and other chemicals and the vast amount of water that it takes in bringing the animal to slaughter, most of which is used to irrigate land growing feed for livestock. If the taste for cow flesh indicates anything, it is that it's an inherently wasteful taste. Every herd of cattle needed to produce steaks and other forms of beef require up to twenty times more land, which leads to destruction of trees and rain forests, ten times more energy and water, and far more pesticides, fertilizer and other resources than vegetarian diets. These factors are hardly in line with the value of *bal tashhit*—not wasting needlessly. Is it ethically elevating to favor a diet that involves the feeding of seventy percent of the grain grown in the United States. to animals destined for slaughter while twenty million people die annually due to hunger? If grain and similar abundant natural resources were used to directly feed starving human beings rather than using up time and resources in the preparation of meat, would that not be a great *mitzvah*?

Is it ethical to support the notion of a diet that involves the wasteful use of land, water, energy and other agricultural commodities and thus perpetuate hunger and poverty that frequently leads to instability and war? It's simply impossible to ignore the profound consequences of animal agriculture. By some estimates, animal agriculture now accounts for nearly fifteen percent of all greenhouse gas emissions, which is more than every car, bus, truck, plane and train on the planet combined. Cattle lead the way, representing sixty—five percent of the livestock sector's emissions.

The tremendous quantity of grains grown to feed animals requires extensive use of chemical fertilizers and pesticides. Much air and water pollution is caused by the production and usage of these products. Various constituents of fertilizers, particularly nitrogen, are washed into surface waters. High levels of nitrates in drinking water have caused illnesses for people as well as animals. Manure produced by cattle raised in feedlots washes into surface waters, which in turn pollutes streams, rivers, and aquifers. Studies have shown that American livestock contribute *five times* more organic waste to water pollution than do people, and twice as much as industry.[21]

---

21 See Richard Schwartz, *Judaism and Global Survival* (New York: Lantern Books, 2002), 173.

Studies have indicated that if the entire American population were total vegetarians, no irrigation water at all would be needed to produce our food.[22] So, theoretically, if we only ate meat on the Sabbath, holidays, and life-cycle events, we would make a tremendous contribution as caretakers of the earth.

Just take a look at slaughterhouses. Slaughterhouses are also prime sources of pollution. They discharge massive amounts of grease, carcass dressing, intestinal waste, and fecal matter into the sewer system which then empty into rivers and other waterways. Because of these factors, the animal products industry pollutes more water than all other industries combined.[23] Indeed, more water is used by the animal production industry in the U.S. than by all other industries combined. Over fifty percent of all water consumed in America is used for animal agriculture, most of which is used to irrigate land growing feed for livestock. The production of one pound of steak uses 2,500 gallons of water, while only twenty-five gallons are required to produce a pound of wheat. So if we only ate meat on Shabbat, holidays, and life-cycle events, we would be making a tremendous contribution as caretakers of the earth.

Just look to California, which over the past several years experienced severe drought conditions. Agriculture accounts for about eighty percent of water use in the state, and the beef industry is one of its thirstiest culprits. According to the Water Footprint Network, producing just a pound of beef requires 1,800 gallons of water. One could shower for an entire year and still would not use as much water as it takes to produce ten burgers. Thus, encouraging people to eat less meat is not only more humane, but a *mitzvah*. It also may improve health, as a National Institute of Health study analyzing 537,000 participants found negative implications in the consumption of a heavy red meat diet increasing risks for a host of chronic diseases including heart disease, diabetes, Alzheimer's disease, and kidney disease. So we can either choose to eat foods that will protect our planet or foods that will destroy it; to eat in a way that will be healthy for our bodies or in a way that will increase the risk of illness. The Gemara suggests this as well: "Our Rabbis taught: 'that a person should not eat meat unless he has a special appetite for it ... Mar Zutra the son of R. Nachman said that a parent should not accustom his son to flesh and wine."[24]

Much of the above description of the assault on our environment is a product of ignorance but this egregious deterioration of the health of our

---

22 Ibid.
23 Ibid.
24 BT *Hullin* 84a.

environment also indicates that malevolent practices inherent in our contemporary society are at odds with authentic Jewish values. Judaism teaches that the "Earth is the Lord's" and we are to be partners with God in protecting the environment. But in much of the world today we follow the creed that the earth is to be exploited for maximum profit, regardless of the long-range ecological consequences.

Continuing that point, Judaism emphasizes *bal tashhit* as a core value. By contrast, wastefulness in the United States is so great that, with less than five percent of the world's people, American use about a third of the world's resources; this has a major impact on pollution and resource scarcities. A Gemara describes a wise person as someone who considers the long-range consequences of his/her actions.[25] We must plan for future generations, but the way of our world often only considers immediate gains.

Indeed, the great disparity of wealth, opportunity, and insensitivity to the vulnerable is symptomatic of moral and spiritual impoverishment. We live in a world not guided by spiritual values but by materialism and short-term pleasure. An increase of Torah and *mitzvot*—or more generally, an elevation of humane values—creates a spiritual antidote to the exploitation of creatures and the Earth that God bestowed on us: "The Holy One blessed be He, wanted to bring purity to Israel. He therefore multiplied their opportunities for Torah and *mitzvot*."[26]

Now it is a time for action. Increasing our *mitzvot*, changing our eating patterns, and practicing vigilance in ameliorating our wounded environment. The Baal Shem Tov—the founder of the modern Hasidic movement—taught that the root of the word *mitzvah* is 'to join;' a *mitzvah* is a joining of souls to the Creator. The *mitzvot* invest our everyday lives and activities with spiritual significance; as 'a way of life' faithfully observed, their effect is to enhance the quality of our lives and the life of the planet. On a deeper level, our pollution of the environment is a moral problem. Our current materialistic society suggests a kinship to the ancient Sodomites who live by the value "What is mine is mine, and what is yours is yours"[27]; *What I am doing benefits me and I do not care what the effects may be on anyone else?* By demoralizing the human being we are encouraging pollution in the deepest and most far reaching sense.

---

25 *Tamid* 32a.
26 See Aryeh Carmell and Cyril Domb (eds.) *Challenge: Torah Views on Science and Its Problems* (New York: Feldheim, 2000 [Second, Revised Edition], 515.
27 *Avot* 5:10.

It is urgent that Torah values, especially righteousness, justice, and equity be applied toward the solution of current environmental problems. This means, for example, an energy policy based on conservation and renewable energy, consistent with Jewish teachings on preserving the environment, conserving resources, protecting human lives, and considering future generations. And this requires a radical shift toward a reduction of meat consumption, since meat-centered diets and the livestock agriculture associated with them causes much pollution, wastes important resources, treats animals harshly, creates water shortages, and contributes to the scarcity of resources throughout the world.

We have the enormous spiritual potential to transform our world. And when spiritual growth becomes the goal, the true needs of all humankind will be reached, instead of the illusory needs created by a superficial ethic that benefits the few and causes harm to the majority.

The powerful waters of Torah and holiness revolutionize life on this Earth by restoring to humankind its true goal as caretaker of our planet as partners with God actualizing soul and beauty in the gift of life bestowed on us. And it will be through the larger community of humankind where spiritual passion and equality for all will be realized.[28] The online media revolution, education, and advertising mediums can all support this Torah aim of creating a world ruled "Not by might and not by power but by my spirit alone."[29] As the Messianic era approaches, we will one day transform the muddy, polluted waters of the streams to the pure holy streams of water of the Torah[30] restoring to humankind its true goal as caretaker of our planet, as partners with God actualizing the gift of life bestowed on us.

---

28 See Aryeh Carmell and Cyril Domb (eds.) *Challenge: Torah Views on Science and Its Problems* (New York: Feldheim, 2000 [Second, Revised Edition], 519–20.

29 Zechariah 4:6.

30 BT *Yoma* 77b.

CHAPTER 2

Humanity and the Tree of the Field

Conservation as a Commandment

Rosh Kehillah Dina Najman

Ice caps are melting, the ozone layer has been damaged, and overall the planet on which we depend for our existence is being destroyed. The culprit: human activity. Is there a Torah obligation, in addition to our ethical responsibilities, to conserve the planet? In this chapter, I will outline two approaches to this question, both yielding an affirmative answer but from the different perspectives of Rambam's rationalism and Ramban's *kabbalism*. Subsequent to this analysis, I will explain how Rabbi Samson Raphael Hirsch draws on both traditions in a masterful synthesis that speaks to us today.

When Adam is first brought into this world, God places him in a garden. The Torah explains the purpose of human beings' presence in the garden:

וַיִּקַּח ה' אֱלֹקִים, אֶת-הָאָדָם; וַיַּנִּחֵהוּ בְגַן-עֵדֶן, לְעָבְדָהּ וּלְשָׁמְרָהּ.

"And the LORD God took the man and put him into the garden of Eden to work it and to watch over it."[1]

A midrash in *Ecclesiastes Rabbah* augments the verse with a narrative: God takes Adam into the Garden of Eden, lets him pass before all the trees and greenery in the garden, and directs him to care for this world:

See my works, how fine and excellent they are. Now all that I created I created for your benefit. Think upon this and do not corrupt or destroy my world. For if you destroy it, there is no one to restore it after you.[2]

---

1 Genesis 2:15.
2 *Ecclesiastes Rabbah* 7:28.

Based on this verse in the Torah, the Sages understand this instruction by God that we, humans, are "co-partners of God in the work of creation."[3] Yet, for details about how to care for the environment, we have to wait until the book of Deuteronomy; this is not accidental. For this is the time when the people, for the first time, are preparing for their entry into the Land of Israel, when they will have a land to call their own. Moses instructs the people:

כִּי-תָצוּר אֶל-עִיר יָמִים רַבִּים לְהִלָּחֵם עָלֶיהָ לְתָפְשָׂהּ, לֹא-תַשְׁחִית אֶת-עֵצָהּ לִנְדֹּחַ עָלָיו גַּרְזֶן--כִּי מִמֶּנּוּ

תֹאכֵל, וְאֹתוֹ לֹא תִכְרֹת: כִּי הָאָדָם עֵץ הַשָּׂדֶה, לָבֹא מִפָּנֶיךָ בַּמָּצוֹר.

When you will besiege a city a long time, in making war against it to take it, you should not destroy the trees thereof by wielding an axe against them; for you may eat of them, but you should not cut them down; for the man is like the tree of the field, that it should be besieged of you.[4]

This discussion of *Bal Tashhit*, with regard to not destroying fruit-bearing trees, even during wartime, serves as a proof-text for the prohibition of purposeless destruction and for an explanation for how we are supposed to cultivate and guard God's world. Rambam clarifies the generality of this *mitzvah*:

ח אין קוצצין אילני מאכל שחוץ למדינה, ואין מונעין מהם אמת המים כדי שייבשו-- שנאמר "לא תשחית את עצה (דברים כ, יט), וכל הקוצץ, לוקה. ולא במצור בלבד, אלא בכל מקום, כל הקוצץ אילן מאכל דרך השחתה--לוקה. אבל קוצצין אותו, אם היה מזיק אילנות אחרות, או מפני שמזיק בשדה אחרים, או מפני שדמיו יקרים; לא אסרה תורה, אלא דרך השחתה.

ט כל אילן סרק--מותר לקוץ אותו, ואפילו אינו צריך לו. וכן אילן מאכל שהזקין, ואינו עושה אלא דבר מועט שאינו ראוי לטרוח בו--מותר לקוצו. וכמה יהיה הזית עושה, ולא יקוצנו--רובע הקב זיתים; ודקל שהוא עושה קב תמרים, לא יקוצנו.

י ולא האילנות בלבד, אלא כל המשבר כלים, וקורע בגדים, והורס בניין, וסותם מעיין, ומאבד מאכלות דרך השחתה--עובר ב"לא תשחית (דברים כ,י; ואינו לוקה, אלא מכת מרדות מדבריהם.

We should not cut down fruit trees outside a city nor prevent an irrigation ditch from bringing water to them so that they dry up, as Deuteronomy 20:19 states: "Do not destroy its trees." Anyone who cuts down such a tree should be given the punishment of lashes.

---

3 BT *Shabbat* 119a.

4 Deuteronomy 20:19.

This does not apply only in a siege, but in all situations. Anyone who cuts down a fruit tree with a destructive intent, should be given lashes.

Nevertheless, a fruit tree may be cut down if it causes damage to other trees or to fields belonging to others, or if a high price could be received for its wood. The Torah only prohibited cutting down a tree with a destructive intent. It is permissible to cut down any non-fruit bearing tree, even if one has no need for it. Similarly, one may cut down a fruit bearing tree that has become old and produces only a slight yield which does not warrant the effort required to care for it.

What is the yield that an olive tree must produce to warrant that it should not be cut down? A quarter of a kav of olives. Similarly, a date palm which yields a kav of dates should not be cut down.

This prohibition does not apply to trees alone. Rather, anyone who breaks utensils, tears garments, destroys buildings, stops up a spring, or ruins food with a destructive intent transgresses the command "Do not destroy." However, he is not lashed. Instead, he receives stripes for rebellious conduct as instituted by the Sages.[5]

Likewise, the *Sefer ha-Hinukh* quotes Rambam before proceeding to explain Rambam's reasoning on the matter:

שרש המצוה ידוע, שהוא כדי ללמד נפשנו לאהב **הטוב והתועלת** ולהדבק בו, ומתוך כך תדבק בנו הטובה, ונרחיק מכל דבר רע ומכל דבר השחתה, וזהו דרך החסידים ואנשי מעשה אוהבים שלום ושמחים בטוב הבריות ומקרבים אותן לתורה, ולא יאבדו אפילו גרגיר של חרדל בעולם, ויצר עליהם בכל אבדון והשחתה שיראו, ואם יוכלו להציל יצילו כל דבר מהשחית בכל כחם, ולא כן הרשעים אחיהם של מזיקים שמחים בהשחתת עולם, והמה משחיתים את עצמם במדה שאדם מודד בה מודדין לו. כלומר, בה הוא נדבק לעולם, וכעניין שכתוב (משלי יז, ה) שמח לאיד לא ינקה רע. והחפץ בטוב ושמח בו נפשו תלין בטוב לעולם זה ידוע ומפרסם.

The root of this commandment is known—it is in order to teach our souls to love the good and the beneficial and to cling to it. And through this, good clings to us and we will distance [ourselves] from all bad and destructive things. And this is the way of the pious and people of [proper] action - they love peace and are happy for the good of the creatures and bring them close to Torah, and they do not destroy even a grain of mustard

---

in the world. And they are distressed by all loss and destruction that they
see; and if they can prevent it, they will prevent any destruction with all
of their strength. But not so are the wicked—the brothers of the destructive spirits. They rejoice in the destruction of the world, and they destroy
themselves—[since] in the way that a person measures, so is he measured; which is to say that he clings to it forever, as the matter that is written (Proverbs 17:5), "the one who rejoices in calamity, will not be cleared
(of evil)." And the one who desires the good and rejoices in it, 'his soul will
dwell in the good' forever. This is known and famous.[6]

When using the term "the good and the beneficial," the *Sefer ha-Hinukh*
alludes to Rambam's understanding of the "goodness" of the world as the natural purposefulness that manifests divine governance. In *Guide to the Perplexed*,
Rambam writes about Moses asking not only for forgiveness for the Jewish
people after the sin of the Golden Calf, but also for the knowledge of God's
attributes:

> וַיֹּאמֶר, אֲנִי אַעֲבִיר כָּל-טוּבִי עַל-פָּנֶיךָ, וְקָרָאתִי בְשֵׁם ה', לְפָנֶיךָ; וְחַנֹּתִי אֶת-אֲשֶׁר אָחֹן,
> וְרִחַמְתִּי אֶת-אֲשֶׁר אֲרַחֵם. כ וַיֹּאמֶר, לֹא תוּכַל לִרְאֹת אֶת-פָּנָי: כִּי לֹא-יִרְאַנִי הָאָדָם, וָחָי.
>
> And God said: "I will make all *My goodness* [emphasis added] pass before
> you, and will proclaim the name of the LORD before you; and I will be
> gracious to whom I will be gracious, and will show mercy on whom I will
> show mercy."
> And God said: "You cannot see My face, for man shall not see Me and live."

Forgiveness is granted, but it is impossible for Moses to grasp the Divine
essence, which is how Rambam understands his request. Instead, God responds
that God will allow all God's goodness to pass before Moses. Rambam explains
that the phrase "all My goodness" alludes to the display to Moses of all existing things of which it is said: "*And God saw everything that He had made, and,
behold it was very good.*"[7] By their display, I mean that he will apprehend their
nature and the way they are mutually connected so that he will know how He
governs them in general in and in detail."[8] In other words, Rambam equates
the concept of *tov* (goodness) to that of wise governance. In this respect, God's

---

6 *Sefer ha-Hinukh*, 529:2 (Sefaria translation).

7 Genesis 1:31.

8 *Guide of the Perplexed*, (trans. Shlomo Pines), I:54, 124.

goodness" means God's "governance" of nature; this becomes apparent when one examines nature.

Later, in the *Guide*, Rambam explains how Divine governance is manifest in biology.[9] Both the structure of living beings—"the gradation of the motions of the limbs, and the proximity of some ... to others"—and their individual development—"the gradual succession of the various states of the whole individual"—manifests "the deity's wily graciousness and wisdom." He refers explicitly to what he considered a work of well-established science: Galen's *Treatise on Human Anatomy and Development*. All of what was orchestrated by God is the gradual development and harmonious organization of organisms, as described by Galen. Indeed, someone who appreciates nature in accordance with science will understand that God did not only create the world, but also continues to govern it by means of the natural purposiveness implanted in each species; this is the goodness of creation that was revealed to Moses.

Thus, Rambam emphasizes the acknowledgment of God's wise governance of nature, an acknowledgment that has both a theoretical and a practical aspect. The theoretical dimension is the study of nature in accordance with science, while the practical side is the commandment of בל תשחית: refraining from undermining Divine wisdom by acting contrary to natural purposiveness and actively supporting divine wisdom through the careful conservation of nature. Rambam's approach depends on the Aristotelian view of nature. The Aristotelian view of nature, not as an aggregate of mechanisms, but rather as inherently purposive in both part and whole.

An alternative approach is developed by Nachmanides, whose emphasis on natural actions as "hidden miracles" makes him less friendly than Rambam to the idea of a natural order intelligible to science. In his derivation of all six hundred and thirteen commandments from the Ten Commandments given at Sinai, Ramban explains the theoretical aspect of his approach: that the *mitzvah* of *Anochi Hashem Elokecha* (embracing "I am the Lord your God) commands us, not to study Divine governance as manifest in natural purposiveness, but rather to appreciate the kabbalistic doctrine that God is at once both *Ein Sof* (infinite), the ten *Sefirot*, and that all of the above constitute a divine unity.[10] To regard any aspect of divinity as separate would be to disrupt Divine unity in thought.

---

9 Ibid., II:32, 525.
10 *Kitvei Ramban*, vol. 2, 546.

The practical application of this for Ramban is *bal tashhit* בל תשחית, which commands us to refrain from performing any wanton destruction. Citing the source for this *mitzvah* in Deuteronomy 20:19, Ramban chooses to emphasize the phrase: *ha-Adam etz haSadeh* האדם עץ השדה. As his commentary on Deuteronomy shows, Ramban understood this phrase, not as a question—"Is the tree of the field a human?"—but rather as a statement: "the tree of the field is the human." In this respect, he follows Ibn Ezra rather than Rashi.[11] In other words, the tree is intimately connected to the human being. Both exhibit the *sefirotic* structure of divinity, a structure that kabbalists often depict as a tree. Wanton destruction of trees is tantamount to the destruction of the divine unity. To the wanton destroyer of nature, Ramban applies the term used of the paradigmatic heretic, Elisha ben Abuya.[12] Such a person is a *kotetz eitzim*: an uprooter of saplings. This transgression of the first of the Ten Commandments is clearly akin to idolatry. Yet, both Ramban and Rambam agree about the principle *Bal Tashhit*, although they differ greatly in their underlying views. Rabbi Samson Raphael Hirsch masterfully weaves together the two positions in a way that also makes practical suggestions about how we can play our designated role of guarding and serving nature:

> 'לא תשחית וגו' "Do not cut down the trees in the environs of the city for the purpose of destroying them; or more precisely: do not destroy them just to cut them down, so that the whole purpose of your action is "the swinging of the ax," destruction. You may eat their fruit; moreover, it is incumbent upon you to keep them as a source of food: ממנו תאכל – מצות עשה, ואתו לא תכרת – זו מצות לא תעשה (*Sifre*). He who needlessly cuts down a food-yielding tree violates both a positive command and a prohibition."
> כי האדם עץ השדה לבא מפניך במצור
> "The tree of the field is the human being, the produce of the soil is the condition for man's existence שחייו של אדם אינו אלא מן האילן (*Sifrei*; עץ השדה is the subject). Ibn Ezra makes the apt comparison to the similar expression "כי נפש הוא חבל" (below, 24:6), where the millstones are called simply "נפש" because the existence of the נפש depends on them. It appears, then, that the meaning of our verse is as follows: Do not cut down the fruit trees of the besieged city, for the fruit trees constitute the existence of man

---

11 See the commentaries of Rashi Ibn Ezra and Ramban on Deuteronomy 20:19, s.v. כי האדם עץ
    השדה".

12 BT *Hagigah* 14b.

and therefore are included in the siege; i.e., they are part and parcel of what you are trying to obtain by the siege. Just as you must not besiege the city in order to destroy it, you must not destroy the trees of the city. They are a part of the besieged city."

Rav Hirsch focuses on purposefulness, not on the unity of nature. He does not, however, focus on the natural purposiveness as thematized by Aristotle and Galen, as Rambam does. Avoiding reliance on specific scientific doctrines that may be replaced by others, he emphasizes the purposefulness of nature for our human activities. At the same time, Rav Hirsch echoes Ramban by citing Ibn Ezra's declarative interpretation of the phrase *ha-Adam etz hasadeh* הָאָדָם עֵץ הַשָּׂדֶה: the tree of the field is the human. There is an intimate connection between the life of human beings and the life of natural things.

He elaborates on the underlying psychology of this *mitzvah* in his book, *Horeb*:

Although you are laying siege to a city, and you are thus about to do harm to man and therefore certainly need not respect the property belonging to man's personality more than man himself, nevertheless you may not destroy this property without reason or purpose .... And from this you should hear the warning of God: 'Do not destroy anything.'

Yea, 'Do not destroy anything!' is the first and most general call of God, which comes to you, man, when you realize yourself as master of the earth. All round you perceive earth and plant and animal; yea, earth and plant and animal already bearing your imprint from your technical human skill; they have been transformed by your human hand for your human purposes, into dwelling-place and clothing, food and instruments, and you have taken them as your property ... Only if you use the things around you for wise human purposes, sanctified by the word of My teaching, only then are you a man and have the right over them which I have given you as man. However, if you destroy, if you ruin—at that moment you are not a man, you are an animal, and have no right to the things around you. I lent them to you for wise use only; never forget that I lent them to you. As soon as you use them unwisely, be it the greatest or the smallest, you commit treachery against My world, you commit murder and robbery against My property, you sin against Me! ... There is a lesser degree of destruction which must nevertheless be avoided; wasting—i.e., discarding the means at your disposal in a manner whereby the desired aim does not correspond to the extent of the divestment. This is an offence of lesser degree, as the things in themselves are not destroyed but are passed to others for their use: nevertheless, it is still destruction, since for you they have been destroyed. Every small or large possession which God grants you brings you the duty to make proper use of it, which also includes parting with it for wise purposes...[13]

In a way that is characteristic of his humanism, Rav Hirsch connects the divine command to conserve nature with the title of *haAdam* האדם, the human. This is not merely the name for a biological species. It is a distinguished title conferred on by God. If we betray our divine mission, we no longer deserve to be called human. Moreover, echoing Ramban's association of wanton destruction with the heresy of "uprooting the saplings," Rav Hirsch cites the rabbinic teaching that one who destroys in anger is an idolater.[14] Thus Rav Hirsch gives us an account of the *mitzvah* of conservation that draws on both Rambam and Ramban without forcing us to choose between Rambam's rationalism and Ramban's *kabbalism*. This is an explanation of the *mitzvah*'s centrality that can appeal to everyone.

These teachings should guide us as we fulfill the mandate of *l'ovdo u'shomro* לעבדו ושומרו from the second chapter of Genesis. While *l'shomro* לשומרו could be understood as a negative commandment of *bal tashhit*—בל תשחית, *U'l'avdo*—ולעבדו presents us with a positive directive: To labor and work in partnership with Divine Unity fulfill the task we were given by God when we were placed in *Gan Eden*. While none of these rabbinic figures thought about the human impact on climate change and the environment, the application of their teachings is clear.

As the Psalmist teaches: "The heavens are the heavens of Adonai, But the earth God has given to the sons of men."[15] We are the caretakers, responsible for the limited resources found on and under the ground on which we walk. As stewards of God, we take responsibility for a healthier and more sustainable planet. This is about morality and justice. This is about today and it is certainly about whether there will be a tomorrow.

---

13 Rav Shimshon Raphael Hirsch, *Horeb*, Section IV, no. 396, 397, 398; 400, 279–81.
14 BT *Shabbat* 105b.
15 Psalms 115:6.

Divine Wisdom or Altering Creation? A Torah Perspective on GMOs

Rabbi Gabe Greenberg

When observant Jews walk into the supermarket, they are immediately concerned with several factors and values that will enter into their decision-making process as to what to purchase. Foremost among these issues will likely be an item's formal *kashrut* status: whether it is inherently kosher—that is, most fruits and vegetables in their raw state—or has been certified kosher by a recognized *kashrut* organization. Other principal concerns will be that of price, availability, taste and preference, and the degree to which the product is part of a healthy diet, among many factors.

Increasingly, kosher consumers are cognizant of additional values that impact their purchase, including whether a food item is organic, cruelty-free, fair-trade, or produced locally. As other essays in this collection have argued, some of these values can be seen either as instantiations of broader Jewish values, or more direct fulfillments of particular *halakhot* or *mitzvot*. Another of these more recent concerns is the presence of genetically modified organisms in our food. The World Health Organization defines GMOs as follows:

> Organisms (i.e., plants, animals or microorganisms) in which the genetic material (DNA) has been altered in a way that does not occur naturally by mating and/or natural recombination .... The technology allows selected individual genes to be transferred from one organism into another, also between non-related species.[1]

The acronym "GMO," thus, stands for "genetically modified organism" and is generally used synonymously with the acronym "GE," or "genetically

---

1 "Q&A: Genetically Modified Food." World Health Organization. Accessed March 27, 2018. http://www.who.int/foodsafety/areas_work/food-technology/faq-genetically-modified-food/en/.

engineered," as well as with the term "food biotechnology." The altering of genetic material can be achieved in one of several ways. One is by using a "gene gun," which shoots metallic particles covered in DNA into plant tissue. Another method is stressing certain strains of bacteria into accepting foreign DNA, and then inserting the bacteria into the new crop. Additional technologies are being constantly developed and refined.[2] And indeed, the issue of GMOs is a widespread one, given the high percentage of food products found in our grocery stores that contain GMOs in some manner; consider the pervasiveness of corn and soy products in packaged food items and note that the vast majority of domestically grown corn and soy is genetically modified,[3] and it is immediately apparent that GMO foods are ubiquitous where we shop.

There is wide-ranging debate and disagreement as to the pros and cons of genetically modified food and food production and we will briefly consider some of them at the conclusion of the essay. Our task here is to investigate the various Torah and rabbinic sources which may cast light on the Torah approach to this issue. Obviously, the technology which allows scientists to manipulate targeted DNA sequences did not exist until recently. Nevertheless, our tradition provides the tools with which to analyze and consider this technology, its use, and how its prevalence affects human and ecological health in the broadest sense.

Torah and Rabbinic Sources: Kilayim

Our initial lens through which to examine GMOs is that of the prohibition of *kilayim*. The Torah verses describe a category of prohibitions known collectively as *kilayim*, or improper mixtures. *Kilayim* makes sense as a starting point in that it deals explicitly with the bringing together, in various ways, of different species/types, while genetic engineering too can involve the insertion of DNA from one species into that of another, thus also constituting a "bringing together" of different species.

The Torah states in Leviticus 19:19:

> You shall not let your cattle mate with a different kind; you shall not sow your field with two kinds of seed; you shall not put on cloth from a mixture of two kinds of material.[4]

---

2 Chelsea Powell. "How to Make a GMO.: Science in the News. August 11, 2015. Accessed March 27, 2018. http://sitn.hms.harvard.edu/flash/2015/how-to-make-a-gmo/.

3 USDA, National Agricultural Statistics Service, *June Agricultural Survey* 2000–2016.

4 All Torah translations taken from the Jewish Publication Society.

This prohibition is repeated, refined, and widened in Deuteronomy 22:9–11:

> You shall not sow your vineyard with a second kind of seed, else the crop—from the seed you have sown—and the yield of the vineyard may not be used. You shall not plow with an ox and an ass together. You shall not wear cloth combining wool and linen.

The prohibitions mentioned above traditionally apply to animal husbandry, clothing, and agriculture. There are lengthy *halakhah* discussions of the applicability and limitations of these *mitzvot*, historically and through the present day. The most commonly relevant of these to the lives of Jews today is the prohibition on wearing wool and linen in our clothing, known as *sha'atnez* (*sha'atnez* is thus a sub-category of the general prohibition of *kilayim*). The prohibition of *lo taharosh*, not working with multiple species at a time—is still in effect, but is relevant only to farmers, carriage-operators, and coachmen.[5] Similarly, *kilay ha-kerem*, the laws of *kilayim* as they relate to the planting varied types of seeds and species, is of limited applicability.

Another contemporary example of *kilayim* which has *halakhah* relevance is tree-grafting (*harkavat ilan*). Given the widespread usage of the technique in modern fruit production, the respective permissibility of engaging in this agricultural technique, or of benefitting from its results, has received treatment from *poskim* (*halakhah* authorities). The *halakha* allows the fruit of grafted trees to be eaten, and as such the particular issue of grafted-fruit is reduced to a limited circle of farmers and advanced gardeners.[6] The one exception here is during Sukkot, during which folks reacquaint themselves with grafting due to the prohibition of utilizing a grafted citron (*etrog murkav*) to fulfill the *mitzvah* of the *arba minim*.

For our purposes in this essay, tree-grafting is important for an additional reason. When contemporary sages and scholars have sought to understand GMOs, the phenomenon of tree-grafting has emerged as the locus of their discussion. The central discussion is found in tractate *Pesahim* 55b–56a. The *mishna* there states: "Six actions were performed by the Jewish residents of Jericho, contrary to common practice. With regard to three, the Sages

---

5   Carriage riders, in Central Park or downtown New Orleans, may be aware as well, as it is prohibited to ride in a carriage or cart which is being pulled by different species; *Yoreh De'ah* 297b:12–13.

6   There is a debate amongst the *poskim* about whether a Jew must uproot fruit trees on their property if they were created through grafting; see *Aruch Hashulhan, Yoreh De'ah* 295:16–18.

reprimanded them, and with regard to three, the Sages did not reprimand them. And these are the ones with regard to which they did not reprimand them: The residents of Jericho would graft palm trees the entire day on the fourteenth of Nisan."[7] The *gemara* explains:

> Rabbi Yehuda said: They brought fresh myrtle, strong beer made from the fruit of the laurel tree, and barley flour that was cast into a vessel, and forty days has not passed since it was ground. They boiled them together and poured the mixture into the core of the palm tree .... Rav Aḥa, son of Rava, said: They placed a branch of a male palm tree on the female, and by doing so the female tree would yield fruit.

The *gemara* explicitly describes a process wherein plant material from one plant is placed within another plant and notes that the sages did not reprimand the residents of Jericho for doing so. Indeed, Rabbi Eliyahu Bakshi-Doron, one of the few contemporary *poskim* who have engaged directly with the question of GMOs, understands the *mishna* as the central proof-text that genetic engineering in plants is *halakhically* permitted: "While this [the gemara's example] does constitute [a form of] grafting between species, since it is not one [independent] plant with another, and it does not change the palm into another species, it does not qualify as a violation of *kilayim*."[8] He additionally cites the early twentieth-century scholar Rabbi Avraham Karelitz (*Hazon Ish, Kilayim* 2:16), who used this *gemara* to rule similarly that, "If one adds something which isn't in itself a plant (i.e., is only derived from a plant), but is instead absorbed in the plant and helps it grow—this is permitted.[9]

In addition to Rabbi Bakshi-Doron and Hazon Ish, Rabbi Shlomo Zalman Auerbach also wrote about the issue of genetic engineering vis-à-vis *harkavat ilan*. A letter he wrote to Dr. Avraham S. Avraham (author of the *halakhah* compendium *Nishmat Avraham*) outlines his general position. First, he deals with the *halakhah* rule of *nireh l'ayin*—the concept which states that, generally speaking, if something prohibited is not visible to the naked eye, then the *halakhah* disregards it. Regarding GMOs, however, Rabbi Auerbach did not think that *nireh l'ayin* is applicable, because "people manipulate the particles [i.e., the DNA] and put them in one species from another—this is considered as

---

7   Translation: The William Davidson digital edition of the Koren Noé Talmud.

8   R. Eliyahu Bakshi-Doron, *Binyan Av*, 4:43:1.

9   Cited in Bakshi-Doron, ibid.

if they are visible to the eye, and not similar to the case of microscopic organisms."[10] Rabbi Auerbach seemed to assign a level of *chashivut*—importance—to the manipulated DNA, such that while it is not visible, it nevertheless cannot be disregarded due to its being microscopic.

> Secondly, Rabbi Auerbach goes on to make an important distinction:
> Regarding animals, in my humble opinion, genetic engineering does not violate cross-breeding [*harva'ah*] because it is only crossing "material" between one animal and another, and this would only be problematic in tree-grafting, even if it were simply the addition of a liquid which on its own would not produce any growth .... [This distinction between animals and plants is because regarding plants] ultimately the "field" is sown with two different species, whereas regarding animals the Torah stated "your animal," and the genetic material does not constitute an "animal" ... [11]

Rabbi Auerbach takes the strongest *halakhah* position against genetic engineering that I am aware of, and yet he only limits the prohibition to plant material. We therefore see that the permissibility of performing genetic engineering on plants is the subject of a *makhloket achronim* (a debate amongst contemporary decisors). However, even R. Auerbach does not believe that the resultant GMOs produced by such technology would be considered prohibited or non-kosher. That is, even the most stringent position only takes issue with the scientific action of creating GMOs, rather than with a company such as the Israeli dairy Tnuva selling products that contain the GMOs themselves; no *poskim* that I am aware of has issued such a ruling which would extend to the commercial companies or consumers themselves.

Beyond the *halakhah l'maaseh* aspect of *kilayim,* a more fruitful approach requires delving into the *taamei haMitzvot,* the reasons behind the laws which the sages have striven to articulate over the centuries. Interestingly, there is an intellectual tradition among the commentators that sees *kilayim* as paradigmatic of a *hok*—a Torah law that has no perceptible reason. Rashi says this explicitly in his commentary on Leviticus 19 cited *supra*: "The term *hukim* means those enactments of the King for which no reason is given."[12] Other interpreters do, however, see meaning in these laws.

---

10 R. Shlomo Zalman Auerbach, *Minchat Shlomo*: 2:97:27.
11 Ibid.
12 Translation from *Pentateuch with Rashi's commentary*, M. Rosenbaum and A.M. Silbermann (Jerusalem: A.M. Silbermann, 1929).

The Static View of Creation

The central understanding of the *mitzvah* is offered by Nachmanides, who argues that the reasoning behind the prohibitions of *kilayim* is rooted in the structure *ma'aseh bereishit*, God's original creation. He notes that Genesis 1 frequently repeats that God made animals and plants *l'minam*: "according to their [particular] kind/species." Nachmanides inferred that if God created these kinds/species initially, then God must want these same species to continue and perpetuate themselves, while concomitantly maintaining this same system of speciation that had been created initially:

> God created in the world various species, and gave them the power of reproduction enabling them to exist forever as long as God will desire the existence of the world; and God further endowed them with a power to bring forth [only] after their kind, and that they should never be changed.[13]

The problem with *kilayim*, then, is that by bringing different species together, we change the Divinely-inspired schema of Creation, in one of two possible ways: new species will be created which did not exist prior, or that hybrid offspring will be created which are themselves sterile, unable to have further offspring (Nachmanides discusses mules as an example). Nachmanides finally adds a subsidiary problem: changing Creation in this way intimates that God's works are not perfect *chas v'shalom*, and that God "needs our help" in populating Creation.[14]

Rabbi Avraham Ibn Ezra (twelfth century, Spain) had a similar understanding to Nachmanides, noting in his commentary on Leviticus 19:19 that, "[Y]ou must not do anything to animals which alters the work of God ... you must *preserve* each species, and not interbreed one species with another."[15] Centuries later, Rabbi Naftali Tzvi Yehuda Berlin again ascribed the law to upholding a stewardship of Creation. He relates the *hok* to a midrashic understanding wherein the word *hok* is etymologically related to the word *chakak*, to engrave. According to this view, *kilayim* preserves a certain essentialism that God "engraved" into the workings of Creation: "and one who mixes one kind with a different kind will ultimately destroy their essential natures."

---

13 Nachmanides Commentary on Leviticus 19:19; See Rabbi Dr. Charles Chavel (trans.), *Commentary on the Torah* (Brooklyn, NY: Shilo Publishing House, 1974).

14 "כאילו יחשוב שלא השלים הקב"ה בעולמו כל הצורך ויחפוץ הוא לעזור בבריאתו"

15 Trans. Jay Schachter, via Sefaria.org.

This same reason is articulated by the anonymous author of the *Sefer ha-Hinukh* in his discussion of a separate *mitzvah*, that of "*Lo LiHaChayot Machshefa*," not to allow a witch to live. He understands that the problem with magic is similar to the aforementioned problems with *kilayim*; namely, tinkering with the Divine order of Creation:

> [God] desires [the world's] settlement and that everything should be administered in a natural way (בדרך הטבע), as nature was at the beginning of creation - and yet this person wants to change everything. And according to my opinion, the problem of magic is that at the beginning of creation, God instilled for each and every thing in the world a nature [through which] to accomplish its action well and straight, for the good of the creatures of the world that He created; and He commanded each one to act according to its species, as it is written about all the creatures "according to its species"(Genesis 1:12). [16]

All of these *m'forshim* agree on a central thesis: God created the world with a particular and regimented organizational structure, and intended for that structure to persist indefinitely. Specifically, the types and kinds of species—of plants and animals, of bacteria and algae—that God created are meant to exist, in their current form, forever. Doing anything that would muddle the different species, or prevent their continued existence, would be religiously problematic and potentially prohibited under the aforementioned *mitzvot*.[17]

* * *

On considering this position, there are two problems that become immediately apparent. First, there is the problem of extinction. We know that countless species of plants and animals have lived and died, and became extinct prior to widespread human control of the planet. While these rabbis may certainly have argued that it is incumbent on us today to stem the tide of species' extinction, how would they understand prehistoric extinction? It's hard to understand how we might reconcile it with the idea that God created the system in such a way that it would be static and self-perpetuating.

Secondly, the sources that we have seen thus far speak against the notion of altering species in any way. But we know that humans have been breeding/domesticating plants and animals for thousands of years, stretching back prior

---

16 *Sefer ha-Hinukh*, Mitzvah 62 (Sefaria translation).

17 Other sources which corroborate this thesis include the Rambam, *Guide to the Perplexed* 3:17, and Malbim to Job 37:24.

to the giving of the Torah. Just one example should suffice to show the difficulty of this position: consider the domestic dog, the *canis familiaris*. Dogs are understood to be the descendants of wolves and have been bred over the millennia for different traits that make them helpful, in a variety of ways, to humans and human society.[18] There is archaeological evidence of dogs having been extant in Biblical Israel during Temple times,[19] and dogs are mentioned in the Torah in different contexts.

According to our Biblical and rabbinic sources, are dogs to be considered a *b'dieved*, "post-facto," creature? If so, why were they so widespread in Biblical Israel? And how would we reconcile that with other Torah perspectives which claim that the dog evinces some important and unique spiritual qualities (most particularly surrounding the Exodus, where we are learn in Exodus 11:7 that "no dog snarled at the Israelites" as they left)?[20] This critique would of course be extended to the manifold animals and plants that we raise and grow for food. So, while a few contemporary rabbis have attempted to offer up some innovative approaches to these issues,[21] it is fair to say that our contemporary understanding of science poses an as-of-yet unresolved challenge to this view of Creation and the world. We will discuss whether aspects of this view can nevertheless be utilized in our thinking about GMO foods.

Divine Wisdom as Manifested in Human Creativity

As opposed to the static and regimented worldview articulated by the *m'forshim* on *kilayim* and *kishuf*, other rabbinic literature seems to advocate for humanity's creative interaction with the natural world. Perhaps most well-known example comes from the *Midrash Tanchuma, Parshat Tazria 5*:

> The wicked Turnus Rufus asked Rabbi Akiva: Whose deeds are better—
> God's or human beings'? Rabbi Akiva replied: Human beings! ... Rabbi

---

18 It is the subject of scholarly debate the degree to which dogs, as we know them today, have adapted to human society. See Adam Miklosi, *Dog Behaviour, Cognition, and Evolution* (Oxford: Oxford University Press, 2015), 21.

19 Lawrence Stager, "Why Were Hundreds of Dogs Buried at Ashkelon?" *Biblical Archaeology Review*, May/June 1991.

20 The Netziv here notes that dogs can "uniquely recognize spiritual realities," and BT *Bava Kamma* 60b: "When dogs howl, it means the Angel of Death has come to town; but when dogs play, it means Elijah the prophet has come to town ... "

21 Rabbi Natan Slifkin neatly describes and outlines some of these approaches in chapter 20 of *The Challenge of Creation* (Israel: Zoo Torah, 2012).

Akiva brought him sheaves of wheat and fresh-baked rolls, and said: These are God's works and these are humans'—are not these better than the sheaves? Rabbi Akiva brought him raw flax and clothes from Bet She'an and said: These are God's works and these are humans'—are not these better than the flax?

This story presents the clearest rabbinic articulation of a worldview which endorses humanity's creative use and harnessing of nature for our own benefit. Not only is this permitted, according to Rabbi Akiva, but it is seen as "more pleasing" (נָאִים יוֹתֵר) to God! Wheat and flax, in their "natural state," are intrinsically good—but they can only reach their fullest potential through humanity's processing and refinement of them into food and clothing, respectively.

Much like the first chapter of Genesis serves as the paradigm for the "static" view of nature and Creation discussed above, so too does it seem to be the template for this midrash. Specifically, Genesis 1:28: "God blessed them [humans] and said to them, "Be fertile and increase, fill the earth and master it ..." The translation of this final verb, "וְכִבְשֻׁהָ," can vary between "master," "subdue," "rule," or "dominate." Whatever the precise translation, it clearly positions humans in a dominant and empowered role vis- à -vis the natural world.

A midrash recounts and further refines the idea that human creativity is pleasing to God:

Rabbi Yosi says two things were planned for creation on the sixth day, but did not get created until Saturday night. On Saturday night, God granted Adam Divine wisdom; Adam took two stones, ground them against one another, and created fire. He also took two animals and mated them, and created a mule (BT *Pesahim* 54a).

According to Rabbi Yosi, the primeval Adam's human creativity is not simply pleasing to God, but is itself a channeling of Divine wisdom and Divine creativity. The crux of the tension between these two worldviews is clearly expressed here, particularly in the second clause of the midrash. Adam's creation of the mule could be understood as a paradigmatic violation of the tenets of *kilayim* (a mule being the sterile offspring of a horse and a donkey). And yet for Rabbi Yossi, not only does this seem permissible, it is praised as being Divinely inspired. For Rabbi Yosi, the directive to human creativity and domination outweighs the concerns of toying with Creation and playing with species.

Divine Wisdom vs. Altering Creation

But that is not the end of the midrash. There is a second opinion, offered by Rabban Shimon ben Gamliel. He does not believe that Adam created the mule. Rather, he believes that "the mule was created later, in the days of Ana [grandson of Esau] ... and just as Ana was impure, so was the impurity he created." Rabban Shimon ben Gamliel's midrash is based on a confusing genealogy described in Genesis 36, wherein Ana is described as first the brother, and then the son, of Zivon. The midrash resolves this by understanding him as the offspring of a prohibited union, and in turn the progenitor of another prohibited creature, the mule.

This midrash offers us a helpful lens to see the tension between the static state model of creation vs. the human creativity model. Two *tannaim*—first and second century Palestinian sages—argue as to whether the combining of species is Divinely inspired, or inherently impure and destructive. We are meant to understand that these worldviews, though potentially competing, are both quite legitimate within Jewish thought—they are both true, *eilu v'eilu divrei Elokim hayim*.

Earlier, I described the *makhloket* between several contemporary *achronim* regarding the *halakhah* permissibility of genetic engineering. I noted that Rabbi Eliyahu Bakshi-Doron ruled leniently on the issue. Rabbi Shlomo Zalman Auerbach, on the other hand, was inclined to rule stringently on the act of genetic engineering (נראה דשפיר אסור), as a violation of *harkavat ilan*, a subcategory of the prohibition of *kilayim*. However, he limited this to genetic engineering of plants, as opposed to animals.

If we were to analyze the topic of GMOs purely from a *halakhah* approach, then, it would seem that any possible *issur* was limited to the narrow of geneticists who research these technologies or work for the large companies like Monsanto or Syngenta that produce the GMOs themselves. When we consider the various *peirushim* and *midrashei aggadah*—commentaries and homiletic elucidations—discussed earlier, however, we understand that the issue of GMO food is not simply limited to the *issur v'heter* question of whether the food is kosher, or the more limited question of whether an observant Jew may participate in genetic engineering. Rather, we are faced with a larger question: How should an observant Jew feel about the preponderance of GMO products in our food system? Should we work towards a world where GMOs are used less, or not at all? What is the Torah-true perspective on GMOs?

The answer lies in the tension suggested in the *makhloket* between Rabbi Shimon ben Gamliel and Rabbi Yossi; namely, that altering Creation is either an example of Divine creativity filtered through human hands, or an unsanctioned exploitation of nature's strictures. Rabbi Joseph Soloveitchik, in his *The Emergence of Ethical Man*, argued that these worldviews are not, in fact, competing. He sees them as complementary forces which we are supposed to harness, and, ultimately, to preserve and keep in fine balance:

> Nature surrenders voluntarily to man's control and rule, she entrusts man with her most guarded secrets. Is more cooperation than dominion, more partnership than subordination? Let us watch out for moments of tension and conflict, when nature begins to hate man and to resent his presence … If nature refuses to be dominated, man is left helpless and weak … This is man's freedom: either to live at peace with nature and thus give expression to a natural existence in the noblest of terms, or to surpass his archaic bounds and corrupt himself and nature.[22]

Rabbi Soloveitchik offered a synthesis between the two positions. Yes, God created the world in a specific, regimented way. However, there is hidden potentiality in that schema, and within those species, which are meant to change, to evolve, and to be utilized. If humans do so "cooperatively," "peacefully," and in "partnership" with nature, then we are free to exercise our creativity; not only free, but in fact mandated to do so. But overstepping our bounds would constitute a violation both of our broad human mission, and perhaps of specific *mitzvot* as well. Notably, Soloveitchik does not tell us what constitutes "overstepping of bounds," but rather describes the emotional-spiritual aspect of such a violation. His articulation is descriptive, rather than prescriptive. Similarly, the author(s) of the *Sefer ha-Hinukh* gives us a relatedly vague recommendation when describing what constitutes magic, which he describes as the improper combining of earthly forces and items:

> … Knowing the difference of these things - which is the mixing God permitted to us, and have no aspect of magic, and which is the type that does have an aspect of magic and is forbidden—this distinction is well-known.[23]

---

22 Joseph Soloveitchik, *The Emergence of Ethical Man* (New York: Ktav Publishing House, 2005), 60.

23 *Sefer ha-Hinukh*, ibid.

Unfortunately, these comments fail to give us precise guidelines as to the scope of genetic engineering which the tradition might consider problematic. Let us now briefly consider certain external factors which may help attune us to what a Torah-approach to GMO usage might look like.

GMO Usage Today

One of the central arguments that proponents of GMO foods make is that the global population will need ever-increasing food yields in order to survive, and that certain foods can be genetically modified into providing higher yields.[24] On its face, this argument seems to parallel Rabbi Akiva's argument to Turnus Rufus: Humans are supposed to extend their control over agriculture in order to feed ourselves. So perhaps widespread GMO usage is a fulfillment of this deeply human-divine mission?

But research that has emerged over the last years illustrates that the promise of higher yields has not come to fruition. Europe has introduced only minimal GMO crops in recent decades, yet its yield-growth has been consistent with the United States over the past twenty years.[25] Not only that, but pesticide use has increased in the United States over that time, despite the claims that GMO crops would necessitate less chemical use.[26] The higher use of pesticides has been linked to a variety of negative health consequences for humans.[27]

On the other hand, a major critique of GMO foods has been that they are themselves inherently less safe and less healthy than conventional foods. This argument has been largely discredited by a wide-ranging and detailed

---

24 Refer to the websites of Monsanto and Bayer, two of the major companies that dominate the GMO market, where the topic of "food security" is articulated as a central pillar of their mission: https://www.cropscience.bayer.com/en/stories/2016/nutrition-and-food-security-food-trends-and-global-hunger and http://discover.monsanto.com/global-food-security-challenge

25 Danny Hakim, "Doubts About the Promised Bounty of Genetically Modified Crops," *New York Times*, October 29, 2016.

26 Some studies have noted that pesticide use for individual crops, such as BT corn, has decreased, but this does not negate the overall rise in pesticide use. See http://advances.sciencemag.org/content/2/8/e1600850.full, accessed July 12, 2017, and https://www.ers.usda.gov/data-products/adoption-of-genetically-engineered-crops-in-the-us.aspx, accessed July 12, 2017. It is worth noting that the companies that make the strongest claims for the benefits of GMO crops are also those who stand to benefit monetarily from both their adoption, as well as the pesticides that are marketed to be used in conjunction with them.

27 http://www.ewg.org/agmag/2015/03/claims-gmo-yield-increases-don-t-hold. Accessed June 25, 2017.

study undertaken by the National Academies of Sciences, Engineering, and Medicine (NASEM) in 2016. The study investigated the health-risks of GMO food consumption. The researchers summarize their findings as follows:

> While recognizing the inherent difficulty of detecting subtle or long-term effects in health or the environment, the study committee found no substantiated evidence of a difference in risks to human health between currently commercialized genetically engineered (GE) crops and conventionally bred crops.[28]

This data helped to dispel one of the central arguments leveled against GMO usage. Given our current understanding of the science, it seems that the major arguments on both sides of the debate are not as strong as once believed. The intrinsic health and safety of individual GMO foods is likely safe, while the long-term effects of increased pesticide use is likely damaging to the environment, and, thus, ultimately to human health. Further, as the NASEM scientists themselves admit, there is a dearth of long-term studies researching the health effects on humans and the environment from GMO usage.

Concluding Thoughts

The debate over the safety and sagacity of GMO usage will likely continue. Hopefully, continued research will help us deepen our understanding of the potential risks and rewards of its use. As Jews, we should welcome and encourage continued research, and be wary of any attempts to stem the tide of increased knowledge. Fulfilling Rabbi Soloveitchik's counsel requires pursuing a path of action which is "cooperative and peaceful" with the natural world; such a path, in turn, necessitates thoughtful, deliberative, and patient observation of the result of our actions. The role of corporations in political advocacy on behalf of GMO adoption should ideally be severely limited, as such companies are inherently *nogeia badavar* (i.e., they should be recused on account of their conflict of interest in honestly assessing the repercussions of their work).

There are contemporary thinkers who suggest that we should view GMO foods as non-kosher. Certainly this would not be the case according to *halakhah*, as discussed earlier, so perhaps this is being suggested along the

---

28 The National Academies of Sciences, Engineering, and Medicine, *Genetically Engineered Crops: Experiences and Prospects—Report in Brief.* May 2016.

lines of a *chumra* or acting *lifnim mishurat hadin*—a supererogatory decision. I believe this is an unwise approach, for several reasons. First, it would severely curtail the amount of available food for the kosher consumer in the supermarket, given the omnipresence of GMO ingredients in our packaged foods today. Secondly, such behavior would fail to substantively address the central issue.

If we are convinced that the Torah-true worldview is one wherein genetic engineering is limited, then a self-imposed "boycott" on GMO foods by the religious community is a poor tactic to accomplish this. Rather, we would need to engage in a more structural, and ultimately political, strategy to advocate for such a position.

Conclusion

Rabbi Dr. Shmuly Yanklowitz

Food is central to human identity, communal life, spirituality, and ethical commitments. Every time we participate in the act of eating, we make countless consequential (but often unrecognized) choices about our physical health, our spiritual well-being, our relationships, and our morals. But how often do we take the time to consider the food in front of us? And going further, how does Jewish wisdom enhance our perspective to make us more equipped to handle the complex decisions of what we consume on a daily basis? Should I eat animals? How should I perceive and engage with institutions tasked with ensuring the highest levels of *kashrut*? Does the positive treatment or abuse of workers affect what food I eat? Should I consume GMOs? How does *kashrut* keep my family and my community together? How does it divide it? How does climate change cause us to rethink the production and consumption process? How might my eating process bring me closer to God? How might each meal help me to refine my character?

Like on most matters, Jewish wisdom has much to offer on emerging trends and issues in contemporary food culture, an oft-overlooked aspect of religious engagement. Indeed, the topics pertaining to the ethical relationship to our food has not been explored enough in modern Jewish thinking. It is my hope and my dream that this volume exploring the breadth and depth of issues pertaining to kosher food ways and ethical consumption becomes an intellectual guide for many readers—and a first resource to turn to—as well as a collection of thought that only spurs productive discussion and debate. It is also my hope that this book will be the first of many Torat Chayim publications to come.

The questions and topics posited by this volume are vast and require a great deal of intellectual analysis and spiritual meditation. How we ultimately understand the Jewish nexus with food and spirituality is a topic that affects us all to our core because without considering food, how are we to live?

On this thought, consider this Jewish folktale about how God decided on the location of the Beit HaMikdash (the location of the Holy Temple in Jerusalem):

> Many thousands of years ago, even before Jerusalem was a city, two brothers lived there in neighboring farms. One brother was married. Every year, he found that his farm did not produced enough food to satisfy his family's needs, and they all lived in poverty. The other brother lived alone, and his needs were easily provided for by his farm. One year, both brothers had bumper crops. When the harvest was completed, the richer brother said to himself: "I have so much more than I need, I will take some of my harvest and leave it in my brother's barn." He decided to do so in the dead of night, so that his brother would not realize what he had done, and would assume that the extra food was part of his own harvest. That same evening, the poorer brother thought to himself: "This year, I finally have more than enough for my family. But for my brother, that which he harvests is all that he has. He has no family, only his possessions." And out of love for his brother he decided that that very evening, he would take some of his harvest to his brother's barn, so that his brother could rejoice the bounty of his crop. During the night, each of the brothers set out in a cart and left part of their harvest in the other's barn. When they awoke in the morning, they saw that their harvest was in no way diminished, and each thought that he had only dreamed about helping the other, but had not actually done so. And so, that night each brother brought food to his brother's barn once more. In the morning, once again, each store of food was undiminished.
>
> On the third night, each made sure to stay up and set out in the middle of the night. This time, they encountered each other on the road, and both realized what the other had done. They ran toward each other and embraced.
>
> Of the spot where they kissed, God said, "This is where I want My Temple built."[29]

God wants to see food bring human beings closer together in holiness, in love, and in respect. Perhaps humans need to eat to sustain ourselves for exactly this reason: that we might come closer to one another in the profound act of

---

29 Rabbi Joseph Telushkin, *A Code of Jewish Ethics, Volume 2: Love Your Neighbor as Yourself* (New York: Random House, 2009), 2–3.

consumption. If we are not convinced by holy altruism, there is an interesting Talmudic teaching that explains how a charitable view toward food is developed out of self-interest:

> Rabbi Chiyya advised his wife: "When a poor person comes to the door, give him food so that the same may be done to you [i.e., our] children." She exclaimed, "You are cursing our children [by suggesting that they may be become beggars]." But Rabbi Chiyya replied: "There is a wheel which revolves in this world."[30]

Indeed, we are uncertain of the future economies of food production and consumption and "there is a wheel which revolves in this world." But, central to Jewish identity is a sense that food (or the lack thereof) evokes deep moral responsibility:

> Abraham … would go forth and make his rounds, and wherever he found travelers, he would bring them to his house. To the one who was accustomed to eating wheat bread, he gave wheat bread to eat. To the one who was accustomed to eating meat, he gave meat to eat. To the one who was accustomed to drinking wine, he gave wine to drink. Moreover, he built stately mansions on the highways and left food and drink there so that ever traveler stopped there and thanked God. That is why delight of the spirit was vouchsafed to him. And whatever one might ask for was to be found in Abraham's home.[31]

Today, nearly twenty million households in America suffer from food insecurity. This is a *shonda*! A travesty! A great injustice! As Jews, what are doing to rectify this problem? Are we truly heeding the words of the Prophets when they teach us that in a just society, vulnerable individuals don't need money to receive basic food to survive?[32] For doesn't it say in the Scriptures that: "Everyone who is thirsty, go to the water, even one with no money, go, buy and eat; go and buy wine and milk without money and without price!"[33]

Indeed, it is not merely how we think about food but how we think about our character and relationships within that food production, consumption, and distribution that matters so much.

---

30 BT *Shabbat* 151b.
31 *Avot d'Rabbi Natan* 7.
32 See Isaiah 55:1.
33 הוֹי כָּל צָמֵא לְכוּ לַמַּיִם וַאֲשֶׁר אֵין לוֹ כָּסֶף לְכוּ שִׁבְרוּ וֶאֱכֹלוּ וּלְכוּ שִׁבְרוּ בְּלוֹא כֶסֶף וּבְלוֹא מְחִיר יַיִן וְחָלָב

If the rich man says to the poor man, 'Why do you not go and work and get food? Look at those hips! Look at those legs! Look at that fat body! Look at those lumps of flesh!' The Holy One, be Blessed, says to the rich person, 'It is not enough that you have not given him anything of yours and helped him out, but you must mock what I have given him?').[34]

Our relationship with food encompasses more than we think at first glance. Food awakens a consciousness of our inner selves and also the consciousness of the *other*. Let us not squander this profound opportunity each day to walk and bask in the compassionate ways of God. Through understanding the choices of what we put inside our bodies, may we have the spiritual fortitude to influence, beautify, and bring out the bounty in the world around us.

---

34 *Midrash Leviticus Rabbah* 34:4: ויקרא רבה (וילנא) פרשת בהר פרשה לד:ד
אמר העשיר לאותו העני לית את אזיל לעי ונגים חמי שקיין חמי כרעין חמי כרסוון חמי קפרן א"ל הקדוש
ברוך הוא לא דייך שלא נתת לו משלך מאומה אלא במה שנתתי לו אתה מכניס לו עין רעה לפיכך (קהלת ה)
והוליד בן ואין בידו מאומה מן כל מה דהות ליה לא ישבוק לבריה ונסיב מומא לנפשיה

Index

A

abstinence from food, 67–68, 78
Adler, Rachel, 92–93
aggadah, 137, 261
agriculture, 40, 62, 64, 123, 145, 150, 156,
　159–161, 163–165, 213–214, 240–241,
　243, 254, 263
alienation
　of food, 122
　of labor, 161
Albo, Yosef, 222–223
Alexandrai, Rav, 163
Alter, Yehudah Aryeh Leib, 134
American Heart Association, 88–89
ana Hashem, 134–135
animal suffering, 39, 182–208, 220, 239
　le-tzorekh ha-adam, 63
　to'elet muhletet, 212
　Tza'ar Ba'alei Hayyim (tbh), 12–13, 63,
　　182–189, 191, 194–196, 199, 203,
　　206–208, 210–212, 216, 239
　tzorekh hiyuni, 213
animal welfare, 130, 208–217
　and *kashrut*, 19–22
anti-Semitism, 12, 40
asceticism, 49, 51, 67–68, 70–71, 116
Ashkenazic tradition, 2, 120, 168n8, 183, 196
Avodah B'Gashmius, 78
Avot of Rabbi Nathan, 165

B

Baal Shem Tov, 51, 55, 71–72, 77, 78, 143,
　154, 242
Bahya, Rabbeinu, 48
Bakshi-Doron, Eliyahu, 255
Bal Tashhit, 64, 122–123, 194–195, 220, 240,
　242, 245, 249, 251
Bamberger, Yitzhak Dov Halevi, 211–212
Bava Metzia, 62, 63, 136, 141, 185–186, 189
beit midrash, 75, 134–135
Berakhot, 50
bizion okhlin, 45

blessings, 51, 60, 65–66, 71–72, 75, 77, 81,
　84, 86, 119–125, 163
blood prohibition for humanity, 37, 238–239
b'nei beitekha, 23
Buber, Martin, 49, 135

C

Carlebach, Shlomo, 165
Carmell, Aryeh, 215
Cassuto, Umberto, 238
charity (*tzedakah*), 22, 84, 168–170
civil society, 7–8, 22
climate change, 25, 158, 164, 219, 251, 266
community
　customs and standards, 5, 20, 138, 139, 199
　dignity of, 194
　forming identity, 156, 198
　inclusive, 144–150, 192
　in diaspora, ix, 20
　regulating and sustainable, 157–158
　religious, 125, 142–144, 198, 208
　sacred, 29, 59–62, 65, 135, 243
compassion, 31 ff., 65, 142, 148–149, 211, 216
　as serving God, 135–136, 141
　God as source of, 32, 40, 93, 142, 148
　to animals, 40, 64
　when eating, 49, 59
composters, 122
conservation as commandment, 235–243
creation, 15–17, 33, 43, 51, 71, 90, 93–94, 135,
　138, 189, 228, 235, 237, 257–259, 261–263
cruelty, 36, 39–40, 63, 140, 148, 151, 185,
　187–191, 195, 197–198, 210–213, 216,
　220, 223, 239, 252

D

Danzig, Avraham
　Hokhmat Adam, 212
Davis, Ellen F., 165
death
　associated with meat production and
　　eating, 37

associated with eating as physical act, 75
defeated by God and Torah study, 90–92,
    95–96
in balance with life, 34, 39, 95
protecting fellow beings against, 101,
    110–112, 197
Dessler, Eliyahu, 84
Dietary Guidelines Advisory Committee, 88
dignity, ix, 20, 33–34, 36, 120, 136, 138, 142,
    149–150
divine image, 134–153
Dresner, Samuel H., 224

E
eating
    act of, 55–57
        accompanying practices, 46–49
        and dignity, 120
        concomitant obligations, 49, 61
        spiritual act, 50–51, 54, 62, 66–86,
            117, 121, 125, 230
    disorders, 116, 119. See also overeating,
        under-consumption, obesity
        bulimia, 116
    ethics of, 19, 39, 61–65, 87–118, 220,
        235–243
        holiness of, 34–36
        physical satisfaction, 78
        social dimension of, 41, 122
        Talmudic guidelines to, 113
Eidels, Shmuel, 169
Elimelekh of Lizhensk, 59–60
environmentalism, 21, 25, 34, 39, 65, 126,
    157, 159, 235–243
Ephraim Shlomo ben Chaim, 11
ethical collapse, 151
ethical decision-making, 96, 150
ethics. See also eating
    and business practices, 5, 8, 21
    as religious value, 32, 49, 90 ff.
    Kosher food supervision, 1–9, 19
    of consumption, 2, 61–65
    of nutrition, 111–117
    ritual and, 135, 138
Ettlinger, Jacob, 212
equality, 133, 144, 149, 243

F
farming
    effect on forests, 157, 215
    factory farming, 19, 39, 157, 214–215, 219
    farmers displacement, 158
    farming villages in crisis, 158–161

organic, 40
    small farmers, 19, 155 ff.
Falk, Marcia, 92–93
fasting, 51, 131, 167 ff.
    as sin, 67–68
Feinstein, Moshe, 3, 63, 183, 201–204,
    206–207, 212
feminist Jewish theology, 92–95
food production, 19–20, 59, 62, 65, 78, 122,
    123, 165, 212–215
    biotechnology and genetic engineering,
        253, 264, 255. See also genetically
        modified organisms
freedom, 15, 41, 136, 146, 262
Freud, Sigmund, 66

G
Garden of Eden, 19, 35, 66, 79, 129–130,
    132–133, 156, 186, 224, 235–236, 244
genetically modified organisms (GMOs),
    123, 235–243
    definition, 252–253
    divine wisdom vs. altering creation,
        261–263
    human creativity, 259–260
    static view of creation, 257–259
    Torah and Rabbinic sources, 253–256
    usage, 263–264
Glasner, Moshe Shmuel, 63
GMOs, see genetically modified organisms
    (GMOs)
God
    gendered metaphors for, 93–94
    God of life, 15–17, 90–94, 97, 101
    good God, 124
    governance of humans and nature,
        104–105, 247–248
Greenberg, Irving, 90, 95, 97, 106

H
halakhah, 12, 20, 37, 43, 56–57, 100–101,
    103, 124, 137, 182, 189
    animal life termination, 216
    animal suffering, 183, 206–207
    and duties of intimacy, 137–138, 217
    caring for one's body, 73, 104–106, 110,
        111, 115
    eating fish and meat together, 123–124
    eating meat and milk together, 14, 37
        animal world, 16–17
        Kabbalah, 15–16
        circle of physical developement, 17
    genetic engineering permissibility, 261

hamira sakanta m'isurah (danger is a more serious prohibition than ritually prohibited foods), 99, 102
hunting for sport, 195–200
(legal) premises, 98–104
maalin ba-kodesh ve-ein moridin, 45
meat consumption, permissibility, 182, 204 ff., 224–226
mixing species
  kilayim, 253–257
  lo taharosh, 254
  sha'atnez, 254
  tree-grafting (*harkavat ilan*), 254–255
regarding possessions, 251
rhetoric of values and, 182–208
rule of *nireh l'ayin*, 255
sakanah (safeguarding oneself from bodily danger), 103, 111
sharing food, 61
technical problems, 215
trustworthiness, 2–5
violation, 199–200
washing hands before and after meal, 111
Halevi, Hayim David, 213
hametz (leavened bread), 14, 102–103, 129
Hartman, David, 94
Hasidic wisdom on spiritual eating, 49–51, 69–76
dangers of over-consumption, 57–59
eating, act of, 55–57
enjoying the taste as holy, 70–71
raising divine spark, 52–54, 71–72
sacred community, 59–62
Hasidism, 51–62, 69–76, 134–135, 146
Hayyim, Yosef, 60
Hazon Ish, 221
health
crisis, 87, 125
eating, 111–113
lifestyle, benefits, 89–90
meat consumption, limiting, 219
public, 87
risks, 112
Heidegger, Martin, 71
Hertz, Joseph, 221
hesed (an act of kindness), 84
Heschel, Abraham Joshua, 137, 149
hibbat ha-kodesh, 54
Hillel, 104
hillul ha-Shem, 216
Hirsch, Samson Raphael, 239, 249
holiness, 27–30, 32–34, 243

areas in life, 37–39
eating and holiness, 34–36
expanding *kashrut*, 39–42
kashrut, 36–37
hok, 256
Horeb: A Philosophy of Jewish Laws and Observances, 239
human creativity, 259–261
Huna, Rav, 113
hunger
global, 219
halakhah, 123
and malnutrition, 34–35
and poverty, 240
relief organizations, 170

I
Ibn Ezra, Abraham, 167, 257
implements of sacrality (*tashmishei kedushah*), 43
injustice, 149–150, 210, 238, 268
Israel. *See also* Jewish history
Chief Rabbinate's monopoly on kosher supervision, 5, 8, 122
communities, 125, 159
eating disorders, 119
debate about breeding species, 256, 259
grace before and after meals, 46, 120
Independence Day celebrations, 41
law of the land, 1, 123, 125, 128–129, 163–164, 186
meat consumption, 219–220
Israel of Kozhenits, 49
Isserlein, Israel, 183–188, 201, 207, 211–212

J
Jerusalem, 168, 267
Jewish cultural memory, 197
Jewish ethics, 164, 183, 188, 267
and ritual, 135–136
Jewish history
post-Talmud period, 184
First Temple period, 167–168
Second Temple period, 167–168
Jewish labor law
boundaries, borders, and slavery, 142–151
halakhah and duties of intimacy, 137–138
labors of love, 138–142
Jewish law, *see halakhah*
Jewish nutrition ethic

anthropological premises, 104–117
ethical premises, 95–98
halakhah (legal) premises, 98–104
healthy eating as a religious obligation,
90–95, 103
Josiah, Ahai ben, 165
Judaism, 13, 94, 98, 120, 150, 220
liturgy, 92–93
values, 18, 41, 59, 98
and holiness, 27–28, 31, 41, 65
and modern comforts, 59
attentiveness, 65, 130
attention to basic needs, 62, 162–164
as religious obligation, 190
avoiding cruelty, 148, 151, 187,
190, 197
based on *kashrut*, 18
bringing joy, 86
community, 42, 65, 142, 143, 164, 242
emulating God through acts of
lovingkindness, 96
equity, 38, 62, 162, 243
forming identity, 197–198, 208
justice, 19, 22–23, 27–28, 32, 243
moderation, 81–82, 164, 221
nutritious eating, 118
reducing poverty, 22
respect of life, ix, 87, 98 ff., 182 ff.,
215–216, 242. *See also* animal
suffering
striving for ideal, 36, 42, 115, 192
supplementing and reforming
religious practice, 20, 32, 138
sustainability, 65, 142, 162
universal applicability, 22, 36, 42,
144, 154
work ethic, 136, 148

K
Kabbalah, 15–16, 251
Kagan, Yisrael Meir, 141
Ahavat Hesed, 141
Hafetz Hayyim, 141, 149
Karelitz, Avraham Yishaya, 221, 255
Karo, Joseph, 99
kashering process, 122
kashrut, 4, 11, 18–19, 36–37, 124, 210, 216
animal welfare, 19–22
environmental realities, 24–26
expanding, 22–24, 39–42
hashgaha, 2, 5, 8
laws of, 10–13, 18, 34
and modern Jewish diversity, 4–5

kavvanah, 55, 134
keviut seudah, 123
Kitzur ha-Shelah, 45
Kivrot ha-Ta'avah, 222
Klatzkin, Eliyahu, 212
kol, 81–82
Kook, Abraham Isaac, 125, 211,
224–225, 237
Kozhenitser Maggid, 49

L
labor, 38, 62, 69, 79, 115, 134–153,
162, 251
Landau, Yehezkel, 183, 192, 196–199, 201
Noda Bi'Yehudah, 192–196
Leibowitz, Nehama, 224
Lev, Sarra, 141
Levenson, Jon, 90
Levinas, Emmanuel, 146
Linzer, Dov, 111
Local Food movement, 122
l'shem shamayim, 22
Luria, Yitzhak, 140

M
Magen Avraham, 44, 48
Maharsha, 169
Maimonidean theology, 92–93
Maimonides, 69, 117, 120, 124, 146, 227,
229–230, 248
Code of Jewish Law, 210
MaLBIM, 152
manna, 78, 80, 114–115
matzahs, 20–21, 40, 131
meat consumption
benefits of reducing, 230–233
case in law, 233–234
concern about excess, 221–222
eliminating, 224–228, 237
self-discipline, 239
health consequences, 219
limiting, 218–234
Mekhilta, 47
Menachem Nachum of Chernobyl, 52, 70
middah, 64, 81–82
midrash, 105, 128, 261–262
Midrash Lekah Tov, 46
Mishnah Berurah, 141
mitzvot, 19, 22, 47, 54, 66, 71, 78, 93, 102, 122,
152, 210, 216, 245, 251, 252, 256, 258
bein adam la-makom
(ritual commandments between
people and God), 49

bein adam le-havero
(ethical commandments between
people and people), 49, 141–142
of *shiluah haken,* 210
of *simhat yom tov,* 85
taking pleasure from physical world, 71
Mobley, Gregory, 91
morality, 5, 144, 201, 210, 216, 224–227,
237–238, 242, 251, 257, 266, 268

N

Nachmanides, 20, 221, 248, 256–257
Nachman of Breslov, 151
"Tale of the Master of Prayer," 151
Nachum, Menachem, 54, 70
National Academies of Sciences, Engineering,
and Medicine (NASEM), 264
naval birshut ha-Torah, 20, 216
Neurlingen, Yosef Yuspa, 45
Yosif Ometz, 45
New England Journal of Medicine, 88
non-kosher food, 256, 264–265
non-kosher animals, 10–11, 13, 19, 29,
195, 209
nutrition, 87–125, 130, 132–133, 224
nutritional value, 18, 22, 54, 79
using religious discourse in, 115

O

Obama, Barack, 25
obesity
and hunger, xii
and poor nutritional lifestyles, 87–89,
102–103
in children, 102, 119
Orthodoxy, 4–6, 19–20, 41, 119, 124, 142,
154, 205–207
in America, xiii, 4, 205–207
in Israel, 5–7
in pre-Holocaust Europe, 142
ultra-Orthodox community, 5–6
Or Yisrael, 48
overeating, 114–116, 133, 221–222

P

panentheism, 51
Perlman, Yeruham Yehudah Leib, 212
Piskei ha-Tosafot, 211–212
Poverty and Famine, 163
price of food, 5, 8, 39, 62, 160, 163–164, 246,
252, 268
production, 19–20, 54, 59, 62, 65, 78–79, 86,
122–123, 125, 165, 206, 212, 219–226,
254, 268

R

rabbinic theology, 93, 96–97
Reeve, Richard, 82
religion, 9, 12, 20, 31–32, 49, 51–56, 67, 73,
90, 98–99, 137, 144
righteousness, 12, 21, 86, 92, 128, 136, 143,
155, 165, 203, 228

S

Sacks, Jonathan, 9
sacred *(kodesh),* 28–30, 32, 36–37, 41, 43, 50,
53–62, 68, 137, 150, 152, 217
sacrifice, 28, 30, 37, 45–47, 56, 75–76,
121, 218–219
satisfaction, 125, 130
Schwartz, Richard, 238
Scripture, Culture and Agriculture, 165
Sears, David, 216
Sefer ha-Hinukh, 64, 245–246, 258
Sefer ha-Rokeah, 47
Sefer Hasidim, 44
sefirot, 61
self-obsession, 49–50
Sen, Amartya, 163
Shabbat
and festivals, 47–48, 131
meal, 120–121, 229–230
meat consumption, 218–234
prohibitions, 99
shekhinah (divine presence), 58–59, 93–94, 122
Shimon ben Gamliel, 261–262
sh'khiah hezeikah (danger is common and
likely to occur), 103
Shulhan Aruch, 2, 45, 47, 99–100, 111,
123–124, 162–164, 196
Shulhan Aruch ha-Rav, 48
Shulhan she Arba, 48
simha, 81, 84, 131
Sirkis, Yoel ben Shmuel, 212
slaves, 27, 142 ff.
and community, 144–148
Israelites, 38, 140, 144, 146–147
slaughter, 12, 19, 39–40, 184, 186, 189, 195,
203, 211, 237–241
shehitah, 12–13, 210
slow cooking movement, 122
smoking, 124
social isolation, 85, 242
social justice, 27, 143, 162, 168
social wrongs *(lifnei iver),* 23
societal change, 22
Sofer, Moshe, 126–127
Sofer, Shimon, 45
Hitorerut ha-Teshuvah, 45

Sofer, Shmuel Benyamin, 45
Soloveitchik, Joseph, 20, 33, 94, 262
    Halakhah Man, 33
source of joy, 227
spark, Divine, 52–54, 70, 135
Spalter, Shalom, 48
Stocker, Thomas F., 25
sustainability, 52–65

T
Talmud, 62, 67, 162–163, 168–169,
    221–222, 254
    accounting for pleasures in afterlife, 41
    foods to be eaten, 113
    portion control importance, 114
Tanach, 135–136, 138–139
    Torah, 10, 14, 18, 74, 79, 147–148,
        224, 242
        as Guide for World, 154–155
        books of Torah
            Exodus, 27
            Leviticus, 29–30
            Deuteronomy, 66, 99,
                104, 112, 130, 238, 245,
                249, 254
        on food, land, and basic human
            needs, 161–165
        protecting life, 94, 96, 216
        refining human character, 216
        values, 96, 183, 189
        obligations, 124
    Prophets
        Isaiah, 168
        Zechariah, 167
tashmishei kedushah, 43
taste (*ta'am*), 54
    as metaphor for goodness, 127–128
Tikkunei Zohar, 52
tikkun, 19, 33, 60, 230
*Treatise on Human Anatomy and
    Development*, 248
trust
    to people (*ne'emanut*), 1–9
    in God (*bitahon*), 80, 210
Trump, Donald, 25
tzedakah, 22
tzedakah (donating money), 84, 151
tzelem Elokim
    ethico-anthropological precepts,
        105–111
    human as symbol of God, 149–150

tzimtzum (self-withdrawal or
    self-constriction), 15, 38
Tzadok Ha-Kohen, 72–75
    on eating meat, 75–76

U
under-consumption, 114–116
unhealthy eating, 89, 101–104, 112, 115
    salt, 34, 40, 88–89, 103, 123, 131
    saturated and trans-fats, 89
    sugar and sweeteners, 34, 40, 83, 87–89,
        102–104, 123, 127–133
    "Sugar Is Killing Us," 88
    junk food, 102–103

V
Vaad (rabbinic committee), 5
values, 3, 22, 41, 59, 86, 90, 136, 138,
    141–144, 150. *See also* Judaism
Ve-Akhalta ("And you shall eat"),
    120–121, 125
vegan(ism), 75, 122
vegetarian(ism), 39, 122, 223, 225–227, 231,
    234, 236, 238, 240–241

W
Waldenberg, Eliezer Yehudah, 212
Water Footprint Network, 241
Weiss, Asher, 63
Wolbe, Shlomo, 81, 83
Wolf, Zeev, 58

Y
Yad HaLevi, 212
Yaffe, R. Mordechai
    Levush, 48
Yehiel Mikhel Weiser, Meir Leibush ben, 152
Yehudah HaNasi, 189–190, 211
yetzer hara, 82
yihudim (unifications), 51, 136
Yohanan, R., 44
Yom Kippur, 131, 168
Yonah, Rabbeinu, 23
Yosef, Ovadiah, 212
Yosef Hayyim (*Ben Ish Hai*), 60

Z
Zalman, Shneur, 94
Zeitlin, Hillel, 142–144
    Yavneh, 142
    Zohar, 44

שמות

בן זומא 172

חזון איש 178

ישראל 173

מהרא״י (ישראל איסרל ן) 172–176, 180

ראי״ה (אברהם יצחק הכה ן) קוק 180

רב אליהו קלצקין 179, 175

רבי 179, 172

רבי יוסי הגלילי 172–173

רבי ישראל איסרליין 171

רבי פנחס בן יאיר 172

רבי שמעון בן אלעזר 178, 174

רבי יוחנן 175

רבן גמליאל 176

רמ״א (משה איסרליש) 173

רש״י (שלמה בן רבי יצחק) 174, 177

ריטב״א (יום טוב בן אברהם אַשְׁבִּיל י) 178–176

רמב״ם (משה בן מימו ן) 178, 180

רמב״ן (משה בן נחמ ן) 180–177

ר״ן (נסים בן ר׳ ראוב ן) 179–177

מונחים

כבילה והנפה 171, 181

צער בעלי חיים 181–171

תועלת לאדם 172–173

תרומת הדשן 172–173, 175